Resistance with the People

HARVARD COLD WAR STUDIES BOOK SERIES

Series Editor
Mark Kramer, *Harvard University*

Redrawing Nations: Ethnic Cleansing in East-Central Europe, 1944–1948
Edited by Philipp Ther and Ana Siljak

Triggering Communism's Collapse: Perceptions and Power in Poland's Transition
Marjorie Castle

Resistance with the People

Repression and Resistance in Eastern Germany 1945–1955

GARY BRUCE

ROWMAN & LITTLEFIELD PUBLISHERS, INC.
Lanham • Boulder • New York • Oxford

ROWMAN & LITTLEFIELD PUBLISHERS, INC.

Published in the United States of America
by Rowman & Littlefield Publishers, Inc.
A Member of the Rowman & Littlefield Publishing Group
4720 Boston Way, Lanham, Maryland 20706
www.rowmanlittlefield.com

P.O. Box 317, Oxford OX2 9RU, United Kingdom

British Library Cataloguing in Publication Information Available

Library of Congress Cataloging-in-Publication Data

Bruce, Gary, 1969–
   Resistance with the people : repression and resistance in Eastern Germany, 1945–1955
/ Gary Bruce.
       p. cm. — (Harvard Cold War studies book series)
   Includes bibliographical references and index.
   ISBN 0-7425-2487-6 (alk. paper)
      1. Opposition (Political science)—Germany (East) 2. Protest movements—Germany
(East) 3. Germany (East)—History—Uprising, 1953. 4. Internal security—Germany
(East) 5. Germany (East)—Politics and government. I. Title. II. Series.

DD286.4 .B78 2003
943'.1087—dc21

                                                                                2002031863

Printed in the United States of America

♾™ The paper used in this publication meets the minimum requirements of American
National Standard for Information Sciences—Permanence of Paper for Printed Library
Materials, ANSI/NISO Z39.48-1992.

For as the interposition of a rivulet, however small, will occasion the line of the phalanx to fluctuate, so any trifling disagreement will be the cause of seditions; but they will not so soon flow from anything else as from the disagreement between virtue and vice and, next to that between poverty and riches.

—Aristotle

Contents

Abbreviations

CDU	Christian Democratic Union of Germany
DBD	Democratic Farmers' Party of Germany
DVdI	German Administration of the Interior
GDR	German Democratic Republic
KPD	Communist Party of Germany
KVP	People's Police in Barracks
LDPD	Liberal Democratic Party of Germany
LOPM	Leading Organs of the Parties and Mass Organizations
LPG	Agricultural production collective
MfS	Ministry for State Security
MVD	(Soviet) Ministry of Internal Affairs
NDPD	National Democratic Party of Germany
NKVD	(Soviet) People's Commissariat of Internal Affairs
RAW	Railway outfitting works
RIAS	Radio in the American Sector
SBZ	Soviet Occupied Zone
SED	Socialist Unity Party of Germany
SfS	State Secretariat for State Security
SMAD	Soviet Military Administration in Germany
SPD	Social Democratic Party of Germany
VEB	Nationally owned enterprise
ZA	Central Committee (of the SPD)

Tables

Acknowledgments

I have the very happy task of giving recognition to those who have assisted me in writing this book, although I admit to some frustration because it must be done in a manner that is far too brief. I would like to thank in particular Professor Peter Hoffmann of McGill University for his careful reading of previous drafts. I have greatly appreciated his thoughtful analysis, unparalleled devotion to accuracy in the writing of history, and apparently endless patience.

During my research in German archives, I encountered first-rate assistance from all archival staff as they patiently explained how the documents were catalogued and helped me to develop a network of contacts. I would like to thank: Dr. Agethen, *Konrad-Adenauer-Stiftung*, Bonn; Dr. Kaff, *Konrad-Adenauer-Stiftung*, Bonn; Herr Sandler, *Archiv des Deutschen Liberalismus*, Gummersbach; Frau Göpel, *Bundesbeauftragter für die Unterlagen des Staatssicherheitsdienstes der ehemaligen DDR (BStU)*, Berlin; Herr Wiedmann, *BStU*, Berlin; Herr Popiolek, *BStU,* Berlin; Dr. Wegmann, *BStU*, Berlin; Dr. Engelmann, *BStU*, Berlin; Frau Ehlich, *Stiftung Archiv der Parteien und Massenorganisationen der DDR (SAPMO)*, Berlin; Herr Lange, *SAPMO,* Berlin; Frau Nestler, *SAPMO*, Berlin; Frau Fruth, *Bundesarchiv, Abteilungen Potsdam*, Potsdam; Dr. Rexin, *Franz-Neumann-Archiv*, Berlin; Dr. Schwabe, *Mecklenburgisches Landeshauptarchiv*, Schwerin; Frau Galle, *DeutschlandRadio Archiv*, Berlin; Herr Marik, *Thüringisches Hauptstaatsarchiv Weimar*, Weimar.

Many gave freely of their advice and their time to help me understand the fascinating history of East Germany. I would like to thank Professor Heydemann, University of Leipzig; Professor Baring, Free University of Berlin; Dr. Mitter, Berlin; Dr. Graf, Free University of Berlin; Professor Longworth, McGill University; and Dr. Charters, University of New Brunswick. I would also like to thank Christian Ostermann, Cold War International History Project, and Mark Kramer of Harvard University for their interest in the project, and for their friendship.

Many others supported my work by providing collegial feedback. Here I would like to thank Professor Schmidt, McGill University; Professor Goldsmith-Reber, McGill University; Hans-Walter Frischkopf, McGill University; Professor Doerr, St. Thomas University; and Glenn Leonard of the University of New Brunswick.

Mary McDaid of McGill University, Carole Hines and Elizabeth Hetherington of the University of New Brunswick, and Anne Marie Macpherson of St. Francis Xavier University provided the critical infrastructure necessary for the timely completion of the project.

I was terribly sad to leave Germany at the end of my research. During my entire stay there, I always felt "zu Hause, " due in large measure to the close friends I made. For warm hospitality and enduring friendship, my heartfelt thanks go to: Dieter Leutert and family, Berlin; Sven Lauk, Berlin; Matthias Putzke, Berlin; Albrecht Meier, Berlin; Armin Mitter and family, Berlin; Samuli Siren and Meri Juva, Berlin; Ines Laue, Leipzig; and Helga Wahre, Bonn.

I gratefully acknowledge the financial assistance of the Social Sciences and Research Council of Canada; the German Academic Exchange Service (DAAD); and McGill University.

The editorial staff at Rowman & Littlefield is the model of professionalism and courtesy. Matthew Hammon, April Leo, and Kärstin Painter have been outstanding collaborators on this project.

For unfailing support, I thank my family. To Antoinette Duplessis, I express my sincerest of thanks for her assistance, commentary, and above all for peace of mind. *Je dis ton nom, et le soleil se lève.*

As always, the merits of this book belong to all whom I have mentioned. Any faults are mine alone.

Map 1
The East German provinces 1945–1952 and their major centers.

Map 2
The "special camps" in East Germany, 1947.

Map 3
East Germany's administrative regions (*Bezirke).*

Chapter 1

Introduction

November is grey in the north German plain. At the beginning of the month, as if on queue, the crisp autumn air turns soggy and the mercury begins its downward march toward winter. It is the month that squarely announces the end of summer, and that a long, unpleasant winter lies ahead. November usually brings little joy to Germans.

But November 1989 was different. In the spring of that year, Poland's Communist government did something that would have been unthinkable in Eastern Europe prior to Mikhail Gorbachev's arrival at the helm of the Soviet Union in 1985—it sat down with the opposition group *Solidarity*, led by the fiery electrician from the Lenin shipyards in Gdansk, Lech Wałęsa, and arranged for partial free elections to be held in June. The results of those elections seem self-evident now although they completely surprised the non-Communist candidates. Opposition candidates swept 99 of 100 seats in the Polish senate, and every one of the contested seats in the Parliament (*sejm*). By September, Poland had a non-Communist Prime Minister. Similarly, reformers in the Hungarian Socialist Workers' Party (the Communist party) began talks with opponents that would end in the thorough trouncing of the former Communists in free elections held in March/April 1990.[1] Peacefully, and with little fanfare, Poland and Hungary had dismantled the Communist system in place since World War II, prompting Lazar Kaganovich, Stalin's last surviving lieutenant, to declare that it was "outrageous" that the Soviet Union was allowing Hungary and Poland to "return to a bourgeois line."[2]

The East German revolution of 1989 contrasted sharply with the reform movements of Poland and Hungary. In September Hungary allowed East Germans to cross unhindered into Austria. Thousands of East Germans who were either vacationing in Hungary or who had arrived in the hopes of finding their way to the West, surged across the border, first into Austria and eventually finding their way to

West Germany. At the same time that East Germans descended upon Hungary to journey through the Iron Curtain, they also swarmed West German embassies in Prague, Budapest, and even East Berlin itself, scaling fences and enduring trying sanitary conditions inside the crowded embassies in the hopes of obtaining permission to leave for West Germany.

Other East Germans thought the time ripe not to leave the country, but rather to reform it from within. In September, the artist Bärbel Bohley, Jens Reich, and other prominent dissidents established *Neues Forum* (New Forum), an oppositional group that aimed to open discussion on the major issues facing East Germany. In Leipzig, the old market city in southern East Germany, increasingly large crowds attended the Monday night peace service at the St. Nikolai church, a service that started in 1982 but with the border through Hungary open, and New Forum and other oppositional groups established, these ordinary church services turned into mass demonstrations.[3] On October 2, following the church service, the security forces brutally disbanded a demonstration of about 20,000 people.

The East German government, under the leadership of the ailing seventy-seven-year-old Erich Honecker, began preparations to deal with the huge demonstration planned for the following Monday, October 9, in Leipzig. Security reinforcements were sent to Leipzig, hospitals alerted to prepare extra beds and blood plasma. Germans considering attending the demonstration that October night in Leipzig had every reason to be fearful—just a few months previously, the Communist party newspaper *Neues Deutschland* (New Germany) boasted that "China's national army defeats counter-revolutionary riot," a chilling view of the Tiananmen Square massacre.[4] In the last hours before the demonstrations, Kurt Masur, the Leipzig Gewandhaus orchestra conductor and later conductor of the New York philharmonic orchestra, succeeded in convincing the party leaders in Berlin not to use force to disperse the crowd. The armed security forces melted into the darkness as demonstrators poured out of the St. Nikolai church and into downtown Leipzig. Demonstrations continued to increase in size culminating in the massive demonstration on November 4, 1989 in East Berlin which attracted between 500,000 and 1 million people. East Germany's noted author Christa Wolf and the legendary head of East German foreign espionage, Markus Wolf, addressed the crowd.

Five days later, on November 9, 1989, at 7 pm precisely, Günter Schabowski, secretary for information for East Germany's ruling Socialist Unity Party, announced at a televised press conference that the government was easing travel restrictions. When asked when this would take effect, Schabowski answered, "immediately," although the changes were in fact supposed to be instituted the following day. In responding to a question by Tom Brokaw of NBC News, Schabowski summarized the meaning of his announcement: "It is possible for them [East Germans—GB] to go through the border."[5] Thousands of citizens of the German Democratic Republic (GDR) immediately began lining up to pass through the concrete wall that symbolized the Cold War. Bewildered East German border guards yielded to the pressure from the mounting crowds and opened the crossings to West Berlin.[6] By midnight, the line of spluttering Trabants containing East Germans eager to reach the long-forbidden western half of the former German capital extended for miles. That night in Berlin demonstrated the different human reactions to the unknown. Some East Berliners swarmed through West Berlin hugging strangers and lining up at sex shops; others forbade their children to leave the house, having fallen for the Communist propaganda about the Wall being an "anti-fascist protective barrier" and believing that West German Nazis would soon overrun their eastern city. The fall of the Berlin Wall paved the way for the first free elections in East Germany in March 1990, and for German unification the following October. Although the nature of the events in 1989 continue to be debated—did the regime simply implode? or did a genuine revolution take place?[7]— it is clear that the people themselves played an important role in forcing the hand of government, and in forcing the pace of change. In the end, the demonstrators of the fall of 1989 in East Germany helped usher in major political changes in East Germany.

The dramatic toppling of the government in East Germany has forced historians to reexamine the history of what was perceived as a fairly stable Communist country, and in this regard earlier resistance in East Germany must come under close scrutiny. The following study examines political resistance in eastern Germany in the first decade after World War II with a particular emphasis on the relationship between repression and resistance. This study deals with the two most tangible manifestations of this resistance: the actions of members of the non-Marxist parties in the GDR—the Christian Democratic Union (CDU), the Liberal Democratic Party of Germany (LDPD), and the Social Democratic Party of Germany (SPD) (banned in eastern Germany except eastern Berlin from 1946)—and the only other mass uprising in East German history, that of June 17, 1953. In essence, both are similar phenomena which fall broadly under the category of *bürgerlich* (bourgeois) resistance, characterized by a rejection of the Communist system, a desire for a united democratic Germany, and the restoration of basic human rights. In both manifestations, the state's abuse of basic rights of its citizens—such as freedom of speech, the right to own property, and personal legal security—played a dominant role in the motivation to resist. Although opposition in the GDR may well have "had many faces," as Ilko-Sascha Kowalczuk has asserted,[8] approaching the topic of resistance from this point of view misses the *communality* of motive to resist.

With regard to the June 17 uprising, this study aims to restore balance to the historiography which has tended to emphasize economic motives of the demonstrators. Indeed, in many accounts of the uprising, the reader comes away with the impression that the Soviet occupation from 1945 to 1949 was completely removed from the uprising; that East German workers were more concerned with spare parts for the factory than with the arrests of their colleagues; and that East Germans were oblivious to the fact that they were living in a dictatorship that systematically abused basic rights.[9] Although economic factors certainly played a role in the uprising, it is appropriate to view the uprising not only in economic terms.

There were other manifestations of fundamental political resistance in this time period. Individuals or groups who worked for anti-Communist groups based in West Berlin, such as the CIA-backed Fighting Group Against Inhumanity

(*Kampfgruppe gegen Unmenschlichkeit—KgU*) and the Investigative Committee of Free Jurists (*Untersuchungsausschuss freiheitlicher Juristen—UfJ*) merit consideration in this regard, as do East Germans who worked "behind the lines" directly for western intelligence agencies.[10] However, these groups are addressed only tangentially in this study because of the dearth of sources and the difficulty in determining the motives of East Germans who worked for these groups. It is telling that recent works, based on declassified American documents, on American efforts to subvert the eastern bloc through guerrilla and intelligence efforts are virtually silent on resisters in Eastern Europe and on the ground operations there.[11]

There is strong evidence that the West, and the United States and United Kingdom in particular, played a role in resistance efforts throughout Eastern Europe in the early postwar period, whether directly by infiltrating agents to support and organize local resistance, as intended in the numerous U.S. operations in Rumania in 1946 and the doomed Albanian efforts of 1950,[12] or indirectly through psychological warfare, such as Radio Free Europe or leaflet drops from balloons. The American government came to prefer psychological operations in any case after bungled infiltration operations confirmed Presidents Truman and Eishenhower's reluctance to run covert operations in Eastern Europe.[13] The extent to which radio broadcasts into Eastern Europe and leaflet campaigns contributed to popular dissent is exceptionally difficult to capture, but nonetheless presents itself as a fertile area of investigation for future historians.[14]

In certain cases, the West had important building blocks of resistance already in place in Eastern Europe. The heavily armed Ukrainian Insurgent Army (UPA) fought a ferocious underground campaign against Communist rule in both Ukraine and Poland.[15] In the Baltics, the British attempted to build on the anti-Soviet "Forest Brothers" partisan group.[16] Other building blocks could be found in the popular discontent that manifested itself in a march that turned into an anti-government rally of 10,000 strong in May 1946 in Cracow,[17] and major labor unrest that paralyzed the textile industry in Łódź in September 1947,[18] that swept through the tobacco factories near Plovdiv and Khaskovo, Bulgaria in May 1953, and that shut down the mighty Škoda factory in Plzeň, Czechoslovakia in June 1953.[19]

The conduct of the Christian churches in the GDR also merits consideration in the topic of resistance. This resistance, however, should be conceptualized in terms of resistance stemming from an institutionalized world view fundamentally different from the Communist world view. Moreover, the ultimate political aims of this resistance are not as tangible as the aims of the subjects under examination in this study. Church resistance therefore merits consideration on its own terms, in terms of a long-established institution attempting to defend its independence.[20] Church resistance represented a different phenomenon to the individual and group resistance discussed in this study. Nevertheless, the fundamental resistance of the churches and the anti-Communist groups like the KgU merit a place in the historiography of resistance in the GDR.

Major European thinkers have contemplated the role of repression in the motivation to resist. In the fifteenth century, Nicholas of Cusa, whom Ernst Cassirer has characterized as "the first great modern thinker,"[21] wrestled with the topic of whether revolution was ever justified given that kings were entrusted by God to stand vigil over society. He concluded that a revolt was justified if the monarch violated the trust of his subjects.[22] Establishing trust between rulers and ruled, in particular where basic rights were concerned, was central to the English Bill of Rights of 1689. The Bill of Rights outlined Parliament's right to participate in the governing process, and affirmed basic freedoms for the English people, including the right to trial by jury and the right to be released from prison if the jailor could not show cause for imprisonment (*Habeas Corpus*).[23] During the Enlightenment, political philosophers came to view the role of the state as guarantor and protector of the natural rights with which all individuals are endowed: the right to liberty, to security of the person, and to property. John Locke, the first philosopher to deal comprehensively with the political consequences of Enlightenment thought, believed that a revolt was justified when the king failed to protect the natural rights of his subjects. Locke argued that if the king failed in this task, his monarchy would be a form of war rather than government.[24] Locke's justification for revolt was closely tied to the intellectual climate of seventeenth and eighteenth century Europe which conceived of political legitimacy resting in individuals and their natural rights. The American Declaration of Independence of July 4, 1776 reflected these aspects of Enlightenment thought. The Declaration proclaimed unalienable rights to be "life, liberty and the pursuit of happiness,"[25] and acknowledged political legitimacy as resting in individuals, claiming that if a government did not secure the above mentioned rights, the people had the right to alter or abolish that government.[26] The classic document of the French Revolution, the Declaration of the Rights of Man and the Citizen, arguably the most important document in shaping the course of nineteenth-century European history, echoed the emphasis on basic rights which had characterized the American Declaration of Independence, declaring basic rights to be liberty, property, personal security, and the right to resist oppression.[27] Furthermore, the Declaration proclaimed that laws would be enacted which would protect citizens against arbitrary arrest, and which would protect the citizen's right to freedom of expression. In the nineteenth century, almost all European nations experienced popular challenges to the state in support of the basic rights brought to the fore by the French Revolution.[28]

Resistance in East Germany in the decade following World War II, like the German resistance to Hitler,[29] follows in this tradition of resistance which justified itself by the fact that the ruling regime failed to serve and protect its subjects and their natural rights. The development of the East German state from 1945 eroded both organized political opponents' and the broader population's belief that the state exercised its authority in the name of the people.[30] The demonstrators of June 17, 1953, like organized political opponents, did not simply demand replacement of the government, but sought a new political system characterized by a government which safeguarded individual freedom and equality before the law, and allowed participation in the political process, both pillars of modern western democracies.[31] The existence of such a political system in neighboring West Germany naturally influenced the resisters' desire for a western democratic system to replace the Communist one.

Historians who deal with resistance in the German Democratic Republic must inevitably turn to the rich historiography on resistance in the Third Reich,[32] but they must be cautious and consider these works as a starting point rather than a reference point. The two dictatorships and their historical circumstances were fundamentally different. That the GDR was not involved in an all-encompassing war or mass murder, and that the GDR formed part of a divided German nation, are a few of the more obvious differences. Nevertheless, the historiography on resistance in Nazi Germany has contributed significantly to the conceptualization of "resistance," and leaves an important legacy for historians of GDR resistance.[33]

The concept of "resistance," and the emphasis on high-level assassination attempts on Hitler, came to be reevaluated in the 1960s, leading to a broadening of the types of activities which could be categorized as resistance.[34] Researchers involved with the Institute for Contemporary History's project "Resistance and Persecution in Bavaria 1933-1945," known simply as the Bavaria Project, carried out the most important work on this topic. The results of this project were published between 1977 and 1983 in a six-volume set entitled *Bayern in der NS-Zeit* (Bavaria in the era of National Socialism). Ian Kershaw has summed up the nucleus of this project: "The emphasis was placed upon the impact of the Nazi regime on all areas of everyday life, allowing a multi-faceted picture of spheres of conflict between rulers and ruled to emerge."[35] Concentrating on "spheres of conflict" inevitably led to an evaluation of resistance. The Bavaria Project initially adopted the following definition of resistance: "Resistance is understood as every form of active or passive behaviour which allows recognition of the rejection of the National Socialist regime or a partial area of National Socialist ideology and was bound up with certain risks."[36] Peter Hüttenberger, a member of the Bavaria Project involved in conceptualizing its approach, promoted this definition which expanded the traditional view of resistance to include actions not specifically designed to overthrow the government. He brought to the fore the importance of "resistance" as a reaction, and therefore a concept of room for maneuver: "Research on resistance must therefore grasp the social relationships, and include the reciprocal mechanisms of power and societal reaction."[37] The Bavaria Project therefore set the criterion for resistance as effect, not motive, and subsequently examined the daily life of Germans in Bavaria during the Nazi era with particular attention to those activities which actually forced the regime to compromise—actions that limited the regime's agenda in some way, no matter how small. In 1981, Martin Broszat, one of the editors of *Bayern in der NS-Zeit*, made a plea for a new concept to describe this type of resistance, believing the term "resistance" was too closely linked to elite resistance and the assassination attempts. In Volume IV of *Bayern in der NS-Zeit*, Broszat fully defined the concept of *Resistenz*, borrowed from the medical vocabulary for a body fighting a foreign presence, which he had cursorily introduced in Volume I of the series. Broszat defined *Resistenz* as "effective defense, limitation, stemming of National Socialist power or claims to power, regardless of motive, interests, or driving forces."[38] *Re-*

sistenz covered a wide range of activity, from factory strikes, to disregarding the ban on being in the company of Jews, to refusing the Hitler greeting. Broszat's approach represented the polar opposite to traditional resistance historiography, as *motive* for actions receded into the background. Broszat defended his position by stating: "In every socio-political system, even more so under a political domination like that of National Socialism, what counts most is that which was *done* and *accomplished*, less that which was only *desired* or *intended*."[39] Ian Kershaw perhaps stated it best when he said that in Broszat's approach, resistance was portrayed in shades of grey, rather than black and white.[40]

Broszat's concept has received a mixed review in the academic world. The primary difficulties in grappling with Broszat's approach are demonstrated by two statements by Peter Hoffmann: "It makes no sense today to demand that every opponent of the regime and of National Socialism had to have been a fanatical potential assassin in order that his opposition be believed."[41] And: "On the whole, at all times from 1933 to 1945 the majority of German voters, indeed of the entire population, supported the government, albeit with varying degrees of willingness."[42] In light of Hoffmann's observations, the lack of analysis of motive in the *Resistenz* concept is glaring. Did *Resistenz* activities imply support of, or opposition to, the Nazi regime? At an international conference of historians in Berlin in July 1984, the Swiss historian Walter Hofer in particular lashed out at the *Resistenz* concept for blurring the distinction between fundamental resistance against the Nazi system and superficial opposition. He argued that motive was of central importance in the discussion on resistance.[43] Klaus Michael Mallmann and Gerhard Paul came to a similar conclusion, stating that Broszat's definition clouded the issue of resistance as, ultimately, *Resistenz* could be interpreted as basic support for the regime, rather than basic hostility to it.[44] The closeness of the terms *Resistenz* and the English "resistance" is therefore misleading. Peter Steinbach has criticized the *Resistenz* approach, arguing that "resistance appears as daily behaviour, not as an escalation of a wide spectrum of resistance behaviour to a decisive and life-threatening act."[45] Timothy Mason has also taken issue with the *Resistenz* concept, arguing that working class strikes were political resistance, not *Resistenz,* as they were politically motivated actions designed to weaken or even overthrow the regime.[46]

Ian Kershaw downplays the criticism of the *Resistenz* approach, stating that Broszat introduced the term as a conceptual device to investigate the effect of National Socialist penetration of society on the "little people" and the extent to which they defended against it, in no way suggesting that *Resistenz* derailed the Nazis from their ultimate objectives. *Resistenz* was thus a manner of conceptualizing Nazi Germany in terms of conflict spheres—as a dynamic relationship between the power structure and the broader society. As Broszat himself stated: "The expansion of the topic of resistance was not meant to open the door to an increasing devaluation of the term resistance. . . . The goal was rather to demonstrate the broad scale of resistance as well as its types of expression—from the occasional or persistent non-conformity to illegal underground work. Above all, it was to demonstrate the abundance of opportunities and circumstances for oppositional behaviour."[47] In other words, the "resistance" which had occupied a prominent place in historiography up to that point represented just the extreme case within Broszat's topic of investigation. To further clarify Broszat's position, Kershaw distinguishes between the *fundamentalist* approach to resistance, which deals with "organized attempts to combat Nazism and . . . high-risk political action [which challenged] the regime as a whole,"[48] and the *societal* approach, which explores "a multiplicity of points of conflict with ordinary citizens."[49] Although Kershaw is correct to point out the distinction between the two approaches, his flattery towards Broszat's *Resistenz* as a conceptual framework is too extreme. The criticisms of historians like Mallmann, Paul, and Hofer must be taken seriously. Broszat has, in fact spawned a school of thought whereby *Resistenz* replaces resistance as "real" resistance. As Broszat states: "If through the investigations of the Bavaria project it becomes clear that active, fundamental resistance against the NS-Regime was fruitless on almost all occasions, but on the other hand effective *Resistenz* can be detected in many different ways in various social sections, then this alone is a result that should cause reflection on the premises of the term 'resistance.'"[50] Fruitlessness, however, cannot be a criterion of determining whether or not something happened.

Robert Gellately's works on the Gestapo, although not directly concerned with the issue of resistance, provide a balance to *Resistenz* historiography, and point to an important criterion in determining the level of acceptance of the regime. In *The Gestapo and German Society* (Oxford: Clarendon Press, 1990), Gellately addressed the high level of cooperation that the Gestapo experienced from the wider society. Gellately concluded that individuals became unofficial enforcers of the regime not only out of fear for their own safety, but due to underlying support for the regime.[51] As Gellately has written: "Instead of (implicitly or otherwise) regarding the German population as largely *passive*, it might be more useful to portray them as more *active* participants who, even as unorganized individuals, from time to time played a role in the terror system."[52] Active participation with the secret police is an important barometer of the regime's support, and is applicable to East Germany. Klessmann has tangentially referred to this point: "The enormous number of [Stasi informants] was actually a substitute for badly functioning spontaneous denunciation."[53] Klessmann's generalization does not apply to the earlier period of GDR history when the informant system was still in its infancy, but the low level of cooperation with the Ministry for State Security even in those days points to a general rejection of this arm of the regime, and by extension the regime itself. A study of East Germany's Ministry for State Security (MfS) in the early years reveals that the MfS had considerable difficulties in gaining popular acceptance.[54]

Historians are presently grappling with the application of resistance research on the Third Reich to the GDR. In a recent publication, Ilko-Sascha Kowalczuk made an initial attempt at categorizing GDR resistance. Kowalczuk believes that the terms "opposition" and "resistance" are synonymous: "In principle, resistance and opposition are understood as a type of behaviour which brought into question, limited, or stemmed the all encompassing claims to political domination. This type of behaviour should be called resistance, which can be organized or not organized, and which can be carried out by groups, individuals or institutions."[55] Kowalczuk described four basic types of resistance: (1) refusal to participate in society (*gesell-schaftliche Verweigerung*), (2) social protest (*sozialer Protest*), (3) political dissent (*Politischer Dissens*), and (4) mass protest (*Massenprotest*). The first was the most common type of resistance in the GDR, a passive protest which could include referring to the Berlin Wall as "the Wall" rather than an "antifascist protective barrier" or refusing to participate in the parties or mass organizations.[56] The most common type of refusal to participate in society involved watching or listening to western television and radio. As in Broszat's approach, the motive for this type of resistance recedes into the distance. The second category, social protest, was tied to various social groups and their reaction to developments in society. The most drastic examples of this type of protest were strikes.[57] Kowalczuk points out that this type of protest flowed easily into political dissent. The third category, political dissent, encompassed reform socialists, "bourgeois" (*bürgerlich*) opposition, and societal or cultural opposition. The latter manifested itself in rock music or hair styles, while the reform socialists played a negligible role in the 1950s, taking on a more prominent role in the 1970s and 1980s. Bourgeois opposition was critical in the 1950s, however, led by small groups but enjoying the widespread support of the population. It was characterized by the rejection of Marxist-Leninist ideology and strove for a free democratic Germany: politics as practiced in West Germany.[58] The last category is self-explanatory, witnessed only on two occasions in the GDR: June 17, 1953 and in the fall of 1989. Kowalczuk's assertion that bourgeois opposition in the 1950s was widespread merits attention. His choice of term to categorize this opposition, "political dissent," is inappropriate, however, for it is associated with the reform movements of the latter years of the GDR, and the term "dissent" detracts from the basic rejection of the Communist regime. It is more useful to conceive of the bourgeois opposition of the later 1940s and early 1950s in terms of fundamental political resistance.

More recently, Rainer Eckert has published "17 Theses" on resistance and opposition in the GDR.[59] The seventeen theses cover a wide spectrum of opposi-tional activity, but are weighted towards opposition in the latter years of the regime. Eckert does not deal specifically with a definition of resistance, although he is careful to stress the need to differentiate between the fundamental resistance of social democrats, Christians, and underground groups like the Fighting Groups Against Inhumanity and the Investigative Committee of Free Jurists, and the oppo-sition of reform-oriented groups of the 1970s and 1980s.[60] Eckert addressed several central issues regarding resistance in East Germany. First, he pointed out that attempts "to approach dictatorial power from the angles of resistance or opposition" are rare among historians,[61] adding that "this approach only makes sense when resistance is accepted as a phenomenon of dictatorship."[62] The leading authority on German resistance to Hitler has already come to this conclusion: "The relation between National Socialism and the Resistance is a key to comprehending the Nazi System."[63] It is important, therefore, to explore East German resistance in conjunc-tion with the development of the dictatorship. Eckert also raised the issues of whether East Germans who worked for foreign spy services, or those who fled the GDR, should be considered resisters. He concluded that those who fled the GDR cannot be considered true resisters because they essentially abandoned hope of changing the regime.[64] The issue of agents is more complicated and will have to await further research and ultimately greater access to documents. It does seem on first analysis that East Germans who conducted subversive work against the GDR out of political conviction should be considered resisters.

The most recent attempt to clarify the term "resistance" has come from Christoph Klessmann in a 1996 article in *Historische Zeitschrift* entitled "Opposition und Resistenz in zwei Diktaturen in Deutschland." Klessmann prefers the term "opposition" for GDR history because "resistance" is associated with the active political fighting of the Nazi regime. To further his choice of word, Klessmann stated: "The examples from the GDR show at least that we are dealing with partial opposition rather than resistance with the goal of toppling the system."[65] This definition may be appropriate for the latter years of the GDR, but is not applicable to the founding years of the regime when there was clear resistance with the aim of overthrowing the Communist system. Neither has Klessmann's analysis contributed to an understanding of the June 17 uprising. The uprising, the most visible example of resistance to the regime prior to 1989, received only one sentence in Klessmann's discussion.[66] Klessmann is correct, however, but saying nothing new in pointing out the importance of motive for differentiating between Resistenz and Opposition, although both involved personal risk: "Historians should attempt . . . to draw the line between Resistenz as (often unintentional) limiting of political power, and opposition as conscious . . . hostility."[67]

Historical works on resistance in the GDR are far fewer than those on resistance in the Nazi era, in part because the East German archives were opened only recently. Because of the vast quantity of sources now accessible, it seems premature for some historians to question the usefulness of the new material. Lutz Niethammer, speaking for a group of historians at a conference of the *Forschungsschwerpunkt Zeithistorische Studien* in Potsdam in June 1993, stated that "studies on the 17 June uprising based on new material can complement, and occasionally, correct the best western studies (such as Baring's), but on the whole show the previous western works to be classics rather than rubbish."[68] Niethammer later committed another disservice to the historical profession, stating that historical analysis on the GDR, especially on the major events, will now depend on evaluation and analysis of what is already known, rather than on new information emerging from the archives.[69] Happily, this attitude was not shared by all historians in attendance. Armin Mitter in particular spoke out against this position.[70]

The lack of historical works on GDR resistance was due in part to the dearth of sources, but also in part to the "political incorrectness" of the topic in the era of *Ostpolitik*. Beginning with the *Generalvertrag* in 1972, West German historians in general became reluctant to investigate topics which might be disparaging to East Germany and jeopardize the precarious friendship which had been established. As a result, the standard western histories of the GDR have only fragmentary information on resistance, usually limited to a crude interpretation of the June 17 uprising and the visible resistance of intellectuals such as Wolfgang Harich and Robert Havemann.[71] This absence becomes noticeable when these works are contrasted with more recent studies of the GDR such as Mary Fulbrook's *Anatomy of a Dictatorship* (Oxford: Oxford University Press, 1995) in which societal reaction to the regime occupies a prominent position. However, Fulbrook concerned herself to a greater extent with the latter years of the regime and acts of opposition which would fall under Broszat's *Resistenz* category. Her intent was to "open up some of the more inchoate, but not less important, forms of popular dissent or 'resistance' in the broader sense of the regime's demands. It is clear that much nonconforming behaviour was not explicitly regarded or consciously intended as such. . . . It was on the whole primarily self-protective, with respect to the defence of an individual's own personal values or interests, rather than actively oppositional in intent."[72] In this approach, motive for opposition occupies a secondary role, yet Fulbrook herself provided an important clue to underlying motive for opposition when she stated: "It was not so much because the GDR lacked national legitimacy, as that it failed to produce a new, intrinsic, legitimacy of its own, that its stability was undermined."[73] As will be demonstrated in this study, abuse of basic rights significantly contributed to the regime's inability to establish legitimacy in the 1940s and 1950s.

Prior to 1989, the only sound work dedicated to opposition and resistance in the GDR was Karl Wilhelm Fricke's *Opposition und Widerstand in der DDR* (Cologne: Verlag Wissenschaft und Politik, 1984). Fricke defined opposition as hostility to the political situation which expressed itself relatively legally and relatively openly, whereas resistance was political opposition which did not have open and legal means to express itself.[74] Fricke's work was not primarily concerned with the development of resistance in association with the development of the repression apparatus, nor with the June 17, 1953 uprising. Fricke's work remains a significant contribution to the literature and an important introduction to the field of GDR opposition.

Within the period under investigation, 1945 to 1955, the most evident demonstration of popular resistance was the uprising on June 17, 1953. This topic has enjoyed a renaissance in the aftermath of the opening of the archives, yet the conclusions that have been reached have been far from uniform. The debate centers around the nature of the uprising. Was it a popular anti-communist revolutionary upheaval? Or was it simply a workers' uprising, the result of poor working conditions and therefore more representative of a "normal" conflict present in any modern society? With regard to the nature of the uprising, Armin Mitter's conclusion is noteworthy: "More conclusive is the fact that June 17 was not about a workers' revolt or workers' movement, but rather that the *resistance potential* within society as a whole against Communist power was activated. Workers were only one part of this resistance potential, if perhaps the most important."[75] This "resistance potential," and the role of abuse of basic rights within the formation of this potential, is investigated in the present work. A full discussion of the literature on the 17 June uprising is found in chapter five of this study.

Based on this historiographical analysis of resistance in Nazi Germany and of literature on the GDR, this study sets out several goals. First, it seeks to return motive to a prominent place in the consideration of resistance. The primary difficulty with a *Resistenz* approach is that it removes motive as a consideration in reaction to the development of the regime.[76] This study, therefore, considers resistance to be acts, organized or not, which arose from a conscious, political motive, aimed at undermining the political system in some way, and bound with a certain degree of risk. Individuals who carried out these acts ultimately aspired to overthrow the Communist system. Organized leaflet distribution by members of the non-Marxist parties and in particular the underground activity of members of the SPD and the June 17, 1953 uprising will therefore be treated as similar phenomena.

Second, this study will detail the history of resistance in the political parties by integrating records from the parties and those of the east German security apparatus. This integrated approach, not available in the present literature, reveals the prominent place of repression in motivation to resist and the presence of resistance in the lower levels of the LDPD and CDU.[77]

Third, this study will argue that a basic commonality existed between aims and motives of resisters in the non-Marxist political parties and those in the broader population. This thesis has been proposed in the literature, but has not been proven conclusively.[78] To prove this hypothesis, one must address the only instance of concerted resistance to remove the Communist system in East Germany during the period under investigation: the revolution of June 17, 1953, and the evidence demands the term "revolution" be applied, rather than the heretofore preferred term "uprising." This study will provide previously unavailable information on the revolution and its aftermath to demonstrate the political nature of the revolution, and thus challenge existing studies which emphasize the economic component of the disturbances. If one sets aside the organizational aspects, the June 17, 1953 revolution was an act of resistance fundamentally similar to the July 20, 1944 assassination attempt. By examining the Soviet Occupied Zone and the GDR from 1945 to 1955, it becomes clear that there existed in the East German population a basic rejection of the Communist system which was intertwined with the regime's disregard for basic rights. Protestors on June 17, 1953 demonstrated for the release of political prisoners and voiced political demands similar to those which had been raised by oppositional members of the non-Marxist parties in the GDR prior to their being forced into line. The organized political resistance in the non-Marxist parties was resistance with the people (*Widerstand mit Volk*).[79]

Fourth, this study seeks to incorporate an examination of the repression apparatus into an analysis of resistance, thereby illustrating the symbiotic relationship between resistance and repression. The material on the Communist repression apparatus which will be introduced will provide a balance to studies which emphasize the role of economic considerations as a source of the revolution.[80]

Because of the collapse of Communism in East Germany, rich sources on the topic of resistance are now available. On resistance in the CDU, documents of the *Archiv für Christlich-Demokratische Politik* (Archive for Christian Democratic

Politics) in the Konrad Adenauer Foundation in Sankt-Augustin are imperative, as records of the CDU *Kreis* and *Bezirk* levels provide a view into the situation in the lower levels of the party, not always reflected in the records of the leadership. These lower level reports also contain situation reports on the East German population after 1953. When used in conjunction with state records and records of the other non-Marxist parties, these records provide valuable insights into the population. Unfortunately, the records of the CDU *Ostbüro* contain only fragmentary evidence on CDU resistance activity in the Soviet zone/GDR.

The holdings of the *Archiv des Deutschen Liberalismus* (Archive of German Liberalism) in the very comfortable Friedrich Naumann Foundation in Gummersbach contain documentation on the LDPD. Like the CDU files, records of the *Kreis* and *Bezirk* level provide information on resistance in the lower levels of the party—in most cases more so than CDU records on the lower levels of the CDU—not reflected in higher levels of the party. Situation reports from the LDPD following the revolution also provide insight into the population. Documentation from the *Ostbüro* of the FDP is, like that of the CDU, fragmentary.

The *Archiv der sozialen Demokratie* (Archive of Social Democracy) in the Friedrich Ebert Foundation in Bonn contains exceptionally useful documentation on SPD underground activity in eastern Germany, especially the statements of those involved in resistance activity and the reports of SPD couriers on activity in eastern Germany. Documentation from the higher levels of the western SPD, on the other hand, is not useful as it does not provide information on SPD activity in the East. The western SPD ran the *Ostbüro* furtively.

The most important holdings on resistance activity in the *Stiftung Archiv der Parteien und Massenorganisationen der DDR* (Foundation Archive of the Parties and Mass Organizations of the GDR) housed in a former department store in Berlin (and since moved) are found in the record groups *Befreundete Parteien* (Befriended Parties), *Amt für Information* (Information Office), *Justiz* (Justice), the papers of leading functionaries, and *Leitende Organe der Parteien und Massenorganisationen* (Leading Organs of the Parties and Mass Organizations). A recent study made extensive use of files in this latter record group; thus these files, unlike the files in the other groups, were not systematically investigated for the present study.[81] The records of the Free German Trade Union (FDGB) should be explored in future research for insights into popular developments.[82]

Documentation generated by the GDR's repression apparatus offers excellent evidence on the development of resistance in the Soviet Occupied Zone and GDR. Records of the Ministry of the Interior (previously held in Potsdam, and now transferred to Berlin-Lichterfelde) offer the most comprehensive documentation on the revolution of 1953. Records of the Ministry for State Security in Berlin held by the German office with a name that puts people off learning German—*Bundesbeauftragter für die Unterlagen des Staatssicherheitsdienstes der ehemaligen Deutschen Demokratischen Republik* (Federal Commission for the Files of the State Security Service of the former German Democratic Republic)—are also valuable in assessing resistance. The holdings of the *Dokumentenstelle* provide information on MfS operations, while the *Sekretariat des Ministers* record group contains the records of leadership meetings. The situation reports collected by the MfS following the revolution are contained in a general record group called the *Allgemeine Sachablage*. These reports are presented for the first time in this study.[83]

In analyzing resistance in the Soviet Occupied Zone and GDR from 1945 to 1955, it becomes clear that resistance was intimately tied to concepts of law, democracy, and the moral basis of power. Emmi Bonhoeffer, at the thirty-seventh anniversary of the July 20, 1944 assassination attempt, reflected on the nature of German resistance in the Third Reich: "Resistance to Hitler was always both: moral protest and political calculation. The moral protest was directed at the cynicism of Hitler and his government, against his attacks on neighbouring peoples, his persecution of the Jews and its infernal result. The political considerations revolved around the destruction of the concept of law, around an analysis of the development of dictatorship, and around the reorganization of the state after Hitler . . . to guarantee a parliamentary form of government."[84] Thus a common link between both resistance in the Third Reich and in the GDR in the 1940s and 1950s was a desire for a state based on the rule of law, a concern for human rights and freedoms, and the protection of the individual from the totalitarian state.

Notes

1. Gale Stokes, *The Walls Came Tumbling Down: The Collapse of Communism in Eastern Europe* (New York: Oxford University Press, 1993), 136.

2. David Remnick, *Lenin's Tomb: The Last Days of the Soviet Empire* (New York: Vintage Books, 1994), 442.

3. Stokes, *The Walls*, 139.

4. Stefan Wolle, "Der Weg in den Zussammenbruch: Die DDR vom Juni bis zum Oktober 1989," in *Die Gestaltung der deutschen Einheit: Geschichte—Politik—Gesellschaft*, ed. Eckhard Jesse and Armin Mitter (Bonn: Bundeszentrale für politische Bildung, 1992), 85.

5. Alexandra Richie, *Faust's Metropolis: A History of Berlin* (NY: Carroll and Graf Publishers Inc., 1998), 834 (footnote 55).

6. Konrad Jarausch, *The Rush to German Unity* (New York: Oxford University Press, 1994), 3-4.

7. Jarausch, *The Rush*, 6.

8. See Ilko-Sascha Kowalczuk's review of Ehrhart Neubert's *Geschichte der Opposition in der DDR 1949-1989* in *Deutschland Archiv* 31 (1998): 135-138. Ehrhart Neubert suggest that there were only four forms of resistance in East Germany: uprisings; resistance stemming from social milieus like political parties and organizations; individual, random acts; and flight from East Germany. See Neubert, *Geschichte Geschichte Opposition in der DDR 1949-1989* (Bonn: Bundeszentrale für politische Bildung, 2000), 31.

9. See the discussion of the literature on June 17, 1953 in chapter 5.

10. The most extensive work on the KgU is Kai-Uwe Merz, *Kalter Krieg als antikommunistischer Widerstand: Die KgU 1948-1959.* (Munich: Oldenbourg Verlag, 1987). The author had access to material in private archives, but the selection of documentation from public archives is limited.

11. Peter Grose, *Operation Rollback: America's Secret War Behind the Iron Curtain*

(Boston: Houghton Mifflin, 2000); Gregory Mitrovich, *Undermining the Kremlin* (Ithaca: Cornell University Press, 2000); Scott Lucas, *Freedom's War: The American Crusade Against the Soviet Union* (New York: New York University Press, 1999).

12. Lucas, *Freedom's*, 48; Grose, *Operation*, 40.

13. Grose, *Operation*, 213; Mitrovich, *Undermining*, 10.

14. Mitrovich points out that western radio broadcasts likely kept the spirit of resistance alive. Mitrovich, *Undermining*, 185.

15. Grose, *Operation*, 44.

16. Grose, *Operation*, 34.

17. Bartholomew Goldyn, "Disenchanted Voices: Public Opinion in Cracow, 1945-46," *East European Quarterly* 32 (1998): 142.

18. Padraic Kenney, *Rebuilding Poland: Workers and Communists, 1945-50* (Ithaca: Cornell University Press, 1997), 121.

19. Mark Kramer, "The Early Post-Stalin Succession Struggle and Upheavals in East-Central Europe," *Journal of Cold War Studies* 1 (1999): 16-19.

20. Ilko-Sascha Kowalczuk, "Von der Freiheit, Ich zu sagen," in *Zwischen Selbstbehauptung und Anpassung*, ed. Ulrike Poppe, Rainer Eckert and Ilko-Sascha Kowalczuk (Berlin: Ch. Links Verlag, 1995), 98. Ehrhart Neubert points out the importance of the religious milieu for opponents of Communism in the GDR. See Neubert, *Geschichte*, 26.

21. Ernst Cassirer, *Individuum und Kosmos in der Philosophie der Renaissance* (Leipzig: B.G. Teubner, 1927), 10. Louis Dubré's treatment of Cusa has also been flattering. Dubré refers to him as "the most original mind of the 15th century." Louis Dubré, "Introduction and major works of Nicholas of Cusa," *The American Catholic Philosophical Quarterly* LXIV (1990): 1.

22. John Morrall, *Political Thought in Medieval Times* (London: Hutchinson and Co. Ltd., 1971), 121.

23. The text of the Bill of Rights is reprinted in Stephen Englehart and John Moore Jr., eds., *Three Beginnings: Revolution, Rights, and the Liberal State* (New York: Peter Lang, 1994), 191-193.

24. John Locke, *Two Treatises of Government*, ed. P. Laslett (New York: Mentor, 1965), 413-416. Thomas Hobbes opposed Locke on this point, arguing that citizens did not possess the right to resistance against the state because it would lead to anarchy, chaos, and war, which, he felt, was far worse than any tyranny. See Thomas Hobbes, *Leviathan*, ed. M. Oakeshott (Oxford: Blackwell, 1947), 114-116.

25. Engelhart and Moore, *Three Beginnings*, 195. The text of the American Declaration of Independence is reprinted in this work: 195-198.

26. Engelhart and Moore, *Three Beginnings*, 195.

27. The text of the Declaration of the Rights of Man and the Citizen is reprinted in Engelhart and Moore, *Three Beginnings*, 201-204.

28. Peter Hoffmann, *The History of the German Resistance 1933-1945* (Montreal: McGill-Queen's University Press, 1996), x.

29. On the historical place of the German resistance to Hitler, see Hoffmann, *The History*, ix-x.

30. On the "people" (das Volk) as the basis of political legitimacy Hermann Heller has written: "Trotz mannigfaltiger Unterströmungen und Gegenwirkungen anderer Art ist spätestens seit dem 18. Jahrhundert als oberster, alle politischen Normen und Formen legitimierender Wert von der allgemeinen öffentlichen Meinung das 'Volk' anerkannt." Quoted in Kurt Lenk, "Probleme der Demokratie," in *Politische Theorien von der Antike bis*

zur Gegenwart, ed. Hans-Joachim Lieber (Bonn: Bundeszentrale für politische Bildung, 1993), 938.

31. Lenk, "Probleme," 939.

32. Mary Fulbrook points out in her recent history of the GDR that it will likely be a number of years before the historiography on opposition in East Germany reaches the same level of sophistication as has been achieved in the literature on resistance in Nazi Germany; Mary Fulbrook, *Anatomy of a Dictatorship: Inside the GDR 1949-1989* (Oxford: Oxford University Press, 1995), 153. On the value of the historiography of Nazi Germany for GDR history in general, see Christoph Klessmann, "Zwei Diktaturen in Deutschland—was kann die künftige DDR-Forschung aus der Geschichtsschreibung zum Nationalsozialismus lernen," *Deutschland Archiv* (hereafter DA) 25 (1992): 601-606.

33. The most important works on German resistance to Hitler in outlining the debates in the field are, in roughly chronological order: Hans Rothfels, *The German Opposition to Hitler* (Hinsdale: Henry Regenery Co., 1948), originally published in English, and in German the following year; Gerhard Ritter's *Carl Goerdeler und die deutsche Widerstandsbewegung* (Stuttgart: Deutsche Verlags-Anstalt GmbH, 1954), which appeared in English as *The German Resistance: Carl Goerdele's Struggle Against Tyranny* (London: George Allen & Unwin, 1958); Hermann Brill's *Gegen den Strom* (Offenbach: Bollwerk Verlag, 1946); Günter Weisenborn's *Der lautlose Aufstand* (Hamburg: Rowohlt, 1953); Hans Mommsen, "Gesellschaftsbild und Verfassungspläne des deutschen Widerstandes," and Hermann Graml, "Die aussenpolitischen Vorstellungen des deutschen Widerstandes," in *Der deutsche Widerstand gegen Hitler*, ed. W. Schmitthenner and H. Buchheim (Cologne: Kipenheuer & Witsch, 1966), published in English in 1970 as *The German Resistance to Hitler*; H.J. Schultz, *Der zwanzigste Juli : Alternative zu Hitler?* (Stuttgart: Kreuz Verlag, 1974); Klaus Mammach, *Die deutsche antifaschistische Widerstandsbewegung 1933-1939* (East Berlin: Dietz, 1974); Peter Hoffmann's *Widerstand, Staatsstreich, Attentat* (Munich: R. Piper, 1969). This work has been revised and expanded several times. It appeared in translation in English in 1977 as *The History of the German Resistance 1933-1945* (Cambridge: The MIT Press, 1977) and as *The History of the German Resistance 1933-1945* (London: MacDonald and Jane's, 1977). In 1985, the fourth German edition was published as *Widerstand, Staatsstreich, Attentat* (Munich: R. Piper, 1985). The latest edition appeared in 1996 as *The History of the German Resistance 1933-1945* (Montreal: McGill-Queen's University Press, 1996). The most important work for an evaluation of the historiography on resistance in the Third Reich for GDR history is Poppe, Eckert, and Kowalczuk, *Zwischen Selbstbehauptung.*

34. The most important summary works on the definition of resistance are: Klaus-Jürgen Müller, ed., *Der deutsche Widerstand 1933-1945* (Paderborn: F. Schoningh, 1986); Jürgen Schmädeke and Peter Steinbach, eds., *Der Widerstand gegen den Nationalsozialismus* (Munich: R. Piper, 1985); Peter Steinbach, ed., *Widerstand: Ein Problem zwischen Theorie und Geschichte* (Cologne: Wissenschaft und Politik, 1987); Peter Steinbach and Johannes Tuchel, eds., *Widerstand gegen den Nationalsozialismus* (Berlin: Akadamie Verlag, 1994); Gerd Ueberschär, ed., *Der 20. Juli 1944: Bewertung und Rezeption des deutschen Widerstandes gegen das NS-Regime* (Cologne: Bund Verlag, 1994).

35. Ian Kershaw, *The Nazi Dictatorship*, 3rd ed. (New York: E. Arnold, 1993), 157.

36. Kershaw, *The Nazi*, 158.

37. Peter Hüttenberger, "Vorüberlegungen zum 'Widerstandsbegriff,' in *Theorien in der Praxis des Historikers*, ed. Jürgen Kocka (Göttingen: Vandenhoeck & Ruprecht, 1977), 122. Because of the importance of language in this debate, all quotations will also be

provided in the original German. "Die Erforschung des Widerstandes muss also die sozialen Beziehungen umgreifen und die wechselseitigen Mechanismen von Herrschaft und gesellschaftlicher Reaktion miteinbeziehen."

38. Martin Broszat, "Resistenz und Widerstand: Eine Zwischenbilanz des Forschungsprojekts," in *Bayern in der NS-Zeit* (Munich: R. Oldenbourg Verlag, 1981), vol. 4, 697. Resistenz was defined as "wirksame Abwehr, Begrenzung, Eindämmung der NS-Herrschaft oder ihres Anspruches, gleichgültig von welchen Motiven, Interessen und Kräften dies bedingt war." For a summary of the main points of the Bavaria Project, see Martin Broszat and Elke Fröhlich, eds., *Alltag und Widerstand—Bayern im Nationalsozialismus* (Munich: Piper, 1987).

39. Broszat, "Resistenz," 698. "In jedem politsch-gesellschaftlichen System, noch mehr unter einer politschen Herrschaft wie der des Nationalsozialismus, zählt politisch und historisch vor allem was getan und was bewirkt, weniger das, was nur gewollt oder beabsichtigt war."

40. Kershaw, *The Nazi,* 158. Broszat and Fröhlich (Alltag, 55) identified three main types of resistance by period, although the borders between them were fluid:
1) Communist and Socialist resistance in the working classes 1933/34.
2) Partial Resistenz/Volksopposition especially in the churches 1935-1940/1.
3) Fundamental opposition and plans for a coup by conservative elite 1938-1944.

41. Hoffmann, *Widerstand* (Munich: R. Piper, 1985), 54.

42. Hoffmann, *Widerstand,* 60.

43. See the discussion comments of Walter Hofer in *Der Widerstand gegen den Nationalsozialismus,* ed. Jürgen Schmädeke and Peter Steinbach, 1119-1158. Marlis Steinert and Klaus-Jürgen Müller shared Hofer's sentiments. Motive has come to occupy an important place in the literature again with Peter Steinbach and Johannes Tuchel, eds., *Widerstand gegen den Nationalsozialismus* (Bonn: Bundeszentrale für politische Bildung, 1994).

44. Klaus Michael Mallmann and Gerhard Paul, "Resistenz oder loyale Widerwilligkeit? Anmerkungen zu einem umstrittenen Begriff," *Zeitschrift für Geschichtswissenschaft* 41 (1993): 99-116. Mallmann and Paul also point out that a weakness in Broszat's approach was the assumption that the all-encompassing totalitarian model of Nazi Germany was accurate. As they stated, the totalitarianism theory came back into the debate through the "back door" of Resistenz research.

45. Steinbach, "Widerstand," 55. "Widerstand erscheint als Verhaltensform des Alltags, nicht aber als Steigerung eines breiten Spektrums von widerständigen Verhaltensweisen zur entscheidenden und lebensgefährlichen Tat."

46. Timothy Mason, "Arbeiteropposition im nationalsozialistischen Deutschland," in *Die Reihen fast geschlossen,* ed. Detlev Peukert and Jürgen Reulecke (Wuppertal: Hammer, 1981), 293. Günther Morsch argues against Mason stating that worker protests in the Third Reich were not politically motivated, and therefore not resistance, but were simply reactions to unacceptable working conditions. Günter Morsch, "Streik im Dritten Reich," *Vierteljahrshefte für Zeitgeschichte* (hereafter VfZ) 36 (1988): 649-689. In Jeffrey Kopstein's work on East Germany, *The Politics of Economic Decline in East Germany, 1945-1989* (Chapel Hill: University of North Carolina Press, 1997), Kopstein uses the term "resistance" loosely, ranging from grumbling, to shirking, to sharing food with colleagues who were not supposed to receive extra rations (26-29). The question remains whether the workers fundamentally rejected the regime.

47. Broszat, "Resistenz," 693. "Die Ausweitung des Widerstandsthemas sollte nicht . . . einer inflationären Entwertung des Widerstandsbegriffs . . . Tür und Tor öffnen. Ihr Ziel

war es vielmehr, die breite Skala der Ausdrucksformen des Widerstandes—von der zeitweilig oder beharrlich resistenten Nonkonformität bis hin zur illegalen Untergrundarbeit aufzuzeigen, vor allem auch die Fülle der Anlässe und Rahmenbedingungen für oppositionelles Verhalten darzulegen." Ian Kershaw provides an excellent summary of the debates surrounding Broszat's Resistenz concept; Kershaw, *The Nazi*, 162-179.

48. Kershaw, *The Nazi*, 167.

49. Kershaw, *The Nazi*, 167

50. Broszat, "Resistenz," 698. In 1982, Richard Löwenthal added to the analysis of resistance by differentiating between (1) political opposition, (2) refusal to participate in society (gesellschaftliche Verweigerung), and (3) ideological dissidence (weltanschauliche Dissidenz). Richard Löwenthal, "Widerstand im totalen Staat," in *Widerstand und Verweigerung in Deutschland 1933 bis 1945*, ed. Richard Löwenthal and Patrik von zur Mühlen (Berlin, Bonn: J.H.W. Dietz GmbH, 1982), 14. Similarly, Hans-Adolf Jacobsen has differentiated between active and passive reistance. Hans-Adolf Jacobsen, *"Spiegelbild einer Verschwörung": Opposition gegen Hitler und der Staatsstreich vom 20. Juli 1944 in der SD-Berichterstattung* Vol. 1. (Stuttgart: Seewald, 1984), 20.

51. Robert Gellately, *The Gestapo and German Society* (Oxford: Clarendon Press, 1990), 10.

52. Robert Gellately, "Rethinking the Nazi Terror System: A historiographical analysis," *German Studies Review* vol. XIV (1991): 30.

53. Christoph Klessmann, "Opposition und Resistenz in zwei Diktaturen in Deutschland," *Historische Zeitschrift* 262 (1996), 457. "Die riesige Zahl von IM war insofern der Ersatz für die schlecht funktioniriende spontane Denunziation."

54. Gellately has suggested that historians of the Third Reich have concentrated either on history from above or from below with little overlap. As a result, recent works on "daily" resistance do not deal adequately with the Nazi security apparatus. He points to Kershaw's analysis of the "Hitler Myth" as an appropriate direction for future historians, as it investigates "both the Führer image-building and image reception"; Gellately, "Rethinking," 27. His comments are also an appropriate reminder for historians of the GDR.

55. Kowalczuk, "Von der Freiheit," 90. "Prinzipiell wird unter Widerstand und Opposition eine Verhaltensform verstanden, die den allumfassenden Herrschaftsanspruch in Frage stellt, begrenzt oder eindämmt. Ein solches Verhalten soll widerständiges heissen. Dabei kann dieses organisiert wie nicht organisiert, in Gruppen, individuell oder institutionell geschehen."

56. Kowalczuk, "Von der Freiheit," 100.

57. Kowalczuk, "Von der Freiheit," 105.

58. Kowalczuk, "Von der Freiheit," 111.

59. Rainer Eckert, "Widerstand und Opposition in der DDR: Siebzehn Thesen," *Zeitschrift für Geschichtswissenschaft* vol. 44 (1996): 49-67.

60. Eckert, "Widerstand," 53.

61. Eckert, "Widerstand," 50.

62. Eckert, "Widerstand," 50.

63. Hoffmann, *German Resistance to Hitler* (Cambridge: Harvard University Press, 1988), 3.

64. Eckert, "Widerstand," 57-58.

65. Christoph Klessmann, "Opposition und Resistenz in zwei Diktaturen in Deutschland." *Historische Zeitschrift* 262 (1996): 455.

66. Klessmann, "Opposition," 479.

67. Klessmann, "Opposition," 460. For a detailed examination of the weaknesses in Klessmann's article, see the review by Peter Hoffmann at www.msu.edu/~german/articles /hoffmann1.html. Accesssed September 6, 1996.

68. Lutz Niethammer's contribution to the discussion in Jürgen Kocka and Martin Sabrow, eds., *Die DDR als Geschichte* (Berlin: Akadamie Verlag, 1994), 65. "Kaum widersprochen wurde schliesslich auch der Einschätzung, dass solche Forschungen die besten zeitnahen westlichen Untersuchungen—wie in diesem Fall Barings—zwar ergänzen, im einzelnen auch korrigieren, sie im Ganzen aber eher zu Klassikern als zur Makulatur machen."

69. Kocka and Sabrow, *Die DDR*, 66.

70. See Armin Mitter, "Der 'Tag X' und die 'Innere Staatsgründung' der DDR," in *Der Tag X: Die "Innere Staatsgründung" der DDR als Ergebnis der Krise 1952/1954*, ed. Ilko-Sascha Kowalczuk, Armin Mitter, and Stefan Wolle (Berlin: Ch. Links Verlag, 1995), 15-16.

71. The basic texts prior to 1989 were David Childs, *The GDR: Moscow's German Ally* (London: Unwin Hyman, 1988); Martin McCauley, *The German Democratic Republic since 1945* (London: MacMillan Press, 1983); Hermann Weber, *Die DDR 1945-1986* (Munich: R. Oldenbourg Verlag, 1988); Dietrich Staritz, *Geschichte der DDR 1945-85* (Frankfurt am Main: Suhrkampf, 1985); M. Dennis, *The German Democratic Republic* (London: Pinter, 1988); Henry Kirsch, *The German Democratic Republic* (Boulder: Westview Press, 1985); Henry Ashby Turner, *The Two Germanies since 1945* (New Haven: Yale University Press, 1987); Christoph Klessmann, *Die doppelte Staatsgründung* (Göttingen: Vandenhoeck & Rupprecht, 1982). It should be noted, however, that David Childs' treatment of the uprising was more advanced than the other analyses. Childs pointed to the important facts that economic demands comprised just one category among the demands voiced by demonstrators on June 17, 1953 and that the demonstrators comprised various societal groups apart from workers. Childs, *The GDR*, 31-33.

72. Fulbrook, *Anatomy*, 153.

73. Fulbrook, *Anatomy*, 279.

74. Fricke, *Opposition*, 14.

75. Mitter, "Der 'Tag X,'" 22. Italics added. Mitter also emphasizes the geistige issue of democracy for the demonstrators; Mitter, "Der 'Tag X,'" 23.

76. Both Peter Steinbach in "Widerstand," 55, and Christoph Klessmann in "Gegner des Nationalsozialismus. Zum Widerstand im Dritten Reich" in *Aus Politik und Zeitgeschichte* B 46/1979 emphasize the importance of political motivation in the concept of resistance.

77. Works on resistance in East German political parties have been scarce. Michael Richter's exhaustive *Die Ost-CDU: Zwischen Widerstand und Gleichschaltung* (Düsseldorf: Droste, 1990) described the process of Gleichschaltung (forcing into line) of the eastern CDU, and offered the most comprehensive study of resistance in the CDU. For this study, his emphasis that the CDU was representative of wider society merits attention. Although one must be wary of counterfactual history, his conclusion that the CDU would have won free elections in eastern Germany in the fall of 1949 is noteworthy. A solid work on the LDPD in the early years of the GDR has yet to be written. Recent works that have contributed to an understanding of the LDPD in the Soviet Occupied Zone and the early years of the German Democratic Republic are Ulf Sommer, *Die Liberal-Demokratische Partei Deutschlands* (Munster: Agenda, 1996) and Jurge Louis, *Die LDPD in Thüringen* (Cologne: Bohlau, 1996). Both works have added a stronger primary source base to the discussion. Ekkehart Krippendorf, *Die Liberal-Demokratische Partei Deutschlands in der sowjetischen*

Besatzungszone 1945-1948 (Düsseldorf: Droste, 1955) remains a sound introduction to the topic.

78. Kowalczuk claims that the democratic resistance in these parties had "massive support in wide sections of the population," but does not support this hypothesis. Kowalczuk, "Von der Freiheit," 111.

79. In 1966, the historian Wolfgang Mommsen suggested that historians' preoccupation with elite opponents of Hitler, and their concerns about the loyalty of the population, led to a distorted view of Widerstand ohne Volk (resistance without the people). Mommsen first introduced this concept in "Gesellschaftsbild und Verfassungspläne des deutschen Widerstandes," in *Der deutsche Widerstand gegen Hitler*, ed. W. Schmitthenner and Hans Buchheim (Cologne: Kipenheuer & Witsch, 1966), 76.

80. Works on the GDR police and judicial systems, both pillars of the SED dictatorship, are valuable for the study of East German resistance. Karl Wilhelm Fricke's *Politik und Justiz in der DDR* (Cologne: Verlag Wissenschaft und Politik, 1979) provided a detailed description of the use of the judicial system for political ends. Wolfgang Schuller's *Geschichte und Struktur des politischen Strafrechts der DDR bis 1968* (Ebelsbach: Gremer, 1980) also investigates the use of GDR justice for political ends. More recently, Falco Werkentin has provided a well-documented study of GDR justice in practice in *Politische Strafjustiz in der Ära Ulbricht* (Berlin: Ch. Links Verlag, 1995). This work is helpful in periodizing the harshness of GDR justice. The MfS in the 1950s has received surprisingly little attention in the literature that has appeared since 1990, making the most important work still Karl Wilhelm Fricke's *Die DDR-Staatssicherheit* (Cologne: Verlag Wissenschaft und Politik, 1989). His conclusion that the MfS was not a state within a state remains valid, but he did not have the source base necessary to provide a thorough treatment of the subject. Recently, several books and articles have appeared on the development of the repression apparatus in the Soviet Occupied Zone, but these have not carried the story into the post-1949 period. See in particular Norman Naimark, *The Russians in Germany*, and Monika Tantzscher, "'In der Ostzone wird ein neuer Apparat aufgebaut': Die Gründung des DDR-Staatssicherheitsdienstes," *Deutschland Archiv* 31 (1998): 48-56. The best source at present for disentangling the various Soviet security organs in the Soviet zone—crucial for an understanding of the development of the East German apparatus is David Murphy, Sergei Kondrashev, George Bailey, *Battleground Berlin* (New Haven: Yale University Press, 1997). David Childs and Richard Popplewell's *The Stasi* (Houndmills: Macmillan, 1996), because of the almost complete lack of new documents, does not further our understanding of the East German security service.

81. See Kowalczuk/Mitter/Wolle, *Der Tag X.*

82. Two initial works based on FDGB records are Gerhard Beier, *Wir wollen freie Menschen sein* (Cologne: Bund Verlag, 1993), and Wolfgang Eckelmann, Hans Hertmann Hertle, and Rainer Weinert, *FDGB Intern: Innenansichten einer Massenorganisation der SED* (Berlin: Treptower Verlagshaus, 1990).

83. For an overview of the holdings of the archive of the former MfS, see my "Update on the Stasi archives," *Cold War International History Project Bulletin* #12 (2000): 348-350.

84. Quoted in Steinbach, "Widerstand," 61.

Chapter 2

Resistance and Repression between the End of the War and the First Elections in the Soviet-Occupied Zone

The Beginning of Political Life in Eastern Germany

On May 7, 1945 in a technical college in the French town of Reims which was serving as the headquarters of General Dwight D. Eisenhower, the Supreme Allied Commander for Europe, Colonel General Alfred Jodl, the Chief of Wehrmacht Leadership Staff in the Supreme Command of the Wehrmacht (OKW), signed the unconditional surrender of the German armed forces. With the repetition of this act in the Soviet army headquarters in Berlin-Karlshorst on the next day, the war that had ravaged Europe for six years effectively came to an end.[1] The Allies arrested on May 23 Germany's government, now headed by Grand Admiral Karl Dönitz whom Hitler had appointed to the position from his bunker as Berlin crumbled around him.[2] The Red Army occupied Berlin and the territory east of the Elbe, while western Allied forces had reached a line stretching from Schwerin in the North and along the Elbe and the Mulde rivers to the south. The western Allies had met up with the Soviets for the famous handshake on the bridge spanning the Elbe near Torgau on April 25.

The leaders of the United States, Great Britain, and the Soviet Union had met twice during the war to plan for the postwar world after their presumed victory, once in Tehran from November 28 to December 1, 1943, and once in the former vacation residences of the Czars in the small Crimean town of Yalta from February 4 to 11, 1945.[3] At Yalta, the leaders agreed that France should participate in the occupation of Germany—the Soviet, American, and British occupation zones had already been decided upon by the London agreements of September 12 and November 14,1944[4]—and on the Allied Control Council and that the Allies were to possess supreme authority in Germany. They could not agree, however, on whether or not Germany should be dismembered, and could only agree in principle to reparations.[5] Although the Yalta conference seemed to prepare the way for joint administration of Germany, Stalin's remark that, in this war, the victor would impose his system as far as his armies reached was a more accurate portrayal of how postwar Germany would be dealt with.[6]

On June 5, 1945 in the same building in the Berlin suburb of Karlshorst where the signing of the unconditional surrender had been repeated, the Allies signed another important agreement regarding Germany's future. The "Declaration in Consideration of the Defeat of Germany" stated that there was no central government in Germany able to comply with the demands of the victorious powers. The governments of France, the Soviet Union, the United States, and Great Britain effectively took over the highest government power in Germany, as had been foreseen at the Yalta conference.[7] While each power was to rule its own zone, the commanders-in-chief, General Dwight Eisenhower, General Bernard Montgomery, Marshal Georgi Zhukov, and General Pierre Koenig, concluded an agreement forming the Allied Control Council to deal with questions concerning all Germany, as well as an Allied Kommandatura to deal specifically with Berlin. The Allied Control Council had one significant drawback: it did not possess the right to intervene in the affairs of the occupation zones.[8] On July 30, the Allies constituted the Allied Control Council in a former courthouse in Schöneberg in the American sector of Berlin, and started its functions on August 30.[9] The Council met regularly until March 20, 1948, when the Soviet representative stormed out. The Council did not meet again.

One month after the end of hostilities, Marshal Georgi Zhukov, commander-in-chief of the Soviet occupation troops and Soviet hero who led the First Belorussian Front in a surge across the Oder River and straight to the Nazi capital, issued Order Number 1 creating a body to administer the Soviet-occupied zone called the Soviet Military Administration in Germany (SMAD in German).[10] Zhukov himself headed SMAD until April 10, 1946.[11] One day after SMAD's founding, Zhukov issued Order Number Two which allowed the founding of anti-fascist political parties and unions in the eastern zone.[12] Order Number 2 meant that political activity in postwar Germany occurred first in the Soviet zone, and much earlier than in the western zones which permitted the formation of political parties only as of August 7, 1945. To Wolfgang Leonhard, a German Communist who lived in exile in the Soviet Union during the war and who has provided historians with rare insights into the Soviet zone in his memoirs, Order Number 2 came as a surprise because the Soviet teachers of the German emigrés had indicated that Germans would be allowed to become politically active again only in the distant future.[13] Order Number 2 was also unexpected because there had been no warning of the announcement in the *Tägliche Rundschau*, the Soviet newspaper that had been appearing in the eastern zone since May 15.[14]

Following Order Number Two, official political life began again in eastern Germany. The Soviets first granted official status to the Communist Party of Germany (KPD). The swift entry of the KPD can be explained by the KPD's preparedness ahead of time for its appearance in the Soviet zone. German Communists living in exile in the Soviet Union during the war had been preparing to set up the KPD in the Soviet zone once the war came to an end. Leading German Communists were organized into three groups, the so-called *Initiativgruppen*, which were responsible for establishing the party in eastern Germany. Walter Ulbricht, a KPD member of the Reichstag who had fled Germany to France in 1933, and after France's fall in 1940 had fled to the Soviet Union, led the Berlin group. Anton Ackermann led the group responsible for Saxony, and Gustav Sobottka led the group responsible for Mecklenburg. Ulbricht's group appeared first in Germany, arriving early in the morning of April 30 on a flight from Moscow, even before the surrender of Berlin on May 2.[15]

Once the war had ended, these groups began disbanding the Antifa (or antifascist) committees that German citizens had founded at the end of the war to restore public works. The Soviet authorities often appointed these committees to exercise public power,[16] but in the eyes of the KPD, these committees posed problems because of their political unreliability; the Antifas often contained members from a mixture of political backgrounds. Communists, Socialists, or a combination of the two established most committees, but there were also committees with a liberal, bourgeois leaning.[17] By June 1945, Antifa committees throughout Germany had been dissolved.[18] The KPD dealings with the Antifa committees are one sign that its agenda in eastern Germany reached beyond merely establishing the administration and cleaning up the rubble; the KPD intended to remove political opponents.[19]

The KPD's proclamation of June 11, 1945, however, demonstrated an apparent change in its political philosophy since the Weimar Republic. Instead of Marxist language like "class struggle" and "the social democratic enemy" permeating the decree, the KPD presented itself as a reformed, broadly based workers' party.[20] In the preamble, the decree even went so far as to claim: "We are of the opinion that it would be wrong to force the Soviet system on Germany, as the present conditions of development in Germany are not suitable for it."[21] In retrospect, the ten points of the KPD program contained signs that the party had not entirely abandoned its dictatorial tendencies. Among calls for the resurrection of democratic rights and freedoms so that all citizens would be equal without regard to race, there was no mention of guarantees for freedom of speech or religion. The proclamation called for parcelling out the land of individuals with large land holdings, without mention of compensation. The proclamation called for justice reform, but on the nebulous grounds of "restructuring the judicial system according to the new democratic way of life of the people." Finally, the call for an anti-fascist, parliamentary, democratic republic lacked detail.[22] The KPD had, however, toned down its rhetoric from the Weimar era, especially with its call for cooperation in a United Front to deal with the tremendous problems facing Germany.

Social Democrats founded the Social Democratic Party of Germany (SPD) four days after the KPD. Various groups of social democrats in Berlin,[23] who had been meeting off and on since the end of the war, came together for the first time on June 7 and elected a Central Committee (*Zentralausschuss*—ZA) with Max Fechner, Eric Gniffke, and Otto Grotewohl as speakers.[24] There were difficulties within the ZA immediately, however, as some members such as Gustav Dahrendorf supported a close relationship with the Soviet Union and rejected Weimar-style democracy, while other members under the leadership of Grotewohl preferred an adherence to a social democratic programme. Individuals also founded SPD groups early in 1945 in other areas of the eastern zone, mainly in centers where the SPD had been strong before the war. In Chemnitz, a group of friends formerly in the SPD formed an SPD group and began meetings in March 1945.[25] In Thuringia and those areas of Saxony which had been occupied by American troops, where political activity was still forbidden, SPD groups met secretly to re-establish contact and form a base for the party. In Freital, for example, the mayor, SPD member Arno Hennig, became involved in the establishment of an SPD group while American troops still occupied the region.[26] Within a few weeks of the withdrawal of American troops from Thuringia in early July 1945, the SPD had amassed 800 members in Saalfeld alone and 1800 in *Kreis* Saalfeld.[27] The predominant pattern of SPD foundings outside of Berlin was one of individual groups growing up parallel with little coordination either between the groups or between the outlying areas and the founding members in Berlin.[28]

There are several important points to note about the founding of the SPD. First, SPD members demonstrated a desire for close cooperation with the KPD as both parties were working-class based, and many members of both parties felt that Hitler's rise to power had been facilitated by the division within the working class movement. In fact, Max Fechner, one of the founders of the SPD in Berlin, sent a letter to Ulbricht after Ulbricht's arrival in the city which proposed cooperation with the Communists in the rebuilding of communal administrations and which hinted at a union of the two parties.[29] On June 16, the SPD followed up Fechner's letter and made a formal offer of unity to the KPD, which the KPD rejected. The SPD position mirrored a view in Europe as a whole, as parties of the left in Britain, France, and Italy were also cooperating more closely.[30] The second, and most important, aspect of the founding of the SPD is that it was a re-founding, which meant that the party ideology of the Weimar era was transferred to postwar Germany. That the SPD was re-founded is repeatedly emphasized by those involved in the early days of the creation of the SPD in the Soviet zone.[31] The SPD rejected dictatorship, rejected the idea of class struggle, rejected the imposition of the Soviet system on Germany, and supported parliamentary democracy—all of which were visible in its founding proclamation.

The SPD proclamation called for an anti-fascist democratic republic and a guarantee of democratic freedoms, including the freedoms of expression and religion which the KPD proclamation did not mention. The SPD proclamation emphasized socializing various industries like banks, insurance companies, and industries that dealt with energy and raw materials. Suspicions that the SPD aimed to install socialism at the expense of democracy can be alleviated by examining the history of the proclamation itself. Of the various proposals for the proclamation, Grotewohl's draft was issued because of its emphasis on democracy. Grotewohl feared that Dahrendorf's draft proclamation did not stress the democratic nature of the SPD sufficiently because it stated that the SPD aimed to "build a socialist state." Grotewohl's draft claimed instead that the main goal of the SPD was: "Democracy in state and community, socialism in the economy and society."[32]

It is perhaps surprising that the founding of political parties did not end with the SPD and the KPD, as the Christian Democratic Union of Germany (CDU) and the Liberal Democratic Party of Germany (LDPD) were two middle-class parties that in many ways represented the antithesis of Communism. The LDPD even advocated capitalism, which, according to Soviet ideology, ultimately led to fascism. Historians still debate the Soviet decision to allow these other parties. One explanation holds that the Soviet Union felt the parties would be kept under control by forming a United Front,[33] while other historians argue that the Soviets believed allowing two clearly oppositional parties might endear themselves to the population.[34] Although the true reasons will likely remain unclear until historians gain full access to Russian archives, for the purposes of this study it is important to recall that both middle class parties were constituted legally in the Soviet zone.

On June 26, 1945, the CDU issued its founding proclamation, but, as had been the case with the SPD and KPD, the preparations for the founding of the party had been under way for several months. One of the primary influences in the embryonic CDU was Dr. Andreas Hermes, a former Reichsminister for Agriculture and member of the Centre party. For his participation in the assassination attempt on Hitler on July 20, 1944, Hermes was arrested and sentenced to death, but the execution was continually delayed due to the efforts of his wife.[35] At the beginning of May 1945, the Soviets released Hermes from a Nazi prison in Berlin-Moabit and a few days later the Soviet commander of Berlin, Colonel-General Bersarin, appointed him to head the Food Office.[36] The first CDU political talks of the postwar period took place in this still intact office at Fehrbelliner Platz in Berlin, (and, indeed, these buildings remain to this day one of the best examples of Nazi architecture in Berlin) which also served as the first meeting point between Hermes and Jakob Kaiser after the war.[37] Jakob Kaiser had also been involved in the July 20, 1944 plot to assassinate Hitler and escaped execution by hiding in a friend's house in Babelsberg. On May 25, Soviet authorities assigned Kaiser as liaison between the Food Office and the municipal council.[38] By the end of May, Kaiser, Hermes, and various members of the former Centre party, as well as a few members of the former German Democratic Party (DDP), unofficially formed the CDU.[39]

The differences between the CDU proclamation and that of the SPD and KPD are notable. The CDU agreed in principle to the redistribution of land, mainly to accommodate the influx into the eastern zone of nearly four million Germans expelled from East Prussia, West Prussia, Pomerania, Silesia, and Czechoslovakia,[40] and also felt that industries essential to communal living, such as those dealing with raw materials, should be put under state ownership. Like the KPD, the CDU announced its support for private ownership.[41] Two important points that the other proclamations did not address were the call for the independence of the judicial system and for law to once again become the basis of public life. The CDU proclamation demonstrated unambiguous support for democracy and the rule of law.

The last of the parties to be founded in 1945 was the LDPD. The first meeting of the founders took place on June 16, 1945 in Berlin at the invitation of Eugen Schiffer, a former Weimar justice minister, and Dr. Waldemar Koch, later chairman of the LDPD in the Soviet zone.[42] This group merged with other liberal groups in the city like the liberal group in the district of Steglitz under Dr. Hamel, who had also been involved in the July 20, 1944 assassination attempt.[43] Outside of Berlin, a number of political groups with a liberal ideology similar to that of the groups in Berlin were formed, including the *Deutsch-Demokratische Partei* which was founded in Weimar and Görlitz, the *Demokratische Partei Deutschlands* formed by a professor in Dresden, the *Demokratische Volkspartei* in Halle, and the *Deutsche Demokratische Einheitspartei* in Netzschkau.[44]

The LDPD proclamation reflected the liberal middle-class basis of the party and provided the clearest contrast to the others, emphasizing the right to private property and voicing only limited support for state-run industries. Like the other parties, the LDPD called for the recognition of human rights without regard to race, class, or age and the reforming of German community life on a true democratic basis. Point 15 of the LDPD proclamation explained that these values were to be upheld through an independent judicial system: "An independent judiciary is to be responsible for safeguarding justice." The LDPD proclamation also emphasized the importance of a free economy, and downplayed the need to socialize industry, stating it would be appropriate only for certain industries, and only when there was an overwhelming interest of the population as a whole.[45] The LDPD proclamation reflected not only the views of the Berlin LDPD groups, but of LDPD groups throughout the Soviet zone. The proclamations of the Leipzig and Netzschkau groups expressed similar sentiments, insisting on democracy and the rule of law.[46] Further evidence of the nature of the LDPD comes from secret instructions sent by the LDPD leadership in Berlin to LDPD leaders in charge of forming groups at the grassroots level. In these instructions, the LDPD leadership advised to look for new members for the party in the circles of former Weimar parties like *Deutsch-Demokratische Partei, Deutsche Volkspartei, Deutschnationale Partei*, and *Wirtschaftspartei*. All of these parties had been based on middle-class values similar to those adopted by the LDPD. The LDPD did not consider it likely to find support among former Centre party members or in areas with a large proportion of Catholics.[47]

In sum, all parties proclaimed their support for basic human rights and democracy and at the same time made clear their rejection of dictatorship, although the LDPD and CDU proclamations provided more detail on the manner in which these aspects were to be safeguarded by emphasizing the importance of the rule of law and an independent judiciary. All proclamations also supported increased socialization of the economy, although the LDPD proclamation was the least enthusiastic.

This interest in socialization reflected a broader sentiment in the wake of the Second World War that a new era was upon Europe which would be characterized by the ascendancy of socialism and the decline of bourgeois capitalism, a sentiment which Jakob Kaiser captured in his famous statement: "The era of the bourgeois order is over."[48] Widespread interest in socialism should not, however, be interpreted as a rejection of democracy. Soviet-style socialism, despite an attitude favourable to socialism, would have found little support in the initial years after the war in eastern Germany.[49]

The SPD, KPD, CDU, and LDPD demonstrated their willingness to cooperate by forming the *Einheitsfront der antifaschistisch-demokratischen Parteien* in Berlin on July 14, known as the Antifa-Block.[50] A Central Committee, comprised of five rotating members from each party, led the Central Block, which was located in Berlin. The parties also formed Antifa-Blocks at the *Ort* (local) *Kreis,* (district), and *Land* (provincial) levels over a period of months following the establishment of the Central Block.[51] The provincial Block for Brandenburg, for example, was not established until November 18, 1945.[52] The fact that all the Block's resolutions had to be issued unanimously made the Block a different political entity from that found in the western democratic tradition, as it meant that there could not be political opposition in the traditional sense. The KPD thus ensured that no party could adopt policies which went against KPD interests, as the KPD could simply refuse to support a resolution forcing it to be either abandoned or amended. The Block, therefore, presented a major obstacle to parliamentary opposition.[53]

Shortly after the formation of the Central Block, Stalin, Churchill, and Truman met in Cecilienhof Castle near Potsdam, in the lush Sanssouci garden and palace complex which had been the summer residence of Prussian kings and German emperors. The Allies convened the Potsdam conference to further plan the postwar world, and set out three objectives in particular regarding Germany: to demilitarize and denazify Germany, to create the foundation for a democratic and peaceful Germany, and to treat Germany as a whole.[54] The Potsdam accord issued at the end of the conference supported basic human freedoms, such as freedom of the press and freedom of speech, and called for a return in Germany to the Weimar state of law. A central government with more power allotted to the provinces was foreseen, but only after the signing of a peace treaty. Until that time, local and regional administrations were to run German affairs.

SMAD had begun administrative restructuring of its zone of Germany immediately prior to the Potsdam conference, and continued this restructuring while the conference took place. Order Number 5 of July 9, 1945 divided the zone into four *Länder* and one *Provinz:*[55] *Land* Mecklenburg-Pomerania (after 1946 simply Mecklenburg) with its seat of government in Schwerin, *Land* Brandenburg (Potsdam), *Provinz* Saxony (Saxony-Anhalt) (Halle), *Land* Thuringia (Weimar), and *Land* Saxony (Dresden). The five provinces were divided into *Bezirke* (districts), and each *Bezirk* divided into city and country *Kreise*. With the provinces established on paper, SMAD then went about establishing provincial administrations for the newly formed *Länder* headed by a president and between three and five vice presidents.

The president was usually a member of the SPD (except in Saxony-Anhalt where the president was Dr. Erhard Hübener of the LDPD), but the KPD invariably supplied the first vice president, who was responsible for the crucial ministries that dealt with internal security. In every province, the KPD controlled that instrument vital to power—the police.

Shortly after the establishment of the provinces, SMAD created another level of government by establishing eleven German central administrations.[56] Nine of the eleven German central administrations were located in the Soviet zone of Berlin, gradually coming under one roof in the former headquarters of Goering's Air Ministry on Leipziger street. SMAD, after receiving recommendations from the political parties in the zone, appointed the heads of the administrations as follows: six presidents and eleven vice presidents from the KPD; four presidents and eleven vice presidents from the SPD; one president and three vice presidents from the CDU; and one president and one vice president from the LDPD.

Due to the confusion caused by the various levels of government, SMAD held a meeting on November 13, 1945 with the provincial and central administrations at which it delineated responsibility.[57] The provincial administrations remained the highest German authority in the first year of occupation taking orders only from SMAD, reducing the central administrations to acting solely in an advisory capacity.[58] Initially, Zhukov believed that the central administrations should not intervene in the provincial administrations but rather advise SMAD on issues common to the entire Soviet zone and coordinate three areas of operation in particular: railways, postal service, and supply.[59] One western report characterized the central administrations as having "only fragmentary information about economic events in the provinces, let alone any power to influence them."[60] Zhukov's support for the provincial administrations over the central administrations was likely a result of the Potsdam accords which forbade central administration in Germany before a peace treaty.[61]

Resistance by the Non-Marxist Parties

The Land Reform

The Central Block functioned smoothly in the summer of 1945, encountering its first problems in August when the KPD proposed a land reform which would dispossess of their land all war criminals and members of Nazi organizations considered criminal by the Soviet authorities (usually referred to as "Nazi criminals" in the documents), such as the SS, and land holders with over 100 hectares. This land was then to be redistributed in parcels of five hectares.[62] The land reform, although also being carried out in other zones, held particular importance for the eastern zone because private estates of 100 hectares or more made up one third of the total land area.[63] There can be little doubt that the economic transformation of the eastern zone in order to create a basis for socializing the economy motivated the KPD to launch a land reform. At a KPD meeting in January 1946 on the party's economic program, KPD member Smolka asked: "What type of societal form do we actually have? Do we have capitalism or socialism? I think we must honestly say that we have, of course, capitalism. I believe it is imperative to fill the higher and middle level posts in the economy with our people in order to create a new order in the means of production."[64]

The process leading to the tabling of the KPD land reform proposal began outside Berlin, where the KPD in the provincial Block in Saxony brought forward a proposal for a land reform on August 29. The LDPD and CDU rejected immediately what they saw as an economically weak and politically motivated land reform, but after two days of discussions were willing to accept the proposal on condition that land owners with over 100 hectares (ha.) who were not tainted by a Nazi past would receive compensation.[65] Various CDU groups in other provinces of the Soviet zone also voiced the need for compensation when the land reform arose in the provincial blocks. The Chemnitz CDU group in Saxony as well as representatives of the CDU and LDPD in Thuringia stressed the importance of compensating those with a clean past. W. Zeller, a prominent member of the youth wing of the CDU, reflected overall sentiment in the CDU when he agreed in principle to the land reform in order to meet the needs of the population, but at the same time expressed concern about the lack of compensation. He believed that the land reform must not be carried out as a *Klassenkampf* (Class War).[66] Only in Mecklenburg did the CDU accept the KPD proposal as it stood.

When the KPD put forward a land reform proposal on August 30 in the Central Block in Berlin,[67] the CDU immediately protested stating that land owners with a clean past must receive compensation for the loss of land. The CDU did agree, however, to a resolution stating that, in principle, a land reform was desirable.[68] By issuing this resolution the CDU gave the impression of endorsing the KPD land reform proposal in its entirety. Andreas Hermes, co-chair of the CDU, then attempted to distance himself from the joint statement by publishing an article which emphasized the differences between the CDU and KPD on the issue of the land reform. After Soviet authorities prohibited the publication of his article in *Tägliche Rundschau*, Hermes turned to the American-licensed *Allgemeine Zeitung* which published the article. Hermes' main concerns were the lack of compensation and the effect that the reforms would have on German unity, believing that a reform of this magnitude could not be carried out in one zone of Germany without an adverse effect on eventual unity.[69] Hermes' vision of democracy also played a role in his concerns about the manner of the land reform. On October 26, the *Tägliche Rundschau* asked Hermes six questions regarding the land reform and related issues. Responding to a question about Block work, Hermes provided a thinly veiled criticism of the KPD: "Joint work of several parties on one task requires a great deal of mutual loyalty and unlimited respect for the different beliefs of the co-operating parties. It would be a misunderstanding of democracy if this co-operation limited the expression of differing opinions of the individual partners or made such opinions impossible. In that case, the *Einheitsfront* would simply be a disguise to secure hegemony for a specific course."[70]

The CDU's fears about the land reform seemed to be confirmed on November 15, when Heinrich von der Gablentz, leader of the CDU political-economic committee, presented to the CDU leadership a variety of letters and documents stating that property owners were being unlawfully thrown off their land. Based on these letters, Gablentz stated: "Thousands of completely untainted families, themselves fierce opponents of the Nazi system and recognized victims of fascism, are, through the use of fascist methods, being expelled from their homes and unjustly ordered out of their towns. They are not only being robbed of their land, but of all their personal belongings." And: "These transgressions can no longer be quietly accepted by the Union [i.e., the CDU]."[71] Hilde Benjamin, the notorious Minister of Justice in the GDR from 1953 to 1967, hinted that there had been excesses in the land reform when, as a professor at the Walter Ulbricht German Academy for Political Science and the Law,[72] she wrote: "The punishment of Nazi and war criminals was closely linked to the dispossession of those criminals and to carrying out the land reform. During this process it was not uncommon to find other criminals who were against the new democratic order."[73] The suggestion here is that "other criminals" were dispossessed because they did not agree with the new way of life in the Soviet Occupied Zone, and not because of their activities during the war.

On November 22, 1945 the CDU formally protested against the manner of the land reform. During the Central Block sitting of that day, the KPD and the SPD presented a proposal entitled "help for the new farmers" to support the new farming economy that had been created by the land reform. The LDPD agreed immediately to the proposal, but the CDU wanted to tie the proposal to a statement by the Central Block against the excesses of the land reform. As the other parties refused to accept the CDU position, they issued the resolution without the CDU signature.[74] Some CDU leaders outside Berlin criticized their central leadership for its conduct during the land reform. In *Provinz* Saxony, the CDU provincial executive committee requested the resignation of Dr. Schreiber, the second CDU chairman. The *Land* executive committee in Mecklenburg also distanced itself from the leadership in Berlin, but in Saxony, Brandenburg, and Thuringia there was only a muted response.[75] The reason for the negative reaction by the CDU outside of Berlin is twofold. First, logistics made it difficult for the central CDU to convey its message to the outlying areas, as the telephone and infrastructure systems were still in chaos.[76] Furthermore, Soviet authorities censored the CDU newspaper, often adding articles to the CDU newspaper from the Communist press in favor of the land reform without reference to the source. Thus, as CDU members outside Berlin were not aware of Gablentz's evidence of injustice in the reform, they were puzzled by the CDU refusal to sign the "help for the new farmers" resolution.[77] Second, SMAD increasingly prodded lower levels of the CDU to challenge the central position. In Halle, for example, the Soviets issued the local CDU group a licence for its newspaper in return for taking a stance against the CDU leadership.[78] Still, SMAD failed to convince the provincial chairmen to issue a vote of no-confidence against the central leadership at a meeting organized by SMAD on December 18, in Karlshorst,[79] forcing SMAD to do something it hoped to avoid. Zhukov had hoped that an inner revolt would take place, and the CDU itself would remove Hermes and Schreiber due to their stance on the land reform. As this did not happen, SMAD removed them from their positions demonstrating publicly that SMAD did not tolerate political opponents.

The issue of the land reform is revealing in a number of ways. First, the executive committees of the CDU in all provinces except Mecklenburg rejected the original KPD proposal without being aware of the Berlin CDU stance, based on its disregard for property rights. This demonstrates a basic commonality throughout the CDU. Second, apart from disregard for property rights, the undemocratic conduct of the KPD and the desire for German unity also motivated CDU members to oppose the CDU.[80] Third, it must be remembered that Soviet authorities constrained CDU conduct. These points suggest that Andreas Hermes had analyzed the situation correctly when he declared after his dismissal that the overwhelming majority of the party outside Berlin agreed with the leadership of the party on the land reform issue.[81]

After the removal of Hermes and Schreiber from their positions due to their stance on the land reform, the CDU looked for new leadership, eventually electing Jakob Kaiser, a CDU member with a background in the union movement who somewhat reluctantly took over as chairman of the CDU.[82] Kaiser immediately began to mold the CDU into a party with more socialist elements in its platform. In an article in *Neue Zeit*, Kaiser stated that his aims for the party arose in part from his experiences in the resistance circle of the former mayor of Leipzig, Carl Goerdeler: "We were all convinced that the future of the German people would be largely determined by socialist ideas."[83] Kaiser's interest in "socializing" the party led to his use of the term "Christian socialism" at the Berlin delegates' conference in the first week of February 1946. He made his position clear again, in dramatic fashion, at the executive committee sitting of February 13, 1946 when he said that the party had to move away from dogmatic Christianity and the middle class. He proclaimed that "the Union is not a middle class party" and "the era of the bourgeois order is over." It was here as well that Kaiser introduced his concept of Germany being a bridge between West and East,[84] rather than firmly entrenched in either camp.

Kaiser forcefully argued for the CDU to be a defender of basic human freedoms. In a *Neue Zeit* article of December 30, 1945 entitled "Zum Weg der Union," he wrote: "At the centre of life is the dignity and freedom of the individual," explaining further that freedom was the basis for all democratic politics.[85] At the February 1946 executive committee sitting he again stressed the importance of the free individual: "We are convinced that the core of true socialism must be the awareness of dignity and the importance of free and responsible individuals."[86] Kaiser also emphasized German unity in his platform, which he stressed in a series of speeches at the beginning of 1946. At one speech in February 1946 he stated: "I can only say that for me, the issue of the form of the Reich lies on my heart like no other."[87] His concern for German unity, and a united CDU, led him to travel to the western zones of Germany where he met with various leaders of the western CDU. By late 1946, however, Konrad Adenauer, leader of the western CDU, opposed Kaiser's socialist position and his notion of Germany being a bridge between East and West, preferring that Germany be solidly entrenched in the western camp, a point he made in no uncertain terms at a meeting in Stuttgart in April 1946 between himself and Kaiser. Adenauer also rejected Kaiser's claim that the Berlin CDU should be the central leadership for all Germany, partly because he believed that Berlin must never again be the capital of a united Germany.[88]

The position of the LDPD on the land reform, in contrast to that of the CDU, is less well known. In Saxony-Anhalt, Saxony, and Thuringia, the LDPD initially rejected the KPD proposal. In Saxony-Anhalt, two LDPD members who had refused to sign the land reform law agreed to sign only after pressure from the KPD to maintain the unity of the Block became too great.[89] In Thuringia, the non-Marxist parties forced a vote on the issue of the land reform for anti-fascist property owners, whereby the KPD conceded a passage in the legislation that stated that anti-fascist property owners would not be stripped of their property.[90] Dr. Koch, chairman of the LDPD, spoke out vehemently against the KPD land reform because of its effects on human rights and property ownership. He emphasized that he would not support a land reform that did not compensate the land owner: "The principle of private property is valid for all classes. With [the land reform], the first step off the path is made. Any other form of dispossession could then easily follow,"[91] a view that met with a severe reprimand by Zhukov.[92] Ultimately, Koch agreed to the land reform, largely in the interest of preserving the Block, but also because of pressure from inside his party, spearheaded by Külz, to cooperate with the occupying power out of political tact. Koch did try to temper the land reform later with proposals for committees that would ensure that the reform was free of injustices.[93]

Although in all of the provinces except Saxony-Anhalt, the SPD initially agreed to the KPD proposal for the land reform, lower levels of the party did not always respond enthusiastically.[94] The SPD and KPD in Thuringia, Mecklenburg, Saxony-Anhalt, and Saxony agreed to hold joint events in support of the land reform, but this cooperation did not always come about. In *Kreis* Güstrow in Mecklenburg, only 5 out of 178 public gatherings were joint functions.[95] Hermann Matern, the leading KPD functionary in Saxony, complained of this lack of cooperation: "The Social Democratic Party was with us from the beginning on the land reform. . . . The Social Democratic Party is, however, passive in carrying out the land reform. It neither conducts farmer assemblies, nor participates officially at farmer conferences."[96] Matern clearly lied a few months later when he declared publicly: "We carried out the land reform together; we mobilized the workforce together."[97] The discrepancy between the immediate acceptance of the land reform by the leaders and the unwillingness at a local level to carry it out may be explained by an underlying opposition to working with the Communists. This trend, as will be seen, was common to the SPD at this time.

The land reform had a major impact on agricultural society, yet did not immediately bring the expected loyalty to the KPD. Overall, 6,330 property owners with over 100 ha. and 8,332 smaller land holders lost their land. The reform affected on average 34 percent of the available agricultural land in the Soviet zone, but this percentage was higher in some areas such as Brandenburg where 38 percent of available agricultural land was affected and Mecklenburg where 52 percent of available agricultural land was affected.[98] About 559,000 people, mostly landless farmers, refugees, and non-agricultural workers, each received on average 5 ha. of land from the land reform, and formed a new societal group known as *Neubauern* (new farmers).[99]

Contrary to the widespread spontaneous jubilation throughout the Soviet zone portrayed in the KPD version of the reform, villagers did not uniformly welcome the land reform.[100] Some villages rejoiced in the announcement and decorated the town with banners and flowers, while others expressed little interest. Overall, the political result of the reform disappointed the KPD. In Mecklenburg, Sobottka complained that the land reform had not caused the expected "flood" of farmers into the KPD.[101] In Saxony, Hermann Matern complained that farmers distrusted the land reform fearing it to be Communist propaganda, and as a result entries into the KPD were disappointing.[102] Matern dwelt on the issue of trust stating that farmers did not possess a fear of Communists (*Kommunisten-Schreck*) as they used to, but brought doubts to his own observation stating that they still maintained a "watchful distance."[103] The KPD representative in Saxony-Anhalt reported more success in recruiting farmers for the party, but concluded that overall farmers did not concern themselves with politics at the moment.[104] A KPD member from Thuringia reported that the KPD was having some success recruiting farmers, but that farmers doubted whether the KPD would really carry out the reform.[105] In Radeburg in Saxony, the KPD representative complained that no farmers would stand for the KPD in the upcoming election, preferring to join the LDPD. As a result, the SED had only one farmer on its list in this rural region.[106] It seems likely, however, that the KPD eventually made political gains from the land reform, although further research will be required to address the extent to which those who benefited from the land reform supported the SED at subsequent elections. KPD membership in Mecklenburg increased from 3,200 in June 1945 to 19,500 in October, and 32,000 in December. In local elections in the fall of 1946, the Socialist Unity Party (SED) (the fused KPD and SPD—see below) secured 75.2 percent of the vote in Mecklenburg, and obtained 72 percent of the *Gemeinde* mayorships in *Land* Brandenburg.[107] SMAD restrictions on CDU and LDPD activity also contributed to this result.[108]

The Sequestering of Factories

In the summer of 1946, the Soviets and the Socialist Unity Party (SED) took another step in the economic transformation of the eastern zone. Both SMAD and the SED pressed for a referendum on the sequestering of factories belonging to war criminals, which caused misgivings in the CDU and the LDPD about the manner in which the sequestering would be carried out after the example of the land reform. The referendum was set for July 16, 1946 in Saxony, and the results were to be taken as representative for the entire Soviet zone. Initially, CDU chairman Kaiser protested the referendum on sequestering because he felt that such a public consultation would have to involve all zones of Germany.[109] As a result of SMAD pressure on Kaiser to temper his oppositional stance,[110] the CDU stated in a resolution issued in the Central Block that it welcomed the referendum but warned that the dispossession should not be a precedent for changing the social and economic structures of society. The CDU leadership expected the sequestering to be carried out in a lawful manner.[111] Many factory owners also suspected that the sequestering was part of a Communist plan for rapid socialization.[112] The CDU repeated its insistence that the action only apply to Nazi and war criminals, voicing displeasure at the number of factories which had already been unlawfully confiscated. The CDU was adamant that each confiscation had to be carefully investigated.[113] At the July 9, 1946 sitting of the Central Block, the CDU complained of the initial SED-incited sequestering taking place in Saxony even before the referendum, stating that factory owners had no opportunity to prove their innocence, and that the police confiscated properties from people who had never been involved with the Nazi party nor any war crimes.[114] The CDU produced an eleven point program for improving the situation regarding sequestering in Saxony, which emphasized providing those individuals in question with a fair hearing.[115] CDU concerns about the sequestering process did not prevent the party from supporting the sequestering in principle. With all parties campaigning in favor of the sequestering referendum, albeit the CDU and LDPD did so reluctantly, the July 16, 1946 referendum passed by a comfortable margin: the handing over of "the factories of war criminals and Nazi criminals into the hands of the people" was approved by 77.7 percent of the voters. Only 16.5 percent of cast ballots rejected the proposal, and 5.8 percent of the ballots were invalid.[116]

The Creation of the Socialist Unity Party and SPD Resistance

From the fall of 1945 the SPD engaged in a political fight with the KPD over the issue of fusion of the two parties.[117] Certain sections of the SPD, however, had been in favor of fusion of the parties since the war. The leader of the SPD in Thuringia, Hermann Brill, personified the desire for fusion of the two parties, founding in July a joint KPD-SPD party localized in Thuringia called the "League of Democratic Socialists."[118] Members of the workers' parties had also cooperated closely in Berlin, Dresden, and Görlitz, and in the latter two a clear majority of members had supported fusion.[119] The SPD in Freital demonstrated its support for close cooperation with the KPD by hanging a picture of Stalin on the wall during its founding meeting.[120] These examples of SPD support for fusion with the KPD were isolated, however. A clear majority of the SPD in the eastern zone opposed immediate union with the KPD,[121] although many members desired close cooperation between the two parties. The Leipzig SPD stood out in this regard as it refused any cooperation with the KPD. Two members of the SPD leadership in Berlin, Eric Gniffke and Ralf

Dahrendorf, made a special trip to Leipzig to attempt to convince the SPD leadership there to work more closely with the KPD.[122]

Throughout the summer and fall of 1945, likely invigorated by the party's steadily increasing membership, the SPD leadership continued to assert its independence and oppose fusion with the KPD.[123] On August 26, 1945, at the first party conference of the SPD in *Bezirk* Leipzig, Grotewohl stated that the SPD had a political right to lead Germany, and that there would not be a united list of SPD and KPD candidates in upcoming elections.[124] He could be buoyed by the fact that the SPD had crushed the KPD at a council election in the enormous *Leunawerk* factory complex, electing twenty-six members to the KPD's one.[125] Grotewohl later gave another speech to thousands of members and functionaries of the SPD in the house of the *Neue Welt* newspaper in the American sector of Berlin, in which he loudly proclaimed SPD independence.[126] The situation became more delicate from September 19, when Wilhelm Pieck, the chairman of the Central Committee of the KPD, suggested fusion of the parties. The SPD, however, maintained its desire for independence.

On October 5 and 6, 1945 at Wennigsen near Hannover in the British zone of occupation, during the first conference between the leader of the western SPD, Kurt Schumacher, and Otto Grotewohl, Grotewohl made clear his opposition to fusion with the KPD.[127] On October 22, 1945, the Central Committee (ZA) supported Grotewohl's position by rejecting the KPD offer of fusion, stating that a majority of SPD members would not accept it. British observers at this meeting stated that they expected that in the future the SPD would follow "a very much stronger line" against the KPD.[128] As a demonstration of this "stronger line," the SPD rejected a KPD proposal to hold a joint function on the anniversary of the November revolution.[129]

SPD members outside Berlin also vigorously opposed joining the parties. In Thuringia, Hermann Brill, who had come to oppose cooperation with the KPD because of SMAD interference and general conduct in the Soviet zone,[130] verbally attacked Heinrich Hoffmann, a member of the SPD *Land* organization in Thuringia, at a sitting of November 26, accusing Hoffmann of treachery in supporting fusion.[131] In Schwerin and Rostock, SPD members Hermann Lüdemann and Albert Schulz gathered members together who were against the pro-fusion stance of the SPD chair for Mecklenburg, Carl Moltmann. They failed to convince the *Land* organization of the dangers of fusion, however, likely because of the relative popularity that the KPD enjoyed in Mecklenburg due to the land reform.[132] In Saxony-Anhalt, Werner Bruschke, the secretary of the Saxony-Anhalt SPD executive committee, voiced his opposition to fusion.[133] In Saxony, Arno Hennig and Arno Wend, under secretaries for *Bezirk* Dresden, travelled to Berlin in an attempt to convince the ZA to remove Otto Buchwitz from his position as chairman of the SPD organization for *Land* Saxony because of his support for fusion.[134] The most common reason given by SPD members for opposition to fusion with the KPD at this time was the disregard that the KPD had shown toward other parties in the administration. For SPD members, this behavior raised the specter of renewed dictatorship.[135]

On November 4, an event in Austria altered political developments in Germany. The Austrian elections were a resounding and shocking defeat for the Communists as the social democrats won 76 of 165 seats in the Austrian national assembly, compared to the communists' four seats.[136] The message for the KPD in the Soviet zone of Germany was clear: It would not win an open and free election against the SPD; therefore fusion of the two parties had to be brought about. Accordingly, the KPD increased its pressure for fusion, but made little progress against the stubborn resistance of the SPD. On December 4, 1945, the first meeting of the SPD Central Committee with the leaders of the provincial and *Bezirk* organizations of the Soviet zone SPD took place. Opponents of fusion clearly emerged victorious from the meeting, as only two present supported fusion: Otto Buchwitz of Saxony and the Central Committee member Karl Litke.[137]

As the pressure from the KPD mounted for at least talks on the possibility of fusion, the SPD agreed to a joint meeting of thirty leading functionaries from each party for December 20 and 21 in Berlin, the so-called *60er Konferenz*. At this conference, Grotewohl made known his displeasure with the KPD by giving a speech listing ten points that suggested why the KPD was, at present, an unsuitable partner. He stressed the fact that the KPD was not acting according to its proclaimed adherence to democracy, and suggested that the SPD would pull out of local administrations if the KPD continued to exert pressure and unwanted influence on the SPD. He phrased it bluntly: "In our membership, a deep distrust of the Communist brother party has materialized."[138] He also pointed to the protection by the Soviet authorities that the KPD enjoyed, in contrast to the harassment and arrests experienced by SPD members. Gustav Kligelhöfer, a secretary of the ZA of the SPD, echoed Grotewohl's concerns about SMAD favoritism saying: "Many of our comrades do not speak that which they have in their hearts, as they want to restrain themselves, need to restrain themselves, out of fears based on previous experiences."[139] Grotewohl did not rule out fusion outright, however, but insisted that the ten points be a basis for it. In these points, he also mentioned the need for a German-wide meeting of the SPD to agree on fusion,[140] as he believed that fusion in one zone would be a disaster for German unity. Grotewohl's stance at this conference deserves close attention, as he did *not* agree to the KPD's fusion proposal. By attaching the conditions that fusion could not occur on a zonal basis, and that there must be separate lists for the upcoming elections, Grotewohl effectively postponed fusion indefinitely.[141] His expression of a desire for unity was crafty maneuvering within the limitations of Soviet occupation, as he simply could not suggest otherwise. Participants at the conference have stated that they saw Grotewohl's speech as a way of avoiding fusion.[142]

The SPD was a divided party after the December Conference, although a majority of members continued to oppose fusion because of the KPD's dictatorial behavior up to that point.[143] One strain within the party, a clear minority, desired immediate fusion. Otto Buchwitz of Saxony and Heinrich Hoffmann of Thuringia expounded this view most vocally, but members at the grassroots level echoed these sentiments, as in the SPD in Görlitz and Güstrow.[144] Another group felt that, due to the circumstances, fusion was inevitable, but that the SPD would be able to continue its policies within the new united party. The undemocratic conduct of the KPD troubled this group but it felt that this would be tempered by a strong SPD presence.[145] The hope of influencing the future party was evident when the chair of SPD *Bezirk* Leipzig, Trabalski, suggested dissolving the SPD rather than join the new united party, but a majority of this SPD group opposed this option despite the clear anti-Communism of the members.[146] Friedrich Ebert in Brandenburg and Albert Schulz in Rostock also felt that the SPD would be able to exert enormous influence on the development of the new party.[147] Even Otto Grotewohl felt that the new party could be manipulated: "Should it come to close contact between both parties, then I know that we Social Democrats will be the stronger section."[148] Although these suggestions may seem naive, it should be remembered that the SPD, like many contemporary observers, believed that the KPD protector SMAD would not be in Germany much longer due to the temporary division of Germany.[149] Without SMAD interference, the SPD might well have been able to influence the new party. A third strand within the party staunchly opposed fusion with the KPD because of the KPD's totalitarian tendencies. Some SPD groups, like those in Wismar, Rostock, and Dresden, expressed this view by calling for a party-wide referendum on the issue of fusion.[150] Hermann Brill made his aversion to fusion clear in an article for the SPD newspaper *Tribüne* after the December Conference, writing that he was pleased to work alongside the KPD, but that he was equally pleased that fusion was not to take place on a zonal level.[151] Brill feared the KPD's version of democracy, and was not alone in his suspicions that the KPD would establish a dictatorship.[152] In Borna, for example, in response to a query by a Soviet officer as to why the SPD and KPD were not working together, the local SPD leader said: "We SPD want true democracy."[153] A resolution from the SPD in Zehdenick was more subtle: "We Social Democrats of Zehdenick have unfortunately determined that, up to this point, the KPD has not acted in a way conducive to union."[154] In Waltersdorf, the fact that the KPD had historically proclaimed the dictatorship of the proletariat and suddenly supported democracy caused SPD members to be suspicious.[155] Lastly, the SPD group in Chemnitz fiercely opposed fusion with the KPD because it believed the KPD would establish a dictatorship. Hans Hermsdorf, a member of the SPD in Chemnitz, said that he refused to negotiate with the KPD where the concept of democracy was concerned, and that he would fight every dictatorship, "however it may name or disguise itself."[156] At one *Bezirk* party meeting, he exclaimed: "Back to democracy, forward to socialism!"[157]

SPD concern about fusion with the KPD caused some members to turn to the western Allies for support. The earliest contact came in October 1945, when Grotewohl approached the British in Berlin asking them for insurance that there would be free elections in the eastern half of Germany. One SPD Central Committee (ZA) member even went so far as to ask the British occupation authorities to ban joint election lists through a Control Council directive. The request did not receive much attention, however, because the British intelligence officer who received the request did not think the issue of much importance, and was suspicious of the SPD in any case.[158] On November 11, in the wake of the intensification of the KPD campaign, Grotewohl became more urgent with his plea for outside help. Visibly unnerved, he informed the British authorities that "there was a danger of people in Eastern Germany considering that they had merely exchanged one party dictatorship for another."[159] It appears that by the beginning of the new year, the British had admitted to misjudging the earlier threat, as one British representative stated: "It seems probable that Grotewohl . . . will give way to the Communist demands, as he sees no hope of outside help until the zonal frontiers have been abolished, and is unwilling to sacrifice his career and that of other good socialists in pointless resistance."[160] It seems, however, that the British occupation authorities also felt that resistance was pointless as they did not offer assistance to the Social Democrats in the Soviet zone.

SMAD's vigorous, multifaceted campaign eventually broke SPD resistance to fusion. During the first months of 1946, in order to break the resistance of the Central Committee of the SPD to fusion, SMAD increased pressure on local SPD groups to cooperate with the KPD to join the two parties.[161] The Soviets hoped that internal pressure would force the SPD to abandon its opposition to fusion. SMAD activities included denunciations of those against fusion as saboteurs and fascists, and arrests of outspoken opponents of fusion.[162] Furthermore, the Soviets banned meetings of SPD groups who opposed fusion and offered material and moral support to local SPD groups that supported fusion.[163] Through these tactics, the Soviets managed to create the necessary conditions for fusion at the local level. In the first months of 1946 local SPD and KPD groups began to join together in a united party and in turn applied pressure on their *Land* representatives to seek agreement on fusion.[164] Ultimately, the Soviet tactic of inducing fusion from below proved effective. During a meeting on February 11, 1946 between the ZA and the SPD *Land* committees, the *Land* committees appealed to the ZA to support fusion based on the "spontaneous" fusion which was taking place at the local level throughout the Soviet zone. Faced with the position of the *Land* committees, and aware of the increasingly severe Soviet measures against opponents of fusion, Grotewohl abandoned his opposition to fusion.[165]

In the days prior to the meeting of February 11, 1946, Grotewohl had, in fact, been considering the possibility of fusion with the KPD given the situation in the Soviet zone. During a dinner meeting on February 4 in West Berlin of Grotewohl, Dahrendorf, and Sir Christopher Steel, the head of the political department in the British military government in Germany, Grotewohl lamented that he could not prevent fusion under the circumstances. Steel reported: "Not only was the strongest pressure brought to bear on them [Grotewohl and Dahrendorf] personally, ([Grotewohl] spoke of being tickled with Russian bayonets), but their organisation in the provinces had been completely undermined. Men who four days before had assured him [i.e. Grotewohl] of their determination to resist were now begging him to get the business [i.e. fusion] over and have done with it."[166] Earlier in Frankfurt am Main, Grotewohl had forewarned SPD members in West Germany: "If any decision should be taken in Berlin that doesn't please you, you can be certain that this decision has only been taken under pressure from the Soviet occupying power."[167]

Given these conditions, Grotewohl came to accept fusion in the hope that the SPD would remain alive within the new party. He made this calculation on the assumption that German unity would soon occur, following which both he and the SPD could again become prominent figures in politics.[168] The alternative, he felt, was to abandon SPD policies in their entirety in the Soviet zone. Grotewohl later regretted his decision to support fusion once he realized that it was a maneuver to remove the SPD in the Soviet zone. Grotewohl attempted to escape the GDR at least once.[169]

Three days after the February 11, meeting, Curt Swolinzky invited a group of between eight and twelve SPD *Kreis* chairmen of Berlin[170] to join him in organizing an SPD party vote in Berlin on the question of fusion. Opponents of fusion won the March 31, 1946 vote handily as 82.6 percent of SPD members who voted rejected immediate fusion with the KPD.[171] The keen interest in cooperating with the KPD also made itself apparent, however. Sixty-two percent of those who voted answered yes to the question of whether they desired cooperation with the KPD.[172]

After the vote, the SPD constituted itself as an independent party in the western zones of Berlin, and watched as the eastern SPD went forward to unity. On April 21 in the Admiralpalast theatre in Berlin, shortly after the opening of the joint SPD/KPD gathering at 10:00 a.m., Wilhelm Pieck and Otto Grotewohl crossed the stage, met in the middle, and shook hands to seal the fusion of the two parties. The handshake remained the symbol of the Socialist Unity Party of Germany (SED) until 1990.

The SPD *Ostbüro*

Members of the SPD who remained in the East after the fusion of the two parties conducted extensive anti-Communist resistance in the Soviet zone, either within the SED in the hopes of reforming the Communist system from within or outside the party carrying on SPD work illegally.[173] Kurt Schumacher, the leader of the western SPD, contributed significantly to supporting SPD resistance in the Soviet zone based on his concern for the erosion of democracy there. On the developing situation in the eastern zone, Schumacher stated: "One cannot declare the principles of democracy, of socialism, of freedom, of the right of self-determination, and then adopt policies which are the opposite."[174] Again in 1947, he stated: "The fact that social democracy in the eastern zone is forbidden, suppressed, and persecuted is not primarily an SPD issue. It is a question of equal rights in accordance with the equality of all German citizens. It is a question of world democracy."[175] Schumacher therefore established the SPD *Ostbüro* (Eastern Office), an organization based in Hannover in the British zone to aid both the eastern members of the party who sought refuge in the West and those who stayed in the East to fight Communism. Schumacher described the *Ostbüro* as "the institution of organized Social Democrats against the Communist claims to power in Germany."[176] The *Ostbüro*, founded virtually simultaneously with the fusion of the KPD and SPD in April 1946, grew out of a section of the party which had been established in February 1946 in Hannover to provide support for SPD refugees from the Soviet-occupied zone (*Sowjetische Besatzungszone—SBZ*).[177] Schumacher envisaged five initial asks for the *Ostbüro*: (1) to be a contact post for SPD members in the Soviet-occupied zone and a coordination post for resistance groups there, (2) to gather information on the Soviet-occupied zone in order to trace the development of the Communist system, (3) to make public this information gathered on the eastern zone, (4) to mount a defense against spies from Soviet and East German secret services in the Federal Republic of Germany, and (5) to assist political refugees from the Soviet occupied zone.[178] Schumacher's desire to maintain links to the eastern SPD in order to build up the party again quickly in the event that the zonal boundaries fell also underlay these tasks.[179] As far as can be determined by the documents, the *Ostbüro* smuggled neither groups of SPD resisters nor weapons into the Soviet zone, but rather supplied groups already in place with information and materials (especially pamphlets) of the western SPD. It should be mentioned, however, that it is not possible to come to a definitive conclusion on this topic as the documentary source base is fragmentary. The Central Committee of the western SPD ran the *Ostbüro* furtively, leaving virtually no documentation on *Ostbüro* operations in official minutes. The following account relies on the reports of individuals involved in SPD resistance which are housed in the Archive of Social Democracy in Bonn.[180]

Underground SPD Resistance

SPD members engaged in underground anti-Communist resistance immediately following fusion of the parties. These early SPD groups, which were composed of anti-fusion SPD members who had been in contact prior to the founding of the SED, journeyed at enormous risk to Ziethenstrasse in Berlin where the SPD was housed. There, they gathered SPD pamphlets, information sheets, and newspapers to distribute in the Soviet zone, and informed their colleagues in Berlin of developments in the zone. Because the SPD was still legal in Berlin due to the city's four-power status, and because of the relative accessibility of Berlin, SPD groups in the SBZ initially contacted Berlin rather than the *Ostbüro* in Hannover. In Halle, a major industrial center in eastern Germany, Fritz Gebuehr, Georg Otten, Günther Eckstein, Klara Laue, Arthur Kuntzmann, and Karl Behle met at the first mention of fusion to plan strategy in case fusion passed. Once the SED had been created, Behle made the long trip to Ziethenstrasse—a journey of several days given that war damage made most roads and railways still impassable—to obtain brochures and newspapers for illegal distribution in the eastern zone. Only at the end of 1946 did a courier from the *Ostbüro* in Hannover contact Behle directly. Soviet forces brought the activities of this group to an end, arresting Behle at his apartment early on the morning of April 9, 1947 and delivering him to the underground investigation cellars in a prison in Halle nicknamed "Red Ox" by the inmates. Red Army officers beat Behle almost on a daily basis for over five months in an attempt to obtain the names of others in the group. After his sentencing to ten years in a labor camp,

Behle was delivered to Sachsenhausen, the former Nazi concentration camp just north of Berlin converted to a "Special Camp" following the war by the KGB forerunner, the Soviet People's Commissariat of Internal Affairs (NKVD). Behle complained about the lack of food and the harshness of conditions in the barracks that the Nazis had built for opponents of the Third Reich, but he was stunned that the Soviets allowed them three newspapers a day and even permitted the "politicals" in his section of the camp to watch films in the camp theater, located in the "nonpoliticals" section.[181] Behle may have considered his sentence fortunate. In May 1946 in Rostock, the NKVD arrested five former secretaries of the SPD in Mecklenburg. Erich Krüger was executed out-of-hand, while Heini Besse, Erich Becker, and Willi Jesse (the former contact person for Mecklenburg for the July 20, 1944 resisters) were each sentenced to twenty-five years in jail. Only Hermann Witteborn managed to flee to the West.[182]

Other SPD resisters elected the dangerous route of contacting the Hannover office in the British zone of Germany. Dieter Rieke's group, based in the town of Döhren in *Kreis* Gardelegen which lay on the Cold War frontier between the eastern and western zones of Germany, furtively contacted SPD members in the nearby towns of Stendal, Magdeburg, and Salzwedel. The mayor of Döhren, a key member of this group, helped smuggle people out of the eastern zone and written materials from the western zones into the Soviet zone and sent reports on the eastern zone to the *Ostbüro* via a courier named Ernst Knippel. Knippel's greatest asset was a forged photo ID, complete with identifying fingerprint, to travel throughout the Soviet zone. In February 1948, Knippel let his guard down while crossing into the Soviet occupied zone[183] and Soviet authorities at the border immediately arrested him. Armed with the names that Knippel revealed, the Soviets blocked all roads in the area leading to the border with the western zones of Germany and began rounding up the resisters. Several of them found themselves delivered to the "Red Ox" prison in Halle, now a historic site in Germany in memory of those who suffered there.[184]

This episode involving Knippel shows how the young *Ostbüro* was no match for the seasoned veteran in the Soviet NKVD. Indeed, it appears that the NKVD penetrated the *Ostbüro* in Hannover at an early stage. Beginning in 1946, in the town of Haldensleben, Arthur Leibknecht secretly spread pamphlets denouncing Communism. He carried out his work uninterrupted until January 4, 1948 when he met an old acquaintance, Arthur Reich, son of a newspaper editor in Thuringia. Reich's social democratic background, and his proof that he had been in the *Ostbüro* in Hannover, proved to Leibknecht that he was trustworthy. After a certain period, Leibknecht felt comfortable enough to provide Reich with anti-Communist pamphlets to distribute. In March, three plain-clothed NKVD agents knocked on Leibknecht's door and pulled him out of his apartment, catching Leibknecht, who was in the middle of preparing underground material, completely by surprise. On his desk sat pamphlets, false ID, maps, and records of meetings. The agents threw Leibknecht in the back of a truck and drove him to Weimar where he was interrogated from 9 pm to 4 am. After a while, he later complained, he could no longer tell on which side of his face the punches landed. Throughout his interrogation, he worked over in his mind the people who knew of his work, and concluded that Reich must have turned him in, and indeed, Reich was later revealed to have worked for the NKVD. Leibknecht was sentenced to twenty-five years labor.[185]

The initial signs of an emerging Communist dictatorship in the east and the brutality of the Soviet occupation were primary factors behind these first SPD underground resistance groups. In Saxony, an underground SPD group, which counted among its members Helmut Wenke, Benno von Heinitz, and Peter Krämer, contacted the Berlin SPD for the purposes of spreading pamphlets. The group, which consisted in large part of students, protested the excesses of the Soviet occupiers and their German helpers by spreading pamphlets entitled "Ivan the Terrible" and painting anti-Communist slogans on the German criminal police building in Bautzen. Heinitz and Wenke were arrested on the night of August 19-20, 1947 and Krämer shortly thereafter. Heinitz and Krämer each received twenty-five years labor, and Wenke received ten.[186]

Communist infringements on personal freedoms also drove the members of Hermann Kreutzer's group to resist. Hermann Kreutzer, still fiery when I interviewed him in 1995, his father, Paul, and his fiancée, Dorothee Fischer, led an SPD group of about 100 centred in Saalfeld/Rudolstadt, Thuringia. The group relied heavily on a contact at the Thuringian chamber of trade because he had at his disposal a much valued commodity in Germany in the 1940s—telephones. Members of the group also occupied positions in the *Kommunalpolitik* branches of the *Kreis* and *Land* administrations which greatly assisted the group as the communications abilities of these departments helped the group maintain contact with other SPD members in the eastern zone.[187] Roughly six months after fusion, and after having considered the possibility of infiltrating the SED from within, the group contacted the SPD in Berlin and met with an *Ostbüro* representative. The group furtively distributed *Ostbüro* pamphlets and provided information on developments in the SBZ to the western SPD. Kreutzer was motivated to act by the restrictions on basic freedoms in the eastern zone, including the right to fair trial and the freedom of expression. After twelve years of Nazism, he refused to let another dictatorship form on German soil.[188] When I asked him his primary motivation to resist, he slammed his fist down on the table in the café and bellowed "Freiheit!" much to the consternation of other patrons. He also believed that German unity would take place in the near future and wanted to maintain SPD contacts in the Soviet zone because of the difficulties in starting the party anew. Kreutzer's group maintained contact with the *Ostbüro* through a neighbouring resistance group in Rudolstadt from January 1947 to the spring of 1949[189] when the three leaders of Kreutzer's group were arrested and sentenced to twenty-five years by a Soviet Military Tribunal. Kreutzer was amnestied in 1956.[190]

Resistance within the SED

Other SPD members believed that they could destroy the new party from within. Siegfried Weisse gathered a group of like-minded Social Democrats to form the resistance group "igel," and turned to Ziethenstrasse for further instructions. There, he received instructions to remain within the SED in order to obtain documents on the administration and the economy. Weisse was an ideal candidate for such information as his position at the head of the Saxony finance administration in Dresden allowed him to see important inner workings of government, and he had a government car at his disposal which allowed him to make contact with resisters outside Dresden. Weisse also had contacts to the secretary of the *Kreistag* office and the president of the *Kreistag*, Elfriede Matschke. Weisse was unaware, however, that a member of the Dresden *Kreis* council for education, Werner Uhlig, also worked for the *Ostbüro*. Weisse regularly contacted his sources about government work and secretly relayed the information to the *Ostbüro*. He also procured important materials for couriers such as stamped service identification in both German and Russian so they could move more easily through the zone. The Soviets were tipped off to Weisse by the actions of an amateur SPD courier from Hanover, who came to provide Weisse with instructions and, finding him away from his apartment, began informing others in the building that he brought important instructions from Hanover and that it was urgent he speak to Weisse. Weisse got wind of his imminent arrest, sneaked out of work early to return to his apartment, gather a few belongings and head for the West. Weisse knew that if he made the connections with the streetcar—his government vehicle was in the shop—he might have a chance. Weisse ran to North Square where he got on the first street car just as the doors were closing, and hurried across the tracks at the Square of Unity to barely make the connection to the second street car. Sweating, he splashed quickly along the sidewalk in the driving rain when a big black truck pulled up beside him and an enormous man jumped out and yelled: "Get in." Weisse kicked him in the stomach and turned to run when he was grabbed from behind and another man from the truck delivered a blow that knocked him out. Weisse came to on the cold steel floor of the truck on its way to the NKVD building on Bautzen street in Dresden.[191]

The most prominent SPD resisters who remained in the SED were Fritz Drescher, ministerial director of the *Land* government for Saxony,[192] and Arno Haufe and Arno Wend, both members of the *Landessekretariat* for the Saxony SED. Drescher and Wend hardly had a break from their resistance activities in the Third Reich before they engaged in renewed resistance.[193] Wend was arrested during a series of SPD arrests on July 7, 1948 and sentenced to twenty-five years labor which he was to carry out in the legendary remote Siberian work camp in Vorkuta, but was amnestied after serving seven years. Fritz Drescher, and the fourteen members in his illegal group, were sentenced on June 17, 1949 to twenty-five years for espionage and anti-Soviet propaganda.[194] Haufe, Wend, and Drescher were amnestied in 1954. Indeed, as has become evident in the cases cited here, the majority of those sentenced in the mid-1940s for SPD-related activity were released between 1954 and 1956.[195]

It appears that a small portion of SPD members in the eastern zone joined either the CDU or the LDPD to avoid persecution and to resist the SED from within these parties. One *Ostbüro* report stated: "A small number of our comrades have fled into the bourgeois parties in order to disguise themselves."[196] One member of the SPD reported that he joined the LDPD in Ronneburg, Thuringia in 1946 and urged people there to vote for the LDPD as a protest against the SED.[197]

The SPD presence in the SED meant that the new party was far from united. In reports to the SED from various Saxony *Kreise*, the difficulties between former SPD and KPD members were evident. In Pirna, an SED member reported that "political differences still exist in some local SED groups because there are functionaries that have not bridged the antagonisms that existed between SPD and KPD prior to 1933."[198] In Auerbach, the SED complained: "The cohesion of the party is deficient."[199] In Kreis Löbau, a meeting of the SED turned to a discussion on the unity of the party during which somebody in attendance stated: "In 1918, the masses were united and the leadership wasn't, today the leaders of the parties are united but there is resistance in the lower levels of membership."[200] *Kreis* Zwickau and *Kreis* Hoyerswerda also complained of poor cooperation between KPD and SPD members.[201]

The Origins of the Communist Repression Apparatus in Eastern Germany

Because of the integral role that basic rights played in the motivation behind political anti-Communist resistance in eastern Germany, both broadly in the population and specifically in the non-Marxist parties, we now turn to the repression apparatus in eastern Germany. Indeed, a history of resistance in eastern Germany would be incomplete without mention of the governmental power structures, for the relationship between resistance and authority was intertwined. The most important pillars of the repression apparatus in eastern Germany were the police and judicial systems.

SMAD established a police force in eastern Germany almost immediately after occupation, although the Soviet commander of the field army exercised ultimate public authority.[202] Local Soviet army commanders created the new police force by appointing police chiefs, usually based on the recommendations of the mayor, to recruit "anti-fascists" for police work. These initial cadres came disproportionately from the working classes; roughly 87.6 percent of all police in the Soviet zone were workers or farmers, and 90 percent held membership in the SED.[203]

In the initial days after the war, police tasks entailed registering inhabitants, carrying out SMAD orders, and enforcing those German laws still valid for the upholding of public security.[204] The police force carried out the third duty with limited success, however. The police posts did not coordinate their activities well, and even the names of the police forces varied according to region, named either *Ordnungsdienst, Ordnungspolizei,* or *Schutzpolizei.*[205] The vast majority of the police force, which by January 1946 numbered a mere 21,973 including clerks, had no policing experience and were often undisciplined or corrupt,[206] which hampered the police's ability to bring the rampant crime of the initial postwar years under control. In Berlin, crime had risen a staggering 88 percent since 1937.[207]

The year 1946 marked the beginning of significant changes in the police force. First, as a result of a declaration of the Allied Control Council of January 1, 1946, the Allies permitted the police to carry weapons, although the shortage of available arms meant that most police continued to use billyclubs.[208] The most important change, however, came as a result of SMAD Order Number 0212 of August 1946 which secretly created a new central administration in the Soviet zone, the German Administration of the Interior (*Deutsche Verwaltung des Innern*—DVdI). The lack of organization in the police force and the related low success rate in fighting crime contributed to the impetus behind the founding of the DVdI.[209] But Erich Mielke, a vice president of the DVdI and from 1957 until 1989 the leader of the East German secret police, was right to see far greater possibilities, calling the DVdI a "sharp weapon for the democratic rebuilding."[210] The leadership of the DVdI consisted of one president, Erich Reschke, and three vice presidents, Erich Mielke, Willy Seifert, and Paul Wagner.[211] Although the DVdI remained small initially, employing only seventy workers by the end of 1946,[212] the SED took an important step in transforming the DVdI in December 1946 into the "sharp weapon" foreseen by Mielke. Ulbricht and Fechner met with the presidents of the provincial interior ministries to transfer supreme authority in police matters from the provinces to the DVdI.[213] The DVdI took over central authority of all agencies that dealt with internal administration, public order, and security, which included the criminal police, the traffic police, the railway police, the water police, and the fire department.[214]

Control of the judicial system was a primary goal of the KPD in eastern Germany after the war, as made evident by a KPD proposal for reform of the judicial system. The proposal envisaged a president, two vice presidents, and six departments, two of which had to be occupied by KPD members: Department II responsible for personnel matters, and Department V responsible for criminal law. The other departments—new jurists, civil matters, and the penal system—could be given up to other parties, although the last had to be occupied by somebody who saw "eye to eye" with the KPD.[215] Filling the personnel post with a reliable Communist was critical to the KPD, because a Communist in this post would permit the KPD to staff the Central Administration for Justice with people sympathetic to Communism. The KPD barely disguised this intention in an internal proposal for justice reform: "The democratic renewal of the judicial apparatus and the judicial administration requires increased recruitment of suitable elements from the broader population. For these purposes, those with no training in law should be taken in if they possess the necessary character and educational qualities to exercise a post in the judicial system."[216] With the assistance of SMAD, the KPD did manage to obtain the important posts in the Central Administration for Justice. Although an LDPD member, Eugen Schiffer, headed the Central Administration for Justice, true power lay with his first vice-president, SED member Ernst Melsheimer, and the head of the personnel department, the reliable Communist Hilde Benjamin.

Starting in 1946, the Central Administration for Justice implemented a six-month course to train these new recruits to become "people's judges" and "people's public prosecutors."[217] SMAD permitted the four parties to nominate candidates for the school, but only allowed "reliable democrats" to attend.[218] The "people's jurists" ushered in the beginning of the Communist takeover of the judicial system, although the impact of the "people's justices" was not immediate. By the end of 1947, only 25 percent of all judges and public prosecutors carried SED membership books.[219] Even GDR historians did not disguise the importance of the "people's justices" for the transformation of the justice system: "The class structure of the judicial system was able to be drastically changed only by relatively quickly producing judges and prosecutors from the working classes. . . . After a brief introduction, they handled those trials which were vital for the protection of the new order: trials against Nazi and war criminals, saboteurs, and speculators."[220] Hilde Benjamin, the later GDR justice minister, put it sharply: "The institution of the 'people's judges' was the truly revolutionary element in the restructuring of the judicial system, and became its symbol."[221] The true element to the training however, was a deprofessionalizing and politicizing of the judicial system.[222]

Characteristics of Life After the War

The concerns of the broader population in the first year of occupation did not revolve around political developments or the behind-the-scenes Communist takeover of power. Daily life was characterized to a much greater degree by eking out an existence amid the rubble and contending with the brutality of the Soviet occupation. In the eastern zone, wartime bombing had destroyed nearly 65 percent of housing in the larger centers and nearly 40 percent of the population lost all their possessions.[223] The majority of the population had to struggle to find temporary housing, often crowding those places still livable or simply living in the streets. The search for food occupied a good portion of the day, but ended more often than not in disappointment. No zone of Germany could provide the inhabitants with the 2000 calories per day necessary for an average person to function properly. The American zone had the highest average at 1330 calories per person per day, followed by the Soviet zone at 1083, the British at 1050, and the French at 900.[224] These conditions forced the German population to turn to the black market to survive, where cigarettes and sexual favors fetched many of the necessities of life. Malnutrition was nevertheless common, leading to an increase in the incidence of diphtheria, tuberculosis, and typhus and a horrendous infant mortality rate. In 1945 in Berlin, the infant mortality rate stood at approximately 60 per 1,000, compared to the norm in industrial countries of 9-12 per 1,000.[225] The rampant crime, noted above, also contributed to the chaos and hardship of everyday life immediately after the war.

Although attempting to eke out a living certainly occupied a majority of the population, this was overshadowed by concerns for personal safety. The five Soviet armies that occupied the eastern zone brought with them primitive feelings of revenge for the brutality of the Nazi occupation of the Soviet Union, feelings that could be unleashed in their role as unchallenged conqueror. Isaac Deutscher, a postwar journalist and later Stalin biographer, wrote in October 1945 about the Soviet zone: "Even now questions of high politics are of little concern to the German civilian compared to the pressing daily problems of personal security for himself and especially for his wife or daughter."[226] Deutscher hinted at who bore the brunt of the revenge: the women of the eastern zone. The rape of German women by Red Army soldiers, which began well before the war ended during the advance on East Prussia, is now beginning to take its place in the historiography of East Germany as a major historical occurrence.[227] The sheer extent of rape has suggested to Norman Naimark that it was a "systematic expression of revenge and power over the enemy . . . deeply rooted in socio-psychology."[228] Although instances of Soviet brutality against German women abound, one example in particular demonstrates the baseness of Soviet conduct. A Soviet army hospital for patients with syphilis granted permission for the patients to have an evening out in the nearby Brandenburg town, but the outing turned grotesque when the patients proceeded to attack and rape local townspeople. For a long period thereafter, nobody in the district left their house at night.[229] Red Army abuses were also prevalent in other regions of the Soviet zone. Robert Murphy, the American political advisor for Germany with the rank of Ambassador, commenting on the situation in Berlin stated that according to reliable reports, the "majority of the eligible female population" had been violated.[230] In Thuringia, the LDPD reported that the population lived in fear because of attacks by Red Army soldiers.[231] An SMAD order curtailing contact between the Red Army and the German population in 1947 drastically reduced the incidence of rape,[232] but the experience left a scarring legacy. As Naimark has concluded: "It is important to establish the fact that women in the Eastern zone . . . shared an experience for the most part unknown in the West, the ubiquitous threat and the reality of rape, over a prolonged period of time."[233] As the female population in the zone outnumbered the male population by about 3 million, this was an issue that affected a clear majority of the population.

The incidence of rape caused a loathing of the occupying force and had serious consequences for the Soviet partner, the SED. Soviet reports indicated that many SED members despised the Russians because of their attacks on German women[234] and the SED was aware of the effect the occupation was having on their political fortune. Fred Oelssner, the head of the Agitprop department in the Central Committee of the KPD, stated: "People have already talked about the attacks of the Russians, they happen and they hurt us."[235] Max Fechner echoed his thoughts: "It [the issue of rape] hurts us [i.e., the SED]."[236] One member of the National Committee for Free Germany, Berut von Kügelgen, also suggested that the Red Army was not helping the Communist cause in Germany, stating that it would have been better for the KPD "if the war had ended before Red Army troops had entered Germany."[237] Hermann Matern indirectly pointed to the tie between the SED's unpopularity and the problem of rape when he commented on the abysmal result for the SED in the 1946 Berlin elections: "We could not, despite all our efforts in this direction, win over the women."[238] Outside of Berlin, local SED groups also complained of their inability to win over women to the KPD. The SED in *Kreis* Freiberg reported that it was having "tremendous difficulties" getting women to stand for election for the SED.[239] A report from the town of Gohlis offered an explanation for the difficulties, stating that not one woman would stand for the SED in Gohlis because of the present "insecurity." [240] The SED in Radeburg even went so far as to put on their election list one female farmer, who was not a member of the SED, as bait for other women. [241] For the purposes of this study, it is important to emphasize that the brutality of the Soviet occupation caused large sections of the population to view with hostility both the Soviets and their allies in Germany, the SED.

The widespread incidence of rape contributed to the brutality of the Soviet occupation, but the conduct of the Soviet People's Commissariat for Internal Affairs (NKVD) must also be examined to understand the hardening of the population's attitude towards the Soviets and their German helpers. [242] The Soviet military personnel who installed themselves in 1945 in the Potsdam headquarters of the Group of Soviet Occupation Forces—a building that the Soviets would leave only in the summer of 1994—brought with them NKVD personnel. Colonel General Ivan Serov, a veteran of the Soviet security establishment and a key player in the mass expulsions of ethnic minorities in the Soviet Union, led the establishment of Soviet security units throughout the Soviet zone. [243] NKVD tasks in the Soviet zone resembled those in the Soviet Union: to secure the Soviet state against real and potential threats. The NKVD used its network to be informed of, and to control all, branches of life in the SBZ, a task made easier by its control of the SMAD branch for civilian affairs. [244] Serov led the NKVD troops in eastern Germany on an intense campaign to remove resistance, real or suspected, to Soviet policies for eastern Germany. Initially, the NKVD targetted SPD members who fought against fusion with the KPD and underground *Werwolf* groups which were suspected of planning a terrorist campaign against the occupying forces. [245] These targets soon gave way to widespread arrests.

Serov established a system of "Special Camps" throughout the Soviet zone to deal with opponents. At first, Nazi and war criminals made up the majority of prisoners in the eleven camps of the Soviet zone, and indeed, all Allies had agreed that camps on German soil should be established as prisons for Nazi and war criminals. [246] By 1946 a number of political opponents and other innocent individuals found themselves in the camps of the eastern zone, especially youths suspected of *Werwolf* activities. [247] Present estimates suggest that the camp system contained about 120,000 prisoners between 1945 and 1949, of which approximately 42,000 died [248] although some estimates range as high as 240,000 inmates of which 95,000 died. The deaths were caused primarily by the dreadful living conditions. [249] Although the estimates vary, they are consistent in that they reveal a death rate among inmates of between 35 and 40 percent.

The arbitrary arrests and camp system caused much duress in the population. When marching prisoners between camps, NKVD officers would often arrest people off the street to make up for prisoners who escaped along the way, which caused general panic in the population at the sight of these marching columns. [250] In October 1946, several groups in Eisfeld wrote directly to the Soviet authorities requesting the release of youths who had been arrested in the region. [251] Similarly, parents flooded Otto Buchwitz, the leading SED member in Saxony, with letters regarding the whereabouts of their missing children after he successfully petitioned SMAD for the release of 500 other detained youths.[252] The deep fear of the occupying power was also revealed by farmers who were worried they would not be able to fill the quotas set by SMAD. One KPD member reporting on the situation in Saxony with regard to agricultural quotas stated: "The orders are central ones [i.e., from SMAD in Karlshorst]. In other words the local Soviet commander himself is enormously fearful lest they not be carried out. This fear has caused clashes in the villages, which always become unpleasant affairs."[253] The hostility in the population to the NKVD was not lost on the Soviet authorities in Germany. In November 1947, General Major I.S. Kolesnichenko, head of SMAD in Thuringia, stated in a letter to General-Lieutenant Makarov that the activities of the NKVD were a main reason behind the hostile attitude toward the Soviet occupiers, hastily adding that the NKVD was of course investigating properly and arrested only guilty individuals, but that the Germans were used to "another system of justice."[254]

The actions of the NKVD negatively affected popular support for the KPD/SED. The KPD in the town of Reichnau reported that the population was concerned because a woman had disappeared after threatening suicide out of fear of imminent arrest. The report concluded that "the rigorous measures of the GPU [this Soviet military intelligence branch was often confused with the NKVD] negatively affect the work of the [KPD] for the upcoming referendum. Perhaps we could determine if these actions are a result of orders from the central authority, or if we are dealing here with overzealous local GPU offices."[255] The SED could sense the waning of their political fortunes due to Soviet conduct. In April 1948, Grotewohl veiled the problem by blaming the West: "Western propaganda about the supposed wave of arrests and lack of freedom seriously undermine the SED's authority in the zone and in Germany as a whole."[256] The disregard for basic rights which characterized the Soviet occupation clearly undermined the legitimacy of the SED.

The First Elections in the Soviet Occupied Zone

The elections of 1946 provided an opportunity, albeit limited, for the population to pronounce judgement on developments in the eastern zone. In the elections to the *Gemeinde* councils between September 1 and 15, the SED obtained 57.1 percent of the overall vote, compared to 21.1 percent for the LDPD and 18.7 percent for the CDU.[257] The reasons for the SED success at the *Gemeinde* level are varied. Although the land reform contributed to the favorable SED result, the difficulty the other parties encountered in standing candidates for election played a greater role in the result.[258] In *Kreis* Döbeln, only three out of thirty-nine *Orte* convinced SMAD to accept their CDU candidate, meaning that East German voters could not vote for the CDU in thirty-six localities in Döbeln. CDU *Land* committees complained of similar occurrences in Thuringia and Mecklenburg,[259] ultimately leading Kaiser in the Central Block sitting of August 22, 1946 to formally complain of the difficulties the CDU encountered in registering their local groups.[260] In many regions where the

CDU and LDPD could not stand candidates for election, the population expressed its displeasure with the SED by spoiling their ballots. The number of spoiled ballots often equalled or surpassed the number of SED votes.[261] The uneven distribution of the limited paper supply in favor of the SED[262] and SMAD arrests of some of the more popular non-Marxist candidates also posed barriers to the non-Marxist parties.[263]

At the *Land* and *Kreis* elections of October 20, 1946, the CDU and LDPD improved their count because SMAD did not require candidates to be registered with them.[264] As a result, the SED was not able to win over 50 percent of the vote in any province. Between the elections, the SED lost 430,000 votes and the CDU/LDPD gained 750,000, although the CDU and LDPD still did not have candidates in all ridings.[265] At the *Kreis* level, the SED received 50.1 percent of the vote, the CDU 25.2 percent, and the LDPD 18.6 percent. At the *Land* level, the SED received 47.6 percent, the LDPD 24.6 percent, and the CDU 24.5 percent. In the provincial assemblies of Brandenburg and Saxony-Anhalt, the bourgeois parties received a majority over the SED and its coalition partner the Association for Farmer Mutual Assistance (VdgB).

Due to the difficulty in getting accurate numbers on the election,[266] it may not be possible to know the true results of the vote, but there are clear indications that the vote count was adjusted in favor of the SED prior to the release of the results. An internal report of the party control commission of the SED in Mecklenburg discussing the October 1946 vote stated that the bourgeois parties had outpolled the SED in *Kreis* Güstrow, Hagenow, Ludwigslust, Neubrandenburg, and Greifswald.[267] The official statistics, however, showed a very close race with the SED ahead in all of these *Kreise*, except Ludwigslust.

That the SED was able to obtain only approximately 50 percent of the vote under extremely favorable conditions suggests that the party did not enjoy overwhelming support in the population. The vote in Berlin and the subsequent reaction of the SED and the Soviets to the first elections in the Soviet zone provide further evidence of the SED's unpopularity, despite the seemingly desirable results of the election. The four power status of Berlin forced the SED to run against the SPD and the bourgeois parties without enjoying any advantages. The results shocked even opponents of the SED. The SED finished in third place behind the SPD and the CDU, obtaining 19.8 percent of the vote, compared to the SPD at 48.7 percent, the CDU at 22.2 percent and the LDPD at 9.3 percent. The SED performed best in the Soviet sector of the city, but still only managed 29.9 percent compared to the SPD's 43.6 percent of the vote.[268] The Berlin vote clearly demonstrated that the SED could not win an open and fair election in the Soviet zone of Germany, a fact that Ulbricht all but admitted when he stated: "The growth of reactionary tendencies in the CDU and LDP requires a strengthening of the SED and close cooperation with these parties, in order to beat back the reactionary influences in the bourgeois-democratic circles."[269]

The Soviets were already so concerned by the results of the *Gemeinde* elections that, without waiting for the *Land* and *Kreis* election results, they formed a Central

Committee Commission to investigate the poor results. During a conference between the Commission and Colonel Sergei Tiul'panov's propaganda administration in SMAD, several members of SMAD forwarded explanations for the SED's poor showing at the *Gemeinde* elections, not, as the numbers might suggest, its relative success. Like Ulbricht, Tiul'panov targetted his anger at the CDU and LDPD,[270] revealing that those parties had indeed gained much influence in the population. Both SMAD and the SED must have been especially displeased with the results of cities with a high percentage of working class voters such as Leipzig, Dresden, Zwickau, Plauen, Halle, Jena, Erfurt, and Bautzen where the CDU and the LDPD received more votes than the SED.[271] The Commission's report to the Central Committee on October 11 further demonstrated Soviet disappointment in the first election results by pointing out "serious deficiencies" in SMAD's propaganda administration, and concluding that virtually all of its leaders should be replaced.[272] Clearly, the results of the elections deeply troubled the Soviet authorities in Germany.

Political anti-Communist resistance in the first year of occupation was a response to transgressions against basic rights. The conduct of the CDU during the implementation of the land reform and the conduct of the SPD both during the fusion debates and in its underground resistance made visible this motivation. Although the LDPD did not engage in resistance to the same degree in this early phase of the Soviet Occupied Zone, the party did voice concerns about excesses in the land reform and excesses in the sequestering of factories. The broader population did not significantly partake in resistance activities during the first year of occupation primarily because merely surviving the dreadful postwar conditions was a feat unto itself. Nevertheless, it is apparent that the SED did not have a solid basis of support in the population, as attested to by the results of the fall 1946 elections and subsequent reaction by SMAD and the SED. To explain popular reluctance to strongly endorse the SED, the nature of the Soviet occupation must be addressed. The widespread incidence of rape and the wanton conduct of the NKVD severely undermined the legitimacy of the SED in the Soviet zone. The infringements on basic rights by the Soviet authorities in Germany provoked a hostile climate of opinion toward the Soviet partner in Germany, the SED.

Notes

1. At this ceremony, Admiral Hans Georg von Friedeburg, Field Marshal Wilhelm Keitel, and General Hans-Jürgen Stumpff signed on behalf of the German Wehrmacht. The full text of the document is in *Das Potsdamer Abkommen: Dokumentensammlung* (Berlin [East]: Staatsverlag der DDR, 1980), 31.

2. Hitler named Dönitz his successor as president of the Reich, war minister, and supreme commander of the armed forces; Jackson Spielvogel, *Hitler and Nazi Germany: A History* (Englewood Cliffs, N.J.: Prentice-Hall Inc., 1988), 227.

3. Churchill is reputed to have said that if the Allies had looked for ten years they could

not have found a worse meeting place than Yalta, and only an adequate supply of whiskey made a stay there bearable; Russell Buhite, *Decisions at Yalta: An Appraisal of Summit Diplomacy* (Wilmington, Del.: Scholarly Resources Inc., 1986), 4-6.

4. David Childs, *The GDR: Moscow's German Ally* (London: George Allen and Unwin, 1983), 2.

5. For the protocols of the proceedings and other related documents, see *Foreign Relations of the United States: The Conferences at Malta and Yalta* (Washington, D.C.: U.S. Government Printing Office, 1955), 562-996.

6. Milovan Djilas, *Conversations with Stalin* (New York: Harcourt, Brace and World, 1962), 114.

7. Karl Wilhelm Fricke, *Politik und Justiz in der DDR* (Cologne: Verlag Wissenschaft und Politik, 1979), 18.

8. Fricke, *Politik*, 18. As we shall see, this drawback became important when eastern politicians appealed to the western Allies for assistance in their zone.

9. Martin Broszat and Hermann Weber, eds., *SBZ-Handbuch* (Munich: R. Oldenbourg Verlag, 1990), 11.

10. SMAD had four main departments: demilitarization, civil administration, economics, and politics.

11. Colonel General V.D. Sokolovski followed Zhukov until March 29, 1949; Sokolovski was succeeded by General V.I. Chuikov to October 10, 1949 and the disbanding of SMAD.

12. Orders were usually made known through the SMAD organ *Tägliche Rundschau*; Fricke, *Politik*, 28.

13. Wolfgang Leonhard, *Die Revolution entlässt ihre Kinder* (Cologne: Kiepenhauer & Witsch, 1981), 345-347.

14. The *Tägliche Rundschau* appeared daily except Monday until June 30, 1955; Siegfried Suckut, *Blockpolitik in der SBZ/DDR: die Sitzungsprotokolle des zentralen Einheitsfrontausschusses* (Cologne: Verlag Wissenschaft und Politik, 1986), 13; Broszat and Weber, *SBZ*, 36.

15. Leonhard, *Die Revolution enlässt ihre Kinder* (Cologne: Kiepenheuer & Witsche, 1981), 341.

16. Gregory Sandford, *From Hitler to Ulbricht: the Communist Reconstruction of East Germany 1945-46* (Princeton: Princeton University Press, 1983), 27; Dieter Mark Schneider, "Renaissance und Zerstörung der kommunalen Verwaltung in der SBZ," *VfZ* 37 (1989): 460.

17. Sandford, *From Hitler*, 26.

18. Schneider, "Renaissance," 467.

19. According to Dieter Mark Schneider, the initiative groups of the KPD in eastern Germany dissolved these committees largely because they were supporters of western-style democracy. Schneider, "Renaissance," 266. Wolfgang Leonhard also indicated that he became skeptical of KPD motives for dismantling these committees, as they functioned smoothly and provided a needed service; Ilse Spittmann, *Die SED in Geschichte und Gegenwart* (Cologne: Edition Deutschland Archiv, 1987), 146. To be fair, it should be mentioned that the western Allies also disbanded the Antifas in the western zones because they believed that the committees represented a potential political opponent. See Christoph Klessmann, *Die doppelte Staatsgründung* (Bonn: Bundeszentrale für politische Bildung,1991), 121-126.

20. *Stiftung Archiv der Parteien und Massenorganisationen der DDR im Bundesarchiv*

(hereafter SAPMO-BA), *Zentrales Parteiarchiv* (hereafter ZPA), RY1/ I 2/3/28, 1.

21. SAPMO-BA, ZPA, RY1/I 2/3, 1-2.

22. SAPMO-BA, ZPA, RY1/I 2/3, 1-2.

23. Otto Grotewohl, Eric Gniffke, and Engelbert Graf formed the first group. Karl Germer, Hermann Schlimme, Bernhard Goering, and Richard Weimann formed a second group, while Max Fechner led a third. Broszat and Weber, *SBZ*, 464.

24. Frank Moraw, *Die Parole der "Einheit" und die Sozialdemokratie* (Bonn-Bad Godesberg: Verlag Neue Gesellschaft GmbH., 1973), 85.

25. Beatrix Bouvier and Horst-Peter Schulz, *"...die SPD aber aufgehört hat zu existieren"* (Bonn: J.H.W. Dietz, 1991), 235.

26. Franz Walter, Tobias Dürr, and Klaus Schmidtke, *Die SPD in Sachsen zwischen Hoffnung und Diaspora* (Bonn: J.H.W. Dietz, 1993), 121. Hennig later participated in an illegal SPD group.

27. Interview with C.E. (Curt Eckhardt); Bouvier and Schulz, *die SPD*, 277.

28. A detailed account of the origins of the SPD in the Soviet-occupied zone can be found in Beatrix Bouvier, "Antifaschistische Zusammenarbeit, Selbständigkeitsanspruch, und Vereinigungstendenz," *Archiv für Sozialgeschichte* 16 (1976): 417-468.

29. Moraw, *Die Parole*, 83.

30. For more on European developments, see Dietrich Staritz, *Einheitsfront, Einheitspartei: Kommunisten und Sozialdemokraten in Ost- und Westeuropa 1944-1948* (Cologne: Verlag Wissenschaft und Politik, 1982), 114.

31. See Bouvier and Schulz, *die SPD*, for their series of interviews on the subject. Helga Grebing, Christoph Klessmann, Klaus Schonhoven, and Hermann Weber, *Zur Situation der Sozialdemokratie in der SBZ/DDR zwischen 1945 und dem Beginn der 50er Jahre* (Schüren: Presseverlag, 1992) also emphasizes the re-founding of the party.

32. Bouvier, "Antifaschistische," 425.

33. Hermann Weber, ed., *Parteiensystem zwischen Demokratie und Volksdemokratie* (Cologne: Verlag Wissenschaft und Politik, 1982), 25.

34. Weber, *Parteiensystem*, 27.

35. J.B. Gradl, *Anfang unter dem Sowjetstern: Die CDU in der SBZ 1945-1948* (Cologne: Verlag Wissenschaft und Politik, 1981), 13.

36. Gradl, *Anfang*, 14.

37. Gradl, *Anfang*, 15.

38. Werner Conze, *Jakob Kaiser: Politiker zwischen Ost und West 1945-1949* (Stuttgart: W. Kohlhammer Verlag, 1969), 10.

39. Notable members from the DDP (by the end of the Weimar period, the name had been changed to *Staatspartei*) included Ferdinand Friedenburg, Ernst Lemmer, Walter Schreiber, and Otto Nuschke. Members from the former Centre party were Andreas Hermes, Jakob Kaiser, Lukaschek, Emil Dovifat, Heinrich Krone, and Hermann Vockel; Manfred Agethen, "Die CDU in der SBZ/DDR 1945-53," in *"Bürgerliche" Parteien in der SBZ/DDR: Zur Geschichte von CDU, LDPD, DBD, und NDPD 1945 bis 1953*, ed. Jürgen Fröhlich (Cologne: Verlag Wissenschaft und Politik, 1994), 49.

40. Jonathan Osmond, "Kontinuität und Konflikt in der Landwirtschaft der SBZ/DDR zur Zeit der Bodenreform und Vergenossenschaftlichung 1945-1961," in *Die Grenzen der Diktatur: Staat und Gesellschaft in der DDR,* ed. Richard Bessel and Ralph Jessen (Göttingen: Vandenhoeck & Rupprecht, 1996), 147.

41. The CDU proclamation is reprinted in Weber, *Parteiensystem*, 129.

42. Ekkehart Krippendorf, "Die Gründung der LDP in der SBZ 1945," *VfZ* 8 (1960):

290; Broszat and Weber, *SBZ*, 545. Four others who took part in the founding of the LDPD were Albert-Willy Meyer, salesman and journalist, Dr. Wilhelm Külz, former Reichsminister of the Interior and mayor of Dresden until 1933, Franz Xaver Kappus, a writer, and Dr. Wilhelm Eich, a professor from Berlin. The founders originally decided to name the party after the former Weimar party *Deutsch-Demokratische Partei.*

43. Krippendorf, "Die Gründung," 292.

44. Krippendorf, "Die Gründung" 292; Hermann Weber, *Von der SBZ zur DDR* (Hannover: Verlag für Literatur und Zeitgeschehen, 1968), 20.

45. The proclamation is reprinted in Weber, *Parteiensystem*, 186. Point 8 on the issue of socialization stated: "Die Unterstellung von Unternehmungen unter die öffentliche Kontrolle ist nur gerechtfertigt, wenn die betreffenden Betriebe hierfür geeignet und reif sind und wenn ein überwiegendes Interesse des Gesamtwohls dies gebietet."

46. Other main points of the Leipzig proclamation were the support of political freedom and basic human freedoms like speech and assembly. The Netzschkau proclamation also emphasized that dictatorship must be eradicated. These proclamations are reprinted in Krippendorf, "Die Gründung," 305.

47. Weber, *Parteiensystem*, 186. This document reflects the underlying hostility between the CDU and the LDPD. The CDU had even tried to prevent the founding of the LDPD. The leading LDPD members Külz and Koch often referred to the CDU condescendingly as a "getarntes Zentrum mit demokratischem Anhängsel"; Krippendorf, "Die Gründung," 300; Conze, *Jakob Kaiser*, 24.

48. Tilman Mayer, *Jakob Kaiser—Gewerkschafter und Patriot. Eine Werkauswahl* (Cologne: Bund Verlag, 1988), 214-229.

49. Sigrid Meuschel, *Legitimation und Parteiherrschaft in der DDR* (Frankfurt am Main: Suhrkamp Verlag, 1992), 38. Meuschel suggests that even Soviet Socialism would not have been thought of as badly as it was later.

50. The formation of the Antifa-Block did not prevent the parties from campaigning vigorously to increase membership in their own parties, however. In the first year of occupation, it appears that the KPD and SPD were much more active in trying to engage the population in their politics than the other parties. In March 1946 in Dresden, for example, the KPD held 745 public meetings, the SPD 722, but the CDU only 118 and the LDPD 100. *Bundesarchiv—Abteilungen Potsdam* (hereafter BA-P), DO 1 7/22, 49. Dresden police report for 1945-1946.

51. Hermann Weber, *DDR: Grundriss der Geschichte 1945-1990* (Hannover: Fackelträger-Verlag, 1991), 26.

52. Suckut, *Blockpolitik,* 21.

53. For differing explanations on why the CDU and LDPD participated in the Block, despite its restrictive nature, see Agethen, "Die CDU," 49; Suckut, *Blockpolitik,* 20-21; and Broszat and Weber, *SBZ*, 553. The first members of the Central Committee of the Block were Wilhelm Pieck, Walter Ulbricht, Franz Dahlem, Anton Ackermann, and Otto Winzer from the KPD; Andreas Hermes, Walther Schreiber, Jakob Kaiser, Theodor Stelzer, and Ernst Lemmer from the CDU; Waldemar Koch, Eugen Schiffer, Wilhelm Külz, and Artur Lieutenant from the LDPD; and Otto Grotewohl, Gustav Dahrendorf, Helmuth Lehmann, Otto Meier, and Eric Gniffke from the SPD. Eric Gniffke, *Jahre mit Ulbricht* (Cologne: Verlag Wissenschaft und Politik, 1966), 52.

54. For the protocols of the conference and related documents, see *Foreign Relations of the United States: The Conference of Berlin (Potsdam)* (Washington, D.C.: U.S. Government Printing Office, 1960), vols. I and II.

55. For the sake of simplicity, these will be referred to collectively as "provinces" in this study.

56. The eleven administrations were transport, information, fuel industries, trade and utilities, industry, agriculture, finances, work and social security, health, education, and justice. These were outlined in SMAD Order Number 17 of July 27, 1945. Five more administrations were added by 1947, the most important being the German Administration of the Interior which was created in August 1946; Broszat and Weber, *SBZ*, 201.

57. Broszat and Weber, *SBZ*, 202-204.

58. The decrees of the provincial administrations were given the force of law by Order Number 110 of SMAD of 22 October 1945; Ingetraut Melzer, *Staats-und Rechtsgeschichte der DDR* (Berlin [East]: Staatsverlag der DDR, 1983), 36-37.

59. Norman Naimark, *The Russians in Germany* (Cambridge: Harvard University Press, 1995), p.49.

60. Naimark, *The Russians*, 45.

61. Naimark, *The Russians*, 49.

62. Siegfried Suckut, "Der Konflikt um die Bodenreform-Politik in der Ost-CDU 1945," *Deutschland Archiv* (hereafter *DA*) 15 (1982), 1083.

63. Sandford, *From Hitler*, 82.

64. SAPMO-BA, ZPA, I 2/12/22, 66. Minutes of a KPD meeting of January 7, 1946 regarding the economic program.

65. Peter Hermes, *Die CDU und die Bodenreform in der SBZ im Jahre 1945* (Saarbrücken: Verlag der Saarbrücker Zeitung, 1963), 115. A reprinted document of September 4, 1945 from the CDU organization in *Provinz* Saxony to the central leadership of the CDU mentions that a Soviet representative attended the land reform discussions and rushed the proceedings along. The CDU would have preferred more time to consider the issue. Also, it would have made more sense to introduce the land reform proposal in highly agricultural Mecklenburg or Brandenburg, but not all parties had been founded in those provinces by August 1945.

66. *Archiv für Christlich-Demokratische Politik der Konrad-Adenauer-Stiftung* (hereafter ACDP), I-255-001/7, NL W. Zeller. Notes from a 1946 speech.

67. Protocol from the Central Block sitting of August 30, 1945; Broszat and Weber, *SBZ*, 201.

68. Reprinted as "Erklärung der "Einheitsfront" in Berlin vom 13. September 1945"; Hermes, *Die CDU*, 123.

69. Suckut, "Der Konflikt," 1086. Hermes stated: "Eine reichseinheitliche Regelung scheint uns gerade in dieser Frage eine unerlässliche Notwendigkeit." Hermes also made his views known in three speeches in Berlin and Dresden at the end of October 1945; Winfried Becker, *CDU und CSU 1945-1950* (Mainz: V. Hase und Koehler Verlag, 1987), 188.

70. Conze, *Jakob Kaiser*, 47.

71. An extract from the protocol is printed in Suckut, "Der Konflikt," 1087; See also Agethen, "Die CDU," 50.

72. Peter Ludz, *The Changing Party Elite in East Germany* (Cambridge: The MIT Press, 1968), 439.

73. Hilde Benjamin, Max Becker, Kurt Goerner, and Wolfgang Schriewer, "Der Entwicklungsprozess zum sozialistischen Strafrecht in der DDR," *Staat und Recht* 18 (1969): 1117.

74. Hermes, *Die CDU*, 133.

75. Suckut, "Der Konflikt," 1089.

76. Suckut, "Der Konflikt," 1086-1089.

77. Peter Bloch, *Zwischen Hoffnung und Resignation. Als CDU-Politiker in Branden-burg 1945-1950* (Cologne: Verlag Wissenschaft und Politik, 1986), 62. Bloch acknowledged that the declaration of September 13 was confusing and that articles in the CDU newspaper did not seem consistent with the party line.

78. Hermes, *Die CDU*, 68.

79. Only Herwegen of the CDU Saxony and Lobedanz of the CDU in Mecklenburg spoke out against the central CDU leadership; Suckut, "Der Konflikt," 1089.

80. Bloch, *Zwischen*, 63-68.

81. Hermes, *Die CDU*, 91.

82. Weber, *Parteiensystem*, 120.

83. Mayer, *Jakob Kaiser*, 186.

84. Kaiser's famous phrase was: "Wir haben Brücke zu sein zwischen Ost und West"; Mayer, *Jakob Kaiser*, 214-229.

85. Mayer, *Jakob Kaiser*, 199.

86. Mayer, *Jakob Kaiser*, 219.

87. Mayer, *Jakob Kaiser*, 229.

88. Conze, *Jakob Kaiser*, 80.

89. SAPMO-BA, ZPA, RY1 2/5/50, 18. September 21, 1945 report of the SED *Bezirk* secretaries on the progress of the land reform.

90. SAPMO-BA, ZPA, RY1 2/5/50, 22. September 21, 1945 report of the SED *Bezirk* secretaries on the progress of the land reform.

91. Armin Behrendt, *Wilhelm Külz: Aus dem Leben eines Suchenden* (Berlin [Ost]: Buchverlag Der Morgen, 1968), 56.

92. At the meeting between Koch and Zhukov on September 5, 1945, Zhukov stated that he was "satisfied" with the role of the KPD and the SPD in the *Einheitsfront*, suggesting that opposition by the SPD leadership was limited; Krippendorf, "Die Gründung," 303

93. Behrendt, *Wilhelm Külz*, 58.

94. Krippendorf, "Die Gründung," 303.

95. SAPMO-BA, ZPA, RY1 1 2/5/50, 13. September 21, 1945 report of the SED *Bezirk* secretaries on the progress of the land reform.

96. SAPMO-BA, ZPA, RY1 2/5/50, 14. September 21, 1945 report of the SED *Bezirk* secretaries on the progress of the land reform.

97. Gert Gruner and Manfred Wilke, *Sozialdemokraten im Kampf um die Freiheit* (Munich: Piper, 1981), 115.

98. Arnd Bauerkämper, "Die Neubauern in der SBZ/DDR 1945-1952: Bodenreform und politisch induzierter Wandel der ländlichen Gesellschaft," in Bessel and Jessen, eds., *Die Grenzen*, 109.

99. Klessmann, *Die doppelte Staatsgründung*, 81.

100. Osmond, "Kontinuität," 143-144.

101. SAPMO-BA, RY1/I2/5/50, 13. September 21, 1945 report of SED *Bezirk* secretaries on the progress of the land reform.

102. SAPMO-BA, RY1/I2/5/50, 13. September 21, 1945 report of SED *Bezirk* secretaries on the progress of the land reform, 15.

103. SAPMO-BA, RY1/I2/5/50, 13. September 21, 1945 report of SED *Bezirk* secretaries on the progress of the land reform, 16.

104. SAPMO-BA, RY1/I2/5/50, 13. September 21, 1945 report of SED *Bezirk* secretaries on the progress of the land reform, 19.

105. SAPMO-BA, RY1/I2/5/50, 13. September 21, 1945 report of SED *Bezirk* secretaries on the progress of the land reform, 24.

106. SAPMO-BA, ZPA, NL 182/908, 88. August 31, 1946 excerpts and summary of reports from the SED *Bezirk* groups in Saxony in preparation for the elections.

107. Bauerkämper, "Die Neubauern," 119-120.

108. Naimark, *The Russians*, 329.

109. Kaiser made his position clear at the first CDU conference on June 16, 1946 in eastern Berlin; Fricke, *Opposition*, 50.

110. Naimark, *The Russians*, 184.

111. The resolution is reprinted in Suckut, *Blockpolitik*, 149; see also Gradl, *Anfang*, 72; Fricke, *Opposition*, 50.

112. SAPMO-BA, ZPA, I 2/2/22, 88. January 7, 1946 minutes of the KPD meeting on the economic programme.

113. ACDP, VII-012-1001. June 5, 1946 CDU statement; May 17, 1946 memorandum on the question of dispossesion in industry.

114. Minutes from the July 9, 46 Central Block sitting; Suckut, *Blockpolitik*, 157.

115. Proposal reprinted in Suckut, *Blockpolitik*, 158-159.

116. Naimark, *The Russians*, 185.

117. For a summary of the debates regarding whether or not the fusion was forced, see the exchange of letters in *DA* 24 (1991): 410-416.

118. Andreas Malycha, *Auf dem Weg zur SED; die Sozialdemokratie und die Bildung einer Einheitspartei in den Ländern der SBZ: ein Quellenedition* (Bonn: J.H.W. Dietz Nachfolger, 1995), LV. For more on Brill, see Manfred Overesch, *Hermann Brill: Ein Kämpfer gegen Hitler und Ulbricht* (Bonn: J.H.W. Dietz Nachfolger, 1992).

119. Werner Müller, "SED Gründung unter Zwang—Ein Streit ohne Ende?" *DA* 24 (1991), 53. Hermann Matern, the KPD leader in Dresden, had to insist on the SPD being founded as leading SPD members wanted a united party immediately; Harold Hurwitz, *Die Anfänge des Widerstands* (Cologne: Verlag Wissenschaft und Politik, 1990), vol. 4, Part 1, 300.

120. Walter et al., *Die SPD*, 122.

121. Malycha, *Auf dem Weg*, XXVIII.

122. Hurwitz, *Die Anfänge*, Part 1, 311-315.

123. By November 1945, the SPD had 380,000 members while the KPD had 305,000; Grebing, *Zur Situation*, 22.

124. Moraw, *Die Parole*, 107.

125. Moraw, *Die Parole*, 108.

126. The speech took place on September 14, 1945; Hurwitz, *Die Anfänge*, Part 1, 347.

127. Schumacher made it clear that he did not want a close relationship with the eastern SPD as he felt it was being too influenced by SMAD; Lucio Caracciolo, "Der Untergang der Sozialdemokratie in der SBZ," *VfZ* 36 (1988), 298.

128. Hurwitz, *Die Anfänge*, Part 1, 479.

129. Malycha, *Auf dem Weg*, LXXI.

130. Brill is reported to have said at an SPD meeting in Weimar on November 11, 1945: "If you want to know what Soviet culture is, you just have to look outside your window and see the Ivans in their filthy uniforms. And *they* want to teach us how to build socialism in Germany!" Naimark, *The Russians*, 263.

131. Moraw, *Die Parole*, 135.

132. Klaus Schwabe, *Die Zwangsvereinigung von KPD und SPD in Mecklenburg-*

Vorpommern (Schwerin: Friedrich-Ebert-Stiftung, 1994), 16; Hurwitz, Vol. 4, Part 1, 497.

133. Hurwitz, *Die Anfänge*, Part 1, 497.

134. Walter, *Die SPD*, 134.

135. This thread is evident in the reports contained in Malycha, *Auf dem Weg*. See in particular: "Bericht Friedrich Eberts über die Neubesetzung des Oberbürgermeisteramtes in Brandenburg vom 27. September 1945"; Malycha, *Auf dem Weg*, 37. In this report, Ebert complains of KPD occupation of the post of mayor arbitrarily. See also "Protokoll über die Sitzung des SPD-Vorstandes der Provinz Sachsen am 17. Dezember 1945"; Malycha, *Auf dem Weg*, 158.

136. Caracciolo, "Der Untergang," 303.

137. Moraw, *Die Parole*, 136-137.

138. Gruner and Wilke, *Sozialdemokraten*, 71.

139. Gruner and Wilke, *Sozialdemokraten*, 146.

140. The speech with these ten points is reprinted in Hermann Weber, ed., *DDR. Dokumente zur Geschichte der Deutschen Demokratischen Republik 1945-1985* (Munich: Deutscher Taschenbuch Verlag, 1986), 55.

141. The Central Committee reiterated its anti-fusion stance at a meeting of January 15, 1946; Spittmann, *Die SED*, 156.

142. Staritz, *Einheitsfront*, 206.

143. The division was partly a result of the misinterpretation of the conference due to communications problems and Soviet censorship. Gustav Kligelhöfer reported on January 3, 1946 that some SPD members were confused because the conference was portrayed in the media as the beginning of the fusion process; Malycha, *Auf dem Weg*, LXXXV.

144. Malycha, *Auf dem Weg*, 88.

145. "Schreiben der Ortsgruppe SPD Oranienburg an Otto Grotewohl 20 Februar 1946"; Malycha, *Auf dem Weg*, 409.

146. Werner Müller, "Sozialdemokraten und Einheitspartei," in Dietrich Staritz, *Einheitsfront*, 155. For the hostility of the Leipzig SPD group to fusion, see Malycha, *Auf dem Weg*, 315: "Aus dem Protokoll über die gemeinsame Sitzung des Landes—und Bezirksleitung Sachsens der KPD und SPD am 28. Januar 1946."

147. Malycha, *Auf dem Weg*, XXXVI, 90.

148. Ernst Lemmer, *Manches war doch anders* (Frankfurt am Main: H.Scheffler, 1968), 268.

149. Malycha, *Auf dem Weg*, L.

150. Malycha, *Auf dem Weg*, 88.

151. Malycha, *Auf dem Weg*, 346.

152. "Rundschreiben Nr.18 des Landesvorstandes der SPD Thüringen vom 6. November 1945"; Malycha, *Auf dem Weg*, 187.

153. "Protokoll über die Unterredung der Bornaer Ortskommandatur mit dem Unterbezirksvorstand der SPD Borna vom 16. Januar 1946"; Malycha, *Auf dem Weg*, 302.

154. Malycha, *Auf dem Weg*, 398.

155. Malycha, *Auf dem Weg*, 104. From a Waltersdorf Meeting on February 8, 1946.

156. "Schreiben von Hans Hermsdorf an dem Bezirksvorstanden der SPD Chemnitz August Friedel vom 31. März 1946"; Malycha, *Auf dem Weg*, 447. The SPD in Magdeburg was also against fusion, as demonstrated by insisting on a German-wide party conference; ibid., LXI. See also Bouvier and Schulz, *die SPD*, pp. 251-262.

157. Bouvier and Schulz, *die SPD*, 255. Excerpts of an interview conducted with Hermsdorf are reprinted in this work.

158. Hurwitz, *Die Anfänge*, Part 1, 479.

159. Caracciolo, "Der Untergang," 302.

160. Hurwitz, *Die Anfänge*, Part 2, 799.

161. Andreas Malycha suggests that the Soviets hoped to present the western powers with a *fait accompli* which would have increased their bargaining position at the Paris foreign ministers' meeting in April 1946; Malycha, *Auf dem Weg*, XV.

162. Works on political prisoners in the first year of occupation are now beginning to emerge in large volume, but a sound scholarly work has yet to appear. See Lutz Niethammer, *Der "Gesäuberte" Antifaschismus: Die SED und die roten Kapos von Buchenwald* (Berlin: Akademie Verlag, 1994); Bodo Ritscher, *Speziallager Nr.2 Buchenwald* (Weimar-Buchenwald: Gedenkstätte Buchenwald, 1995); Gunter Agde, *Sachsenhausen bei Berlin: Speziallager Nr. 7 1945-1950* (Berlin: Aufbau Taschenbuch Verlag, 1994). For an earlier account, see Gerhard Finn, *Die politischen Häftlinge der Sowjetzone 1945-1958* (Berlin: Kampfgruppe gegen Unmenschlichkeit, 1958).

163. Klessmann, *Die doppelte Staatsgründung*, 139.

164. Hermann Weber, *Die Sozialistische Einheitspartei Deutschlands 1946-1971* (Hannover: Verlag für Literatur und Zeitgeschehen, 1971), 10.

165. Eric Gniffke has labelled this meeting the "rebellion of the *Land* committees"; Moraw, *Die Parole*, 149.

166. Caracciolo, "Der Untergang," 312.

167. Alexander Haritonow, "Freiwilliger Zwang," *DA* 29 (1996), 410.

168. Caracciolo, "Der Untergang," 316-318.

169. Caracciolo, "Der Untergang," 318.

170. Hurwitz, *Die Anfänge*, Part 2, 1082.

171. 71.8 percent of Berlin SPD members took part in the vote, which was permitted to take place only in western Berlin; Grebing, *Zur Situation*, 37.

172. Klessmann, *Die doppelte Staatsgründung*, 141.

173. Fricke, *Opposition*, 36.

174. Helmut Bärwald, *Das Ostbüro der SPD* (Krefeld: SINUS, 1991), 32.

175. Dieter Rieke, *Sozialdemokraten als Opfer gegen die Rote Diktatur* (Bonn: Friedrich-Ebert-Stiftung, 1994), 24. For more on Schumacher himself, see Gunther Scholz, *Kurt Schumacher-Biographie* (Dusseldorf: ELON Verlag, 1988); Willy Albrecht, *Kurt Schumacher. Ein Leben für den demokratischen Sozialismus* (Bonn:Verlag Neue Gesellschaft, 1985); Dietrich Orlow "Delayed Reaction: Democracy, Nationalism, and the SPD 1933-1960," *GSR* XVI (1993), 80.

176. Rieke, *Sozialdemokraten*, 25.

177. The leader of the refugee support branch in Hannover was Rudi Dux; Buschfort, *Das Ostbüro*, 17.

178. Bärwald, *Das Ostbüro*, 29.

179. Buschfort, *Das Ostbüro der SPD* (Munich: R. Oldenbourg Verlag, 1990), 20. The most recent treatment of the SPD *Ostbüro* is found in Wolfgang Buschfort, *Parteien im Kalten Krieg: Die Ostbüros von SPD, CDU und FDP* (Berlin: Ch. Links, 2000).

180. Documents on SPD activity are also available in the holdings of the first eastern German political police, K-5. This special branch of the police force was not founded until 1947, however. Documents from K-5 on SPD activity are presented in the following chapter.

181. *Archiv der sozialen Demokratie* (hereafter AdsD), SPD-PV-Ostbüro 0421 8 March 1954 report of Karl Behle Bonn. See also ADSD SPD-PV-Ostbüro 0394. Behle was amnestied in 1954.

182. *Franz Neumann Archiv* (hereafter FNA), VII/8. Unsigned, Undated report to Franz Neumann. Confirmed in ADSD, SPD-PV-Ostbüro 0394. December 16 ,1954 summary of the fates of certain SPD members in the eastern zone. Jesse was amnestied in 1954. Whether the others were released before finishing their sentences remains undetermined.

183. AdsD, SPD-PV-Ostbüro 0421, July 25, 1956 report on the history of the arrest of the Rieke Group, Gardelegen, 1.

184. AdsD, SPD-PV-Ostbüro 0421, July 25, 1956 report on the history of the arrest of the Rieke Group, Gardelegen, 2.

185. AdsD, SPD-PV-Ostbüro 0421, August 1, 1956 report on Arthur Leibknecht's arrest by Soviet security organs. Leibknecht was amnestied in 1956.

186. AdsD, SPD-PV-Ostbüro 0420 B/I, August 15, 1951 report by Helmut Wenke.

187. Interview with Hermann Kreutzer, Berlin, April 24, 1995.

188. Bärwald, *Das Ostbüro*, 38.

189. Bärwald, *Das Ostbüro*, 38.

190. Interview with Hermann Kreutzer, Berlin, April 24, 1995.

191. AdsD, SPD-PV-Ostbüro 0421, February 4/5, 1954 report by Siegfried Weisse. Other members of Weisse's group were Fritz Bauer, Gerth Hoppe, Herbert Schäfer, Günter Flach, Herbert Unger, Jochen Müller, and Gerhard Ungerade. See also AdsD, SPD-PV-Ostbüro 0394, November 26, 1956 report; undated report by Source 47670 on illegal group "igel" of the SPD from 1946 to March 1949.

192. Fricke, *Opposition*, 39.

193. Fricke, *Opposition*, 39.

194. The fourteen members of Drescher's groups were Helmut Hoffmann, Halle; Willi Korn, Halle; Erich Bunk, Merseburg; Günter Meier, Halle; Emil Fuchs, Schkopau; Kreist, Merseburg (no first name given); Albert Lebbin, Bitterfeld; Alfred Fritze, Sangerhausen; Hans Donner, Bitterfeld; Willy Thorwandt, Weissenfels; Erich Schmidt, Pouch bei Bitterfeld; Hermann Polenz, Hettstedt; Artur Wagner, Schkeuditz; and Fritz Drescher, Weissenfels. Two received twenty years labor, all the others twenty-five years; Fricke, *Politik*, 118.

195. The releases were due in part to a relaxation of the judicial following the June revolution and in part to a similar relaxation in the wake of de-Stalinization; Wolfgang Buschfort, "Gefoltert und geschlagen," in Rieke, *Sozialdemokraten*, 30.

196. AdsD, SPD-PV-Ostbüro 0361/2. November 11, 1955 report on arrests and releases of comrades in the Soviet zone.

197. AdsD, SPD-PV-Ostbüro 0394, March 9, 1948 personal report; AdsD, SPD-PV-Ostbüro 0361/2, November 10, 1955 report on arrests and releases of comrades in the Soviet zone. Hans Lehmann and Dr. Shade of Görlitz were also SPD members who joined the LDPD.

198. SAPMO-BA, ZPA, NL 182/908, 81. August 10, 1946 report from SED Pirna to the SED *Landesvorstand* Saxony.

199. SAPMO-BA, NL 182/908, 82. August 31, 1946 excerpts and summary of SED *Bezirk* reports on the state of preparations for the upcoming elections in *Land* Saxony.

200. SAPMO-BA, NL 182/908, 83. August 31, 1946 excerpts and summary of SED *Bezirk* reports on the state of preparations for the upcoming elections in *Land* Saxony.

201. SAPMO-BA, NL 182/908, 84. August 31, 1946 excerpts and summary of SED *Bezirk* reports on the state of preparations for the upcoming elections in *Land* Saxony.

202. Fricke, *Politik*, 13.

203. Rüdiger Wenzke, "Auf dem Wege zur Kaderarmee. Aspekte der Rekrutierung,

Sozialstruktur und personellen Entwicklung des entstehenden Militärs in der SBZ/DDR bis 1952/1953," in *Volksarmee schaffen—ohne Geschrei: Studien zu den Anfängen einer "verdeckten Aufrüstung" in der SBZ/DDR 1947-1952*, ed. Bruno Thoss (Munich: R. Oldenbourg Verlag, 1994), 209.

204. Wolfgang Eisert, "Zu den Anfängen der Sicherheits- und Miltärpolitik der SED-Führung 1948 bis 1952," in Thoss, *Volksarmee*, 147.

205. BA-P, DO 1 7/270, 37. 21 October 1947 annual report for the year 1946-47.

206. Richard Bessel, "Die Grenzen des Polizeistaates," in Bessel and Jessen, *Die Grenzen*, 226-227; Naimark, *The Russians*, 356. On average, 5 percent of the police force had prewar police experience; Wenzke, "Auf dem Wege," 209.

207. Similarly, Saxony reported crime four to five times higher than before the war; Bessel, "Die Grenzen," 225.

208. Bessel, "Die Grenzen," 227.

209. Naimark, *The Russians*, 358; Kurt Arlt, "Das Wirken der Sowjetischen Militäradministration in Deutschland im Spannungsfeld zwischen den Beschlüssen von Potsdam und der sicherheitspolitischen Interessen Moskaus 1945-1949," in Thoss, *Volksarmee*, 130.

210. Eisert, "Zu den Anfängen," 150.

211. Eisert, "Zu den Anfängen," 150. Seifert was in charge of the administration police, and Wagner the Schutzpolizei; BA-P, DO 1 7/550, 3. Report on the initial division of powers of the DVdI in the SBZ.

212. Eisert, "Zu den Anfängen," 150.

213. Naimark, *The Russians*, 358.

214. BA-P, DO 1 7/253. Schematic breakdown of the DVdI in 1946.

215. SAPMO-BA, ZPA, NL 182/1118, 50-51. Undated proposal by KPD member Melsheimer for the structure of the Central Administration of Justice.

216. SAPMO-BA, ZPA, NL 182/1118, 64. October 5, 1945 proposal of the Central Committee of the KPD for a reform of the judicial system.

217. The empowerment of judges and lawyers was prescribed in a SMAD order from December 17, 1945. There were initially 5 schools set up for the training of "people's jurists." These schools were centralized into one center in Potsdam-Babelsberg with the founding of the GDR in 1949; Melzer, *Staats- und Rechtsgeschichte*, 51.

218. Josef Streit, "Zur Geschichte der Staatsanwaltschaft der DDR," *Staat und Recht* 8 (1969): 1264.

219. Falco Werkentin, *Politische Strafjustiz in der Ära Ulbricht* (Berlin: Ch. Links Verlag, 1995), 21.

220. Melzer, *Staats- und Rechtsgeschichte*, 51.

221. Benjamin, "Der Entwicklungsprozess," 1119.

222. Gerhard Dilcher, "Politische Ideologie und Rechtstheorie, Rechtspolitik und Rechtswissenschaft," in Hartmut Kaelble, Jürgen Kocka, Hartmut Zwahr, eds., *Sozialgeschichte der DDR* (Stuttgart: J.G. Cotta'sche Buchhandlung Nachfolger, 1994), 475.

223. Kirsten Poutros, "Von den Massenvergewaltigungen zum Mutterschutzgesetz. Abtreibungspolitik und Abtreibungspraxis in Ostdeutschland, 1945-1950," in Bessel and Jessen, *Die Grenzen*, 174.

224. Klessmann, *Die doppelte Staatsgründung*, 45.

225. Dennis Bark, David Gress, *From Shadow to Substance 1945-63* (Oxford: Basil Blackwell, 1989), 131.

226. Quoted in Klessmann, *Die doppelte Staatsgründung*, 55.

227. See the excellent chapter "Soviet Soldiers, German Women, and the Problem of

Rape," in Naimark, *The Russians*, 69-140.

228. Norman Naimark, "Die Sowjetische Militäradministration in Deutschland und die Frage des Stalinismus," *ZfG* 43 (1995), 294.

229. Norman Naimark, "Die Sowjetische," 295.

230. Naimark, *The Russians*, 80. Estimates on the number of German women raped varies widely, from about 30,000 to 2 million. Naimark, "Die Sowjetische," 296.

231. *Archiv des Deutschen Liberalismus* (hereafter ADL), LDPD #14802. April 1946 report from LDP *Kreisverband* Langensalza.

232. Naimark, "Die Sowjetische," 294.

233. Naimark, *The Russians*, 107.

234. Naimark, *The Russians*, 117.

235. Naimark, *The Russians*, 118.

236. Naimark, *The Russians*, 119.

237. Naimark, *The Russians*, 120.

238. Naimark, *The Russians*, 120.

239. SAPMO-BA, ZPA, NL 182/908, 88. August 31, 1946 summary of reports from the SED in 18 *Gemeinden* in Saxony.

240. SAPMO-BA, ZPA, NL 182/908, 88. August 31, 1946 summary of reports from the SED in 18 *Gemeinden* in Saxony

241. SAPMO-BA, ZPA, NL 182/908, 88 August 31, 1946 summary of reports from the SED in 18 *Gemeinden* in Saxony.

242. For an excellent introduction to the various Soviet security organs, and of great assistance in deciphering the number of acronyms, see David Murphy, Sergei Kondrashev, and George Bailey, *Battleground Berlin* (New Haven: Yale University Press, 1997), 30-33.

243. Murphy, Kondrashev, and Bailey, *Battleground*, 29.

244. The Russian archives have yet to release the documents of the civilian affairs branch of SMAD.

245. Naimark, *The Russians*, 382.

246. See "Berichte über sowjetische Internierungslager in der SBZ", *DA* 22 (1990): 1804-1810; Achim Kiliam, "Die "Mühlberg-Akten" im Zusammenhang mit dem System der Speziallager des NKWD der UdSSR," *DA* 26 (1993): 1138-1159.

247. Barbara Kühle and Wolfgang Titz, *Speziallager Nr.7 Sachsenhausen 1945-1950* (Berlin: Brandenburgisches Verlagshaus, 1990), 15.

248. The eleven camps were located in Bautzen, Berlin-Hohenschönhausen, Buchenwald, Frankfurt/Oder, Fünfeichen bei Neubrandenburg, Jamlitz bei Lieberose, Ketschendorf bei Fürstenwalde, Mühlberg bei Riesa, Sachsenhausen, Torgau, and Weesow bei Werneuchen; Kühle and Titz, *Speziallager* 7.

249. Naimark, *The Russians*, 378.

250. Kühle and Titz, *Speziallager*, 13.

251. ACDP, I-298-001/4. October 1946 letter from the mayor of Eisfeld, the Antifa women's committee, and the Free German Youth to the Soviet authorities in Eisfeld.

252. Naimark, *The Russians*, 390.

253. SAPMO-BA, ZPA, RY1 I 2/5/50, 20. September 21, 1945 report of KPD *Bezirk* secretaries on the progress of the land reform.

254. Naimark, "Die Sowjetische," 298.

255. SAPMO-BA, ZPA, RY1 I 2/5/50, 20. September 21, 1945 report of KPD *Bezirk* secretaries on the progress of the land reform.

256. Naimark, *The Russians*, 391.

257. Fricke, *Opposition*, 51. The SED received 5,093,144 votes overall, the CDU and LDPD 3,553,939.

258. The right to active vote applied to everyone over eighteen, while the right to passive vote applied to everyone over twenty-one who had not been a member of the SS or SD and was not a war criminal; SAPMO-BA, ZPA, I 1/2/90, 7. Minutes from the first *Reichskonferenz* of the KPD, 2 and 3 March 1946.

259. Agethen, "Die CDU," 51; Gradl, *Anfang*, 73; Conze, *Jakob Kaiser*, 107; Mattedi, *Gründung*, 88-89.

260. Minutes of the Central Block sitting of August 22, 1946; Suckut, *Blockpolitik*, 163.

261. Fricke, *Opposition*, 51.

262. Agethen, "Die CDU," 51; Conze, *Jakob Kaiser*, 106; Bloch, *Zwischen*, 74-75.

263. See the statement of Aloys Schaefer in Brigitte Kaff, ed., *"Gefährliche politische Gegner": Widerstand und Verfolgung in der sowjetischen Zone/DDR* (Düsseldorf: Droste, 1995), 197.

264. Agethen, "Der Widerstand," 25.

265. Fricke, *Opposition*, 52.

266. Peter Lapp's study on East German election practices (Peter Lapp, *Wahlen in der DDR* [Berlin: Holzapfel, 1982]) was published before access to archival material, and thus had to rely on official SED statistics. Since 1989, more information on the extent to which the elections were manipulated has been trickling out of the archives, but information on the early elections remains scarce.

267. *Mecklenburgisches Landeshauptarchiv* (hereafter MLHA), IV L 2/4/1214, Landesleitung der SED Mecklenburg LPKK.

268. Broszat and Weber, *SBZ*, 422-423.

269. Fritz Reinert, *Blockpolitik im Land Brandenburg 1945 bis 1950* (Potsdam: Brandenburger Verein für Politische Bildung Rosa Luxemburg, 1992), XXIX; Fricke, *Opposition*, 52.

270. Naimark, *The Russians*, 332.

271. Naimark, *The Russians*, 329; Fricke, *Opposition*, 51.

272. Naimark, *The Russians*, 335.

Chapter 3

Dictatorship and Resistance, 1946–1949

The SED Repression Apparatus

The emerging police state in the eastern zone progressed considerably in 1947 as the police came under the influence of the SED, and correspondingly began to take on tasks related to political crime. One police report characterized the new direction as follows: "In the anti-fascist democratic republic, it is necessary to develop a new order. . . . The goals of this new order are the protection of the individual and his material assets, and the prevention of future evils against the state, community, and the individual."[1] The author of this report did not provide a definition for "evil." An internal classified report on the situation in the police was more specific:

> In our young republic [i.e., the Soviet zone—GB], the police are the first and only bearers of arms. They deal with not only criminal and traffic matters, but rather I see one of their most important tasks as constantly protecting . . . against attacks on our young democratic state. The imperative precondition for this is the absolute political reliability of all of those in the service of the police.
>
> There are clear signals in the police which are frighteningly similar to those in the developing stages of the police in the Weimar Republic. If this development continues, there is a great danger that if a sudden political situation occurred, we [the SED—GB] would not have enough control of the police (uniformed as well as the criminal police), to use them as a protective instrument.[2]

The political transformation of the police resulted in regular crimes, and even non-crimes, becoming politicized, especially where the economy was concerned. A police report from 1947 suggested that the politicization of certain crimes contributed to the unpopularity of the police: "The police are very often forced to take action against 'hoarders' [*Klein-Hamsterei*] who sell their surplus to improve their food situation. Members of the police force are required to confiscate even the smallest amount. As the population does not understand the need for this, these police measures are seen as unjust treatment. It has even happened that 'hoarders' and those who steal from fields etc. attack the police and their assistants."[3] In one case, police attempts to confiscate three horses led to a "threatening" crowd being formed, forcing the police to abandon their attempt at confiscation.[4]

The historian Richard Bessel has pointed to the reason for the unpopularity of the police, so candidly admitted in the above report. As Bessel has written: "The *Volkspolizei* during the later 40s and early 50s was increasingly occupied with problems to which the solutions gave the impression that they served a foreign political elite and a foreign occupation authority."[5] Bessel concluded that the *Volkspolizei* had to contend with legitimacy problems from the beginning.[6] This transformation of the police into a party weapon was not only unpopular in the population, but also within the police. An internal SED report complained:

> The majority of police employees in the Cottbus police administration lack clear political direction. I also have reason to believe that this disease is present in other district administrations. In general, there is a dangerously negative attitude towards the Russian occupying power. It is mainly these members who also never see their tasks from a political perspective, and who reject or disapprove of any political activity by the police. In many cases they even sabotage such activity.
>
> It is not uncommon to find cases of even high ranking police officers who, when we receive requests from the Russian occupying power, say: "Why should we work for the Russians? They steal from us too." Or they say: "The police has nothing to do with politics, the police must remain apolitical."[7]

The author of the report was aghast that a member of the Berlin police force, who found an SPD *Ostbüro* pamphlet that poked fun at Pieck, Grotewohl, and the Russians, passed it first around the office and then to another police station, before somebody reported the incident. The author complained how widely spread the pamphlet had been before someone reported the incident: "What use is our work of educating the public, and what use are our threats against people who spread these types of pamphlets, when, with the acquiescence of high ranking police officers, these types of things are possible in the police?"[8]

As the police became increasingly politicized throughout 1947, it also became more coordinated and centralized, as demonstrated in the development of the border police (*Grenzpolizei*). In November 1946, each provincial police force formed a separate department for the border police, which took over the task of patrolling the borders of the eastern zone originally held by the Soviet occupation troops. Initially, the border police units of the provinces were poorly clothed, armed, and housed, and the organization of the units differed between provinces. To unify the work of the border police, SMAD issued orders to coordinate the various provincial border police.[9] The Central Administration of the Interior (DVdI) assumed overall authority for the border police the following year. The creation of an internal telex network (*Fernschreibernetz*) for the entire zone by August 1947 contributed significantly to the coordination of the police.[10] Despite greater coordination and centralization, material difficulties still plagued the police. In Saxony-Anhalt, Brandenburg, and Mecklenburg, only 10-15 percent of the police force had the solid blue *Schutzpolizei* uniforms which became standard attire with the founding of the DVdI in 1946. Police vehicles were characterized as an "urgent necessity,"[11] and socks and shoes were also in high demand.[12]

The most important step in the creation of the SED's political police was the expansion of the fifth department of the criminal police (K-5) in 1947.[13] SMAD and SED formed K-5, originally led by Ernst Lange until August 1948 when it was taken over by Erich Jamin, immediately after the war to monitor the police force and judicial system for unreliable elements.[14] Following the announcement of SMAD Order Number 201 on denazification in August 1947, K-5's importance grew as it became responsible for removing former active Nazis still in leading positions in state, societal, and economic administrations. K-5's duties went beyond denazification though, as demonstrated by the vice president of the DVdI Erich Mielke's definition of its task as the defence of "the democratic institutions . . . and economic rebuilding of the Soviet occupied zone from attempts to undermine them."[15] K-5's internal divisions also indicate the extent of its duties: (1) political crimes, including violation of SMAD orders, (2) violations of Allied Control Council directives, (3) sabotage of the rebuilding, (4) antidemocratic activity, and (5) general technical matters.[16] K-5's duties were so politically sensitive that its leaders made clear that no one who had been employed in the Nazi security services Gestapo or SD would be permitted to work in K-5. This did not apply in other branches of the criminal police.[17]

SPD activity in the Soviet zone preoccupied K-5. Indeed, at K-5's founding, Erich Mielke claimed that the greatest danger to the democratic rebuilding would come from "Schumacher agents."[18] In its yearly report for 1947, K-5 in Saxony reported that beginning in the summer of 1947, a "massive distribution" of SPD pamphlets was taking place in the Soviet zone.[19] In contrast to the previous year, K-5 reported that the SPD was conducting "systematic work" against the SED, which reached its zenith with the distribution of the SPD newspaper *Sächsische Zeitung* during the SED provincial party conference in Dresden.[20] In comparison to 1946, K-5 in Saxony reported that the number of incidents of SPD pamphlets or graffiti had risen from 160 to 536.[21] K-5 was pleased to report, however, that Order Number 201 had reduced the incidence of SPD activity. This admission suggests that Order Number 201 served a dual purpose of bringing to an end the denazification process in the Soviet zone and eliminating political opponents.

There is some evidence to suggest that K-5 was also excessive in carrying out the denazification aspects of Order Number 201.[22] The Mecklenburg police leadership admitted that the police often charged alleged Nazi criminals with crimes much more severe than they had actually committed. The police leadership explained this behavior by the fact that the investigative units were mostly comprised of those who had suffered severely at the hands of the Nazis, and who were therefore sometimes "excessive."[23] The excesses also likely undermined the fortunes of the SED. As the police chief of Schwerin stated: "It might reach a point where the methods of the investigative units could burden us as a party."[24]

K-5 reported directly to the Soviet security forces in Germany, but was housed in the DVdI in Berlin. DVdI's responsibility for K-5 was part of the general centralization of the criminal police branches under the German administration of the interior, which had taken place by March 1947. After this point, the provincial ministers of the interior exerted little control over the direction of the police, responsible instead for simply carrying out DVdI orders.[25]

In October 1947, in order to be better informed about the general situation in the eastern zone, Walter Ulbricht, vice chair of the SED, suggested to SMAD that an information and intelligence service be established within the DVdI. Upon SMAD's acceptance of the idea, Mielke established the Intelligence and Information Department (*Abteilung Nachrichten und Information*) in the DVdI on November 11, 1947. Mielke felt that the new department should inform the population of government measures and that it should also be able to inform the government on the general attitude in the zone.[26] The SED explanation for the creation of the Intelligence and Information Department suggests that oppositional behavior within the SPD and the non-Marxist parties was on the rise in 1947. The SED stated that "certain elements" were trying to destroy cooperation within the SED and that "reactionary groups" within the non-Marxist parties were supressing the "progressive" members of the parties.[27] The SED then argued that the Soviet zone had to be equipped with the necessary tools to fight these tendencies: "All efforts to tear apart these forces [i.e., those who supported close work between the KPD, SPD, and the non-Marxist parties] will be fought by Democracy [through] the further expansion of agencies into institutions which . . . will defend against all attacks by reactionaries."[28] Both K-5 and the Intelligence and Information Department had as a primary goal the removal of political opponents, particularly in underground SPD groups and among oppositional members of the non-Marxist parties.

The information offices in the individual provinces (*Landesnachrichtenämter*), which had previously focused on gleaning information from newspapers and transmitting government resolutions to the press, rather than monitoring occurrences in the population,[29] ran the Intelligence and Information Department.[30] Following the addition of the Intelligence and Information Department, the information offices influenced public opinion by planting articles and photos in newspapers and monitored the population through a network of informants. *Landesnachrichtenämter* duties were captured succinctly in a report: "The *Landesnachrichtenämter* take the pulse of all internal developments, come up with a diagnosis and when necessary, prescribe the most effective 'medicine.'"[31] By 1947, the German Central Administration of the Interior had become a powerful instrument of the SED to further its agenda in eastern Germany.

The SED accompanied its takeover of the police apparatus in the Soviet zone with maneuvering to gain control of the judicial apparatus. Of those students who attended the college to become "people's jurists" in 1946 and 1947, 79.6 percent were SED members, 9.7 percent LDPD members, 6.2 percent CDU, and 4.4 percent had no political affiliation.[32] The effect of SED dominance among students was not immediately obvious. By 1947, only 20 percent of judges and 28.2 percent of public prosecutors were SED members, but by 1950, those percentages had risen to 54 percent and 87 percent respectively.[33] These new jurists dealt primarily with the sentencing of Nazi and war criminals, a task with which most courts in the Soviet zone were concerned after SMAD Order Number 201 quickened the denazification process. The number of people tried as Nazi or war criminals in the Soviet zone rose exponentially from 873 to 4,549 over the course of the year 1947-1948.[34] The SED presence at the trials was not only visible in the judges and lawyers, but in the jurors as well. The SED held classes to instruct jurors to see things "from the Party's viewpoint."[35]

Initially, the SED made limited use of the judicial system in the Soviet zone for its political purposes. To a much larger degree, SMAD used the Soviet judicial system and occupation statutes to remove opponents of the SED in eastern Germany. The denazification process in eastern Germany provided an opportunity for SMAD to remove political opponents, based on an article in the Allied Control Council Directive 38 which permitted punishment of postwar crimes. Article III of Section II stated that individuals could be punished, who "after May 8 endangered the peace of the German people or of the world . . . by spreading National Socialist or militaristic propaganda, or by inventing and spreading tendentious rumours."[36] During the era of Soviet occupation, Soviet Military Tribunals (SMT), rather than German courts, were involved in the removal of political opponents. Soviet Military Tribunals in theory tried only crimes against the Soviet occupying power, but in practice crimes against the Soviet program in Germany were also considered crimes against the occupying power. These cases were tried under Russian law, specifically Article 58 of the 1927 criminal code of the Russian Federated Socialist Republic which dealt with "counter-revolutionary activity," the same article that had sent millions of Soviet citizens into the Gulag.[37] The definitions of counter-revolutionary activity were vague enough to be applied broadly for Soviet political ends. For example, Soviet authorities considered counter-revolutionary activities "propaganda or agitation which incites the overthrow, undermining or weakening of Soviet political authority . . . as well as the spreading, production, or storing of materials with similar contents."[38] The maximum penalty for such crimes was execution, although the death penalty was banned under Soviet law from May 26, 1947 to January 12, 1950, during which time the maximum penalty was twenty-five years internment.[39] Until the founding of the GDR, the SED did not have to get its own hands dirty removing political opponents.[40]

Resistance to Repression, 1947

While SMAD and the SED maneuvered to secure the SED's prominent place in the emerging Soviet zone government, the brutality and lawlessness of the Soviet occupation continued, turning the population against the Soviet occupiers and their German assistants. The wide occurrence of rape, outlined in the previous chapter, continued unabated in 1947, as did its accompanying negative effect in the population, until the winter of 1947-1948 when the Soviets restricted Red Army contact with the civilian population.[41] K-5's work also contributed to insecurity in the population, drawing comparisons between it and the Gestapo.[42]

Continuing NKVD/MVD excesses also caused underlying resentment of the occupying power, a fact revealed in the records of local CDU groups. (In 1946 the Soviets renamed the NKVD, the People's Commissariat of Internal Affairs, the MVD, the Ministry of Internal Affairs. Both East Germans and Soviets continued to refer to the MVD as the NKVD for a number of years.) In April 1947, CDU, LDPD, and SED members wrote to the Soviet authorities in Köppelsdorf requesting the immediate release of eleven youths who had been arrested, forced to confess, and then sentenced.[43] In May, a Leipzig CDU group appealed to the party leadership for assistance in releasing a CDU member and four youths who had been wrongly arrested.[44] A Thuringian CDU group complained to the central CDU leadership in Berlin that there had recently been a series of wrongful arrests and requested that the party leadership talk to SMAD in Karlshorst about the issue.[45] By December 1947, the Soviets themselves had become concerned about the effect of the arrests. General I.S. Kolesnichenko, head of SMAD in Thuringia, wrote to SMAD in Karlshorst saying that CDU and LDPD politicians sympathetic to the Soviet Union reported that the main reason for the hostility in the population toward the Soviets was the "activities of the NKVD."[46] Kolesnichenko suggested that the NKVD should make their arrests known publicly, as the secrecy surrounding arrests and internment was causing "great fear" in the German population.[47]

Letters from Germans in the eastern zone to Franz Neumann, the chair of the Berlin SPD, offer further insight into the insecurity in the population. The letters repeatedly complained about the use of force stating that it was urgent that the NKVD "special camps" be dissolved. One letter complained that the situation in the Soviet zone made the Nazi era look like "child's play." Another letter, after describing the attempts of one SPD member to fight the SED's "policy of force" which ended in his disappearance, pleaded: "How much longer must these conditions continue? Criminals control the situation here."[48] Neumann was already well informed about the injustices in the eastern zone and had often spoken out publicly against them. Throughout 1947, he gave speeches critical of the Soviet zone, often indirectly comparing the SED to the Nazis with phrases like: "Where the SED rules, there is no political freedom. Where the SED rules, dictatorship rules. Where the SED rules, the concentration camp rules."[49]

SPD Resistance

The desire for democratic conditions in the Soviet zone— such as the guarantee of basic rights, freedom of opinion, assembly, and equality before the law—was the primary motivation behind SPD resistance groups in 1947, a year that witnessed the establishment of an increased number of SPD resistance groups. The increased number of groups led to a vigorous campaign against the SPD under the guise of Order Number 201, as outlined above. The K-5 reports which indicated that SPD resistance increased in 1947 are supported by records in the Archive of Social Democracy in Bonn. The following discussion encompasses all SPD resistance groups or individuals which could be identified through archival sources.

For Heini Fritsche, the manner of the SED seizure of power was a primary motivation to resist. Fritsche, a rare contact for the SPD *Ostbüro* in the *Volkspolizei*, contacted the SPD at Ziethenstrasse in Berlin because he was disturbed by the arbitrary takeover of power which raised parallels in his mind to the Nazi seizure of power.[50] In Freital, Richard Netsch began a resistance group of roughly twenty former SPD members because of the lack of freedom and the "Nazi-like" conditions in the Soviet zone.[51] The conduct of Netsch's group again exposed the inexperience of SPD members that took part in underground activity. The SPD *Ostbüro*, which had as one of its main tasks the assistance of SPD resisters in the Soviet zone, continually sent couriers to Netsch to remind him to act furtively. The *Ostbüro* was especially alarmed that Netsch had sent it a list through the regular mail of all those involved in his group.[52]

SPD resisters also fought random arrests. In Münchenbernsdorf, Thuringia, an SPD member organized illegal SPD work after witnessing the conduct of the NKVD.[53] Another SPD member listed the "25,000" in the NKVD's "special camp" at Buchenwald, a former Nazi concentration camp near Weimar, as his motivation to resist.[54] In Cottbus, an SPD group spread pamphlets demanding the release of the political prisoners in the eastern zone.[55] Other SPD members began working for the SPD *Ostbüro* not solely because of NKVD conduct, but because of the terror of the occupying power and "its SED assistants."[56] The deep insecurity in the zone was visible in an SPD group which provided the *Ostbüro* with information on which Germans were informants for the NKVD, in order that this information be broadcast into the Soviet zone as a warning for other Germans.[57] SPD members complained that these NKVD informants were "dirtier" than in the Nazi era.[58] SPD reports of 1947 repeatedly point out that this insecurity resulted in a deep distrust in the population towards the SED. According to one report, the population was especially bitter because instead of the promised socialism, "Russian fascism" was the order of the day.[59]

At the University of Jena, Wilhelm Wehner, Konrad Abel, and Günther Höfer initiated contact with the *Ostbüro* of the SPD in August 1947 under the guise of the Kurt Henschke group.[60] Dr. Josef Witsch, a publisher, and Ricarda Huch, an author, also came to be involved in the group. As recounted by Wehner himself, his belief in freedom of the individual[61] and his concern for the Sovietization of Germany drove him to resist. Soviet authorities arrested Wehner in March 1948 and, after two years awaiting trial, an SMT sentenced him to twenty-five years labor. Wehner was amnestied in June 1956.[62]

The blatant example of the brutality of the occupation in the Wismut mining operation caused some Social Democrats to engage in resistance. Due to the importance for its development of an atomic bomb, the Soviet Union delighted in discovering that the Erzgebirge region of southern Saxony contained significant uranium deposits. By 1947, the Soviets had secured the area and had begun extensive mining operations. The Soviets realized that Germans would not readily volunteer for this work and thus conscripted roughly 100,000 Germans for the harsh work, most coming from the nearby large cities in Saxony, but the Soviets also conscripted laborers from as far away as Mecklenburg.[63] After learning of the forced labor in the uranium mines in southern Saxony and the miserable living standards, an SPD member of the SED attempted to address the issue within the party but was warned not to broach the subject.[64] He then travelled to Ziethenstrasse in Berlin, where he received various pamphlets, brochures, and copies of Schumacher's speeches for distribution in the Soviet zone. In return, he provided the *Ostbüro* with reports on the eastern zone and the situation within the SED.[65] Within sight of the old city hall on the market square, the SPD member secretly spread pamphlets, including boldly slipping anti-Communist literature into the programs handed out during the annual trade fair for which Leipzig was rightly famous. He also stuck anti-Communist slogans in phone booths and covered the massive walls of the train station, Europe's largest dead end train station, with anti-Communist stickers. During his trial following his arrest in March, he gave an emotional speech in which he exclaimed: "Germany must finally be free!" The speech found little resonance with the judge. The SPD member spent eight years in Bautzen prison before obtaining early release in 1956. While in Bautzen, he did not want for social democratic company, as numerous other SPD resisters were there at the same time, including Dieter Rieke, Albert Lebbin, Paul Schubert, Heinz Brennecke, Fritz Ohlman, and Paul Trautner. The social democrats in the prison were so numerous that other prisoners referred to them as the prison's own "SPD-Faction."[66]

The lack of freedom of expression caused Herbert Braun, a political commentator on Radio Leipzig from February 1947 to May 1948, to engage in resistance. Braun, who had joined the SPD in 1945 and the SED in 1946 in order to provide a "counterweight" to the Communists in the party, resented the fact that Soviet authorities continually subject his manuscripts for the radio to excessive censorship. The ongoing censorship of his views, and the fact that from the end of 1947 the SED was becoming more dependent on the Soviets, caused Braun to request leave from his job as commentator in December 1947. In February 1948 he gave his last commentary on the radio, and in May left the station. Because he was "politically suspect," K-5 arrested him and brought him to trial under accusations of spying for the western powers. As there was little evidence to support this accusation, the charge was changed to cooperation with the Nazis, but the jury found him innocent.

In June, he and his family fled the Soviet zone and settled in Frankfurt.[67]

The infringement on freedom of expression was evident during the trial of an SPD member of the "Lukas Cranach" group in Weimar, named after the noted German renaissance painter, to which Curt Eckhardt and Herbert Wehner belonged. After six months of secret contact with the *Ostbüro* in Berlin, one of the members of the group was awakened in the middle of the night by the screeching of a car outside his apartment followed by banging on his door and the sound of voices. When the resister opened the door, he was faced with two Red Army officers, a translator, a German police officer, and the resister's sister, who had been forced to reveal the whereabouts of her brother. The Soviets ripped through everything in his apartment in their search for underground literature. Finding none, they satisfied themselves of the man's guilt by uncovering West German newspapers and a copy of the American constitution, and took him into custody for questioning. At his trial, the SPD member stated that he was innocent because the Soviet zone was a democracy and therefore a variety of political persuasions were supposed to be allowed: "In every western democracy, this type of expression of opinion would not be punishable."[68] These pleas fell on deaf ears, as this resister, Eckhardt, and Wehner were all sentenced to twenty-five years in a labor camp. Another member of the group found that his talents as an architect earned him special favors while serving time. Recalling his six years in labor camps, the member spoke with some pride of the prison hospital that he had constructed in Weimar and the extension that he built on the prison in Hohenschönhausen outside Berlin, and boasted how the Soviets even offered him a job on the show piece Stalinallee when he was released in 1954.[69]

The initial transformation of the SED into a Marxist-Leninist cadre party also drove SPD members to resist. The transformation of the SED into a Soviet-style Communist Party, a "Party of a New Type," began in the summer of 1947 at the Second Party Congress (*Parteitag*) when the SED announced that parity in the party and government administrations was not necessary because there was no longer a difference between KPD and SPD members of the party.[70] SPD members in the party naturally showed little enthusiasm for this resolution. The SPD-dominated SED group in Gaschwitz stated that the resolution of the Second Party Congress did not aid the party in tackling the tasks ahead, as it undermined the unity of the working class.[71] On a trip through Thuringia in late 1947, Kurt Fischer, the president of the Central Administration of the Interior, noted that at a local gathering of the SED in Glauchau-Rothenback, a member of the party suggested that the leadership of the SED was wrong to embark on this course and that it should follow Kurt Schumacher's vision of socialism. There was a similar occurrence in *Kreis* Rudolstadt where members of the SED stated: "We want to remain Marxists, but not become Leninists. We don't want to become Communists."[72] Evidently, the SPD presence in the SED was still strong in 1947.[73]

At the University of Jena, an active center for resistance throughout the history of the GDR, Gustav Tzschach, an SPD member in the SED and former soldier in the Wehrmacht, founded an SPD resistance group in 1947 with his high school friend Heinz Gunzler due to the changes in the SED, believing that the SED's path of "bolshevizing" Germany was harming the country. Eight humanities students and one science student, ranging in age from twenty-one to twenty-nine years, participated in the group's covert activities. Tzschach believed in Social Democracy, but not Communism, which he stated clearly during the founding of the National Democratic Party of Germany's (NDPD) branch at the University of Jena by mounting a table at the university cafeteria and yelling: "What we need is not a national democratic party, but a social democratic party."[74] The co-founder, Heinz Gunzler, a philosophy student at the university, left the SED after its proclamation of a "Party of a New Type" and joined the LDPD. For Tzschach and the others in the group, the transformation of the SED was part of the general trend in the eastern zone towards dictatorship and abuse of basic rights. The main topics that the group discussed at their secret meetings reflected their concerns: the transformation of the SED into a "Party of a New Type," the transfer of the Russian system onto Germany, the use of force to solve all problems, the increasing suppression of opinions, and the division of Germany.[75] The group contacted the SPD *Ostbüro* in order to receive instructions and to provide the *Ostbüro* with information on developments in the Soviet zone for distribution,[76] particularly to the western press who, the group hoped, would bring international pressure to bear on the Soviet zone. Within the Soviet zone, the group spread information by speaking with small groups of students in tucked-away corners of the university because they judged the danger of leaflet distribution to be too high. After being denounced by a former Nazi press official, the Soviet officers, accompanied by a translator, conducted interrogations only at night and forced Tzschach to remain awake during the day. Dazed and exhausted from the lack of sleep, he signed the thick protocol shoved in front of him and confessed to whatever crime the entirely Russian text convicted him of.[77]

The trend towards dictatorship in the SED even caused some ardent supporters of SPD-KPD fusion to engage in resistance. In Halle, a strong proponent of fusion became disillusioned with the SED and turned to Ziethenstrasse in order to establish an SPD resistance group in Saxony-Anhalt.[78] Paul Szillat, the SED mayor of Rathenow, also became disillusioned with the SED and began working for the western SPD until 1951 when he, his son, and five others were sentenced on counts of sabotage and "social democracy."[79] Ironically, Szillat served his sentence in the notorious prison in Brandenburg which had been built under his administration.[80] In Magdeburg, the pro-fusion Max Fank, a member of the SED *Kreis* executive in Stralsund and member of the Mecklenburg provincial assembly, was arrested on March 9, 1949 for his social democratic activity and sentenced to twenty-five years in a labor camp.[81]

The Soviets adopted strong methods to remove social democratic opponents in the party. During the Easter week of 1947, Halle, Gera, Leipzig, and Dresden witnessed arrests of 130 social democrats in the SED. Additionally, prisons in Zwickau, Dresden, and Buchenwald noted high numbers of SPD inmates.[82] Among the more prominent SPD members arrested were Dr. Konitzer, former president of the Central Administration for Health, and Dr. Rudolf Friedrichs, minister president of Saxony.[83]

Although a majority of SPD members who contacted the SPD *Ostbüro* in 1947 were engaged in underground resistance, a small number contacted the *Ostbüro* because of a rumor circulating in the Soviet zone that the SPD would be reinstated. These members simply desired that the western SPD know of their reliability in order to build up the party again should the ban on the party be lifted, rather than to engage in underground resistance. Wilhelm Pieck, vice chair of the SED, helped to fuel the rumour of SPD reinstatement in the Soviet zone by publishing an article in *Neues Deutschland* at the beginning of 1947 in which he questioned why Schumacher had not yet asked SMAD for permission to reestablish the SPD in the eastern zones of Germany.[84] The "Lukas Cranach group," for one, initiated contact with the SPD *Ostbüro* in Berlin in June 1947 after considering the article. The members of the group desired information on the direction of the western SPD and instructions for reestablishment of the party in the eastern zone.[85] In Cottbus, the notion that the SPD might be permitted again in the eastern zone caused an SPD member of the SED to contact Ziethenstrasse in Berlin in September 1947 to obtain instructions on a course of action. The *Ostbüro* instructed him to gather names of reliable Social Democrats in his district. He then contacted SPD members in the region in order to have them at the party's disposal in the event the party was re-licensed. He was eventually arrested in May 1948, along with four others with whom he had contact.[86]

Repermitting the SPD in the eastern zone had, in fact, been considered at a high political level. In January and February 1947, Pieck, Ulbricht, Grotewohl, and Fechner had travelled to Moscow to discuss with Stalin the situation within the SED. As has been noted, internal strife, emanating largely from the former SPD members but also from the far left elements among KPD members, plagued the SED.[87] At this meeting, Stalin suggested legalizing the SPD in the eastern zone in exchange for the SED obtaining a licence in western Germany. Stalin believed that the SED might be able to split Schumacher's SPD by attracting left-wing elements of the western SPD to the SED.[88] Ulbricht and his colleagues immediately rejected the proposal for an SPD in eastern Germany,[89] essentially acknowledging their own unpopularity and the strength of the SPD one year after its ban.

The capture of Waldemar Kasparek, one the *Ostbüro*'s main couriers, on April 8, 1947 dealt a severe blow to SPD resistance in the eastern zone. Kasparek revealed the names of various SPD individuals and groups in the zone who worked for the *Ostbüro*, including Paul Peters, director of government publications in Halle and head of the SPD for Saxony-Anhalt, Fritz Drescher, a ministerial director of the provincial government for Saxony, Kurt Weiss, leader of municipal department in the SED provincial association in Halle, and the main SPD figure in Magdeburg, government counsel Brendenbeck.[90] He also exposed Professor Brundert, Willi Hesse, Willi Bernhard, Willi Rössner, and Otto Runge as belonging to an SPD organization in Saxony-Anhalt.[91]

In order to deal with the increased SPD resistance activity in 1947, and the correspondingly increased fight by the Soviet Ministry of the Interior (MVD), the SPD *Ostbüro* hired more staff and purchased more modern equipment. Günther

Weber, a former Leipzig police president who joined the *Ostbüro* on April 27, 1947, also helped to run the *Ostbüro* more like an intelligence organization.[92] The organization went through another change in July 1947 when Sigi Neumann and Stephan Thomas (alias Grzeskowiak) replaced Rudi Dux as head of the *Ostbüro*, although the transition was not entirely smooth. Many SPD members were suspicious of Neumann due to his membership in the KPD during the Weimar era.[93] Thomas' and Neumann's first task was to rebuild the courier network which had been compromised by Kasparek's capture.

LDPD Resistance

The SED's disregard for basic rights especially in the industry reform continued to provoke a hostile response by the LDPD in 1947. Due to the repeated unjust confiscations of property from those with an untainted past, the LDPD insisted that wherever the past was debatable, the case had to be brought before the provincial commission on sequestering.[94] Leading LDPD members, including Elster and Külz, officially complained about the manner of sequestering properties,[95] for they felt that it was a basic requirement of humanity that individuals be given a chance to defend themselves.[96] From the beginning, the LDPD had insisted that legal procedures be followed in carrying out the reforms. At the founding sitting of the Central Block on July 13-14, 1945, Dr. Eugen Schiffer (LDPD) insisted that legal security (*Rechtssicherheit*) must accompany confiscation: "The claim to *Rechtssicherheit* is not merely a legal issue, but rather a requirement of life in a modern parliamentary democracy. Life, freedom, honour, property and all other rights must be protected through guarantees."[97]

Lower levels of the party supported the position of the party's leadership. At a public meeting of the LDPD in November 1947 in Beelitz, the speaker attacked the SED due to its disregard for the rights of the middle class, and complained that the Soviet authorities still determined policy for the eastern zone. He added that capitalism allowed people a more comfortable life, whereas socialism only brought poverty and misery.[98] The right to property was at the center of the complaints of Dr. Hans Müller-Bernhardt, LDPD member of the Saxony provincial assembly, when he stated that the "people's factories" should be returned to private hands.[99] In the Thuringian provincial assembly, the LDPD/CDU and a few SED members were in fact able to return some factories to their previous owners. In Brandenburg and Berlin, the opposition parties prevented the SED from socializing cinemas.[100] These protests were not without risk, however. After speaking out against the dispossession of theater owners in Mecklenburg, the deputy minister of the interior, Dr. Spreche, visited the chair of the LDPD fraction in the Mecklenburg provincial assembly, Dr. Scheffler. Spreche tried to persuade Scheffler to change his stance, suggesting that for doing so he would receive additional rations.[101] Refusal of Spreche's bribe led to Scheffler's arrest and trial as a Nazi.

The situation in Thuringia regarding the injustices in the industry reform was particularly tense. LDPD members in *all Kreise* were so appalled by the injustices that they refused to participate in the sequestering commissions, causing the LDPD in Thuringia to approach the Thuringian Minister of the Interior Gebhardt for review of the sequestering procedures.[102] Referring to the sequesterings, Dr. Karl Hamann, an LDPD member of the Thuringian provincial assembly, stated: "Every day, new injustices discredit democracy."[103]

CDU Resistance

As with the LDPD, the CDU voiced its concerns regarding injustices in the sequestering of factories. The CDU newspaper *Neue Zeit* was a vocal critic of the SED's conduct during sequestering.[104] At the Central Block sitting of October 31, 1947, the CDU proposed regulating the sequestering actions through a "Zonal Commission for Sequestering Disputes," a proposal that was quickly dismissed.[105]

SMAD and SED repression of opponents, and unjust incarcerations in the population at large, provoked several leading CDU members to resist, including Wolfgang Seibert, head of the CDU youth group *Junge Union* in Thuringia. Seibert had been a strong proponent of liberal democracy since the end of the war. In 1946, deeply moved by the injustices he was witnessing, Seibert gave speeches throughout the Soviet zone which stressed the importance of basic freedoms for a democracy, such as the freedoms of speech, opinion, and press. In July, he delivered a speech on the nature of dictatorship and democracy, stressing that one of the key differences was the fact that all citizens in a democracy were equal before the law. Seibert also complained that developments in the eastern zone had damaged the population's belief that justice and humanity would be reinstalled in Germany.[106] In a letter to Georg Dertinger, the general secretary of the CDU in the eastern zone, Seibert criticized the CDU's role in contributing to this insecurity. He stated his displeasure with the CDU's work and its apparent blindness to the injustices in the zone: "Things have happened which will always remain a blemish, and unfortunately from which the CDU is not free of guilt." He further lamented that two years after the founding of the CDU, nothing had been done to remove "a Gestapo and its terror." Because Seibert was preoccupied with the policing methods of the zone, he distributed the CDU pamphlet: "We did not fight against terror in order to watch new despotism emerge," at over 120 public gatherings.[107] By June, Seibert could no longer tolerate the injustices in the zone. He wrote to the CDU chair Jakob Kaiser explaining that he would be leaving the party because of its silence, and therefore complicity, in the injustices in the Soviet zone. Seibert wrote: "I do not wish for my name to be associated any longer with a party leadership which over and over publicly bows to an occupying power, whose measures could in no way find the approval of a Christian." He clarified that he was not against the Soviet Union, but rather the Sovietizing of eastern Germany.[108]

At the University of Berlin, a group of students headed by Georg Wrazidlo, chair of the CDU university group and medical student, published a student journal critical of Communism. Their protests began on May 1, 1946 when Wradzilo, at that time leader of the students' working committee, adopted a resolution against decorating the university with Communist emblems.[109] Wradzilo believed that the university served "scholarship and education" and should not be a "party institution."[110] The group, which also included the Catholic students Gerhard Rösch, Schipke, Wolf, and Klein (who was also a member of the central council of the FDJ)[111] were sentenced for conducting underground fascist activity and for possession of weapons. The SED certainly manufactured these charges, considering that Wradzilo was a member of a resistance group against Hitler and a recognized "Victim of Fascism."[112] The arrests disturbed the CDU faction in the Berlin city parliament, who insisted that the Allied Kommandatura be contacted to find out more about the arrests.[113] At the same sitting Annedore Leber (SPD) stressed that the "rechtliche Unsicherheit" (legal insecurity) must come to an end, and demanded that arrests and verdicts be made public.[114] Wradzilo, Klein, and nineteen others served nine years each in eastern prisons.

In 1947, Jakob Kaiser spearheaded CDU resistance to the increasing Communist dictatorship. He resisted one-party rule by opposing the entry of the mass organizations into the Central Block, accusing the SED of undermining the independence of the other parties in an attempt to assume the leading role.[115] In a dramatic speech on July 12, 1947 to the CDU leadership in the Soviet zone, which came to be characterized as "the opposition speech," he proclaimed that the CDU would follow an independent path "especially now," and rejected the SED campaign to intensify Block work.[116] At the same speech, he provided insight into the situation in the Soviet zone and his own motivation to resist the SED when he stated that the population lived in a state of constant trembling because of the "incarcerations and the lack of personal security."[117] In a clear rejection of Communism, Kaiser refused to take part in the celebrations marking the thirtieth anniversary of the October revolution.

Kaiser hoped that the deteriorating situation in the Soviet zone could be arrested by the unification of the zones of Germany and looked forward to a meeting of February 5-6 in Königstein of CDU representatives from all zones of Germany. At this point, relations between eastern and western CDU were still amiable. At Kaiser's prompting, an executive working committee of the CDU and CSU of Germany was elected at Königstein and met in Berlin from March 13 to 15 to work out a political representation for all zones of Germany. The committee sent out letters to the other parties in Germany to help create this representative body. When Kurt Schumacher, the leader of the western SPD, rejected this "National Representation" on May 28, Kaiser's hope to achieve German unity in this manner died.[118] The division of Germany was solidified when the Moscow conference of Allied foreign ministers failed to produce a plan to run Germany as a whole, and the Munich conference of provincial leaders also proved fruitless.[119]

By the fall of 1947, the eastern CDU's opposition to the emerging Communist dictatorship was becoming unpleasant for the Soviet authorities. At the CDU's party conference of September 4 to 8 in Berlin's Admiralspalast, a conference that Gradl has named "The Resistance Conference,"[120] Kaiser delivered his famous statement on the CDU's position towards dictatorship: "We must be, and we want to be, a breakwater against dogmatic Marxism and its totalitarian tendencies."[121] Other speeches by leading CDU members at the conference echoed Kaiser's view. Karl Arnold, a CDU representative from the British zone, spoke out for the importance of the individual in a society. Robert Tillmanns, a CDU member of the Saxony provincial assembly, ignored the presence of Colonel Sergi Tiul'panov, SMAD's information officer, to lash out against Marxism and the SED.[122] Party members demonstrated their support of Kaiser's course by delivering him a resounding 248 of 249 votes for party chair. Equally important, delegates rejected Dr. Reinhold Lobedanz as the third vice chairman because, according to Ernst Lemmer, a member of the CDU executive, he was more willing to compromise with the SED than Dr. Erich Fascher, the choice of the delegates.[123]

This clear support in the party must have given Kaiser added impetus to firmly resist the SED during the *Volkskongress*. After the failure of the Moscow conference of Allied foreign ministers, and due to the lack of progress at the London foreign ministers' conference of November 1947, the SED and SMAD came to the conclusion that a united Germany under Communist domination was a distant wish. The SED therefore called for parties, organizations, and large factories from all Germany to send delegates to Berlin for December 6 and 7 to form a *Volkskongress*, a popular representation, which would discuss German reunification and elect a delegation to bring their views to London, where the foreign ministers' conference was still under way.[124] At the Central Block sitting on November 24, Kaiser spoke out against the SED's plan for a German representative body on the grounds that it would not be representative of all zones of Germany.[125] His grave fear, however, was that this body would not be apolitical but rather a pretense for the SED to put forth its political agenda in all zones of Germany, an agenda which Kaiser opposed on the grounds that it did not fulfil the requirements of parliamentary democracy.[126] Kaiser made his motivations for opposition to the *Volkskongress* clear in a speech to the CDU in the Weimarhalle: "I can only be responsible for a party that is based on freedom." He also emphasized the importance of freedom of the individual: "My friends, we are bound by the requirements of humanity, of freedom, of the unassailable rights of the individual."[127] On December 2, for these reasons, Kaiser rejected official CDU participation at the *Volkskongress*, although he permitted CDU members to attend if they desired.[128]

The *Volkskongress* divided the CDU. Kaiser had elected to resist the Soviets once and for all, whereas a minority of members believed that not to take part in the *Volkskongress* would mean the end of CDU work in the Soviet zone. Otto Nuschke spearheaded this group which had come to put its faith in a path of compromise with the Soviets in the hope that free elections would take place, and that the CDU would subsequently be a major political force. Nuschke was not entirely naive in his expectation of free elections, stating that the western Allies would be the ones to bring about free elections.[129] Most CDU provincial chairmen supported Nuschke, and agreed to attend the *Volkskongress* due to pragmatic reasons.[130] As a result, 219 CDU members attended the *Volkskongress*, including leading functionaries such as Lobedanz, Nuschke, Wolf, Herwegen, and Trommsdorf.[131] In all, over 2,200 delegates attended the *Volkskongress*, including 600 representatives from the West.[132]

Wilhelm Külz, the leader of the LDPD, also agreed to support the *Volkskongress* movement because he felt that only through compromise with the Soviets and the SED could hope be kept alive of exercising liberal politics in the Soviet zone. He realized the error of his ways, however, as shortly before his death on April 10, 1948 he pleaded for a state ruled by law and against the arbitrary confiscation of property.[133] The support of the higher levels of the party for the *Volkskongress* did not translate into automatic support by the lower levels. In the Brandenburg provincial assembly, Dr. Walter Kunze spoke out against the *Volkskongress*. His anti-Communist stance carried over into the dedication of the Hennigsdorf steel works, where, in front of a gathering of workers, he ridiculed the socialist mottos and slogans adorning the plant. For his actions, he was removed from his position as finance minister in the provincial government, and was accused by the Brandenburg Minister of the Interior Bechler of being a western agent.[134]

Citing their "anti-democratic" stance regarding the *Volkskongress*, SMAD removed the CDU chairs Lemmer and Kaiser on December 19, 1947.[135] Kaiser and nine of the fourteen members of the CDU executive then moved to West Berlin, where Kaiser continued to attack the developing Communist dictatorship in the eastern zone by establishing the *Büro Kaiser* to maintain contact with the *Kreis* groups of the CDU in the zone, the majority of which still stood behind him.[136]

Following the removal of Kaiser, SMAD instructed Dertinger to form a *Koordinierungsaussschuss* (Coordinating Committee) to run the CDU on an interim basis under the leadership of Nuschke, Dertinger, Wolf, Hickmann, and Lobedanz.[137] The *Büro Kaiser* thus offered an alternate leadership for the CDU in the Soviet zone to the one under Dertinger and Nuschke.[138] By December 1947, the provincial leaders clearly distanced themselves from Kaiser[139] because of the belief that, ultimately, one had to compromise with the occupying power.[140] Peter Bloch, a CDU member of the provincial assembly in Brandenburg, explained that he stayed in the CDU after Kaiser's removal because he felt that compromise was necessary in order for the CDU to maintain a presence in the Soviet zone. He later admitted that this belief was naive: "We simply did not comprehend, despite our experience in the Third Reich, the . . . inevitability of a dictatorship, be it Nazi or Communist."[141]

The evidence suggests that the majority of the CDU membership had already come to the conclusion that Bloch only came to later. The executive of the CDU received letters from all over the Soviet zone in support of Kaiser.[142] Furthermore, all five provinces witnessed a polarization between the provincial leadership, which distanced itself from Kaiser, and the *Kreis* level which supported him, especially in Saxony where a majority of CDU members firmly stood behind Kaiser on the grounds that there could be no further compromise with the SED and the Soviets.[143] The CDU youth group *Junge Union*, which had been formed in the summer of 1945 in Berlin and Thuringia by young members of the CDU, and eventually spread to all areas of the Soviet zone, stood firmly behind Kaiser. During the Kaiser crisis of 1947-1948, the *Junge Union* and its roughly 42,000 members vowed allegiance to Kaiser and refused to take part in the *Koordinierungsausschuss* and the *Volkskongress*, and because of these actions, SMAD banned the *Junge Union* in the Soviet zone.[144] On February 1, 1948, the *Junge Union* leaders Fred Sagner and Dr. Josef Bock wrote to all *Junge Union* members instructing them to lay down their work until democratic conditions emerged in the eastern zone.[145] Previous to this announcement, the youth groups *Junge Liberaldemokraten, Jungsozialisten*, and *Junge Union* joined together in Berlin in a demonstration against Communism, carrying banners which read "Anti-Communism is a democratic duty."[146]

Although the *Junge Union* work which had been permitted by the authorities had come to an end, the *Junge Union* conducted underground work. Sagner built up *Junge Union* groups throughout the Soviet zone in conjunction with the *Büro Kaiser*,[147] which formed important "spiritual and political resistance centres in the academic arena."[148] These underground groups sometimes cooperated with SPD groups in the Soviet zone. SMAD and SED arrests of a large number of these resisters brought the majority of the underground *Junge Union* work in the Soviet zone to an end.[149] Commenting on his resistance work in the Soviet zone during these years, one young CDU resister stated: "The fear of Siberia was colossal."[150] Kaiser's removal also prompted limited underground resistance by other CDU members. In Niesky and Freital, the local CDU groups contacted the *Büro Kaiser* and began distribution of western CDU pamphlets.[151] The fragmentary archival holdings of the CDU *Ostbüro* unfortunately do not permit the identification of other CDU groups who began to engage in underground resistance as a result of Kaiser's dismissal.

In sum, by the end of 1947, SED and SMAD abuse of basic rights provided a major impetus for underground SPD resistance groups. This motive also drove the active resisters in the CDU and LDPD—notably Jakob Kaiser—who enjoyed widespread support at the lower levels of the party. One CDU member clearly stated his opposition to the anti-democratic nature of the SED: "There are efforts underway to transfer these methods [i.e., as in the Third Reich] into the present and to prevent the emergence of a true democracy. In countless localities, only one party determines policy, a party that has set out a goal of not tolerating those who have different ideas. . . . Impatient people are presently trying, often with dubious and dangerous methods, to revive the spirit of dictatorship."[152] The increased resistance in the non-Marxist parties fueled the repression cycle. As the above discussion of the security apparatus in the Soviet zone has demonstrated, K-5 began an intense campaign to remove this resistance after the announcement of Order Number 201 in August 1947.

Dictatorship and Resistance
between the First *Volkskongress* of December 1947
and the Third *Volkskongress* of May 1949

The Emerging Dictatorship, 1948

By 1948, the deepening Cold War was having a major effect on the development of the eastern zone. After the London foreign ministers' conference of December 1947 failed to resolve the division of Germany, the western Allies believed a negotiated solution to the German problem no longer to be feasible. As a result, the United States and Britain invited the Benelux countries and France to London in the first half of 1948 for a conference on the future of Germany. The conference was held in two sessions, from February to March and from April to June, and it was at this second session that the countries involved decided to lay the foundation for a German government in the western zones of Germany. Because the Reichsmark was devalued and unstable, one of the most important prerequisites for the formation of this government was a currency reform.[153] As the Soviet Union showed little interest in this currency reform, the western Allies introduced the new currency, the D-Mark, into their zones of Germany, but not Berlin, in June 1948. The Soviet Union responded quickly to the introduction of the new currency, claiming that it had to take necessary measures to ensure that the currency did not enter Berlin.[154] On June 18, 1948, the Soviet security forces in Germany, with substantial help from east German police units, stopped all land access to West Berlin from the western zones. The Berlin Blockade then commenced.

Although these measures were harsh, the Soviets were within their rights to prevent ground transportation into Berlin. The western Allies had no written agreements with the Soviet Union guaranteeing land access to Berlin from their zones of Germany. They did, however, have a written agreement guaranteeing three air corridors.[155] The western Allies used these corridors to mount Operation "Vittles." In order to deliver the millions of pounds of supplies per day necessary to sustain the Berlin population, a plane landed in Berlin roughly every thirty seconds.[156] The airlift continued through the inclement winter of 1948 until May 1948 when Stalin lifted the blockade, realizing that there was no further point to it as the Berlin population would be able to easily survive the upcoming summer and subsequent winters. Furthermore, the western counter blockade was starting to negatively affect the Soviet zone's economy.[157]

The growing antipathy between East and West caused the SED to expand its security apparatus to defend its position in eastern Germany. The SED considerably strengthened the police force in the aftermath of the failed Moscow foreign ministers' conference in March 1947, doubling its manpower from the previous year,[158] although low morale and desertions still plagued the police force.[159] At a conference of the *Landespolitik* department of the Central Secretariat of the SED in Werder in

July 1948, the SED decided that the police must not only be expanded, but strictly subordinated to the SED.[160] As a result, the transformation process which had begun the previous year was noticeably advanced, especially as the SED now required the leadership of the police to swear an oath of loyalty to the SED and its policies.[161] The provincial ministries of the interior were also transformed into instruments of political control. In a telling statement, Gebhardt, the Thuringian Minister of the Interior, reported on a conference of the interior ministers saying: "The Ministry of the Interior will be in the future more of a political ministry. For this reason, various jurisdictions are being removed from the interior ministry [i.e., the construction department]. . . . The interior ministry will control central and political power. . . . The new situation in the class war requires new methods."[162]

Furthermore, the SED realized that police alone could not solidify SED dominance in the eastern zone, and as early as the spring of 1948 began preparations for forty "barracked" police units, the future cadres of the National People's Army.[163] Due to the deepening Cold War, the border police were also expanded and brought under the control of the Central Administration of the Interior, rather than the provincial ministries of the interior.[164] The development of departments within the police to monitor the political reliability of police officers, *Politkultur* departments, also ensured SED loyalty in the police force.[165] One SED member made clear at a meeting of the SED leadership in September 1948 that the centralization of the police force served political ends: "Use of force does not just mean that a small group of armed revolutionaries captures power, but rather that we carry out a vigorous class war with the power of a new people's democracy, with the vigorous use of the police etc."[166]

SED efforts to consolidate the instruments of control under its authority would prove successful. By the summer of 1949, the SED, with the help of SMAD, had occupied the leading posts in the Central Administration for Justice and the Central Administration of the Interior.[167] The SED had also succeeded in centralizing power in the central administrations and thus subordinating the provincial authorities to the administrations. By the spring of 1949, the political police branch of the criminal police, K-5, had been fully removed from the authority of the provincial administrations and worked exclusively for the DVdI and SMAD.[168] The SED's leading position in the Soviet zone was secure by 1949, and placed it in a favorable position to dominate the new German Democratic Republic which was founded in the fall.

The changes in the judicial system in the eastern zone in 1948 meant that there would be little recourse against the "power of the new people's democracy," as Eugen Schiffer discovered. Schiffer, the LDPD head of the German Central Administration for Justice, attempted to reform the justice system along liberal democratic lines. Schiffer realized the importance of an objective judiciary for the German population, writing in 1946 that after the experience of the Nazi era, "there could be no doubt that the German population demanded an objective, just, and nonpartisan judicial system."[169] In early 1948, Schiffer wrote to the Soviet authorities arguing for a simplification of the judicial process and for a ban on the election of public prosecutors for provincial courts by the provincial assemblies. In itself, the election independence of the judiciary was compromised, but Schiffer recognized the general trend in the Soviet zone and realized that these elections would be the first step in the complete elimination of separation of powers.[170] On April 29, 1948, SMAD rejected Schiffer's requests for reform of the justice administration, which signalled the coming end to Schiffer's political career. By August 1948, through maneuvering by the SED, Schiffer was forced to retire. In September, SMAD removed a further eight leading functionaries of the Central Administration for Justice, all previously SPD members, so that by the end of 1948 the SED occupied all leading positions in the judicial administration and had removed all potential opponents in that administration to the political transformation taking place.

The SED also worked to secure loyalty in the new generation of jurists by politicizing their training. At a January 1948 sitting of the SED executive, Max Fechner, deputy chair of the SED, insisted on a political education of the "people's judges."[171] The delegates at the second jurists' conference of the SED in November supported Fechner by calling for a widening of the "sociological" content in the training of jurists.[172] On October 2, 1948, Max Fechner became president of the Central Administration for Justice.[173]

The increasing SED exertion and centralization of power was also reflected in major changes to the party itself. The transformation of the party, which began in 1947, received a powerful impetus at the eleventh session of the SED on July 29, 1948, at which the SED leadership issued measures for "cleansing the party from enemy and degenerate elements." The SED was to become a Communist party like that of the Soviet Union, a "vanguard of the working class" instead of the "people's party" as it had proclaimed itself previously.[174] In accordance with becoming a party similar to the Communist Party of the Soviet Union, Anton Ackermann admitted that he hadn't entirely thought things through and that his view of a "German way to socialism" had actually been entirely wrong.[175] To carry out the transformation of the party and afterwards ensure its "purity," the SED created a Central Party Control Commission (ZPKK), Provincial Party Control Commissions (LPKK), and *Kreis* Party Control Commissions (KPKK).[176] These commissions removed "unreliable" members from the SED, the vast majority of which belonged previously to the SPD. Between 1948 and 1950, approximately 200,000 members were purged from the party.[177] By January 1949, at the first SED party conference (*Parteikonferenz*), the SED officially proclaimed its desire to become a "Party of a New Type."

Resistance, 1948

SPD Resistance

The increased attack on SPD members in the SED as a result of the transformation of the party drove some SPD members to resist the Communist dictatorship in the Soviet zone. In *Kreis* Dresden, an SPD member expelled from the SED sought out other SPD members to form a resistance group.[178] In Grimma, an expelled SED member joined with other expelled SED members to form an oppositional group.[179] Other SPD members expelled from the SED opted to join the non-Marxist parties to carry out their oppositional politics. One SPD member writing to the *Ostbüro* stated that in *Kreis* Niederbarnim in Brandenburg, the local CDU group was comprised mainly of former SPD members.[180] The transformation of the SED also caused many SPD members to leave the party voluntarily, as it became clear to them that their hopes for socialism would not be fulfilled. One member felt that the "Communist" road to socialism, by which the decisions were taken away from the people and put in the hands of the party, was wrong, and that—much as Rosa Luxemburg believed—the road to socialism was one of a slow and difficult convincing of the masses.[181] One worker who wrote to the *Tribüne* also rejected the SED's approach to socialism and boasted: "The SPD will rise again."[182] The idea that the SED had hijacked socialism was a common theme of opponents of the SED.

The incidence of SPD resistance dropped dramatically in 1948, however, because of the intense campaign that the Soviets and K-5 had launched in the fall of 1947 under the guise of carrying out Order Number 201. Whereas at least fourteen new SPD resistance groups were founded in 1947, only three could be identified by archival evidence as being founded in 1948.[183] The SPD and its *Ostbüro* were the main targets for Soviet security organs, who believed that Schumacher was the leading puppet master in a vast capitalist conspiracy to undermine the Soviet Occupied Zone.[184] In May, Soviet authorities arrested a large number of SPD members with *Ostbüro* contacts in Gardelegen, Haldensleben, Stendal, Burg, and Jena. In the fall and winter, sweeping arrests of SPD members took place in Magdeburg, Eisleben, Halle, Frankfurt on the Oder, Dresden, and Zwickau. The arrests led to further arrests based on confessions. Hermann Kreutzer, a leading SPD resister, has estimated that 70 percent of eastern SPD members were caught through other members confessing their contacts, although he could not verify if these were forced confessions.[185] In the winter of 1948-1949, SPD members in the Soviet zone were dealt a further blow when K-5 kidnapped from West Berlin the secretary of the *Ostbüro* of the SPD, Heinz Kühn. During his interrogation by the MVD, he exposed a number of SPD members engaged in resistance in the Soviet zone, which led to a massive wave of arrests including the Kreutzer group in April 1949.[186] The intense campaign against SPD resistance curtailed the distribution of pamphlets. K-5 in Saxony proudly reported that many of the leading SPD resisters had been arrested in 1948 and that "the illegal propaganda activity of the SPD was negligible during the year."[187]

Couriers continued to be a weak link in SPD work. In January 1948, Richard Lehners, an *Ostbüro* courier, could not recall the name he had adopted for the current assignment, and blurted out the wrong name when he presented his ID to Soviet authorities during a verification. The Soviets did not arrest him immediately but followed him hoping that he would lead them to other resisters, which he did. In March 1948, he returned to the Soviet zone and stayed with a number of SPD resisters, including Curt Eckhardt who was arrested on the day after his visit. It is also likely that Lehners' bungle led to Arno Wend's arrest in July.[188]

Due to the MVD campaign against the SPD, illegal SPD resistance in 1949 was negligible. The *Ostbüro* acknowledged the reality of what was already taking place and officially discouraged resistance *groups* as building blocks of a future party, and concentrated on individual exchange of information.[189] The concern for the safety of its members in the Soviet zone led to greater use of RIAS to spread its message and in 1952 to the use of balloons as a manner of infiltrating material into the East.[190] In fact, the MVD felt that SPD resistance in the Soviet zone had been eliminated so thoroughly by 1949, that it and the SED abandoned the fight against the SPD *Ostbüro* between 1950 and 1953 and, indeed, there is no archival evidence for the creation of illegal SPD groups in 1949.[191]

CDU Resistance

The increasing Stalinization of the eastern zone, combined with the removal of Kaiser and Lemmer from their positions as leaders of the eastern CDU in December 1947, caused widespread discontent in the lower levels of the CDU in the Soviet zone in 1948. In Mecklenburg, SMAD forced the CDU member Werner Jöhren to step down because of his continuing support of Kaiser. He eventually fled to the West and became leader of the *Ostbüro* of the CDU.[192] One CDU member, alarmed by the meaning of the removal of Kaiser for democracy in the eastern zone, proclaimed publicly: "I say this openly: the majority of our Union friends [i.e., CDU members] still stand behind our democratically elected Jakob Kaiser. We demand from the provincial CDU committees that participation in the Block be brought to an end. We do not want to be guilty of the great tragedy which the SED is bringing upon us. We demand *Gemeinde* elections. Should these not occur, we will take the initiative ourselves."[193] The speaker also wished to withdraw the CDU representative for the district from the *Volkskongress*.

The SED use of force to put through its agenda was at the center of CDU opposition. At a public meeting of the CDU in August 1948 in Zerrenthin, Brandenburg, one CDU member lashed out at the SED for not treating the other parties as legitimate, and even accused the SED of terrorist activities.[194] At a CDU meeting in Bentwisch on June 5, 1948, the CDU leader of the ministry for education in Potsdam attacked the SED for its lack of respect for democracy stating: "As we were against Hitler's dictatorship, so are we fundamentally against every other dictatorship, be it from whichever direction, including the dictatorship of the proletariat."[195]

This opposition was representative of the general membership. At provincial party congresses of the CDU throughout 1948, the membership consistently elected pro-democracy leaders—and therefore more often than not pro-Kaiser candidates. In Brandenburg, Dr. Wilhelm Wolf, chair of the CDU provincial association for Brandenburg, who spoke out for ties to the western CDU and personal freedoms, was elected but died under mysterious circumstances in a car accident in Berlin 5 days later.[196] In Thuringia, the pro-Kaiser Georg Grosse received the most votes, but SMAD disallowed his candidacy. In Saxony, delegates elected Hugo Hickmann as they believed he was working with the Soviets merely out of political necessity, but they elected the Kaiser-supporter Rudolf Schmidt as deputy provincial chair.

SMAD also forbade Schmidt from taking office. Similarly in Mecklenburg, Lobedanz was elected chair, but the second and third chairs elected, Karl Heinz Kaltenborn and Hans Krukenmayer respectively, were Kaiser supporters and thus forbidden by SMAD from taking office.[197]

The CDU also resisted the SED's attempts to control the economy. At the eleventh and twelfth sessions (*Tagungen*) of the SED in June and July 1948, the SED laid claim to the leading role in the economy, meaning that its economic plans were to be implemented in the Soviet zone regardless of the other parties' positions. The other parties realized that a leading role in the economy could not be separated from a leading role in society.[198] At the Central Block sitting of September 7, 1948, the CDU stated that the German Economic Commission (DWK) must come under parliamentary control, as at the moment it was governing "dictatorially."[199] In Mecklenburg, Brandenburg, and Saxony-Anhalt, the CDU criticized the DWK's favoring of the SED's Two Year Plan,[200] and therefore the SED's leading role. In a rare example of bowing to opposition, the SED did propose a way in which all parties could participate in the DWK decision-making process, to which the CDU agreed.[201] Hickmann also felt that the SED had gone too far with its claim to the leading role, and hoped the CDU would give an "offenes Stopp" against renewed dictatorship.[202] CDU concerns surfaced at a meeting of the extended CDU executive, at which the CDU demanded the securing of parliamentary democracy, a ban on one party claims to the leading role, issuing a date for elections, and the formation of an all German government in the near future.[203] By the Third Party Congress of the CDU in Erfurt in September 1948, the CDU had still to be fully coopted into the Communist system. Otto Nuschke put forward a CDU program which insisted on parliamentary democracy, free elections, private property, and which rejected the SED's "people's democracy," although continuing to favor a close relationship between Germany and the East.[204]

Due to CDU opposition to the SED, which had been made clear at the provincial party congresses, the Soviets began a wave of arrests against middle and lower level CDU members, especially in Brandenburg and Saxony-Anhalt.[205] During one of these waves in the spring of 1948, Soviet security organs shot outright the CDU chair of *Kreis* Delitzsch, Hans Georg Löser, in his apartment.[206] The CDU mayor of Falkensee, Hermann Neumann, was arrested and died in prison. On December 31, the entire executive of the CDU in Woltersdorf (*Kreis* Niederbarnim) was arrested.[207] After a trip to Saxony-Anhalt, one CDU correspondent reported that the "NKVD" was playing a decisive role in forcing the CDU into line.[208] Because of the repression of its members, the CDU refused to participate in the Block until August.[209]

The actions of the Soviet security apparatus produced mixed results. They were successful in removing some opposition, but convinced other members to engage in underground resistance. In Borna, a member of the CDU *Kreis* leadership reported that the "attitude in the population was growing more hostile to Russia day by day. . . . Active members of the Union [i.e., CDU] are already trying to contact illegal SPD circles."[210] The CDU provincial association in Saxony-Anhalt even encouraged underground work by reporting an increase in the work of the SPD, and saying that "true" CDU members should contact them.[211] There is only limited archival evidence of underground CDU groups, however, due to the secrecy with which these groups were guarded by the western CDU. It is likely that the following cases were not isolated. In Apolda, one CDU member was able to build up a substantial illegal CDU group throughout 1948. He was so successful in keeping alive contacts to the old CDU that he managed to get elected in the first elections of the GDR in October 1950 in *Kreis* Weimar. He also aided others, through his own financing, in escaping to the West.[212] There was also a CDU group with contacts throughout the zone, which tried to build a resistance group against the Communist dictatorship, but was arrested before it achieved its goal.[213]

A speech by Hugo Hickmann in which he criticized the conduct of the SED provides further insights into motives behind CDU resistance, and also into the developing Communist dictatorship. At a CDU meeting in Luchau, at which approximately 100 people attended, Hickmann outlined his displeasure with SED tactics. He regretted the continuing division of the country and attributed it to the wartime Allies' inability to come to an agreement, but blaming the United States in particular. He was more conciliatory to the people of West Germany, who, he suggested, desired German unity. This statement received a chorus of "bravos."[214] Hickmann further complained of the SED methods of filling administration posts, such as inserting Dr. Kurt Fischer from Saxony as head of the Soviet zone police to replace Erich Reschke.[215] His complaints centered on the increasing control of the instruments of power by the SED: "We demand a police apparatus that will remove the dictatorial regulating of police matters, as has just occurred in Berlin [i.e., appointing Fischer without consultation—GB], and places the Berlin central police leadership under parliamentary control." He criticized in particular the SED's control of the DWK, stating that the CDU was not allowed to be involved in any decision-making, referring to it as "absolute economic dictatorship" and exclaiming: "It cannot continue this way!"[216] He forcefully argued against the increasing one-party state, saying it was becoming like the Nazi era when one encountered obstacles if one did not belong to a certain party, and cited the recent increase in CDU membership as a result of popular discontent with the SED. The discussion after Hickmann's speech showed concern by those in attendance that the SED was squeezing the CDU out of effective participation in government.[217]

LDPD Resistance

Elements within the LDPD continued to resist the SED installation of a dictatorship, including, for a short time, the leader of the party. After Külz's death in April 1948, Arthur Lieutenant, the finance minister for Brandenburg, assumed the leadership of the LDPD and guided the party on a more confrontational stance, criticizing the DWK as being merely a power tool of the SED, criticizing the Two Year Plan as disrupting the economy unnecessarily as German unity would be achieved soon, and criticizing the confiscation of property from those with an untainted past.[218] In July 1948, the LDPD responded to attacks on its policies by the

Tägliche Rundschau with a declaration of the party leadership.[219] In this statement, the party outlined eight points that SMAD had brought up including the newly introduced Two Year Plan, Block cooperation, sequestering of property, and the eastern borders of Germany. In all points, the LDPD was careful to say that it was not fundamentally opposed to the issues as presented by the SED, but that it felt they should be modified. In short, these protests were opposition to the leading-role claim of the SED. Under pressure from SMAD, Lieutenant resigned on October 9, 1948 and was replaced by Karl Hamann, who immediately abandoned Lieutenant's confrontational stance.[220]

The LDPD nevertheless continued to show concern about an SED dictatorship. At the August 5, 1948 sitting of the Central Block, Dr. Kastner worried that the population felt one-party rule had returned to Germany. He felt that this impression was created by pictures of Marx, Engels, Thälmann, and Bebel adorning the Block plenum and by the public statements of certain SED members. At a recent gathering of all political parties, for example, the SED member Jendretzky proposed a toast to the victory of socialism.[221] Shortly after that sitting, the LDPD issued guiding principles which emphasized LDPD support for a parliamentary democratic republic and LDPD insistence that the German republic should be a state based on the rule of law.[222] Many of these elements were echoed in the Eisenacher Program of the LDPD of February 28, 1949, in which the LDPD outlined its main platforms as a guarantee of basic rights and the establishment of a parliamentary, democratic Germany based on a private economy.[223]

The LDPD was most concerned with the unjust dispossessions taking place in the Soviet zone. Dr. Hamann realized the political implications of the injustices stating: "It is . . . frightening to see how great insecurity in the country is with regard to sequestering and the land reform. . . . We will only make progress in political and economic developments when absolute order and absolute legal security are introduced." Hamann's pronouncements were met with cries of: "Exactly Right!" and: "We reject force!"[224] In February 1948, the LDPD in Thuringia unanimously resolved to withdraw its representatives in the local and provincial commissions responsible for carrying out SMAD's sequestering orders 124 and 126,[225] stating: "The conduct of the sequestering commissions at the moment goes against all requirements for the guarantee of rights . . . and runs into pure despotism. Apparently orders 124/126 are to be misused to bring about the socializing of the entire economy." Another LDPD member added: "One must also say that in the local commissions, personal revenge often plays a role. On top of that are attacks by the police. In general, the intrusions and attacks of the investigation units hinder the work considerably. We have no influence on these units."[226] These comments reveal that the police were engaged in excesses in carrying out the reform and confirm that, already by 1948, the police answered only to the SED.

Wolfgang Natonek, the chair of the Leipzig University LDPD group and from February 1947 the chair of the student council, actively resisted the SED dictatorship in eastern Germany. At the Second Party Congress of the LDPD in July 1947, he said that he had had no intention of entering politics, but political developments forced him to reconsider: "We see, however, that it is necessary to engage in party politics in order that we are not dominated by another party. We know what is at stake."[227] Natonek was also incensed that admissions to the university were based on class rather than ability.[228] Natonek's primary motivation to resist, however, was his belief that the new system in eastern Germany was built on force and coercion. After the following experience which took place after a lecture at the university, Natonek decided to enter politics: "A young man came up to me whom I did not know. Clearly he had confused me with someone else. He asked me: is it your turn or mine to deliver our notes to the tower today? Back then, the SED-headquarters was in the Kroch tower on Augustusplatz. I thought to myself, it cannot be possible that something is happening once more that we all thought was behind us for good: namely a state in which one person spies on the next, in which everyone is afraid to say what he thinks."[229] On November 11, 1948, Natonek and a large group of students were arrested. Natonek received twenty-five years labor for "conspiracy with the capitalist west," and the LDPD group at the university was banned.[230] His arrest led to the founding of another short-lived resistance group at the university that rejected the unjust incarcerations.[231]

At the University of Jena, the chair of the LDPD group, Wolfgang Möhring, approved of developments at the university until 1948, when the suppression of opinion, as evidenced by the attempt to remove the philosophy professor Leisegang, and the continuing incarcerations, convinced him to join a resistance group. Möhring's proclamation at a student rally that Marxism was the "devil's math" led to his arrest by Soviet security organs.[232] The student council at Rostock also witnessed fairly vocal opposition in 1948 and 1949, especially by the LDPD member Dieter Riessner who protested against the silencing of oppositional voices and SED control of the university and was subsequently forced to flee to the West.[233]

The stifling of the non-Marxist parties in Berlin had the opposite effect from the one intended by the Soviets and the SED. The harassment at the University of Berlin, especially of the students Otto Stolz, Joachim Schwarz, and Otto Hess, led to a show of solidarity among the students and outside the university as well. As Ilko-Sascha Kowalczuk has written: "Suddenly, the struggle at the university became a struggle for democracy in Berlin."[234] Overall, it appears that young people who did not support the SED turned to the LDPD to express their views. Members under twenty-five years of age made up 24.3 percent of the membership in the LDPD, while members under twenty made up only 2.6 percent of CDU and 6.1 percent of SED.[235]

Opposing the SED, the Sovietization of the eastern zone, or the Soviet Union was at no point in the history of the Soviet zone or the GDR a safe undertaking, as the case of Arno Esch made clear. Esch eagerly joined the LDPD in 1946 and helped establish the local Rostock LDPD group before commencing his law studies at the University of Rostock in the fall. By 1948, he was a rising star in the party, making a number of public appearances, including at the LDPD provincial congress in Stralsund and strongly condemning the Block as a method for the SED to silence democracy. His political abilities earned him growing allegiance, and in February

1949 he helped draft the party's program for the Eisenacher party congress. Esch wanted the LDPD to become a broadly based left liberal party, believing that this would put the party in a good position at all-German elections which he expected would take place soon. For Esch, the founding principle of liberalism was individual freedom. He felt that the world encountered a series of severe problems, principally the atom bomb, and that the key to overcoming them was liberalism and its belief in the basic goodness of humanity. He also believed that one's world view, rather than nationality, should be the deciding factor in politics, which led to his famous phrase: "A liberal Chinese person is closer to me than a German Communist." Esch believed that the last great work of liberalism was the Weimar constitution.[236]

Because of his anti-Communism, he refused to take part in the third *Volkskongress*, and left the sitting of the LDPD central executive which accepted the founding of the GDR. On the night of October 19, 1949, Soviet security officers arrested him while leaving an LDPD meeting. The SMT in Berlin sentenced Esch and seven others to death by shooting for "preparing an armed revolt," and sentenced the other ten in the group to twenty-five years labor. The verdicts were based on Article 58, Paragraph 2, of the Russian civil code which prescribed the death penalty for "preparation of an armed revolt." On July 24, 1951, Esch was executed in the Soviet Union and, although the other executions have not been confirmed, the others sentenced to death were not heard from again.[237] Clearly, Esch's theories of liberalism conflicted with the aims of the SED to Sovietize the eastern zone.[238]

Given these incidences of LDPD resistance, it is not surprising to find that K-5 also noted a high degree of lower level LDPD resistance. Reporting on the LDPD membership, K-5 wrote: "It has been determined that certain LDPD members have a progressive attitude and cooperate in the democratic rebuilding. Larger sections of the party, especially younger members, exhibit reactionary tendencies. This is most prevalent at universities."[239] The evidence suggests that the examples of LDPD resistance outlined above reflected an oppositional stance which was prevalent in the majority of the LDPD membership.

SMAD actions, particularly their establishment of two other parties in an attempt to draw supporters away from the CDU and LDPD, reveal that Soviet authorities in eastern Germany feared popular support of the non-Marxist parties. In April 1948, the Democratic Farmer's Party (DBD) was formed, followed by the National Democratic Party of Germany (NDPD) in May. The CDU and the LDPD, angered by the competition, even contemplated uniting the CDU and the LDPD to combat the new parties.[240] SMAD's decision to delay the *Gemeinde* elections to the fall of 1949 to coincide with the provincial elections also amounted to an admission of CDU and LDPD popularity. LDPD reports suggest that the Soviets were correct to fear an open election, revealing that the decision to delay the *Gemeinde* elections was rejected by the widest majority of the population because they wanted to give expression to their opinions. People repeatedly asked: "Why do we even have a constitution?"[241] The delay of the election provided an opportunity for the Soviets to proceed against oppositional LDPD and CDU members. In Thuringia, the LDPD fraction chairman Hermann Becker was arrested on July 23 and sentenced to twenty-five years labor.[242] On December 31, 1948, the LDPD *Kreis* chairman for Niesky, Konrad Brettschneider, was arrested for anticommunist activities and sentenced to twenty-five years labor by an SMT. Overall, the arrests of CDU members increased by over 40 percent between 1947 and 1948.[243]

By the end of 1948, both the CDU and LDPD remained independent parties that supported a democratic system characterized by basic freedoms, especially legal security, and political plurality. The general membership showed more opposition to compromise with the SED and the Soviets than the leadership and paid for this opposition with punishments ranging from harassment to arrest. In sum, a majority of the general membership of the non-Marxist parties opposed the SED out of democratic conviction. Some of these members then turned to underground resistance because of the accompanying repression.

Furthermore, SMAD and SED actions against these parties suggest that the non-Marxist parties enjoyed support in the broader population and that therefore there was, at least, resistance sentiment in the general population. In an anonymous letter to the organ of the Free German Trade Union (FDGB), the *Tribüne*, one worker claimed that "90 percent of workers were against the SED."[244] Although this number was certainly exaggerated, the popular opposition to the SED was, at a minimum, sufficient to cause grave SED and SMAD concern. Even the SED member Fritz Wolf admitted: "Our policies in the eastern zone, land reform, industry reform, school and judicial reform are a considerable success, thanks to the support of the SMA. What we haven't achieved is actually winning over the masses."[245] In a captured report of the SED factory group in Mückenberg, SED members candidly admitted that the population stood behind the SED in 1945 and 1946, but that this was no longer the case.[246] The lack of support for the SED combined with the support for the CDU and LDPD suggests that the population was prepared to jettison the Communist system in the eastern zone for a democratic system as early as 1948.

Popular Resistance to the SED Dictatorship

Historians face a difficult task in determining with certainty motives behind popular resistance in the Soviet occupied zone. In the absence of modern polling techniques, historians must rely on archival sources to tap into popular beliefs. By analyzing the records of the non-Marxist parties, the SPD, the police, and the SED, it becomes apparent that SED and SMAD abuse of basic rights occupied a prominent position in motivating popular resistance to the Communist dictatorship. Repression by SMAD and SED may have succeeded in removing certain opponents in the population, but it contributed to insecurity within the population at large. The *Volkskongress* elections of 1949, as will be discussed, attest to this point.

The following episodes help to illustrate the extent to which SMAD and SED repression contributed to popular insecurity. During a black market trial in Ilmenau, the accused, in a statement that had little to do with the trial, explained that his son had left for West Germany because he feared arrest by the Russians. The accused added casually: "There have, after all, already been a few arrested." The outraged public prosecutor claimed that this statement was an attack on the occupying power and would not be permitted in the court. The director of the provincial court, Dr. Otto, was so appalled by the prosecutor's comments that he resigned from the case immediately, drawing loud applause from the public in attendance. The judge adjourned the case for a few days, during which time the SED declared that the tickets issued up to that point to attend the trial were no longer valid, and new ones were issued which could only be obtained at the SED office.[247] Popular insecurity was also made evident during an SED rally in Magdeburg in September 1948, with 4-5,000 in attendance. The initial address was followed by some questions concerning the food situation. One person in attendance then stood up and said that Germany had suffered through twelve years of terror only to experience a new terror, with people disappearing from the eastern zone everyday. When the SED representative responded that the arrests were carried out in accordance with the law, an ensuing tumult caused the session to be terminated immediately.[248]

Although the insecurity continually contributed to popular resistance to the SED, some SED members seemed to have little regard for the result. The SED mayor of a small town threatened villagers with the "Red Army" or with being "locked up in a basement" in order to push the party platform through. These threats naturally turned the villagers away from the SED, and in this case to the CDU. One member of the CDU stated: "Believe me, we have the SED mayor Böhm to thank for the fact that there is a local CDU group here."[249]

Situation reports of the non-Marxist parties and the SPD offer important evidence that the above examples were a reflection of deep resentment in the broader population to the SED, based on the abuse of basic rights in the Soviet zone. In January 1949, after Max Fechner's reassurances about the judicial system, the LDPD reported that "the declaration by Max Fechner will contribute to the strengthening of *Rechtsicherheit* (legal security) and order, and therefore the *trust of the population in the zone*." [250] The *Kreis* Borna LDPD reflected that the population did not accept the injustices, no matter how they were couched. The representative from Pagau reported: "Another issue is law and justice. One often hears the words these days 'new societal order.' With these words, Germans are stricken stone-dead"—to which he received thunderous applause.[251] Further examples of the concern for justice come from the LDPD *Ortsgruppe* Lubbenau which stated that in August 1948 the chair of their group had been arrested by the Soviets without reason, and thus they were not filling his position until they heard an explanation from the Soviets.[252] The Jena LDPD representative Dr. Schomerus reported: "Especially now, we should emphasize liberal thought concerning the individual in order that personal rights be respected and guaranteed. To exert pressure and terrorize people is inhumane. . . . We should not forget the individual. People also expect rights from the state. The SED is striving for the totalitarian state." He later added: "I no longer see any sign of the principles of the constitution." Dr. Schomerus's criticism of the SED pressure on the LDPD is intriguing, for it reveals the restrictions in the eastern zone: "We are not Communists. We do not want our nation to become Communist. We are no different from the people in the West. Over there, where people are free, there are only 6-8 percent Communists. From that, one could probably conclude that there aren't too many more here."[253] The LDPD member in Altenburg spoke out against the injustices of the sequestering saying that the LDPD must fight these injustices: "We as liberal democrats must step in where basic rights are affected." The Altenburg member also echoed Schomerus's comments on the hostility in the population to the SED: "The SED is rejected by the entire population. If an election were held, the liberal philosophy would be much more at the fore than the totalitarian philosophy of the SED."[254] In Mecklenburg, one LDPD member admitted what was apparent: "It is probably clear to everyone that the majority of the population do not have Marxist leanings."[255] During a speech in Chemnitz, Hugo Hickmann, a CDU member for Saxony, also hinted at the injustices in the eastern zone: "Without parliamentary control of those who govern, there is no democracy. We place no value on an East German state [*Oststaat*]. A new democratic order must be created, so that our zone can present itself before the world as a zone that guarantees democracy." His speech was met with loud applause.[256]

Situation reports from SPD *Ostbüro* informants from 1948 and 1949 repeatedly mention that the population was fed up with the SED's policy of "Gewalt geht vor Recht" (Force before Rights) especially in matters of dispossession.[257] The most common reasons given in the reports for popular rejection of the SED were the constant feeling of insecurity due to the "terror methods" of the NKVD and SED and a food situation that was abysmal.[258] Of particular interest is the analysis in the reports that the SED, because of the initial support for socialism after the war, had had a basis of support but had lost this support because of the legal insecurity of the Soviet occupation, not personal economic difficulties.[259] The reports often cite the presence of the NKVD as the only reason an uprising had not taken place already.[260]

The widespread injustices in the Soviet zone in the late 1940s caused certain individuals to establish in West Berlin anti-Communist groups. One of the most prominent, and later most violent, was the Fighting Group Against Inhumanity (*Kampfgruppe gegen Unmenschlichkeit*—KgU) founded by Rainer Hildebrandt, who would go on to run the one museum in Berlin that all backpackers visited, the *Haus am Checkpoint Charlie*. In its founding proclamation of April 25, 1949, Hildebrandt appealed to voters in the eastern zone to oppose the upcoming *Volkskongress* election, claiming that whoever voted for it would be voting for a "system of inhumanity."[261] At a press conference two days later, Hildebrandt stated that one of the ultimate goals of the KgU was to free those wrongly imprisoned in the Soviet zone.[262] The KgU also aimed to record all "crimes against humanity" which were taking place in the Soviet zone. Within a few years, the CIA would come to use the anti-Communist potential of the KgU by having the organization conduct an underground terrorist campaign in the GDR.[263]

Horst Erdmann (alias Dr. Theo Friedenau) founded another of the major anti-Communist groups, the Investigative Committee of Free Jurists (*Untersuchung sausschuss Freiheitlicher Juristen*—UfJ), in the fall of 1949.[264] In September and October 1948, Erdmann had already written articles in western journals critical of the judicial system in the zone and the practices of the NKVD.[265] In one article, he suggested how severe the terror system was by issuing instructions on how to avoid NKVD spies, thereby saving oneself from "considerable damage." Erdmann believed that the Communist system could be fought with justice itself and that enough external pressure on the GDR might force it to follow its 1949 constitution, which would result in the end of the regime because the constitution called for free elections.[266] The UfJ also documented the injustices taking place in the eastern zone with the aim of conducting a "new and better Nürnberg."[267] Thus, the injustices were at the core of both the KgU and the UfJ, and given the commonality of purpose it is not surprising that there had even been brief mention of joining the two organizations.[268]

There were signs in 1948 that the Soviets themselves were becoming concerned about the lack of legal security in the eastern zone. The military government in the Soviet zone declared an amnesty on March 18, 1948 for Nazi criminals who were serving less than one year, as well as those accused of minor crimes who had not yet been sentenced. In the summer of 1948, the Soviets released 28,000 prisoners from the "special camps" in the eastern zone, causing the closure of eight of the eleven camps.[269]

The Soviet release of prisoners did not immediately allay the tension between the police and the population, as noted by both SED and LDPD party members. In Mecklenburg, the SED complained of the strained relationship between the *Volkspolizei* and the broader population,[270] and added that the population still distrusted and opposed the party. The LDPD in Zittau also commented on the relationship with the police, stating that the singing of "Wir sind die junge Garde des Proletariats" (We are the young Guard of the Proletariat) by the *Volkspolizei* when they showed up in public would not improve the popularity of the police.[271] In East Berlin, an expelled SED member led an oppositional group specifically against the *Volkspolizei* because of his belief that the organization was a continuation of "fascist militarism."[272]

The election of candidates to the third *Volkskongress* on May 15 and 16 provides an opportunity, although limited, to gauge popular opposition to the SED. The third *Volkskongress* was the last step in the formation of an East German state. A major step toward establishing an East German state had been taken with the second *Volkskongress* in 1948. For this second *Volkskongress*, the leadership of the parties and mass organizations appointed, rather than elected, delegates to attend the gathering in Berlin on March 17 and 18. The delegates to this *Volkskongress* elected a *Volksrat* (People's Council) which formed a constitutional committee under the CDU member Reinhold Lobedanz to draft a constitution. The CDU attempted to obtain a constitutionally outlined separation of powers by insisting on a supreme court, but was unsuccessful due to SED opposition. Apart from this aspect, the constitutional proposal resembled a constitution of a liberal parliamentary democracy.[273] On August 3, 1948, the constitutional committee officially revealed the constitutional proposal.

The final step in the creation of East Germany came in 1949. In May, a second *Volksrat* was elected from the delegates to the third *Volkskongress*, and on October 7-8 1949, the second *Volksrat* constituted itself as the provisional *Volkskammer* (People's Assembly) of the GDR.

For the purposes of this study, the election to the third *Volkskongress* is of greater importance than the role of those delegates in creating the GDR. The statement put forward for the election to the third *Volkskongress* was: "I support the unity of Germany and a just peace treaty. I therefore vote for the following list of candidates for the Third German *Volkskongress*."[274] The right to vote applied to all citizens who had reached the provincial voting age, except those who had been sentenced under Order Number 201 or the Allied Control Council Directive 38 and the mentally ill. There was, however, another category of citizens excluded from voting, which may have affected the result. All those who were sentenced for "sabotaging" the new anti-fascist democratic order, or for adopting a "confrontational attitude" towards the occupying power, were not permitted to vote, even if they had been released by a Soviet "act of mercy."[275] The local election committees registered eligible voters, and the provincial, *Kreis*, and *Gemeinde* administrations were responsible for providing the local election committees with the necessary materials to conduct the election, including election boxes and booths.[276]

Despite the skewed question, the SED could not win an overwhelming majority to its cause. The official results reported 66 percent "yes" votes, but the manner in which the vote was conducted leads to doubts about the accuracy of the tally. It is most probable that the "no" vote was higher and that the Soviet authorities and the SED adjusted the vote, as the following events illustrate. Hermann Hieke, CDU *Kreis* chair of Wolmirstedt, Saxony-Anhalt, stated that reports from the voting locales which entered the *Kreis* election committee once the locales had closed indicated a majority "no" vote, even reaching as high as 70 percent in Kolbnitz, Samswegen, and Rogätz. For the *Kreis* overall, the numbers stood at 55 percent "no," 38-40 percent "yes," and the rest were spoiled. The next day, the Ministry of the Interior ordered the election committee to count all empty and invalid ballots as "yes" votes. Hieke resigned from the committee, but his actions proved fruitless as on Monday, *Kreis* Wolmirstedt announced a result of 55 percent "yes" and 45 percent "no." Hieke also reported that K-5 arrested the chair of the election committee in *Gemeinde* Greater Ammensleben for refusing to falsify the vote count.[277] SPD reports on the *Volkskongress* also indicate that a high "no" vote prompted the SED to order recounts. In Magdeburg, the "no" vote was said to have reached 70 percent.[278]

Police reports also suggest that the population opposed the *Volkskongress*. In Saxony-Anhalt, the police reported that in nearly all *Kreise*, posters dealing with the upcoming election had been torn down "in numbers not seen since before 1945."[279] The police blamed "reactionaries in the Church and CDU/LDPD" for spreading negative propaganda about the vote, and feared that the CDU may have fallen completely into the hands of "reactionaries," stating: "It appears that the reactionary wing is in command. These signs are most evident in the CDU."[280] The police also attributed much of the pamphlet propaganda to Schumacher groups which were said to be "actively at work."[281]

The *Volkskongress* elections reveal significant regional differences in support of the movement and, by extension, the SED. From the results on the following pages, it is apparent that Mecklenburg was the only province that did not witness a significant rejection of the *Volkskongress*. The city of Berlin and the provinces of Brandenburg, Saxony, and Thuringia recorded a significant number of *Kreise* which did not reach the average "yes" vote and which had a higher than average number of spoiled ballots. The urban *Kreise* of Saxony-Anhalt also witnessed opposition to the *Volkskongress*, although the rural *Kreise*, on the whole, supported the movement. In Mecklenburg, the weakest support for the *Volkskongress* came from the industrial centres along the Baltic.

Table 3.1. Results of the *Volkskongress* vote: Districts that did not reach the average "Yes" vote of 66.1 percent and districts with a higher than average "No" vote (in parentheses)

Land	District	Yes Vote (in percentage)	No Vote (in percentage)
Mecklenburg Urban Districts	Wismar	65.7	—
	Rostock	64	—
Mecklenburg Rural Districts	Schönberg	57.7	(42.3)
	Hagenow	59.5	(40.5)
	Ludwigslust	61.5	(38.5)
	Usedom	64.1	(35.9)
Saxony-Anhalt Urban Districts	Salzwedel	60.1	(39.9)
	Halle	60.9	(39.1)
	Magdeburg	62.4	(37.6)
	Weissenfels	62.8	(37.2)
	Zeitz	64.7	(35.3)
	Naumburg	65.4	(34.6)
Saxony-Anhalt Rural Districts	Jericho II	62.5	(37.5)
	Liebenwerda	63.8	(36.2)
	Osterburg	65.4	(34.6)

Table 3.1 Continued

Land	District	Yes Vote (in percentage)	No Vote (in percentage)
Saxony Urban Districts	Plauen	39.8	(60.2)
	Zwickau	53.2	(46.8)
	Görlitz	54.8	(45.2)
	Leipzig	55.4	(44.6)
	Chemnitz	64.3	(35.7)
	Dresden	62.0	(38.0)
Saxony Rural Districts	Plauen	41.2	(58.8)
	Auerbach	47.5	(52.5)
	Glauchau	52.7	(47.3)
	Ölsnitz	54.6	(45.4)
	Zwickau	55.5	(44.5)
	Zittau	56.7	(43.1)
	Leipzig	61.1	(38.9)
	Kamenz	61.9	(38.1)
	Rochlitz	62.0	(38.0)
	Chemnitz	63.1	(36.9)
	Bautzen	64.2	(35.8)
	Löbau	64.3	(35.7)
	Dresden	65.5	(34.8)
Brandenburg Urban Districts	Potsdam	53.2	(46.8)
	Forst	58.5	(42.5)
	Guben	59.0	(41.0)
	Cottbus	61.1	(38.9)
	Wittenberge	63.4	(36.6)
Brandenburg Rural Districts	Lübben	54.5	(45.5)
	Teltow	54.7	(45.5)
	Luckau	57.2	(42.8)
	Cottbus	62.2	(37.8)
	Guben	62.3	(37.7)
	Luckenwalde	62.5	(37.5)
	Angermünde	63.2	(36.8)
	Westpriegnitz	64.1	(35.9)
	Zauch-Belzig	65.9	(34.1)

Table 3.1 Continued

Land	District	Yes Vote (in percentage)	No Vote (in percentage)
Thuringia Urban Districts	Apolda	47.1	(52.9)
	Greiz	47.3	(52.7)
	Gera	49.7	(50.3)
	Eisenach	51.6	(48.4)
	Jena	52.5	(47.5)
	Weimar	54.4	(45.6)
	Mühlhaus	58.0	(42.0)
	Gotha	58.3	(41.7)
	Altenburg	58.9	(41.1)
	Arnstadt	59.6	(40.4)
	Erfurt	62.5	(37.5)
Thuringia Rural Districts	Worbis	47.2	(52.8)
	Greiz	50.0	(50.0)
	Gera	51.2	(48.8)
	Sohleiz	52.4	(47.6)
	Stadtroda	56.7	(43.3)
	Saalfeld	60.6	(39.4)
	Langensalza	60.9	(39.1)
	Mühlenhausen	61.0	(39.0)
	Sonneberg	61.5	(38.5)
	Nordhausen	61.3	(38.7)
	Weimar	63.2	(45.6)
	Eisenach	63.5	(36.5)
	Altenburg	65.6	(34.4)
Berlin Voting district I		60.6	(39.4)
Voting district II		57.8	(42.2)
Voting district III		55.8	(44.2)

Source: SAPMO-BA, ZPA, DY 30 IV 2/5/201. The following note was attached: "Throughout Thuringia, unlike in other provinces, youths voted as poorly as adults."

By 1949, a trend in north-south division of the Soviet zone in terms of popular opposition had become evident. In the elections of 1946, popular support for the non-Marxist parties had been strongest in Saxony, Saxony-Anhalt, Thuringia, and Brandenburg, despite the obstacles placed by SMAD. In the provincial assemblies of Saxony-Anhalt and Brandenburg, it should be remembered, the CDU and LDPD formed a majority. In Saxony, the cities in which the CDU and LDPD had received more votes than the SED in 1946—Leipzig, Dresden, Zwickau, Plauen, and Bautzen—witnessed, with the exception of Bautzen, higher than average rejection of the *Volkskongress* election in 1949. The Central Block sittings in the aftermath of the *Volkskongress* vote demonstrate that the SED had understood the meaning of the election: popular rejection of its programme in eastern Germany. Furthermore, these sittings demonstrate that, in the opinion of several leading politicians, legal insecurity was the overriding component of this popular opposition. During the tumultuous Central Block sittings in the wake of the *Volkskongress* vote, the SED sought to place blame for the "poor" results, indicating the SED was not pleased with its apparent victory. Grotewohl lashed out at a number of groups including the SPD *Ostbüro*, the Schwennicke branch of the LDPD, and the Kaiser CDU. He also saw the handiwork of the Jehovah's Witnesses in the poor *Volkskongress* results.[282] Grotewohl insisted that the LDPD and the CDU remove the reactionary elements in their parties who had campaigned actively against the SED.[283] Hamann did not dispute Grotewohl, stating that Schwennicke and Kaiser elements within the respective parties had to be dealt with and shown the "correct way,"[284] but he carefully pointed out what he believed to be the true reasons for the result: legal insecurity, disunity of the parties, and "certain social complexes."[285] At the same sitting, Wilhelm Pieck also sought to place the blame for the results. He attacked the Bishop of Berlin and Brandenburg, Otto Dibelius, for his public call for resistance against the regime and his comparisons of the K-5 to the Gestapo, the *Volkskongress* vote to manipulation reminiscent of Hitler, and the "people's justices" to Hitler's system of justice. Pieck also directed his criticism against Pfarrer Kirsch of Chemnitz.[286] Pieck further complained of opposition within the CDU and LDPD, stating: "We have nothing against the leadership of the other parties. On the contrary, we want to help the leaders to overcome resistance in their parties."[287] The CDU leader Nuschke agreed: "During the elections, we noted resistance in the individual parties to the *Volkskongress* movement."[288]

Like the LDPD, the CDU leadership bowed to the SED and said it would "clean up" the party, but the CDU also pointed out the true reason behind the "poor" results. Dertinger and Nuschke complained specifically of popular insecurity, saying that the number of arrests likely had something to do with the high "no" vote. Dertinger complained of the lack of fair trials according to standard rules (i.e., plaintiff, defendant, etc.) and provided an important insight when he said: "The issue of so called legal security (*Rechtssicherheit*) and its practical implementation is in my opinion more important than all the other aggravating circumstances such as economic difficulties, social difficulties and so on. These are after all a result of the legacy that Hitler has left behind. The laws of the constitution and criminal proceedings must be, and in my opinion could be, guaranteed."[289] Both Nuschke and Dertinger urged a meeting with the Minister of the Interior, Dr. Kurt Fischer, to discuss arresting procedures.[290]

This emphasis on legal security, combined with the election results, suggests that Soviet and SMAD repression was more evident in Thuringia, Brandenburg,

Saxony, and the cities of Saxony-Anhalt than in Mecklenburg. This hypothesis is difficult to prove in the absence of accurate statistics on the numbers of eastern Germans sentenced by SMTs because of their opposition to Communism, not their activities during the Third Reich, and in the absence of statistics on NKVD/MVD incarcerations.[291] K-5 statistics are slightly more useful because they separate Order Number 201 arrests from other arrests, but it is still not possible to determine if anti-Communist opponents were sentenced under manufactured charges such as sabotage, possession of weapons, or being a western agent. Furthermore, these statistics have only been located for the Saxony K-5.[292] In 1947 in Saxony, K-5 opened 23,017 cases, of which 5,760 dealt with Order Number 201. In 1948, K-5 in Saxony opened 51,236 cases, of which 12,674 dealt with Order Number 201.[293] Clearly, there were many investigations which did not deal with denazification, but with other opponents of the SED.

There is other evidence, however, which suggests that repression was more prevalent in those areas which showed a greater than average rejection of the *Volkskongress*. Repression of the non-Marxist parties was clearly greater in these provinces, with arrests of oppositional CDU members being most numerous in Saxony, Saxony-Anhalt, and Brandenburg.[294] There are at present no statistics available for the distribution of LDPD arrests prior to 1949. The LDPD in Thuringia, however, was the most vocal of all the provincial LDPD executives in complaining of intimidation of its members.[295]

Furthermore, unjust incarcerations of individuals not involved in the non-Marxist parties appears to have been greater in the southern provinces. It should be remembered that the head of SMAD in Thuringia, General Kolesnichenko, suggested to the SMAD leadership in Karlshorst that NKVD excesses were causing great fear in the population. It was these injustices that had led the head of the CDU's youth group, *Junge Gemeinde*, to emigrate to the western zone of Germany. Police excesses during the sequestering of factories had been the impetus behind the Thuringian LDPD's withdrawal from the sequestering commissions. Additionally, LDPD reports on the population mention popular insecurity more often in the reports from Saxony, Saxony-Anhalt, Brandenburg, and Thuringia than in those from Mecklenburg.[296]

The Founding of the German Democratic Republic

By 1949, the division of Germany was becoming permanent. In August, based on the agreements of the London Conference of 1948, the West German state, the Federal Republic of Germany, came into existence. Shortly afterwards, Pieck, Grotewohl, Ulbricht, and Oelssner travelled to Moscow to begin the preparations for the founding of the East German state, the German Democratic Republic.[297] There was then much discussion in eastern German political parties in the first week of October regarding elections to the *Volkskammer*, and not about the actual decision to found the GDR or the composition of the government, because the election process would determine whether the GDR would be a parliamentary republic with competitive parties as laid out in the constitution, or if it would be founded as a *Volksdemokratie*, a people's democracy with one-party rule as had been instituted in the countries of East Central Europe and the Balkans.[298] The documents revealed by Siegfried Suckut in 1991 of the SED executive sittings of October 4 and 9 demonstrate that the SED never intended to hold competitive elections and that the GDR was "from the beginning, seen by the Communist Party of the Soviet Union and the SED as a 'people's democracy.'"[299] These documents explain SED insistence on delaying both the first elections to the *Volkskammer*, and to the provincial assemblies to coincide with the *Kreis* and *Gemeinde* elections set for October 1950.

At the joint sitting of the *Volksrat* and Central Block on October 5, the non-Marxist parties supported the delay of the elections, although both Kastner and Hamann had previously absolutely rejected delaying the provincial elections.[300] The communiqué calling for the *Volksrat* to be transformed into a provisional *Volkskammer* therefore passed without objection.[301] It is difficult to ascertain precisely the reason the non-Marxist parties offered such little protest to the delay of the elections. Part of the reason was certainly SMAD pressure to conform. Nuschke, for example, came to support the GDR's founding after Vladimir Semyenov, the head of the Office of the Political Advisor to the Soviet Commander-in-Chief, informed him on October 5 that SMAD would not accept CDU opposition to the founding of the GDR.[302] It is also possible that the party leadership believed that free elections would take place, because these were, after all, guaranteed in the constitution.[303] Kastner of the LDPD, for example, insisted that the *Volkskammer* was provisional and that elections were a necessity.[304] On October 7, the *Volksrat* became the provisional *Volkskammer* of the newly proclaimed German Democratic Republic and on the following day ordered the five provinces to delay provincial elections for a year.[305]

The founding of the GDR met with reserved CDU support. Although all provincial executives made their support contingent on the holding of free elections, lower levels of the CDU were often unwilling to voice this limited support. In Brandenburg, Peter Bloch called the GDR founding a "coup d'état" as it took place without an election.[306] On October 9, at a CDU conference of *Kreis* functionaries, lower-level CDU members protested the founding of the GDR on democratic principles and some CDU groups left the party on the announcement of the vote delay.[307] The CDU in Luckau complained that the founding of the GDR was anti-constitutional because "according to the constitution, the *Volkskammer* is elected by the people. In the meantime, the constitution has already been promulgated. By whom? From the outset, the founding of the GDR demonstrates several breaches of the constitution." He also complained that while the DWK no longer existed, the government still had the same people: "It is the same SED dictatorship."[308] The delay of the vote also met with criticism from the Saxony-Anhalt CDU groups in Schönberg, Bernburg, and Waren.[309] In Chemnitz, the local CDU group issued a resolution which stated that a people expresses its will through free, equal, secret, general, direct elections, not demonstrations (i.e., *Volkskongress*) and therefore rejected the postponement of the elections.[310] A leading SED functionary, Otto Buchwitz, stated that he had received a series of letters from CDU fractions in the Soviet zone insisting that the provincial constitutions obliged them to hold elections.[311]

In Saxony, the founding of the GDR ran up against considerable opposition in the provincial assembly, where a majority of members, mostly CDU, refused to issue a resolution supporting the new government. The Saxony CDU even wrote to Kaiser saying that the party members opposed Nuschke's treasonous policies.[312] The SED then proceeded violently against these CDU members. Members of the SED and FDGB even visited their homes to curse at the politicians and pressure the members to either reverse their stance or stop their political activities altogether. In most cases the CDU members stopped their political activity quickly; only two CDU members refused to give into the mob pressure.[313] Nuschke had tried unsuccessfully to convince those oppositional members in Saxony to support the government until an election, which he expected to take place in March 1950.[314]

At the October 4, 1949 sitting of the SED executive, Pieck confirmed general resistance at the lower levels of the non-Marxist parties to delaying the elections. He claimed that there were many "reactionaries" in the CDU and LDPD who did not agree with the present policies (i.e., the decision to postpone elections). Five days later, Grotewohl said that on mention of delaying elections to October 1950, a "revolution" in the CDU and LDPD nearly broke out.[315]

Limited CDU resistance to the election postponement was still evident at the Fourth Party Conference of the CDU on November 12, 1949. A leading CDU functionary from Brandenburg, Peter Bloch, stated that the breaching of law and the constitution must finally come to an end. He specifically called for an end to SED attempts at a one-party dictatorship, a statement which met with loud applause.[316] Siegfried Witte, Minister Kirsch, and Saxony's economic minister Gerhard Rohner also criticized the SED.[317] Kirsch defiantly proclaimed that there would never be a unified Germany under Communist domination.[318] The resistance demonstrated at this conference was noticeably less than at previous CDU conferences, however. The Fourth Party Conference marked the emergence of pro-Communist elements within the CDU and the nearing end of its existence as an independent party.[319]

Protest against the delay of the elections is less visible in the LDPD. In Saxony, the *Kreis* leaders supported the leadership's approval of the delay of the elections, but indicated that their membership did not generally support their position.[320] Protests by the LDPD membership are not documented in the minutes of the provincial leadership meetings for the other provinces. However, Grotewohl's comment that "a revolution" almost broke out in the CDU and LDPD on announcement of the delay of the elections, combined with the history of opposition by the LDPD membership to the SED, suggests that the LDPD membership rejected the delay of the election.

It is likely that the population rejected the delay as well. LDPD situation reports for 1949 from the party association in Mecklenburg to the party leadership generally paint a favorable picture of the situation in the GDR and work within the

LDPD. Lapses in this pattern are therefore striking. In November 1949, the LDPD provincial association in Mecklenburg reported that in spite of a "thorough education effort," the population did not understand the postponement of the election.[321] In Saxony, the LDPD reported similar sentiments in the population. One LDPD member reported: "The one thing that I have not been able to do is convince people that it was right that the elections did not take place."[322] Popular protests in his *Kreis* appealed to the rule of law, stating that elections had to be held because they were proscribed by the constitution.[323] SPD reports also emphasized the population's displeasure at the founding of the GDR and the delay of the elections to the following year.[324]

By the time the GDR was founded, there was clear resistance in the membership of the non-Marxist parties to the SED dictatorship in the Soviet zone. The SMAD and SED campaign against these members produced a differentiated response. On the one hand, it eliminated opponents in these parties. On the other hand, it drove some members into active underground resistance and contributed to insecurity in the broader population. The most successful anti-resistance campaign came against the SPD. The NKVD/MVD had eliminated virtually all SPD groups in the Soviet zone by 1949, and through this intimidation prevented the establishment of new groups. Opposition to the SED was visible in the population, as witnessed by the results of the *Volkskongress*, although the opposition was more evident in the provinces of Thuringia, Saxony, Brandenburg, and the cities of Saxony-Anhalt than in the northern province of Mecklenburg. Support for the non-Marxist parties in the Soviet zone, combined with the opposition demonstrated at the *Volkskongress*, illustrates that popular opposition was of a political nature: the population opposed the Communist system in eastern Germany. The evidence presented in this chapter suggests that a primary reason behind the political opposition was the abuse of basic rights by SMAD and the SED. Stroking his cat in his comfortable Potsdam living room in 1995, Karl Schirdewan, the longest living member of the SED Politburo from the 1950s, frankly admitted to me that "repression was the SED's greatest error."[325] Schirdewan accurately pointed to a major reason the SED encountered difficulties in garnering popular support.

Notes

1. Wolfgang Eisert, "Zu den Anfängen der Sicherheits-und Militärpolitic der SED-Führung 1948 bis 1952," in *Volksarmee schaffen—ohne Geschrei*, ed. Bruno Thoss (Munich: R. Oldenbourg Verlag, 1994), 154.

2. Bundesarchiv-Potsdam Abteilungen (BA-P), DO 1 7/205, .34. August 10, 1947 report: "Zur Lage in der Polizei" from Otto Hanschke, member of the executive of the Cottbus SED *Kreis*, department of police and justice, to the SED *Instrukteur* for Brandenburg, Pfeiffer.

3. Richard Bessel, "Die Grenzen des Polizeistaates," in *Die Grenzen der Diktatur*, ed. Richard Bessel and Ralph Jessen (Göttingen: Vandenhoeck & Rupprecht, 1996), 235.

4. Archiv für Christlich-Demokratische Politik (ACDP), II-204-055/4, KV Worbis. 10

May 1948 report from *Kreis* police leadership Mühlhausen to *Kreis* police office.
5 Bessel, 235.

6. ACDP, KV Worbis May 10, 1948 report, 236.

7. BA-P, DO 1 7/205, 34. August 10, 1947 report from Otto Hanschke, member of the executive of the Cottbus SED *Kreis*, department police and justice, to Pfeiffer, SED *Instrukteur* for Brandenburg.

8. BA-P, DO 1 7/205, 34. August 10, 1947 report from Otto Hanschke.

9. BA-P, DO 1 7/270, 421. October 21, 1947 annual report for head of the *Schutzpolizei* on the *Schutzpolizei.*

10. BA-P, DO 1 7/270, 40. October 21, 1947 annual report.

11. BA-P, DO 1 7/270, 41. October 21, 1947 annual report

12. BA-P, DO 1 7/270, 41. October 21, 1947 annual report

13. A political police existed in a disorganized form prior to 1947, but in January of that year these units were centralized and coordinated under K-5. Jens Gieseke, *Die hauptamtlichen Mitarbeiter der Staatssicherheit* (Berlin: Ch. Links, 2000), 55.

14. Archiv der sozialen Demokratie (AdsD), SPD-PV-Ostbüro 0005. September 9, 1948 report on DVdI by "reliable source."

15. Norman Naimark, *The Russians in Germany* (Cambridge: Harvard University Press, 1995), 360.

16. *Bundesbeauftragter für die Unterlagen des Staatssicherheitsdienstes der ehemaligen DDR* (BStU), *Zentralarchiv* (ZA), *Allgemeine Sachablage* (AS) 229/66,372-373. January 8, 1948 overview of K-5 duties in K-5 yearly report for 1947 signed by Nindl, head of K-5 for Saxony.

17. BStU, ZA, AS 229/66, 365. January 8, 1948 overview of K-5 duties.

18. Karl-Wilhelm Fricke, *Die DDR-Staatssicherheit* (Cologne: Verlag Wissenschaft und Politik, 1989), 22.

19. BStU, ZA, AS 229/66, 374. January 13, 1948 yearly report for 1947 for K-5 Saxony.

20. BStU, ZA, AS 229/66, 374. January 13, 1948 yearly report for 1947 for K-5 Saxony.

21. BStU, ZA, AS 229/66, 385. January 13, 1948 yearly report for 1947 for K-5 Saxony.

22. BA-P, DO 1 7/441, 34, 36. Protocol of February 3, 1948 meeting of the Mecklenburg provincial *Volkspolizei.*

23. BA-P, DO 1 7/441, 39. Protocol of February 3, 1948 meeting of the Mecklenburg provincial *Volkspolizei.*

24. BA-P, DO 1 7/441, 39. Protocol of February 3, 1948 meeting of the Mecklenburg provincial *Volkspolizei.*

25. Naimark, *The Russians,* 361.

26. Naimark, *The Russians,* 364-365.

27. BStU, ZA, AS 229/66, 267. November 11, 1947 report: "Aufbau einer Abteilung Nachrichten und Information in der DVdI."

28. BStU, ZA., AS 238/66, 343-344. An undated report on K-5 duties lists the main targets as underground SPD groups, "enemies in licensed political parties," religious sects, and fascist organizations.

29. BStU, ZA, Sekretariat des Ministers (SdM) 324, 23. July 29, 1947 letter from Dünow of the press office to Mielke.

30. BStU, ZA, Sekretariat des Ministers (SdM) 324, 279. July 29, 1947 letter from

Dünow of the press office to Mielke.

31. BStU, ZA, AS 229/66, 280. November 11, 1947 report: "Aufbau einer Abteilung Nachrichten und Information in der DVdI."

32. Andrea Feth, "Die Volksrichter," in *Steuerung der Justiz in der DDR*, ed. Hubert Rottleuthner (Cologne: Bundesanzeiger Verlag, 1994), 358.

33. The CDU and LDPD did agree to the SED's system of "people's justices" because of the necessity to rebuild the justice system in the wake of its infiltration by the Nazi party, but both parties felt that it must be a temporary measure; Feth, "Die Volksrichter," 369.

34. Falco Werkentin, *Politische Strafjustiz in der Ära Ulbricht* (Berlin: Ch. Links Verlag, 1995), 23.

35. BA-P, DO 1 7/441, 32. Protocol of February 3, 1948 meeting of the Mecklenburg provincial *Volkspolizei*.

36. Werkentin, *Politische Strafjustiz*, 23.

37. Karl Wilhelm Fricke, *Politik und Justiz in der DDR* (Cologne: Verlag Wissenschaft und Politik, 1979), 106.

38. Excerpts of Article 58 are reprinted in Fricke, *Politik*, 106-109.

39. Fricke, *Politik*, 110.

40. Werkentin, *Politische Strafjustiz*, 25.

41. Naimark, *The Russians*, 79.

42. One SED member complained that the brutal methods of the criminal police caused the population to fear it as much as it had feared the Gestapo; Naimark, *The Russians*, 360.

43. ACDP, I-298-001/4, NL W. Seibert. April 9, 1947 letter from the CDU, LDPD, and SED to Soviet authorities in Köppelsdorf.

44. ACDP, I-298-001/4, NL W. Seibert. May 23, 1947 letter from the CDU local group Libertwollkwitz-Saxony to the CDU *Kreis* leadership in Leipzig.

45. ACDP, I-298-001/4, NL W. Seibert. May 12, 1947 letter from the CDU provincial association in Thuringia to the CDU in Berlin (Seibert.)

46. Naimark, *The Russians*, 393.

47. Naimark, *The Russians*, 393.

48. Franz Neumann Archiv (FNA), VII/3. May 1949 anonymous letter to Neumann; 4 June 1948 anonymous letter to Neumann; April 20, 1948 letter to Neumann from "the Comrades of the illegal SPD"; March 19, 1948 anonymous letter to Neumann.

49. FNA, IX b 1, "Reden." Notes from speeches of October 20, 1947 and December 12, 1947.

50. Fritsche was arrested on August 15, 1951 and sentenced to twenty-five years labor by an SMT. He spent 4 years of his sentence at the Siberian labour camp in Workuta before obtaining early release; Helmut Bärwald, *Das Ostbüro der SPD* (Krefeld: SINUS, 1991), 44.

51. Franz Walter et al., ed., *Die SPD in Sachsen zwischen Hoffnung und Diaspora* (Bonn: J.H.W. Dietz, 1993), 149.

52. Netsch was arrested in 1951 and sentenced to prison. Other members of the group fled to the West; Walter, *Die SPD*, 149.

53. AdsD, SPD-PV-Ostbüro 0361. May 26, 1947 letter from an SPD member in Münchenbernsdorf.

54. AdsD, SPD-PV-Ostbüro 0046 a-g. May 30, 1949 report from a student.

55. AdsD, SPD-PV-Ostbüro 0421. July 27, 1956 report on Gruppe Behnisch I and Gruppe Behnisch II; July 15, 1947 refugee report.

56. AdsD, SPD-PV-Ostbüro 0421. February 2, 1954 report by Julius Brendenbeck.

57. AdsD, SPD-PV-Ostbüro 0421. July 19, 1956 report on the Keil, Rost, Weck group.

58. AdsD, SPD-PV-Ostbüro 0394. April 3, 1947 anonymous letter to Schumacher.

59. AdsD, SPD-PV-Ostbüro 0361/1. July 24, 1947 report. See also reports of July 23, 1948 and June 4, 1948.

60. Waldemar Krönig and Klaus-Dieter Müller, eds., *Anpassung, Widerstand, Verfolgung: Hochschule und Studenten in der SBZ und DDR 1945-1961* (Cologne: Verlag Wissenschaft und Politik, 1994), 259.

61. Helmut Bärwald, "Terror als System," in *Verfolgt—verhaftet—verurteilt: Demokratie im Widerstand gegen die Rote Diktatur—Fakten und Beispiele,* ed. Günter Scholz (Berlin: Westkreuz Verlag, 1990), p. 29.

62. Bärwald, *Das Ostbüro,* 40.

63. For more on the Wismut mining operation, see Naimark, *The Russians,* 238-250.

64. AdsD, SPD-PV-Ostbüro 0421. July 26, 1956 report from "Source" on his arrest.

65. AdsD, SPD-PV-Ostbüro 0421. July 26, 1956 report from "Source" on his arrest.

66. AdsD, SPD-PV-Ostbüro 0421. July 26, 1956 report from "Source" on his arrest. The unjust imprisonments led to a small prisoners' revolt in Bautzen a few years later. In March 1951, prisoners waved towels out of windows and shouted: "We are not criminals!" to which people on the street shouted back their support; FNA, VII/3, "SBZ/DDR." Undated report from Georg Friedrich on his time in Bautzen.

67. AdsD, SPD-PV-Ostbüro, 0330I. August 28, 1948 personal account of Herbert Braun.

68. AdsD, SPD-PV-Ostbüro 0421. July 25, 1946 report on the Soviet military tribunal arrest and sentencing.

69. AdsD, SPD-PV-Ostbüro 0421. July 24, 1956 report by Hermann Fabian; July 25, 1956 report on SMT arrest and sentencing.

70. Excerpts from SED report on the Second Party Congress; Hermann Weber, *Parteiensystem zwischen Demokratie und Volksdemokratie* (Cologne: Verlag Wissenschaft und Politik, 1982), 84. At the fusion of the SPD and KPD, parity between the parties in the leading functions of the SED from *Kreis* up was guaranteed.

71. "SED Ortsgruppe Gaschwitz an die Delegiertenkonferenz des Arbeitsgebietes Markkleeberg. 15.8.47"; Weber, *Parteiensystem,* 79-80.

72. Frank Thomas Stössel, *Positionen und Strömungen in der KPD/SED 1945-1954* (Cologne: Verlag Wissenschaft und Politik, 1985), 339.

73. FNA, VII/3 "SBZ/DDR." April 25, 1947 letter from Dresden. "We Social Democrats of Saxony are prevented from taking part as guests at your party conference from April 25 to 27, 1947 in Berlin due to the political conditions within the SBZ. In spite of this, we feel tied to you, although we presently work in the SED, and offer you our warmest greetings as socialists."

74. AdsD, SPD-PV-Ostbüro, 0421. May 16, 1956 report on the activities that led to the arrest of the nine-person SPD resistance group from Jena and Sonneberg in 1949.

75. AdsD, SPD-PV-Ostbüro, 0421. May 16, 1956 report on the activities that led to the arrest of the nine-person SPD resistance group from Jena and Sonneberg in 1949..

76. AdsD, SPD-PV-Ostbüro, 0421. May 16, 1956 report on the activities that led to the arrest of the nine-person SPD resistance group from Jena and Sonneberg in 1949..

77. Jena was not the only university that witnessed SPD resistance. The University of Halle also saw SPD activity during the latter half of the 1940s. An SPD group under Karl Frankenberger, a member of the student council, was formed after the war and remained active until April 16, 1947 when Frankenberger fled because of imminent arrest. Another group in Halle had been actively distributing pamphlets on behalf of the SPD from 1948 to

1950; AdsD, SPD-PV-Ostbüro, 0368a-c Report on illegal work in Halle; ibid., SPD-PV-Ostbüro 0394 April 17, 1947 report of student Karl Frankenberger Haale/Saale.

78. FNA, VII/3, "SBZ/DDR." August 19, 1946 report from the courier Kasparek to Franz Neumann.

79. Karl Wilhelm Fricke, *Opposition und Widerstand in der DDR* (Cologne: Verlag Wissenschaft und Politik, 1984), 42.

80. AdsD, SPD-PV-Ostbüro 0420 B1. June 6, 1955 report on SPD prisoners in Brandenburg from former inmate; Hermann Kreutzer confirmed that Szillat served his sentence in Brandenburg prison. Author's interview with Hermann Kreutzer, April 24, 1995.

81. Fank was amnestied on January 24, 1954; Fricke, *Opposition*, 39.

82. Stössel, *Positionen*, 194.

83. Stössel, *Positionen*, 194.

84. AdsD, SPD-PV-Ostbüro, 0421. July 25, 1956 report from "Source" on his arrest and sentencing by a Soviet Military Tribunal.

85. AdsD, SPD-PV-Ostbüro, 0421. July 25, 1956 report from "Source" on arrest and sentencing by a Soviet Military Tribunal, p. 3. This group, which had contact to Curt Eckhardt's group in Erfurt, was arrested on the night of March 11, 1948. On January 19, 1950, Willi Wehner, Curt Eckhardt, and the leader of the Lukas Cranach group were sentenced to twenty-five years labor.

86. *Brandenburgisches Landeshauptarchiv* (BLHA), Ld.Br. Rep. 332, L IV 2/4/187, SED Landesvorstand Brandenburg. May 10, 1948 police minutes on interrogations of SPD members, signature blacked out.

87. The topic of Communist elements in the SED which were unhappy with the fusion of the parties has received little attention in the scholarly literature. For an introduction, see Stössel, *Positionen*.

88. Naimark, *The Russians*, 298.

89. Naimark, *The Russians*, 298.

90. Stiftung Archiv der Parteien und Massenorganisationen (SAPMO-BA), ZPA, IV 2/4/383, .236. August 25, 1948 report by the Central Party Control Commission.

91. SAPMO-BA, ZPA IV 2/4/383, 244. September 10, 1948 report by the Central Party Control Commission.

92. Wolfgang Buschfort, *Das Ostbüro der SPD* (Munich: R. Oldenbourg Verlag, 1991), 21.

93. Buschfort suggests that Neumann was selected because his background in the KPD might be helpful in penetrating the SED; Buschfort, *Das Ostbüro*, 22.

94. Brigitte Itzerott, "Die Liberal-Demokratische Partei Deutschlands," in *Parteiensystem zwischen Demokratie und Volksdemokratie*, ed. Hermann Weber (Cologne: Verlag Wissenschaft und Politik, 1982), 191-193.

95. Archiv des Deutschen Liberalismus (ADL), LDPD #2780. Protocol of Thuringian LDPD executive sitting of November 28, 1947.

96. Itzerott, "Die Liberal-Demokratische," 191-193.

97. "Verlauf der Gründungssitzung am 13. und 14.7.45. Gedächtnisprotokoll von Erich Gniffke"; Suckut, *Blockpolitik*, 63.

98. BLHA, Ld.Br. Rep. 203, MdI Nr. 25, p. 343. November 8, 1947 interior ministry report from Beelitz.

99. Fricke, *Opposition*, 53.

100. Fricke, *Opposition*, 53.

101. Mecklenburgisches Landeshauptarchiv (MLHA), IV L 2/12/530, Justiz, 45. March

18, 1949 memorandum from Dr. Scheffler to the High Division for Criminal matters of the provincial court in Schwerin.

102. ADL, LDPD #2780. Protocol of Thuringian LDPD executive sitting of November 28, 1947.

103. ADL, LDPD #2780. Protocol of Thuringian LDPD executive sitting of November 28, 1947.

104. Siegfried Suckut, *Blockpolitik in der SBZ/DDR* (Cologne: Verlag Wissenschaft und Politik, 1986), 221; Fricke, *Opposition*, 53.

105. Minutes of the Central Block sitting of October 31, 1947; Suckut, *Blockpolitik*, 233-237.

106. ACDP, I-298-001/2, NL W. Seibert. Notes from a speech of March 1947.

107. ACDP, I-298-001/3, NL W. Seibert. February 18, 1947 letter from Seibert to Dertinger.

108. ACDP, I-298-001/3, NL W. Seibert. June 12, 1947 letter from Seibert to Kaiser.

109. AdsD, ZASS t/c 16. March 31, 1947 newspaper report: "Aufklärung über Studentenverhaftungen."

110. John Connelly, "East German Higher Education Policies and Student Resistance, 1945-48," *Central European History* 28 (1995): 273.

111. AdsD, ZASS t/c 16. *Telegraf.* March 23, 1947 newspaper report: "Verhaftung von CDU-Studenten."

112. AdsD, ZASS t/c 16. March 31, 1947 newspaper report: "Aufklärung über Studentenverhaftungen."

113. AdsD, t/c 16 1947. Internal report.

114. AdsD, ZASS, t/c 16 1947. *Kurier* March 28, 1947 newspaper report: "Diskussionen über Studentenverhaftungen."

115. In the Brandenburg provincial assembly, Zborowski (CDU) rejected the FDGB in the Block because he believed that extra-parliamentary organizations should not be involved too closely in party work; Manfred Agethen, "Die CDU in der SBZ/DDR 1945-53," in *Bürgerliche Parteien in der SBZ/DDR*, ed. Manfred Agethen and Jürgen Fröhlich (Cologne: Verlag Wissenschaft und Politik, 1994), 53.

116. Agethen, "Die CDU," 53; J.B. Gradl, *Anfang unter dem Sowjetstern* (Cologne: Verlag Wissenschaft und Politik, 1981), 106-107.

117. Fricke, *Opposition*, 53; Werner Conze, *Jakob Kaiser* (Stuttgart: W. Kohlhammer Verlag, 1969), 156.

118. Conze, *Jakob Kaiser*, 144. Schumacher refused the "National Representation" because he believed that responsibility for representing the German people lay with the parties, not with delegates to the proposed "National Representation." Furthermore, as long as the SPD was forbidden in the Soviet zone, Schumacher would not participate in functions that involved SED representation; Klessmann, *Die doppelte Staatsgründung*, 187.

119. Martin McCauley, *The German Democratic Republic since 1945* (London: MacMillan Press, 1983), 34. In May 1947, the minister presidents of all provinces met in Munich in an effort to maintain the unity of Germany, but the eastern representatives left after a few hours because the delegates could not decide on an agenda.

120. Gradl, *Anfang*, 109.

121. Gradl, *Anfang*, 117.

122. Gradl, *Anfang*, 120; Conze, *Jakob Kaiser*, 172.

123. Agethen, "Die CDU," 54; Conze, *Jakob Kaiser*, 172.

124. Agethen, "Die CDU," 54.

125. Minutes of the Central Block sitting of November 24, 1947; Suckut, *Blockpolitik*, 242; See also Gradl, 128.

126. Agethen, "Die CDU," 54.

127. ADL, #2928. Report on speech by Kaiser September 21, 1947.

128. Conze, *Jakob Kaiser*, 190.

129. Michael Richter, *Die Ost-CDU 1948-52* (Düsseldorf: Droste, 1995), 34.

130. Richter, *Die Ost-CDU*, 32; At the *Volkskongress* Luitpold Steidle of the CDU openly criticized the CDU leadership for not participating; Norbert Mattedi, *Gründung und Entwicklung der Parteien in der Sowjetischen Besatzungszone Deutschlands 1945-49* (Bonn: Deutscher Bundes-Verlag, 1966), 109.

131. Agethen, "Die CDU," 54.

132. Conze, *Jakob Kaiser*, 192. The Committee elected to represent Germany at the London conference never did attend; Gradl, *Anfang*, 132.

133. Fricke, *Opposition*, 57. At the Central Block sitting of November 24, 1947, the LDPD supported the SED proposal, while the CDU rejected it; minutes of the Central Block sitting of November 24, 1947; Suckut, *Blockpolitik*, 32.

134. Fritz Reinert, *Protokolle der Landesblockausschusses der antifaschistisch-demokratischen Parteien Brandenburgs 1945-50* (Weimar: Verlag Hermann Böhlaus Nach-folger, 1994), 196. See also Gerhard Papke, "Die Liberal-Demokratische Partei Deutsch-lands in der sowjetischen Besatzungszone und DDR 1945-52," in *"Bürgerliche" Parteien in der SBZ/DDR*, ed. Manfred Agethen, Jürgen Fröhlich (Cologne: Verlag Wissenschaft und Politik, 1995). The reaction of the lower levels of the LDPD to the *Volkskongress* has not been addressed in the literature and requires further research. It is likely, however, that the LDPD did not enthusiastically support the *Volkskongress*. An SED declaration of August 14, 1947 complained of insufficient Block work at the lower levels and that joint cooperation was often limited to higher levels of the parties. The declaration is reprinted in Suckut, *Blockpolitik*, 230.

135. Richter, *Die Ost-CDU*, 32.

136. See Gradl, *Anfang*, 149 for a list of the members who joined Kaiser in West Ber-lin; Richter, *Die Ost-CDU*, 59.

137. Richter, *Die Ost-CDU*, 35.

138. Richter, *Die Ost-CDU*, 35.

139. Conze, *Jakob Kaiser*, 203.

140. The Berlin CDU was an exception among the provincial leaderships. The Berlin CDU, under its chair Walter Schreiber, broke with the CDU in the Soviet zone and put its full support behind Kaiser in April 1948; Gradl, *Anfang*, 140.

141. Peter Bloch, *Zwischen Hoffnung und Resignation* (Cologne: Verlag Wissenschaft und Politik, 1986), 99.

142. Richter, *Die Ost-CDU*, 42.

143. The head of the Saxony CDU, Hugo Hickmann, is a complex figure. He supported Kaiser and Lemmer, but also felt that compromise with the Soviets was necessary, a belief he later regretted; Richter, *Die Ost-CDU*, 49.

144. ACDP, III-013-870 "Die Arbeit der Jungen Union in der SBZ ruht" by Fred Sagner, 3.

145. ACDP III-013-870 "Die Arbeit der Jungen Union," by Fred Sagner, 5.

146. Richter, *Die Ost-CDU*, 77.

147. Agethen, "Der Widerstand der demokratischen Kräfte in der CDU," in *Die CDU in der sowjetischen besetzten Zone/DDR 1945-52*, ed. Manfred Agethen and Alexander Fischer

(Sankt Augustin: Konrad-Adenauer-Stiftung, 1994), 38.

148. Agethen, "Der Widerstand," in Agethen and Fischer, *Die CDU*, 38. Overall in universities across the Soviet zone, the non-Marxist parties proved to be more popular than the SED. The SED was unable to obtain a majority at any university during the first student council elections in the winter of 1946-1947; Thomas Ammer, *Universität zwischen Demokratie und Diktatur* (Cologne: Verlag Wissenschaft und Politik, 1969), 13-14.

The failure of the SED to win a majority of students to its cause was troubling for the party, and convinced it that the influence of the other parties was too prevalent at universities. The influence of these "bourgeois" elements in the universities was a main reason the SED formed a *Hochschulausschuss* (University Committee) on May 16, 1947. The *Hochschulausschuss* increased pressure for universities to develop a Marxist world view, which in turn caused a large number of professors to leave to the West; Ammer, *Universität*, 34.

149. Agethen, "Der Widerstand," 38; Richter, *Die Ost-CDU*, 80.

150. ACDP, III-013-800. February 5, 1948 report on the visit of a female student from the eastern zone.

151. Richter, *Die Ost-CDU*, 52.

152. BLHA, Ld. Br. Rep. 203, MdI Nr. 25, 299. October 25, 1947 letter from CDU Beeskow to CDU *Kreis* association Ostprignitz.

153. Henry Ashby Turner, *Germany from Partition to Unification* (New Haven: Yale University Press, 1992), 23-24.

154. Turner, *Germany*, 24.

155. Turner, *Germany*, 26.

156. Turner, *Germany*, 26.

157. Klessmann, *Die doppelte Staatsgründung*, 192.

158. The numbers on the police force vary. Richard Bessel claims the police force comprised 68,148 workers by September 1948 (Bessel, *Die Grenzen*, 229), whereas Norman Naimark puts the number at 80,971 (Naimark, *The Russians*, 374).

159. Naimark, *The Russians*, 375.

160. Wolfgang Eisert, "Zu den Anfängen der Sicherheits- und Militärpolitik der SED-Führung 1948 bis 1952," in Thoss, *Volksarmee*, 173.

161. Eisert, "Zu den Anfängen," 173.

162. *Thüringisches Hauptstaatsarchiv* (hereafter THSA) IV L 2/3-032, BPA Erfurt Landesleitung Thur-Sekretariat. Protocol of the SED secretariat sitting of May 8, 1948.

163. Rüdiger Wenzke, "Auf dem Wege zur Kaderarmee. Aspekte der Rekrutierung, Sozialstruktur und personellen Entwicklung des entstehenden Militärs in der SBZ/DDR bis 1952/53," in Thoss, *Volksarmee*, 214.

164. Eisert, "Zu den Anfängen," 177.

165. See Naimark, *The Russians*, 366-368.

166. Eisert, "Zu den Anfängen," 174.

167. For the new structure of the Central Administration of Justice from January 1949, see Thomas Lorenz, "Die Deutsche Zentralverwaltung der Justiz (DJV) und die SMAD in der Sowjetischen Besatzungszone 1945-49," in *Steuerung der Justiz in der DDR*, ed. Hubert Rottleuthner (Cologne: Bundesanzeiger Verlag, 1994), 146.

168. Naimark, *The Russians*, 363.

169. Lorenz, "Die Deutsche," 165.

170. Lorenz, "Die Deutsche," 139.

171. Andreas Gängel, "Die Volksrichterausbildung," in author collective for an

"Ausstellung des Bundesministeriums der Justiz," *Im Namen des Volkes? Über die Justiz im Staat der SED* (Leipzig: Forum Verlag, 1994), 53.

172. Andreas Gängel, "Die Volksrichterausbildung," in author collective for an "Ausstellung des Bundesministeriums der Justiz," *Im Namen des Volkes? Über die Justiz im Staat der SED* (Leipzig: Forum Verlag, 1994), 53.

173. Lorenz, "Die Deutsche," 140; see also Werkentin, *Politische Strafjustiz*, 21-22. By 1949, the only nominal non-SED member in the administration was Dr. Helmut Brandt, the vice president of the German central administration for justice.

174. Stössel, *Positionen*, 169.

175. Reprint of Ackermann's personal admission, September 24, 1948; Hermann Weber, *DDR. Dokumente zur Geschichte der DDR* (Munich: DTV, 1986), 129.

176. Reprinted *Neues Deutschland* article from September 21, 1948; Weber, *Parteiensystem*, 105.

177. Turner, *Germany*, 63.

178. SAPMO-BA, ZPA, IV 2/4/385, 126. January 5, 1950 report by the Provincial Party Control Commission for Saxony. He was arrested in January 1950.

179. SAPMO-BA, ZPA, IV 2/4/385 ZPKK, 409. October 28, 1948 report by the SED *Kreis* executive for Grimma.

180. AdsD, SPD-PV-Ostbüro, 0394. March 9, 1948 anonymous letter.

181. AdsD, SPD-PV-Ostbüro 0394. May 6, 1949 report entitled: "Mein Austritt aus der SED" Signed Lamp'l.

182. SAPMO-BA, ZPA, IV 2/4/383 ZPKK, 11. August 12, 1948 letter to *Tribüne*, the newspaper of the FDGB.

183. See the documents in AdsD, SPD-PV-Ostbüro 0394.

184. Naimark, *The Russians*, 387.

185. Interview with Hermann Kreutzer, Berlin, April 24, 1995.

186. Fricke, *Politik*, 119.

187. BStU, ZA, AS 229/66, 628. Yearly report for K-5 in Saxony for 1948.

188. Buschfort, *Das Ostbüro*, 39-40.

189. Buschfort, *Das Ostbüro*, 65.

190. Buschfort, *Das Ostbüro*, 75.

191. Buschfort, *Das Ostbüro*, 116.

192. Richter, *Die Ost-CDU*, 57.

193. ACDP, III-013-800. Report on CDU gathering in Tivoli August 24, 1948.

194. ACDP, III-013-800. August 19, 1948 report by Siegfried Tscheschner.

195. SAPMO-BA, ZPA, DY30 IV 2/15/1. Report on the CDU meeting in Bentwisch on 6 September 1948.

196. Richter, *Die Ost-CDU*, 82.

197. Richter, *Die Ost-CDU*, 83-86.

198. Suckut, *Blockpolitik*, 33-34.

199. Minutes of the Central Block sitting of September 7, 1948; Suckut, *Blockpolitik*, 291.

200. Richter, *Die Ost-CDU*, 96-99.

201. Minutes of the Central Block sitting of October 8, 1948; Suckut, *Blockpolitik*, 315.

202. Richter, *Die Ost-CDU*, 108.

203. Richter, *Die Ost-CDU*, 113.

204. Weber, *Parteiensystem*, 163.

205. Richter, *Die Ost-CDU*, 48.

206. Richter, "Vom Widerstand," 50.

207. Richter, *Die Ost-CDU*, 237.

208. ACDP, III-013-800. March 31, 1948 report from a correspondent entitled: "Das politische Gesicht Sachsen-Anhalts."

209. Agethen, "Der Widerstand," 31.

210. ACDP, III-013-800. January 30, 1948 report on the personal visit of *Kreis* executive member fromBorna.

211. ACDP, III-013-800. February 26, 1948 report from personal conversation with members of the provincial association for Saxony-Anhalt.

212. ACDP, III-013-630/3. Undated report regarding (name blacked out), industrialist.

213. Richter, *Die Ost-CDU*, 108.

214. BA-P, DO 1 7/38, 33b. Secretariat report on CDU meeting in Luchau on September 3, 1948.

215. Fischer, having spent his war years in Moscow, was a more reliable Communist than Reschke who had been in a concentration camp during the war; Naimark, *The Russians*, 366.

216. BA-P, DO 1 7/38, 34. Secretariat report on CDU meeting at Luchau on September 3, 1948.

217. BA-P, DO 1 7/38, 36. Secretariat report on CDU meeting at Luchau on September 3, 1948.

218. Rüdiger Henkel, *Im Dienste der Staatspartei* (Baden-Baden: Nomos, 1994), 153-154.

219. The LDPD declaration is reprinted in Suckut, *Blockpolitik*, 255-256.

220. Norbert Mattedi, *Gründung und Entwicklung der Parteien in der Sowjetischen Besatzungszone Deutschlands, 1945-49* (Bonn: Deutscher Bundes-Verlag, 1996), 142.

221. Minutes from the Central Block sitting of August 5, 1948; Suckut, *Blockpolitik*, 276-277.

222. Brigitte Itzerott, "Die Liberal-Demokratische Partei Deutschlands." In Hermann Weber. *Parteiensystem zwischen Demokratie und Volksdemokratie: Dokumente und Materialien zum Funktionswandel der Parteien und Massenorganisationen in der SBZ/DDR* (Cologne: Verlag Wissenschaft und Politik, 1982), 199-200.

223. "Das Eisenacher Programm"; Weber, *Parteiensystem*, 202-205.

224. ADL, LDPD #2782. Speech by Dr. Hamann in Erfurt on October 31, 1948 entitled: "Political and Economic Questions of the Day."

225. For details on SMAD orders, see Jan Foitzik, *Inventar der Befehle des Obersten Chefs der SowjetischenMilitäradministration in Deutschland (SMAD) 1945-1949* (Munich: K.G. Saur, 1995).

226. ADL, LDPD #2780. Protocol from the meeting of the LDPD provincial association for Thuringia on February 8, 1948.

227. Fricke, *Opposition*, 61.

228. Hans-Uwe Feige, "Die Leipziger Studentenopposition (1945-48)", *DA* 26 (1993): 1061.

229. Quoted in Connelly, "East German," 274.

230. Fricke, *Opposition*, 61; AdsD, ZASS T/C 15 1948-49. Article from Volk F. newspaper of February 5, 1949: "Studenten kämpfen in der Sowjetzone." Natonek was amnestied in 1956

231. Connelly, "East German," 296.

232. Wolfgang Möhring, "Von der Legalität zum Widerstand," in Rektor der Friedrich-

Schiller-Universität, ed., *Vergangenheitserklärung an der Friedrich-Schiller-Universität Jena* (Leipzig: Evangelische Verlagsanstalt, 1994), 45. On Leisegang, see Robert Gramsch, "Der Studentenrat im Umbruchsjahr 1948" in above, 59-63.

233. Ammer, *Universität*, 42.

234. Ilko-Sascha Kowalczuk, "Die studentische Selbstverwaltung an der Berliner Universität nach 1945," *DA* 26 (1993): 919.

235. Ammer, *Universität*, 158.

236. ADL, #2509. May 16, 1949 speech by Esch to the Rostock LDPD group.

237. Ammer, *Universität*, 48-53.

238. December 9, 1955 letter from Trautmann to Naase regarding the matter of Arno Esch. Other members of the LDPD connected to Esch who were arrested were:Wiese, Posnanski, Kiekbusch, Mehl, Behrens, Kuhrmann, Neitmann, Groth, Krumm and Albrecht, all of whom were sentenced to twenty-five years labor. All were eventually released between 1953 and 1955; ADL, #2509

239. BStU, ZA, AS 229/66, 629. Yearly report for the K-5 for Saxony for 1948.

240. ACDP, III-013-800. May 14, 1948 report from Saxony-Anhalt on a May 9, 1948 CDU meeting of the *Kreis* association of Sangerhausen.

241. ADL, LDPD # 24914. August 20, 1948 report by LDPD *Ortsgruppe* Hohenstein-Ernstthal.

242. He was eventually released from the Soviet Union on October 16, 1956; Fricke, *Opposition*, 59.

243. Statistics compiled by the *Konrad-Adenauer-Stiftung*, 29. May 1996. Number 94RKO1. In 1947, 93 CDU members were arrested. In 1948, 133 CDU members were arrested. These numbers reflect only those cases which could be identified with the use of CDU documents. The true numbers were certainly higher. Karl Wilhelm Fricke suggests that 1948 marked the beginning of a "new era" in the removal of political opponents in the Soviet occupied zone; Karl Wilhelm Fricke, "Opposition, Widerstand und Verfolgung in der SBZ/DDR," in Brigitte Kaff, '*Gefährliche politische Gegner'* (Düsseldorf: Droste, 1995), 10.

244. SAPMO-BA, ZPA, IV 2/4/383 ZPKK, 11. August 12, 1948 letter to *Tribüne*.

245. SAPMO-BA, ZPA, IV 2/4/383, 415. October 11, 1947 resolution by Comrade Fritz Wolf at the party congress of the SED. Wolf was investigated by a party commission for his comments.

246. AdsD, SPD-PV-Ostbüro. September 15, 1947 report; June 11, 1948 report of the SED Betriebsgruppe Werk Mückenberg to the *Kreis* leadership of the SED in Bad Liebenwerda.

247. AdsD, SPD-PV-Ostbüro 0046 c. June 18, 1949 report from Ilmenau.

248. AdsD, SPD-PV-Ostbüro 0361/1. September 4, 1948 report.

249. Quoted in Osmond, 143.

250. ADL, LDPD #10383. January 31, 1949 report from the LDPD provincial association Mecklenburg to the party leadership. Italics added.

251. ADL, LDPD #13822. Protocol of the meeting of the LDPD of the *Kreis* association for Borna on October 26, 1949.

252. ADL, LDPD #12887. February 3, 1949 letter from the LDPD Lubbenau to *Kreis* association of Calau.

253. ADL, LDPD # 2782. Protocol of the sitting of the extended executive for the provincial association of Thuringia on November 26, 1949.

254. ADL, LDPD #2782. Protocol of the sitting of the extended executive for the pro-

vincial association of Thuringia on November 26, 1949. These insights into the population are rare. In the protocols of the LDPD provincial associations of Thuringia, Saxony, Saxony-Anhalt, Brandenburg, and Mecklenburg, there is very little sense of the view of the population. This absence is likely due to the Soviet representative's presence at these meetings.

255. ADL, LDPD #2782. Protocol of the extended executive of the LDPD provincial association of Thuringia on October 15, 1949.

256. SAPMO-BA, ZPA, DY 30 IV 2/15/1, Abteilung Massenagitation. Protocol of speech by Professor Hickmann in Chemnitz on 27 September 1949.

257. See the reports in AdsD, SPD-PV-Ostbüro, 0361/1.

258. AdsD, SPD-PV-Ostbüro 0360/1. There is an entire series of reports in this signature that repeat these themes. In particular, report from Mecklenburg May 28, 1949, Leipzig (undated), Report of May 12, 1949, Report of May 28, 1949, of November 23, 1948, and of July 28, 1949.

259. AdsD, SPD-PV-Ostbüro 0360/1 ibid. Especially report on travel impressions from the Russian zone June 26, 1949.

260. AdsD, SPD-PV-Ostbüro 0360/1. An July 8 ,1949 report on Aue noted that the Soviets had stepped up security in the region because of fear of worker unrest.

261. Kai-Uwe Merz, *Kalter Krieg als antikommunistischer Widerstand: Die KgU 1948-1959* (Munich: R. Oldenbourg Verlag, 1987), 60.

262. Merz, *Kalter Krieg*, 60. Hildebrandt also expressed to me that the many unjust imprisonments in the Soviet zone motivated him to found the KgU. Interview with Rainer Hildebrandt, Berlin, March 2, 1995.

263. See Merz, *Kalter Krieg*, 53-57.

264. Erdmann's background remains unclear. It appears, however, that he was involved in law practice in the eastern zone; Frank Hagemann, *Der Untersuchungsausschuss Freiheitlicher Juristen 1949-1969* (Frankfurt am Main: Peter Lang, 1994), 20-21.

265. Hagemann, *Der Untersuchungsausschuss,* 21.

266. Interview with Siegfried Mampel, April 4, 1995, Berlin.

267. Hagemann, *Der Untersuchungsausschuss,* 22.

268. Interview with Siegfried Mampel, April 4, 1995, Berlin.

269. Naimark, *The Russians*, 395.

270. MLHA, IV L2/4/1179. Position of the LPKK on the questions of the ZPKK from August 10, 1949.

271. ADL, LDPD #9139. Protocol of business committee of the LDPD provincial association for Saxony with the chairs of the *Kreis* associations on December 15, 1949.

272. SAPMO-BA, ZPA, IV 2/4/384. November 25, 1949 report on oppositional groups in the Berlin *Kreis* Treptow.

273. Richter, *Die Ost-CDU,* 72.

274. Dietrich Staritz, *Geschichte der DDR 1949-1985* (Frankfurt am Main: Suhrkamp Verlag, 1985), 23.

275. BA-P, DO 1 7/72, 16. April 21, 1949 orders by Dr. Fischer: "Bestimmungen für die Beihilfe bei den Delegierten-Wahlen zum Deutschen Volkskongress."

276. BA-P, DO 1 7/72, 16. April 21, 1949 orders by Dr. Fischer: "Bestimmungen für die Beihilfe bei den Delegierten-Wahlen zum Deutschen Volkskongress."

277. ACDP, III-013-630/3. March 5, 1952 report by Hermann Hieke, 1-2. See also AdsD, SPD-PV-Ostbüro 0361/1. Report on *Volkskongress* of May 15 -16, 1949 states that recounts were ordered by the SED.

278. AdsD, SPD-PV-Ostbüro 0361/1. Report on *Volkskongress* of May 15 and 16,

1949; Ibid., 0357/1 report. The historian Dietrich Staritz also claims that on the night of May 15, the Central Administration of the Interior ordered the provincial ministers of the interior to recount the disqualified ballots as "yes," but Staritz does not have archival evidence to support the claim; Staritz, 23-24.

279. BA-P, DO 1 7/72, 28. May 17, 1949 letter from Saxony-Anhalt police department to Kurt Fischer, signed Hegen.

280. BA-P, DO 1 7/72, 28. May 17, 1949 letter from Saxony-Anhalt police department to Kurt Fischer, signed Hegen.

281. BA-P, DO 1 7/72, 28. May 17, 1949 letter from Saxony-Anhalt police department to Kurt Fischer, signed Hegen.

282. Minutes of the Central Block sitting of June 8, 1949; Suckut, *Blockpolitik*, 408. Carl-Hubert Schwennicke was chair of the West Berlin LDPD provincial association which from 1947 opposed the LDPD leadership in the rest of the zone. In 1948 the two organizations formally split. Schwennicke's group, which included Hans Reif, Anton Schöpke, William Borm, and Waldemar Koch, believed that the path of compromise with the Soviets that Külz had adopted was a disaster because the Cold War was deepening, and the Soviet Union would not be willing to bend; Henkel, *Im Dienste*, 153.

283. Minutes of the Central Block sitting of June 8, 1949; Suckut, *Blockpolitik*, 411. At the same sitting, Goldenbaum of the DBD stated that CDU members of the election committee in Leipzig said during the counting of votes: "Another vote for us, a no vote."

284. Minutes of the Central Block sitting of June 8, 1949; Suckut, *Blockpolitik*, 415, 440, 467. Kastner also admitted that the LDPD had many disgruntled members: "Large sections, decisive sections of the LDPD are consciously cultivating a damaging bureaucracy, in order to sabotage our economic construction and our economic plan; ADL, LDPD # 2509. Letter of June 1949 from Trautmann, Berlin branch of LDPD *Ostbüro* to RIAS stated that many LDPD members were arrested in June 1949.

285. Minutes of the Central Block sitting of June 17, 1949; Suckut, *Blockpolitik*, 430.

286. Minutes of the Central Block sitting of June 17, 1949; Suckut, *Blockpolitik*, 433-435.

287. Minutes of the Central Block sitting of June 17, 1949; Suckut, *Blockpolitik*, 436.

288. Minutes of the Central Block sitting of June 17, 1949; Suckut, *Blockpolitik*, 440.

289. Minutes of the Central Block sitting of June 17, 1949; Suckut, *Blockpolitik*, 441-445.

290. Minutes of the Central Block sitting of June 17, 1949; Suckut, *Blockpolitik*, 441-445.

291. It is likely that SMT statistics, once compiled, will not prove definitive because the SMTs couched the sentencing of non-Nazi anti-Communists under the generic heading of "fascist." See above discussion. The inaccessibility of NKVD/MVD documents and the documents of the civilian affairs branch of SMAD hinders any attempt at obtaining arrest statistics.

292. The BStU continues to undertake the enormous task of locating and ordering material of the MfS archives. It is likely that once this process is complete, K-5 statistics on the other provinces will be available.

293. BStU, ZA, AS 229/66, 596. Yearly report for K-5 Saxony for 1948.

294. Richter, *Die Ost-CDU*, 48.

295. See the protocols of the LDPD provincial executives for Brandenburg, Mecklenburg, Saxony-Anhalt, Saxony, and Thuringia in ADL, LDPD #23921, 10320, 10399, 9138, 2782, 2780 and 7516.

296. LDPD reports from the Mecklenburg *Kreise* of Rostock and Schwerin do not contain mention of popular insecurity, whereas popular insecurity is mentioned in reports of local groups in Saxony and Thuringia, as well as in the reports of the provincial leadership in Thuringia. See the LDPD reports for the *Kreise* Bad Langensalza, Dessau, Borna, Erfurt, Gera, Rostock and Schwerin in the ADL. The CDU archive in the *Konrad-Adenauer-Stiftung* has yet to catalogue the *Kreis* level CDU documents which it received after the fall of the GDR. Thus the LDPD reports offer better evidence at present to regional differentiation in repression.

297. Suckut, "Die Entscheidung zur Gründung der DDR," *VfZ* 39 (1991): 126.

298. Suckut, "Die Entscheidung," 129.

299. Suckut, "Die Entscheidung," 131.

300. Suckut, "Die Entscheidung," 131.

301. Suckut, "Die Entscheidung," 133.

302. Richter, *Die Ost-CDU*, 193.

303. Suckut, "Die Entscheidung," 133.

304. Mattedi, *Gründung*, 153.

305. Richter, *Die Ost-CDU*, 199-203.

306. Richter, *Die Ost-CDU*, 202; Bloch, 143.

307. Richter, *Die Ost-CDU,* 202; Bloch, 145.

308. Protocol from October 9, 1949 *Kreis* conference; Suckut, *Blockpolitik*, 526. The head of the CDU in Luckau even put forward a proposal for a vote of no-confidence against Nuschke. The proposal was defeated; Reinert, 304.

309. Protocol reprinted in Suckut, *Blockpolitik*, 526.

310. Resolution printed in Suckut in Weber, *Parteiensystem*, 165-166. Reprinted *Union Teilt mit* 1949, Vol. 1 admits that there was much discontent within the CDU for agreeing to delay the vote and accepting the transformation of the *Volksrat* into the provisional *Volkskammer.*

311. Minutes of the October 4, 1949 meeting of the SED party executive, reprinted in Suckut, "Die Entscheidung," 161.

312. Mattedi, *Gründung*, 154.

313. ACDP, III-013-793 March 6, 1952 Report by Wilhelm Rost.

314. ACDP, III-013-793 March 6, 1952 Report by Wilhelm Rost.

315. Minutes of October 9, 1949 meeting of SED party executive, reprinted in Suckut, "Die Entscheidung," 170. The non-Marxist parties must have been anxious to hold elections. The parties were well aware of the widespread discontent, and internal polls suggested the parties would win 70 percent of the vote if elections were held in 1949; Siegfried Suckut, "Innenpolitische Aspekte der DDR-Grüdung," *DA* 25 (1992): 371.

316. Richter, *Die Ost-CDU*, 211.

317. Richter, *Die Ost-CDU*, 211.

318. Agethen, "Die CDU," 58.

319. Richter, *Die Ost-CDU*, 211. Agethen, "Der Widerstand," 35.

320. ADL, LDPD #9139. Protocol of the meeting of the LDPD executive of the provincial association of Saxony on November 3,1949 with the *Kreis* chairs.

321. ADL, LDPD #10386. November 1, 1949 situation report from the LDPD provincial association Mecklenburg to the party leadership.

322. ADL,LDPD #9139. Protocol of the meeting of the LDPD executive of the provincial association for Saxony on November 3, 1949 with the *Kreis* chairs. Member from Plauen speaking.

323. ADL, LDPD #10386. November 1, 1949 situation report from the LDPD provincial association Mecklenburg to the party leadership.

324. AdsD, SPD-PV-Ostbüo 0361/1. November 1949 report from Doberlug.

325. Interview with Karl Schirdewan, Potsdam, March 18, 1995.

Chapter 4

Dictatorship and Resistance in the New State

The Development of the Instruments of the SED Dictatorship

The Ministry for State Security

The present literature on East Germany's legendary secret police, the Ministry for State Security (MfS), is dominated by memoirs and journalistic accounts of the latter years of the organization, no doubt due to a thirst for information by those whose lives were recently affected by the MfS. Very little scholarly material on the earlier years of the MfS based on new sources has been written.[1] For a proper understanding of resistance in the early years of the GDR, however, both MfS reports on the population and a knowledge of MfS operation are important. The dynamic relationship between resistance and repression was amplified by the creation of the Ministry for State Security.

In December 1948, the Soviets and the SED dissolved K-5 and replaced it with the Main Directorate for the Defence of the Economy and the Democratic Order under the German Central Administration of the Interior. Leading Soviet security officials in East Germany were thereby forced to abandon their resistance to expanding German security services. The Main Directorate for the Defence of the Economy and the Democratic Order became one of three directorates within the Ministry of the Interior with the founding of the GDR on October 7, 1949.[2] On February 8, 1950, the *Volkskammer* of the new German

Democratic Republic removed the Main Directorate for the Defence of the Economy and the Democratic Order from the Ministry of the Interior and, with little fanfare, instated it as the Ministry for State Security, an organization that was dissolved in 1989 just a few months shy of its fortieth anniversary, at the time East Germany's largest employer, and an organization that oversaw a network of informants far thicker than that of Nazi Germany. In closed discussions, leading East German communist functionaries and members of the Soviet security apparatus in Germany pored over the records of candidates for the top posts in the new Ministry, finally settling on two veterans of the Spanish civil war to head the Ministry. Wilhelm Zaisser was named Minister of State Security, and Erich Mielke State Secretary.[3]

Although the *Volkskammer* resolution of February 8, did not outline the duties of the MfS, the SED certainly founded the MfS to secure the position of the SED in the GDR, as its motto "Shield and Sword of the Party" made clear. Initially, however, the SED's position was to be guaranteed by a hunt against specific oppositional elements, rather than blanket surveillance of the population.[4] These targets were primarily the non-Marxist parties and the anti-Communist resistance groups in West Berlin. In the end, Mielke's rhetoric that the MfS was founded to secure the societal system of the GDR against the "increased activity of spies, saboteurs and agents" proved somewhat truthful.[5] MfS concentration on spies and agents related directly to the increasing hostility between the Cold War adversaries. By 1950, the SED viewed the United States and its "satellite" West Germany as the GDR's principal enemy.[6]

In its early years, the MfS bore little resemblance to the gigantic system of infiltration that it had become by the 1980s. From a humble complement of 2,700 workers in 1950, the MfS grew to 4,500 by 1951, and to 5,000 by the spring of 1952. These numbers contrast sharply with the 91,015 official employees by 1989.[7] In 1955, Ernst Wollweber, head of state security from 1953 to 1957, talked of the original MfS as an organization in which "everybody knew everybody."[8] His statement that the number of informants from the broader population had increased dramatically to total "several divisions" by 1955 suggests that the number of informants, quite apart from the regular employees, in the initial years of the organization was also small.[9] Recent estimates suggest that 5,200 people were recruited as informants in 1950, 14,000 in 1951, and 15,000 in 1952. These figures must be treated with caution, however, as these do not indicate the number of active informants, nor the duplication in recruitment.[10]

The fact that KGB officers held leading positions in the MfS is well documented. In 1955, Wollweber revealed the extent of KGB influence in the organization: "Eight or 5 years ago, the apparatus of the Friends did the majority of the actual operative work of the Secretariat for State Security."[11] "The Friends" was SED vocabulary for the Soviets. KGB officers were intimately involved in the establishment and running of the MfS until the mid-1950s, when, partly as a result of the Soviet Union's recognition of GDR sovereignty, it withdrew many of its KGB advisors, although still retaining close links.[12] The MfS did not hide the role of the KGB in the early years of the MfS. Indeed, the MfS often proudly pointed to the close cooperation between the two intelligence organizations.[13]

The MfS was founded with a central headquarters in East Berlin and branches at all the *Land* (provincial) and *Kreis* (local district) levels. [14] Following the dissolution of the provinces in 1952, the SED correspondingly divided the MfS into *Bezirk* (regional district) levels. Important sites such as the sprawling Leuna factory complex, or the sensitive uranium mining operation in the Wismut region, also had their own branches.[15] The MfS was originally divided into departments (*Abteilungen*), which over time, and not uniformly, became Main Departments (*Hauptabteilungen*).[16] Key departments in the MfS at this time were Department V, headed by Fritz Schröder and his first deputy, Erich Jamin,[17] which was responsible for monitoring and fighting underground opponents such as the anti-Communist organizations based in West Berlin; Department VI, responsible for the non-Marxist parties in the GDR, the churches, and "sects"; Department III, which was responsible for protecting economic installations; and Department II which was responsible for intelligence operations in West Germany.[18] Although Department II conducted operations in West Germany, the MfS was not equipped with a foreign espionage division. A small GDR foreign espionage service was established within the Foreign Ministry, rather than the MfS, in 1951.[19]

Department V conducted all observations and penetrations of oppositional groups and forwarded the information to the department responsible for carrying out arrests, Department VIII.[20] Although Department V was not responsible for arrests, these had to be approved by Department V first.[21] It remains unclear which department was in charge of penetrating organizations in West Germany and West Berlin, but it is likely that Department V's Section 5 responsible for "western operations" (*Westarbeit*) and Department VIII, which, apart from arrests, planned and executed measures against individual persons, groups, and sites in the "operations theatre" of West Germany and West Berlin, combined on these operations.[22] Additionally, Department VIII coordinated contacts with the *Volkspolizei*.

The *Volkspolizei* and the MfS cooperated closely in fighting opposition in the GDR. The *Volkspolizei* deferred all cases that had even slightly political overtones to the MfS for further investigation, including cases relating to workers who had been negligent on the job, for example, because of their attempts to "sabotage" the GDR's economy.[23] The *Volkspolizei* played an important role in carrying out MfS orders dealing with opponents of the regime, including arrests and house searches.[24]

At an early stage, the MfS began compiling a card catalogue of elements in the GDR that were "undermining" socialism and of former active Nazis. A directive from September 1950 called for the systematic registration of these "enemies," which it listed as: agents of foreign spy services, terrorists, saboteurs, participants in "illegal Schumacher work" (a reference to SPD resistance), Trotskyists, former members of illegal fascist organizations, former members of the Gestapo, the SD, and the *Abwehr*, leading figures in the administration of National Socialist concentration camps and prisons, former members of the SS and SA, leading functionaries in the NSDAP and the government, members of religious sects, and "other people." Although the "other people" category was all-encompassing, and given that any resistance could be termed "terrorism" by the SED, the SED nonetheless clearly focused on former active Nazis and western agents.[25] In fact, as we will see below, the campaign against western agents even took precedence over registering former active Nazis. If information from informants or official sources such as police investigations revealed that one of those registered was engaged in "enemy activity," a file would be started on that person. The MfS organized the files into *Einzelvorgänge* for individuals and *Gruppenvorgänge* if a group of individuals was involved in subversive activity. Initiating a file required the consent of the Minister of State Security himself or one of his designated representatives such as the leaders of the MfS in the provinces.[26]

Among the initial orders which provided guidelines for the new organization were orders on the registration of individuals arrested by the MfS. People engaged in "anti-democratic" activity could be arrested with the approval only of the Minister for State Security, the State Secretary, the leaders of the Departments, the leaders of the MfS in the provinces, or their deputies.[27] Mielke paid at least lip service to legal procedure, noting that an arresting order had to be issued before the arrest and that a judge or public prosecutor had to be informed of the upcoming arrest. This document offers further evidence of the concern with western-based enemy organizations. The guidelines directed MfS workers to register criminals by the "severity" of the crime. Someone charged with, for example, having been a Gestapo agent and an American spy was to be registered under the "more important" crime of being an "Agent of the USA."[28]

On September 9, 1950, Mielke issued an order for the registration of informants from the general population, which separated informants into the categories of "secret coworkers" (*Geheime Mitarbeiter*), individuals who did not publicly work for the MfS but because of their direct contacts with enemy elements could provide information on "espionage and other illegal, anti-democratic" activities, and a second category called "informants" (*Informatoren*), individuals who were able to provide information not because of their contacts but rather their position, such as hotel owners, waiters, and insurance agents. A third category encompassed those who provided their homes as meeting places for the MfS. The orders warned to thoroughly examine individuals who provided these meeting places to avoid "treasonous" acts.[29] The instructions for recruiting these unofficial members of the MfS were vague, stating only that the recruitment had to take place in an MfS building and after a report on the individual in question had convinced the leader of the local MfS branch that he was a suitable candidate. If the individual agreed, the MfS required that he sign a form stating that he was willing to cooperate unofficially with the MfS.[30] It was not until the fall of 1952 that the MfS issued a detailed directive on the recruitment of informants. The MfS registered all informants in the central Department of Registration and Statistics on a 10 cm by 15 cm card which contained the following information: first and last name, birthdate, place of birth, address, class, occupation, nationality, political affiliation, date of recruitment, name of the MfS officer who had recruited the individual, and code name.[31] The registration and statistics department of each provincial ministry for state security compiled monthly reports on the fluctuations in the numbers of informants.[32]

MfS secret coworkers paid particular attention to the CDU in 1950. In November 1950, Mielke revealed the fact that lower levels of the CDU continued to oppose the SED by instructing MfS secret coworkers to penetrate the CDU. Mielke justified the penetration by claiming that the leading CDU functionaries who had recently fled to the West had left "bases" (*Stützpunkte*) in the eastern CDU. His claim was a thinly disguised reference to the fact that there were many CDU members who sympathized with those who had fled. In order to determine these opponents of the SED, Mielke ordered secret coworkers to investigate the contacts that members who fled had had in the CDU in the GDR.[33]

Although the MfS used secret coworkers to obtain information on specific oppositional elements of the eastern German population as illustrated in the above case, a web of informants for internal surveillance was not the main priority. In May 1951, the MfS expanded its information-gathering in the GDR modestly because of upcoming political activities such as a referendum and the world youth games in Berlin. Department VIa was to be expanded and situation reports from various sections of society to be collected.[34] Department VIa, however, was tiny and could not be a true center to evaluate the situation in the GDR. In the initial years, the recruitment of informants for the penetration of visible oppositional groups, especially those in West Berlin, took precedence. An internal MfS history alluded to this point, stating: "The [informants] were, from the beginning, the main strength of the MfS for penetrating the conspiracy of the enemy."[35] Directive 7/51 to combat the League of German Youth indicates that the MfS already had informants in this West Berlin organization by May 1951.[36] Likewise, in orders to secure the May Day celebrations in 1952, the MfS instructed the use of informants to determine "enemy" plans to disrupt the activities, and pointed out where to concentrate these efforts: the anti-Communist groups in West Berlin, such as the Fighting Group Against Inhumanity (*Kampfgruppe gegen Unmenschlichkeit*—KgU); the Investigative Committee of Free Jurists (*Untersuchungsausschuss Freiheitlicher Juristen*—UfJ); the Union of the Victims of Stalinism (*Vereinigung der Opfer des Stalinismus*—VOS); the League of German Youth (*Bund Deutscher Jugend*—BDJ); and the Soviet emigré organization National Labour Alliance (NTS).[37]

The KgU sabotage activities in the GDR, which included blowing up railway bridges, destroying monuments, and damaging factories, naturally drew the attention of the MfS. In April 1952, Wilhelm Zaisser called the fight against the

KgU one of the MfS's "most important tasks" and issued Order Number 60/52 instructing a more concerted fight against the KgU whereby all information on the KgU from any MfS department was to be passed on immediately to Department V.[38] The MfS furthermore believed that the KgU was infiltrating agents into all levels of the GDR government to bring the GDR to a standstill in preparation for "Day X," the day of an American-sponsored war against the socialist world. The greater number of MfS attacks on its workers in West Berlin and show trials of its members working in the GDR made visible the increased attention accorded the KgU. In 1952, two elaborate show trials against the KgU took place in the First Criminal Division of the Highest Court of the GDR with Hilde Benjamin, the soon-to-be Minister of Justice, presiding.[39] In February 1953 Mielke issued a directive to combat the KgU which included the by then familiar steps of finding suitable informants in groups likely to be targetted by the KgU and using these contacts to penetrate the center of the KgU.[40]

The MfS was initially, therefore, a small organization that dealt with clear opponents of the SED, such as the non-Marxist parties and the anti-Communist groups situated in West Berlin. The days of blanket surveillance of the general population were yet to come.

The *Volkspolizei*

The SED's establishment of para-military police forces marked the most important development in the police force in 1949. In that year, the SED began the establishment of a 45,600 strong para-military force out of the *Bereitschaften* units in the DVdI. This force consisted of twenty-four infantry units, eight artillery units, and three tank units.[41] After the founding of the GDR, the SED renamed the *Bereitschaften* department *Hauptverwaltung Ausbildung* (Main Department for Training—HVA) within the Ministry of the Interior and appointed Wilhelm Zaisser, the future Minister of State Security, its leader. The HVA continued to provide military training to these units, usually with weapons delivered from the Soviet Union.[42] The SED dominated the embryonic East German army, comprising 92.3 percent of the officers in the HVA.[43] The HVA also began to develop a navy and air force, founding the *Seepolizei* and the *Luftpolizei* in 1950.[44] The international tensions caused by the outbreak of the Korean War provided further impetus for the SED to increase the military training in the HVA. The HVA ranks grew by over 20,000 to number 52,000 by 1951, and they received more modern equipment.[45]

The SED had difficulty finding these new recruits, however, and the ones they did recruit often proved unreliable. Many young people were reluctant to undertake military training so quickly after the end of the war, and the unpopularity of the *Volkspolizei* solidified their reluctance. A Thuringian police report stated: "In general it must be said that the youth have little inclination for the *Volkspolizei*."[46] At a 1950 public election meeting in Batzow, one high school student criticized the *Volkspolizei* use of tanks and their conducting of nighttime detonation drills. He added: "I do not want anything to do with these people."[47] Furthermore, the units suffered from poor material conditions and low pay. These factors led to general discontent in the HVA and many desertions. In 1950, 600 men deserted from the HVA; in 1951, 395; and in 1952 nearly 1200.[48]

The SED also continued to secure its dominance in the regular police force. In September 1949, Heinrich Hoffmann, a vice president of the German Central Administration of the Interior, emphasized the importance of political reliability by proclaiming one of the main tasks of the police as "the fight for its internal consolidation."[49] To ensure that the police force was loyal to the SED, the SED expanded the *Politkultur* department within the police, and founded a *Politkultur Hochschule* in the fall of 1949 in Bad Freienwalde (which moved to Biesenthal in 1950) to train the expanded ranks of *Politkultur* officers.[50] The SED also attempted to secure political reliability by running intensive education sessions in the police, focusing on the history of the Communist Party of the Soviet Union and Marxism-Leninism.[51] The SED also formed reading groups within the police to discuss Soviet literature, such as Nikolai Ostrovski's *Wie der Stahl gehärtet wurde*, Michail Scholochow's *Neuland unterm Pflug*, and Alexander Fadejev's *Die junge Garde*.[52]

The Judicial System

The judicial system also came to be molded by the SED into an instrument to carry out the Communist program in the GDR. After the founding of the GDR, the government renamed the German Central Administration for Justice the Ministry of Justice but it did not undergo any significant structural changes. Max Fechner, former head of the German Central Administration for Justice, became Minister of Justice.[53] On December 7, 1949, the *Volkskammer* passed a law creating the *Oberstes Gericht* and the *Oberste Staatsanwaltschaft*,[54] which established an *Oberstes Gericht* to decide cases of "outstanding importance" of the first and last instance, and was under the leadership of the NDPD member Kurt Schumann.[55] The Politburo (later the *Sekretariat*) of the SED nominated the judges for the *Oberstes Gericht*, thus closely linking the judiciary to one party.[56] The SED dominated all levels of the judicial apparatus in the early 1950s, supplying 53.6 percent of judges by April 1950 and 86 percent of public prosecutors.[57]

As was the case with the *Volkspolizei*, the SED sought to improve the political reliability of the judicial apparatus. On December 11, 1951, the Politburo issued "measures for the improvement of the justice departments and their work in the GDR" which called for increasing the ideological level of those employed in the judicial field and an improvement of SED work within this field.[58] By 1952 there were eighty-one SED members employed in the Ministry of Justice, compared to four CDU members, one LDPD, and forty-nine who were without political affiliation. The SED was pleased with its political domination in the Ministry of Justice by 1952, reporting that there were no "enemies of the party" among the Ministry of Justice's employees, but also noted room for improvement, recommending that more "proletarian" elements be introduced into the SED leadership in the Ministry of Justice.[59] To ensure that the provinces could not oppose the central government on legal issues, the SED downgraded the provincial ministries of justice to *Hauptabteilungen* (except in Thuringia which was permitted to keep a Ministry of Justice until 1952), and removed prisons from provincial jurisdiction and placed them under the control of the *Volkspolizei* in the Ministry of the Interior.[60]

The GDR showcased its judicial system at the "Waldheim trials" of 1950. The SED leadership had requested from Stalin in September 1949 that the three remaining NKVD/MVD "special camps" be closed in order to boost the popularity of the SED in the GDR which was to be founded the following month.[61] The Soviet Union acquiesced and closed the three camps, releasing 15,038 prisoners and transferring 10,513 to the GDR's Ministry of the Interior for the remainder of their sentences. The release of prisoners did not necessarily improve the SED's standing. In Osterburg, the SED was concerned with a rumor circulating that those released from the "special camp" in Sachsenhausen were so weak that "the ditches along the road from Sachsenhausen were filled with ex-prisoners too weak to carry on."[62] Following the closure of the camps, the Soviets handed over 3,432 prisoners to the GDR's Ministry of Justice for sentencing.[63] The sentencings took place in the criminal division of the Chemnitz provincial court in Waldheim, Saxony, where the prisoners were being held. Dr. Hildegard Heinze, a *Hauptabteilung* leader in the Ministry of Justice handpicked the judges and prosecutors.[64] The trials, which often lasted only a few minutes,[65] took place behind closed doors with little regard for due process. In most cases, the judges refused to admit evidence, and sentenced the accused based on the Soviet protocol of the initial interrogation.[66] By June 1950, 2,981 of those handed over to the GDR for sentencing had been tried and sentenced.[67] Beginning on June 20, the SED attempted to demonstrate that all previous sentences were justified by staging show trials of handpicked war criminals from the remaining prisoners. The SED bussed in daily a carefully selected public to the Waldheim city hall where the trial was being staged.[68] The Waldheim trials launched the vigorous use of the judicial system as a political instrument in the newly founded state.[69]

Resistance to the SED Dictatorship

Resistance in the Non-Marxist Parties

In order to circumvent the free elections outlined in the GDR constitution, both the SED and the Soviet Control Commission pushed for the elections of October 1950 to the *Volkskammer* to be based on "unity lists."[70] In this type of election, a voter did not indicate a preference from a list of candidates, but either supported or rejected the list in its entirety. The leadership of the non-Marxist parties opposed unity lists but the Soviet Control Commission in the GDR stifled their protests. In January 1950, Vladimir Semyenov, the Soviet ambassador to the GDR, let the leader of the CDU know his views on unity lists: "You can have elections immediately, Mr. Nuschke, but only with unity lists. The elections that you desire are driven by mood, and affect the security of the occupying power."[71] At the March 15, 1950 Central Block sitting, both Nuschke and the leader of the LDPD, Hermann Kastner, still spoke out against unity lists.

The position of the leadership reflected sentiment at the lower levels of the party. Gerald Götting, general secretary of the CDU, stated: "There is sharp opposition to the unity lists everywhere in the Union,"[72] and added that "everywhere in the CDU, pamphlets were being distributed against the abolition of free elections."[73] Lower levels of the LDPD demonstrated similar opposition. The LDPD in Borna opposed unity lists fearing that they would facilitate an SED dictatorship.[74] In Gera, the LDPD stated that the independence of the individual parties must be maintained under all circumstances and that unity lists must be rejected. Still believing in the rule of law, these local LDPD groups justified their stance by citing the constitution's articles on free elections.[75] In *Kreis* Annaberg, the LDPD clearly rejected unity lists.[76] The rejection of unity lists was most prevalent in Thuringia where, of the thirty-two LDPD members of the provincial assembly elected in 1946, none offered themselves as candidates at the October 1950 election. Similarly, only four of the twenty CDU elected members offered themselves as candidates again.[77]

LDPD documentation suggests that the broader population also rejected unity lists. Dr. Hans Loch, the LDPD finance minister of the GDR, summarized the attitude of the population at the time as: "Opposition at all costs!" Dr. Walter Koenig, a member of the LDPD executive for Thuringia, also stated that the population was attempting to defend itself against the dictatorship of the SED by expressing a desire for separate election lists.[78] Popular lack of interest in the fall elections, discussed below, also suggests that the population opposed unity lists.

After three months of opposing unity lists, the non-Marxist parties in the GDR accepted unity lists on March 28, 1950, and officially announced at a Central Block sitting in May that unity list elections would take place.[79] The seats in the *Volkskammer* were allotted before the election, so that the SED received 25 percent of the seats, the CDU and LDPD 15 percent each, the NDPD and DBD 7.5 percent each, and the rest were reserved for the mass organizations such as the FDJ. At this election, and all subsequent, the *Volkskammer* issued an election act which listed the number of seats each party or organization was to receive in the next *Volkskammer*, regardless of the results of the election.[80] There are two reasons why the non-Marxist parties accepted this arrangement. As noted above, the parties abandoned opposition to unity lists given the position of the Soviet Control Commission in Germany. Second, as Michael Richter makes clear, CDU members did not want to push any issue too far, given the show trials of opponents taking place in the countries of Eastern Europe.[81] The acceptance of unity lists meant that the GDR became a *Volksdemokratie* and not a liberal parliamentary democracy which the constitution prescribed.

The SED took advantage of the newly founded Ministry for State Security to conduct extensive arrests of suspected political opponents throughout the GDR. In 1950 alone, there were over 78,000 people tried as political opponents.[82] Although there is still no definitive breakdown of the 78,000 sentences, certainly a considerable number would have been a result of the above mentioned purges within the SED and a result of removing oppositional CDU and LDPD members. The show trial of Leo Herwegen and Willi Brundert, discussed below, provides a clear example of this type of sentence. The sentencing of Günter Stempel, the LDPD general secretary, in December 1950 to twenty-five years for his opposition to unity lists is another example of the sentencing of political opponents.[83] The lack of CDU support for unity lists led to a wave of arrests of CDU members after the fall elections.[84] A portion of the verdicts were also handed down against individuals who conducted underground work in the GDR on behalf of anti-Communist groups in West Berlin, such as the eighteen high school students in Werdau. In sum, the SED used its system of justice against any politically dangerous opponent, which included both obvious opponents such as members of the non-Marxist parties and those who distributed anti-Communist pamphlets or disgruntled workers who called for strikes.[85] The number of "true" political opponents among those sentenced must await further research.

In 1950, the CDU suffered its largest number of arrests in one year in the GDR in the period under investigation.[86] On March 29, 1950, the MfS arrested Frank Schleusener, a CDU member of the Brandenburg legislature and mayor of Brandenburg, and allegedly killed him by torture.[87] The MfS claimed that he had committed suicide, but refused to return his body to the family.[88] The CDU mayor of Potsdam, Erwin Köhler, and his wife, Charlotte Köhler, were arrested in early 1950 and sentenced to death on December 2, 1950 for espionage and anti-Soviet propaganda. Soviet authorities quietly executed the Köhlers in the Soviet Union on April 10, 1951.[89] In *Kreis* Mühlhausen, Thuringia, the entire CDU *Kreis* leadership was removed from office and expelled from the CDU. In

Kreis Worbis, fifty CDU mayors were arrested. Leading CDU functionaries in Mecklenburg and Saxony-Anhalt were arrested. In Potsdam, the SMT sentenced thirty-four persons, nearly all CDU members, to twenty-five years labor.[90] In June 1950, the CDU mayor of Gransee, Meyer-Wüstenhagen, was expelled from the Block supposedly because he had "smeared" Communism (*Hetzer*).[91] The CDU chair in Wittenberge, Schätzel, was expelled for the same reason.[92] In Plauen, the SED orchestrated the arrest of thirty members of the CDU group there.[93] At the University of Halle, ten members of the CDU university group were arrested, nearly all of whom were sentenced to twenty-five years in prison.[94] By the end of 1950, attacks on CDU members had become so numerous that Otto Nuschke launched a formal complaint with the SED.[95]

The LDPD also suffered SED persecution. In March 1950, the chair of the LDPD *Kreis* association in Forst, Wilhelm Tietz, was expelled from the Block for being a "reactionary."[96] In August, the MfS arrested LDPD general secretary Günter Stempel and handed him over to the Soviet secret police. The Soviets later tried him and sentenced him to twenty-five years labor and deported him to Siberia. Stempel was released in 1956.[97] The MfS also arrested a number of LDPD members in Schwerin in October.[98]

The SED justified these attacks on members of the non-Marxist parties by claiming that they were cooperating with foreign secret services. An SED declaration of August 1950 stated: "It has been proven that in both 'bürgerliche' parties, in the CDU and the LDP, Kaiser's spy centre has formed a solid basis."[99] The MfS directive dealing with penetrating the CDU, outlined above, demonstrates that the SED employed the MfS to determine which CDU members had contacts with, or held beliefs similar to, Kaiser.

The SED further used show trials to legitimize to the public its conduct against the non-Marxist parties. At a trial appropriately held in the Dessau theater, the largest in Germany, Leo Herwegen, the CDU minister for Work and Social Policy in Saxony-Anhalt, Dr. Willi Brundert, a former SPD member of the SED, and others were accused of economic sabotage.[100] SED jurists believed in show trials as an instrument to frighten the population into obedience, and therefore arranged for massive propaganda to accompany them.[101] During the Dessau show trial, the SED tried to promote its legitimacy by "exposing" the West German/American "imperialists" who sent spies and saboteurs into the GDR.[102] The Dessau show trial took place in April and May 1950, in front of roughly 1400 people who were bussed in daily.[103] There were simultaneous broadcasts on the radio as well, all of which suggests that Willi Brundert's conclusion about the trial was accurate: "It wasn't about the truth; it was about propaganda." After a month of the trial, the SED launched a massive press campaign to convince the population that there was a capitalist conspiracy at work through Brundert and Herwegen, and invited the entire town to attend the announcement of the verdict on the square in front of the theater on May 4, 1950. The SED also issued a series of pamphlets to advertise the upcoming verdict.[104]

Although Dessau had a population of roughly 90,000, only 300 showed up to hear the sentencing of Brundert and Herwegen to fifteen years in prison.[105]

The persecution of non-SED party members, and other widespread injustices, caused several members of the non-Marxist parties to speak out. CDU member Peter Bloch complained of injustice and despotism at a sitting of the CDU faction of the Brandenburg provincial assembly in early 1950.[106] In March, the CDU party executive removed him from his position and expelled him from the party,[107] causing Bloch to seek refuge in the West.[108] Alfred Gruner, a member of the CDU executive for Saxony-Anhalt and *Kreis* chair of Genthin, announced he was resigning from his posts because of the lack of CDU opposition to the SED. In his letter of resignation, he emphasized the lawlessness in the GDR, stating that his rejection of the CDU's political course during the past few months brought risks to his own safety, and he wanted to be careful that he did not follow the same path of other CDU members who had "disappeared without a trace" in 1947 and 1948. He added: "I could name many more sentencings of youths to 15-25 years labour, the last of which occurred when the GDR was presumably sovereign, and therefore for which the government of the GDR is guilty."[109] He also complained that Nuschke's silence in these matters made him an accomplice. In the town of Wachstadt, the CDU chair proclaimed at a public farmers' assembly that "an anti-Marxist Block" had to be founded.[110] In *Kreis* Leipzig, Krahmer of the CDU said he would only work with the SED if they curbed the activity of their "Politicians of the Fist" (*Faustpolitiker*).[111] In January 1950, the Soviet Control Commission removed Hugo Hickmann, the chairman of the CDU in Saxony, from his position for having criticized the SED's use of force and its leading-role claim. Hickmann remained in the GDR after his removal and died in Saxony in 1955.[112]

Lower levels of the LDPD echoed these concerns about the use of force to remove real and potential SED opponents. In *Kreis* Döbeln, Dr. Werner, the vice chairman of the Hainichen LDPD, thundered: "With the Nazis it was bad enough, but what we have today is an even bigger terror."[113] During an LDPD public election meeting in preparation for the elections in the fall of 1950, one LDPD member brought out SED persecution: "People should carefully reflect on what they will be electing on October 15. Members of the SED report to the authorities the names of those who listen to RIAS [Radio in the American Sector of Berlin], and these people are then arrested."[114] LDPD opposition during the preparations for the October vote found resonance in the population. In Saxony-Anhalt, at an election meeting in Schochwitz (Halle) the LDPD candidate Buchholz said: "After the election, I am going to resign and work only for my party. I am no friend of the Soviet Union, and if I am rejected for standing as a candidate, that doesn't scare me."[115] He received tumultuous applause for his comments. In Gottscheina (Leipzig), the LDPD candidate Christina Hack viciously attacked the SED: "Those who are in at the moment are criminals just like Hitler. God wanted Thälmann to be murdered in a concentration camp. Pieck and Grotewohl will get theirs soon."[116]

As was the case during the era of Soviet occupation, the campaign against political opponents produced a differentiated response. The SED campaign against the CDU on the one hand removed many political opponents and caused other oppositional members to leave the party, but on the other hand drove still others to resist the SED more strenuously.[117] A number of CDU resistance groups in the GDR were founded in 1950 including the *Arbeitsgemeinschaft Alte Union*, the *Jakob-Kaiser-Gruppe*, the *Christlich-Demokratischer Kampfbund in Mitteldeutschland, Deutsche Freiheitsliga, Immer bereit sein, Camemberth*, and *Deutsche Widerstandsbewegung gegen den Kommunismus*.[118] The groups, often working with the more aggressive anti-Communist groups stationed in West Berlin, the Fighting Group Against Inhumanity and the Investigative Committee of Free Jurists, spread pamphlets, sent secret radio reports to the West, listened to western broadcasts, delivered reports to the CDU *Ostbüro*, painted anti-SED graffiti on public buildings, and put up anti-SED posters.[119]

Repression in the GDR motivated Norbert Sommer, a CDU member, to engage in resistance work. For over a year, he secretly distributed pamphlets in Sonderhausen that proclaimed: "Freedom for the eastern zone!" and "Against Stalinism!" before abandoning his activities for fear of the authorities closing in.[120] His fears turned out to be justified, as he was arrested in September 1952, and sentenced to seven years in prison. He was amnestied on July 10, 1956 and settled in West Germany.[121]

One of the larger CDU resistance groups, the group "Michael" based in Halberstadt, consisted of between fifty and sixty people—a staggering number under the circumstances—composed mostly of former *Wehrmacht* officers who had joined the CDU or the LDPD. Werner Westermann, the CDU mayor of Waldersleben served as a contact between the CDU *Ostbüro* and the group. The group furtively spread anti-bolshevik pamphlets and posters, but may well have had bigger plans. The group "Michael" stood out for its sizeable possession of arms, including grenades, one machine gun, two artillery pieces, and enough weapons for 300 people, all of which the group stashed in the Langensteiner mountains. After a trip to Berlin on December 6, 1950, two members of the group, Engelbert Lohse and Rudi Fuhrmann, were arrested; shortly thereafter, fifty-five other members of the group were taken into custody. It appears that Fuhrmann exposed the group, as he was released shortly after the arrests. The fate of these resisters remains undetermined, although Westermann suspected that they had been deported to the Soviet Union.[122]

In May 1951, the LDPD resistance group "Scherenfisch" used small rockets to send pamphlets raining over a crowd of 30-40,000 at a sporting event at an unspecified location in the GDR.[123] Later in the year, eight LDPD members in Weimar, including Otto Sickel, an LDPD *Kreis* member of parliament, were arrested for distributing anti-Communist pamphlets. A Soviet Military Tribunal sentenced all members of the group on October 3, 1951 to twenty-five years labor.[124] These groups did not always confine themselves to distributing pamphlets, but also engaged in espionage. Various CDU *Ostbüro* informants reported on the number of Soviet tanks near certain bases; the types of fighter craft seen in the skies; and the number of landings at certain airfields such as Frankfurt/Oder. The barracks of both Soviet and East German forces also came under scrutiny.[125]

The number of groups or individuals who distributed anti-Communist pamphlets began to wane by the end of 1950 because of the development of other methods to distribute pamphlets. Western-based anti-Communist organizations increasingly adopted balloons as a manner of distributing oppositional pamphlets in the GDR. Launching balloons from the western zones of Berlin or from West Germany both greatly reduced the risk to individuals involved in distribution and increased the area covered.[126]

The Communist pressure which had begun in force during the debate on unity lists succeeded in placing pro-Communist candidates at the head of all CDU provincial associations by the end of 1950. By the Fifth Party Congress of the CDU in September 1950, the CDU had been essentially forced into line (*gleichgeschaltet*).[127] All CDU provincial associations reported that the CDU cooperated to a greater degree with the SED in carrying out the SED-sponsored "referendum against remilitarization and for the conclusion of a peace treaty" of 1951 than it had done during the 1950 elections.[128] In October 1951 the CDU abandoned Kaiser's "Christian Socialism" platform for the party and adopted the pro-Communist "Christian Realism." After the Second Party Conference of the SED in July 1952, the CDU officially recognized the leading role of the SED in all branches of state and society. By the Sixth Party Congress of the CDU in September 1952, the CDU had fully become an instrument of the SED.[129] CDU support for Communism translated into a decrease in its membership from 206,114 in 1950 to 164,250 in 1952.[130] The drop in membership related directly to opposition to the CDU's course. In 1950, 59.2 percent of those who left the party did so because of political considerations; 32.1 percent left because they moved (likely to the West); 4.2 percent of the decline was due to death; and only 1.7 percent were expelled from the party.[131]

The LDPD followed a path similar to that of the CDU in bowing to Communist pressure, becoming nearly fully coopted by 1951. One LDPD member even reported that members of the party in Dresden felt it was "undesirable" to discuss liberalism at the party meetings.[132] After Stempel's arrest in 1950, the new general secretary of the LDPD, Herbert Täschner, led the LDPD on a pro-Communist course, beginning by adopting the "democratic centralism" model of the SED for the LDPD's governing structure. At the LDPD Party Congress in Eisenach in July 1951, the LDPD agreed to support the SED in integrating the remaining private enterprise into the socialist economy of the GDR,[133] thus abandoning one of the central tenets of the party. This course did not find unanimous support in the general membership. During the party vote of 1951, one third of the candidates opposed Dr. Hans Loch's candidacy for chair of the party because of his support for the Eisenacher programme.[134] The LDPD also suffered a significant drop in membership. In December 1949, the LDPD comprised 184,842 members. By June 1951, that number had been reduced to 155,417.[135] The LDPD leadership likely acquiesced to the SED dictatorship due to fear of reprisal. Manfred Gerlach, an LDPD member who publicly supported the SED, is reported to have said: "If all-German talks do not come about in the near future, and the present conditions persist, nobody will be able to save our party from liquidation. The wave of arrests which will take place will be the likes of which we haven't seen."[136]

Popular Resistance to the SED

Historians attempting to trace developments in the East German population prior to 1952 face source constraints. As outlined above, there was no systematic reporting within the MfS on developments in the broader population as the Department charged with generating reports on the population—Department VI a—was a small department within a small organization. The reports of this branch have, in any case, yet to be located within the labyrinth of the former MfS-archives,[137] yet it would be surprising if this information contained systematic evaluation of the situation in the GDR given the size of the department. The expansion of the MfS information-gathering network after the June 17 revolution provided future historians with a much broader source base and systematic internal evaluations on which to judge popular developments. Although the police did not engage in full-scale monitoring of the population, it did collect information during crucial events. *Volkspolizei* situation reports are employed in this study.

Similarly, and perhaps surprisingly, the leading organs of the Communist Party, the Politburo and the Central Committee, did not establish until 1952 a department for systematic evaluation of the situation in the GDR. The Central Committee department *Leitende Organe der Parteien und Massenorganisationen* (Leading Organs of the Parties and Mass Organizations) provided the SED leadership with systematic assessment of popular developments and provided future historians with a wealth of information. Prior to 1952, the Central Committee relied on lower level reports from party members on specifically requested information, such as the state of the harvest.

Reports of the CDU and LDPD also have limitations. The LDPD reported only sporadically on popular developments prior to 1953, and no information reports survived from local CDU groups prior to 1953.[138] The records of the Free German Trade Union (FDGB), although limited to analysis of the situation in factories, hold promise for future researchers.[139]

Given the restrictive source situation, historians must look to manifestations of popular will. Two points in particular suggest that a fundamental resistance to the Communist system was present in the population. First, the period between 1945 and 1949 demonstrated widespread popular support for the non-Marxist parties in the GDR. The support for these parties was at once a rejection of the SED and support for the end of the Communist system in eastern Germany. The evidence presented in this study furthers Michael Richter's assertion that elections in the fall of 1949 would have returned a majority vote for the CDU and the LDPD.[140] The conduct of the SED and SMAD outlined in the previous chapter certainly suggested a great fear of the popularity of these parties. Popular support for the non-Marxist parties continued in 1950, but support waned as these parties became coopted into the Communist system.

Second, the repressive measures adopted by the SED dictatorship from 1945 to 1950 undermined popular trust in the political system in the GDR. This attitude was most evident in the popular rejection of the SED's instruments of control, making the situation in the GDR at this time indeed comparable to that of a latent civil war.[141] The historian Wolfgang Eisert's conclusion is accurate: "In so far as the police increasingly became an armed instrument of the SED, it aided in undermining the conditions necessary for democracy. Police protective functions . . . lost out to the pushing through of the SED's claims to power."[142]

Popular Support for the Non-Marxist Parties

The rejection of the SED meant that the non-Marxist parties continued to enjoy widespread support in the early months of 1950, before they were forced to embark on a pro-Communist course. In the province of Mecklenburg, the CDU and the LDPD called for new elections in February because of their certainty of victory. Both parties issued orders to their members at the *Kreis* and *Gemeinde* level to request the dissolution of the local assemblies and the holding of new elections. Although both parties knew of the deep disenchantment with the SED, they had to appear non-confrontational. The LDPD proposal for new elections carefully worded the popular opposition to the SED: "To successfully rebuild, local administrations must have considerable support. They can only gain this support when they have the confidence of the people. This is evidently not the case today. It is most probable that the SED majority would disappear."[143] The LDPD leadership in Mecklenburg added: "Whoever rejects the application for the dissolution of the *Kreis* and *Gemeinde* assemblies proves his fear of new elections, and of the true opinion of the people."[144]

The SED did, in fact, note the popularity of the non-Marxist parties in Mecklenburg and Brandenburg. In May 1950, the SED in Mecklenburg complained of the strength of the CDU in *Kreis* Malchin. In one *Gemeinde*, the SED dropped from thirteen members to two, and the newly formed CDU group immediately received twenty members.[145] In the *Gemeinde* Joachimsthal, an LDPD membership campaign resulted in 100 new members.[146] In *Kreis* Angermünde, the SED complained about how quickly the LDPD succeeded in establishing a local factory group.[147] One SED report concluded that the widespread support for the LDPD and CDU was hindering the development of a "democratic consciousness" in the population.[148] The strongest evidence of significant popular support for the CDU and LDPD remains the conduct of the SED. The insistence on unity lists and the vigorous MfS campaign to force the parties into line reveal the grave fear in the SED of these parties' popularity. Moreover, it should be remembered that the Soviets established two other parties, the NDPD and the DBD, in order to siphon away supporters of the CDU and LDPD.

The Relationship of the Population to the Volkspolizei

Popular rejection of the *Volkspolizei*, which emerged in the earlier years under investigation in this study, continued in the 1950s. In an internal report on the 1950 elections, the police complained that during random identification checks in restaurants, patrons usually insulted and often attacked the police officers.[149] In the week prior to the elections in 1950, seventy-nine assaults on *Volkspolizei* personnel took place in the GDR.[150] The impact of repression on the East German population is further revealed in *Volkspolizei* reports on the election meetings (meetings at which candidates were presented to the public) and rallies prior to the election. Between September 17 and October 2, the *Volkspolizei* authored six reports summarizing the situation at election-related events throughout the GDR. Repression was a primary topic at these events. At a public election meeting at a shoe factory in Brandenburg, one man in attendance stated: "These days nobody has the nerve to open his mouth. Everyone is scared of being picked up. . . . The population is numb from the continuous politics accompanied by marching music on the radio."[151] At an LDPD meeting in Tauer, Brandenburg, an undercover *Volkspolizei* officer questioned the LDPD candidate on his position during the Third Reich. The vast majority of those in attendance became suspicious, called the man an SED spy, and forced him to leave the hall.[152] At the end of an election rally in Storkow, Brandenburg, a miner was arrested for criticizing the GDR, the *Volkspolizei*, and the Oder-Neisse border.[153] In the six police reports written between September 17 and October 2 on public election meetings throughout the GDR, the topic of repression or hostility toward the *Volkspolizei* was mentioned most frequently. There was again regional differentiation here. Saxony-Anhalt and Brandenburg reported these types of incidents, while in Saxony, Thuringia, and Mecklenburg, specific anti-repression sentiment was not expressed in the election meetings.[154]

Reports from SPD *Ostbüro* informants in the GDR at the time of the election also reflected popular fears due to insecurity. The reports stated that the low standard of living, combined with the surveillance and spying, was causing the population to be increasingly disgruntled.[155] Letters from individuals in the GDR to the western SPD asserted that the vast majority of the population rejected the "terror regime," but that the population felt that there was little that could be done as long as the "Russians and the NKVD" remained in Germany.[156] One SPD member who escaped from prison in Bautzen and spent eleven days en route to West Germany was astonished at how ordinary people helped his escape: "The most striking experience of my escape was the willingness of other people in the Soviet zone to help me."[157]

Several church members also spoke out against the repression. In *Kreis* Niesky, a Protestant minister declared: "[The SED] talks of peace, but spreads hate. [The SED] talks of freedom, but subjugates others."[158] In March 1950,

Otto Dibelius, the bishop of Berlin-Brandenburg, and Heinrich Grübner, the provost of the Marienkirche in Berlin, met with Grotewohl to discuss the "prevailing questions of the day," which included SED "hate propaganda" and prisoners in the GDR.[159]

These incidents of popular resentment of the *Volkspolizei* because of its role in repression in the GDR represented a general trend against the *Volkspolizei.* Ulbricht acknowledged that this was the case during a speech to the *Volkspolizei* in Rostock in August 1950. Ulbricht candidly stated that the population did not assist the *Volkspolizei* in fighting opponents of the GDR: "Everyone knows where the enemy sits in the GDR, except the instruments of our state."[160] Ulbricht believed that a more "scientific" approach to police work would improve the *Volkspolizei's* relationship with the population. He said that if such an approach were adopted, the population's view of the police would change, and in situations "when enemies attack *Volkspolizei* officers and the officers retaliate, then the population will accept this and support the police officers," indicating that this had not been the case up to that point. Ulbricht was concerned about police excesses because of their negative effect on German unity: "To win over patriotic forces in West Germany, the question of how things look in the German Democratic Republic is of utmost importance. Is it orderly and democratic? Are democratic laws upheld? Our recommendations for unity will have greater resonance if things look orderly, than if the population talks of . . . conflicts with the police etc. That means that each police officer must be aware of the heavy responsibility that he has with regard to upholding democratic laws, and the importance this has for peace, the unity of Germany, and the preparation for all-German democratic elections."[161]

One aspect of police work which does not fit this pattern was the development of a volunteer system, enabling citizens to assist the *Volkspolizei.* The SED introduced this system in 1952 and obtained 27,000 volunteers by March and 35,000 by June 1953.[162] The rise in the number of volunteers does not necessarily indicate support for the police force, however, as there were attractive perks for volunteering. Police surprise at the revolution of June 17, 1953 suggests, in any case, that the volunteer system was deficient,[163] although part of the rise in the number of volunteers should nevertheless be attributed to those acting out of political conviction.[164]

MfS difficulties in recruiting informants from the general population also suggest a distrust of the SED's instruments of control. During "Operation Twilight" against a religious sect in the GDR, Mielke complained that informants often refused to cooperate with the MfS and that those who did were often negligent.[165] After the 1953 revolution, Ernst Wollweber, the new head of state security, issued Directive 30/53 which called for a substantially increased informant net and better qualified informants.[166] The extensive public relations campaign of the Secretariat for State Security[167] in the aftermath of the June 17, 1953 revolution to soften its image and convince the population to cooperate with it also suggests that the MfS had had difficulty gaining popular support.[168]

The Relationship of the Population to the Judicial Apparatus

Popular rejection of the SED's repressive system of justice is also discernible in the early 1950s. The show trials, far from garnering support by "exposing enemies" in the population, alienated the population and eroded its confidence that the government genuinely represented its interests. Thomas Mann alluded to this effect in a 228-page letter to Ulbricht in 1951, in which he complained about the Waldheim trials and compared them to Hitler's *Volksgerichte.*[169]

Mann was not alone in voicing his concerns about the judicial system. At a trial in Plothen, the audience took up such a position against the public prosecutor, the judge declared the accused innocent out of fear of reprisal.[170] The sentencing of young people particularly angered the East German population. On January 10, 1951 in Dresden, the eighteen-year-old high school student Hermann Joseph Flade was sentenced to death for distributing anti-police pamphlets. The *Oberlandesgericht* of Dresden reduced the sentence to fifteen years in prison.[171] On October 3 1951, eighteen young people, mostly high school students from Werdau, were sentenced to a total of 124 years in prison for spreading pamphlets and having contact with the KgU.[172] The SED publicized the verdicts because the regime wanted to send a clear message to the population on the harsh treatment which opponents of the regime could expect.[173] The verdicts, however, simply contributed to the basic distrust of the regime, a result that was not lost on the SED. In 1951, the Ministry of Justice reported that: "The legal position of the *Obersten Staatsanwalt* in Berlin up to now has been that the 'young offender's act' [which limited sentences for youths who had committed crimes— GB] was not applicable in political cases. This will now be changed because it has led to undesirable results. In the future, these types of verdicts are not to be handed down, even in political cases. Although our judicial system has been accused of light sentencing in political matters, it is now accused of the opposite. If it is expected that prison sentences over ten years will be handed down, the verdict, if indeed such a verdict is deemed an absolute necessity, must be discussed beforehand with the Ministry of Justice of the GDR. . . . Public prosecutors are no longer permitted to request the death penalty."[174] This report revealed not only the popular discontent with SED judicial practice, but the close relationship between the SED and the judicial system. Franz-Josef Kos perhaps summed up best the relationship between the judicial apparatus and the population: "Political justice in the GDR, and especially the show trials, did not contribute to the legitimacy of the state, but rather burdened the relationship between the citizen and the judicial apparatus."[175]

The First Elections in the GDR, October 1950

The *Volkspolizei*-authored reports of the fall 1950 summarizing election-related events in the GDR reveal, at a minimum, that the forthcoming elections did not capture popular interest. In Bautzen, the police reported that the population avoided election meetings.[176] The population in *Gemeinde* Struholmersdorf and in Schmellbach, in Thuringia, stayed away in droves. In Schmellbach, only eight out of a population of 826 attended the election meeting.[177] When Fred Oelssner gave a speech at the world-famous Zeiss optics plant in Jena, workers sat without reaction, except to "laugh loudly" when Oelssner claimed that the living standard in West Germany was comparable to that of the GDR. At 4 pm, with Oelssner in mid-sentence, approximately one-third of the audience left because it was the end of their shift.[178] Workers at the Maxhütte factory in Thuringia refused to attend election rallies saying that they were fed up with the "complete overdose of political events."[179] In general, the press vastly overreported the numbers of those in attendance at election-related events because of the poor attendance, a practice that did not go unnoticed in Dresden where residents complained that the press had inflated attendance numbers at Prime Minister Grotewohl's speeches in Freital and Dresden.[180] Four of the six summary police reports on election gatherings taken between September 17 and October 2, 1950, reported a lack of interest in election-related events, a phenomenon that was particularly noticeable in Saxony and Thuringia.[181]

East Germans protested the elections by removing and/or defacing election posters, attacks which became so numerous that in the days before the election, the police established special detachments to guard election posters. These measures curtailed the number of defacings considerably, but the police still reported an alarming number of incidents of anti-SED graffiti or destruction of election posters. In the week before the elections in Mecklenburg, 567 cases of anti-SED graffiti or destruction of election posters were reported; in Brandenburg, 308; in Saxony-Anhalt, 246; in Thuringia, 320; and in Saxony 413, for a total of 1,864 incidents.[182]

SED election propaganda seems to have contributed to popular opposition. During a conversation on a streetcar, one man said to his companion that clearly the Russians had begun the war in Korea. Another passenger challenged the man stating that the Americans had begun the war, and was drowned out by laughter and shouting of the other passengers.[183] At a farmers' meeting in Bendeleben, *Kreis* Sondershausen, propaganda also played a role. One farmer pleaded with his colleagues: "We want to set aside politics once and for all and talk about farming issues. . . . Farmers, let me say something. Parties come and go. It was earlier so, and will always be this way. Farmers, let me say one thing. We will continue to exist. There will always be farmers."[184]

An episode in Joachimsthal also reveals the extent to which the population had become distrustful of SED propaganda. The SED had removed the LDPD mayor, Quast, and a CDU member of the *Kreis* council, Lipp, because of their alleged corruptness and unwillingness to work with the SED in the Block.[185] The SED organized a mass demonstration against the two politicians, but the propaganda display caused skepticism in the population. A rumor in the *Kreis* that youths armed with billy clubs were waiting at bus stops for Quast to drive him out of town confirmed popular suspicion. Upon hearing this rumor, people throughout the *Kreis* complained that the entire affair must have been the working of the SED in order to secure a favorable result at the fall elections. One person reported to a member of the SED that 90 percent of the population stood behind the deposed politicians, despite the massive propaganda display.[186] The popular discontent with the propaganda was made evident by the LDPD in March 1952 when the LDPD reported to the Soviet Control Commission in Erfurt: "There is great disappointment in the population because the propaganda and reality very often cannot be reconciled."[187]

The elections in October 1950 were, like the *Volkskongress* elections of the previous year, neither free nor secret. To achieve a place on the unity list, a candidate had to present himself to a panel of mainly SED, FDJ, and FDGB members. If the candidate responded in a manner displeasing to the panel, the panel rejected his candidacy. An example given by one witness said that in response to a question relating to war, the candidate was not to answer: "I am against all war," but rather that he was against an "unjust, imperialistic or capitalistic war," but not against a "justified, revolutionary war against an imperialist aggressor." In *Kreis* Wolmirstedt, all CDU candidates had to be replaced by more "reliable" ones.[188] The voting procedure itself was also dubious. Voters received ballots upon their arrival at the voting station, which they simply placed unmarked in the ballot box if they supported the list. In Thuringia, this led to confusion among election officers during the vote count because they were unable to distinguish the piles of uncast ballots sitting beside the boxes from the unmarked ones which "supported" the candidates.[189] If, however, the voter did not approve of the names, he went into a booth to vote. A member of the Communist Party youth group, the Free German Youth, noted the name of the voter as he entered the booth and requested that the voter fold the ballot, thus making it easier to identify the ballots that supported the list.[190] Clearly, voters who used election booths ran tremendous risk of reprisal. In Thuringia, the SED went so far as to adorn election booths with signs reading: "Whoever votes in a booth is a war monger."[191] The SED-dominated *Volkspolizei* secured the election gatherings and the election sites; East Germans could not turn to the security organs for assistance.[192]

The first elections in the GDR, at which 98 percent of the electorate participated, returned 99.72 percent support for the unity lists. Because of the agreed upon formula for distributing seats, the SED received 100 of the *Volkskammer*'s 400 seats, the CDU and LDPD sixty each, the FDGB forty, the NDP and DBD thirty each, the *Kulturbund* and FDJ twenty each, the *Demokratischer Frauenbund Deutschlands* and the *Vereinigung der Verfolgten des Naziregimes* fifteen each, and the VdgB and *Genossenschaften* five each.[193]

The SPD in particular conducted an underground campaign against the election of 1950. In May, a certain Müller gathered a group of former SPD members and drove to the Berlin office of the SPD *Ostbüro*, where they passed on crucial information on the police and the sensitive uranium mining operation in the Wismut region. Throughout September 1950, the group met at night in Müller's home in Zwickau and produced hand-written pamphlets urging voters to vote against the candidates in the October election. On the night of September 22, the group met as usual, writing pamphlet after pamphlet. As two members of the group slipped out of the house to distribute the material, the police emerged from around a corner and arrested both men. Other police officers then rushed in to Müller's house and arrested the rest of the group. The sentences for the group ranged from three months to four years in prison for "smearing [*Boykoktthetze*] against democratic institutions."[194] Other East Germans working for the SPD *Ostbüro* adopted a variety of methods to resist the elections of 1950, including sending 300 anti-Communist letters to Communist party members, and placing anti-Communist stickers in mailboxes and house entrances. These stickers often appeared elsewhere in town, having been passed on by unknown opponents of the regime. [195]

The SPD *Ostbüro* report on this group demonstrated shortcomings of the *Ostbüro*. The author complained that "only" 300 letters could be sent to SED members because of a lack of financial support, and that the *Ostbüro* had failed to provide materials such as leaflets ahead of time. Because of this organizational lapse, SPD members in the GDR attempted to obtain pamphlets at the last minute which led to unnecessary arrests. The author of the report wrote: "Luckily, we had already safely brought material here eight to ten weeks before the vote. If it had been handled this way in all cases, the personnel losses from acquiring the material at the last minute would have been avoided."[196]

The *Volkspolizei* increased its presence on the streets of the GDR to prevent further acts of resistance, and launched three operations: "Gustav," "Heinrich," and "Fritz" to combat underground pamphlets entering the GDR.[197] The *Volkspolizei* believed, as it happened correctly, that the material was being delivered by train from the western sectors of Berlin, and therefore concentrated on this target. The train lines Berlin-Erfurt via Wittenberg, Halle, Merseburg, and Weimar, and Berlin-Plauen, via Wittenberg, Bitterfeld, Leipzig, and Werdau were particularly active in the transport of oppositional material.[198] Police officers were formed into undercover units which boarded the trains and stationary units which remained in the stations. Stationary units patrolled waiting rooms, package counters, and platforms looking for suspicious packets. The distribution of the police units provides insight into the areas in which oppositional flyers were most prevalent. Brandenburg had six mobile, and six stationary units; Saxony eight and nine respectively; Saxony-Anhalt two and eighteen respectively; and Thuringia six and one respectively.[199] Saxony-Anhalt received the lion's share of police attention, while Mecklenburg apparently did not experience enough pamphlet activity to merit any additional police units. The operations prevented many resistance pamphlets from being distributed in the GDR. On September 24, the *Volkspolizei* captured SPD material bound for an SPD group in Plauen. On the same day, the *Volkspolizei* intercepted a CDU member working for the KgU who was distributing material. In Thuringia, the *Volkspolizei* confiscated "considerable amounts" of western-licensed newspapers.[200] In one week in September, the *Volkspolizei* reported confiscation of the following amount of "smear" material: Brandenburg 84,271, Mecklenburg 10,303, Saxony 55,373, Saxony-Anhalt 28,406, Thuringia 16,846, for a total of 195,201.[201]

The Saalfeld Disturbances[202]

The town of Saalfeld in southern Thuringia lies near the uranium mines of the Erzgebirge region, near the border with Czechoslovakia. The Soviet Union, which discovered the uranium in the hills along the border following the war, moved quickly to establish an extensive mining operation to remove valuable uranium for its atomic bomb projects. The Soviets realized that Germans would not readily volunteer to work the mines and thus conscripted roughly 100,000 Germans for the harsh work. Most workers were conscripted from the nearby large cities in Saxony, but the Soviets also conscripted laborers from as far away as Mecklenburg.[203]

Shortly after 6:30 pm on August 16, 1951, two rowdy and drunken workers from the Wismut mines stumbled through Saalfeld's market square and into the hands of *Volkspolizei* officers who promptly arrested the pair.[204] Word of the arrests quickly spread through town, causing nearly forty people to join a protest in front of the police station against the arrests. Several of the demonstrators forced their way into the police department to demand the release of their arrested friends. After being thrown out of the police office for the third time, these demonstrators joined the increasingly hostile crowd in front of the police station. The crowd soon began to loudly swear at the police officers, resulting in the arrests of two other demonstrators.[205]

The second set of arrests sparked further unrest. Because the demonstrators were aware that they did not have sufficient numbers to effectively protest the arrests, the demonstrators retreated into the town of Saalfeld to garner support. The leader of the local *Volkspolizei* took advantage of the absence of demonstrators to discuss the situation with his colleagues. During the respite from unrest, the head of the local *Volkspolizei* station, Commander Schaller, met with the head of the criminal police section of his station, *Oberrat* Hoeg, the head of the *Politkultur* section, *Rat* Kirch, and the Soviet leader of the Wismut complex. During the meeting, the Soviet representative declared that he would ensure that the proper safety precautions were taken within the Wismut complex, but he insisted that the *Volkspolizei* would be responsible for maintaing public security.[206] The trust that the Soviet representative put in the young *Volkspolizei* is notable. Shortly after the meeting had ended, renewed protests took place at the *Volkspolizei* office. Two women urged the now "large mass of people" to attack the station in the name of their comrades. The crowd surged into the lobby, shouting: "Free our mates (*Kumpel*)."[207] Neither the police officers on duty, nor a representative of the Soviet Control Commission were able to disperse the crowd through words alone. After making little progress, several women suggested that the time for negotiation had passed and that the demonstrators should resort to other measures to free the prisoners.[208]

At roughly 9:30 pm, nervous police officers in Saalfeld contacted the head of the criminal police in the provincial *Volkspolizei* office (*Landesbehörde*) for Thuringia, Inspector Zahmel, and informed him of the situation in Saalfeld. At the same time, they contacted the police stations in nearby Maxhütte and Rudolstadt, requesting reinforcements. The demonstrators shoved and insulted the thirty-six police officers from the Maxhütte station as they entered the station.[209] With the reinforcements, the number of police officers in the Saalfeld station rose to fifty.[210] Shortly after the arrival of the extra troops, Inspector Zahmel ordered that "under no circumstances" were weapons to be used.[211] Zahmel had received this order from Erich Mielke, State Secretary for State Security, who had been instructed by the SED General Secretary Walter Ulbricht. Clearly, the disturbance was of such a magnitude that the leadership of the Communist Party and of the security apparatus had been informed, and involved in how to deal with the disturbances.

The tense standoff in the police station continued. At one point, a police officer approached the crowd and tried to explain that the men who had been arrested had to remain in the police station because they had broken the law. The police officer could not finish his speech, however, as he was nearly pulled into the crowd. What happened next certainly came as a surprise to this officer, if not the entire complement of the station. At roughly 10 pm, after having discussed the situation with Wilhelm Zaisser, the Minister for State Security, Inspector Odpadlik at the provincial police headquarters for Thuringia ordered Inspector Zahmel to release the prisoners.[212] The crowd cheered but quickly interpreted the release as a sign of weakness, and correspondingly increased their demands. The crowd demanded the handing over of the *Volkspolizei* officers Hoeg and Enders, as well as the release of all other prisoners, who they assumed were in the police station. The crowd, strengthened by the addition of Wismut workers who were driving past the police station because of the shift change, soon turned violent. About fifty demonstrators broke into the upper levels of the building, and threatened the police officers with axes and picks, yelling: "Where are the scoundrels" and "Throw them out the window." The demonstrators smashed telephones, typewriters, and other office equipment and stole documents which were later burned on the market square.[213] Outside, several demonstrators threw rocks at the police station windows.[214]

As the situation still had not been brought under control by 11 pm, the Saalfeld police requested motorized forces from the provincial office for Thuringia, as well as extra officers from nearby police stations.[215] At roughly 11:15 pm, Odpadlik, Zahmel, Chief Inspector Menzel, who was at once a leading officer in the Thuringian police and Minister for State Security for Thuringia, appeared before the crowd.[216] Odpadlik climbed on top of a truck parked on the market square and addressed the crowd: "Mates! There is nothing wrong with Wismut workers drinking. (Applause.) What has happened here today however, is not right. I promise you, that the guilty officers will be reprimanded and that starting tomorrow, Saalfeld will have a true people's police, one that will represent the interests of the working class."[217] It was not until 2 am that demonstrators finally vacated the police station.[218]

The courthouse and its prison were also sites of unrest on August 16. The crowd released two Wismut workers there and threatened to hang the *Volkspolizei* officer on duty. This hatred directed at the *Volkspolizei* was notable later in the evening as well. At 1 am, workers in a truck drove around town shouting: "End the *Volkspolizei!*" It was not until 2 am that calm had returned to the streets of Saalfeld.[219]

Officers of the *Volkspolizei* in the town of Saalfeld feared further disturbances. During the night of August 16-17 1951, 530 *Volkspolizei* officers and 250 *Bereitschaftenpolizei* officers from Erfurt and Gera arrived in Saalfeld.[220] The arrival of approximately 800 police officers indicates the extent to which SED authorities deemed the situation in Saalfeld to be extremely precarious.[221] No major disturbances took place on August 17 however. For the most part, Wismut workers went to work peacefully, with one exception being a group of Wismut workers that, when passing by the court jail at approximately 10:00 am, shouted to the prisoners that they would be freed that night. The police suspected that the workers would steal explosivers from the mining complex in order to carry out the release of the prisoners.[222]

At 4:30 pm on August 17, the Thurigian Minister of the Interior Gebhardt, several officers from the Wismut mining operation, and *Volkspolizei* inspectors Engelmann and Zahmel met to discuss the situation. Gebhardt emphasized again that police officers were not to fire on the demonstrators.[223] The group agreed that the best approach to defusing the situation would be to bring in about 2,000 SED functionaries (Agitatoren) to introduce an element of stability to the demonstrations and to dissuade demonstrators from drastic action, thereby, in Gebhardt's words, "isolating the ring leaders." The job of organizing the functionaries was given to a high-ranking SED member, the SED first secretary for Thuringia.[224]

At approximately 5 pm, disturbances broke out once again in Saalfeld. Unlike the previous day, the main center of activity on August 17, was the court prison, where the demonstrators demanded the release of all Wismut workers. Gebhardt attempted to engage the approximately 150 demonstrators in dialogue, but was continually interrupted by "workers and Saalfeld business people" hurling insults such as: "Shut up you lying pig."[225] In order to quell the unrest, the crowd was permitted to select a delegation of three Wismut workers who would be allowed into the prison. The delegation determined that there were, in fact, no Wismut workers in the prison, and the crowd began to disperse.

SED members who had been sent to the market square to ensure that the small group demonstrating there did not escalate contributed to a minimization of the disturbances. A few demonstrators tried to break into the police department, but for the most part the demonstrators did not undertake any violent action. There were no serious disturbances on August 17, in Saalfeld.[226]

The police gravely feared popular reprisals after the disturbances. On August 24, the Saalfeld police reported: "Members of the *Volkspolizei* no longer feel secure even in their homes. They are especially concerned when duty calls them away and their wives are alone in the house."[227] One police officer refused to go to Weimar to investigate matters there as instructed, preferring to stay home and "protect his wife and family."[228] Fearing future attacks, the head of the *Volkspolizei* in Thuringia ordered increased security for stations in the area, including Saalfeld, Rudolstadt, Arnstadt, and Ilmenau.[229]

For our purposes, two aspects of the demonstrations in Saalfeld are worth stressing. First, the social makeup of the demonstrators deserves consideration. Although Wismut workers formed the bulk of the demonstrators, other social groups participated. As noted in the above account, "Saalfeld business people" and "vegetable dealers" actively participated in the demonstrations, making it perhaps understandable that the Saalfeld police concentrated on tracking down business people who had participated in the demonstrations. The willingness to engage in civil disobedience was not limited to workers.

The fact that these demonstrations lacked political overtones is also noteworthy. Political slogans and demands were absent, and political symbols of the regime left intact. As one officer noted: "It is extremely noteworthy that the bandits did not touch one political slogan, picture or poster during the plundering of the police department, not even in the slightest. For example, 'Der Ruf,' the newspaper of the [Free German Youth] remained in tact in the middle of a window, while the panes on either side of it were smashed."[230] The lack of political demands contrasts sharply with the June 1953 revolution, as discussed in the following chapter, and suggests that the events in Saalfeld resulted to a large degree from the population's distrust of and hostility toward the police.

Between the founding of the GDR and the beginning of 1952, the SED had succeeded in removing the most visible anti-Communist resisters in the non-Marxist parties. By the fall of 1951, both the CDU and the LDPD were well along the path to becoming instruments of the SED. This transformation resulted in an exodus of members from these parties, and at the same time limited, but more rigorous, underground resistance by representatives of these parties.

Between the founding of East Germany and early 1952, popular hostility toward the SED's repression apparatus is discernible. There was a visibly strained relationship between the population and the SED's instruments of control—the MfS, the *Volkspolizei*, and the judicial apparatus—although because the MfS was still in its infancy and concentrated on West Berlin targets, popular scorn tended to be directed toward the other two instruments. The Saalfeld disturbances provide an important case study of the tension between the *Volkspolizei* and the population.

In an automobile repair shop in Güstrow, Mecklenburg, one SED member commented on the day-to-day manifestation of the relationship between the population and the SED. "The workers are not open with me. It was like this as well with the Nazis. At that time, if a couple of workers were talking, and somebody came up to them wearing the party symbol, they would stop talking. When workers in our factory are talking and I come up to them, they immediately change the topic."[231] Beginning in the summer of 1952, the increased repression that accompanied the "building of socialism" pressured the strained relationship between the population and the SED, and contributed significantly to the explosive upheavals of the summer of 1953.

Notes

1. For memoir literature, see Josef Schwarz, *Bis zum bitteren Ende* (Schkeuditz: GNN-Verlag, 1994); Reinhardt Hahn, *Ausgedient: Ein Stasi Major erzählt* (Halle: Mitteldeutscher Verlag, 1990). The most important journalistic accounts include: David Gill, *Das Ministerium für Staatssicherheit* (Berlin: Rowohlt, 1991); Anett Schwarz, Arianne Riecker, Dirk Schneider, *Stasi intim: Gespräche mit ehemaligen MfS-Angehörigen* (Leipzig: Forum, 1991); Liehard Wawrzyn, *Der Blaue* (Berlin: K. Wagenbach, 1990); Peter Siebenmorgen, *"Staatssicherheit" der DDR* (Bonn: Bouvier Verlag, 1993). More scholarly works include Karl Wilhelm Fricke, *MfS intern* (Cologne: Verlag Wissenschaft und Politik, 1989) and the documentary edition Armin Mitter and Stefan Wolle, *Ich liebe euch doch alle!* (Berlin: Elefanten Press, 1990). The most useful work on the early years of the MfS remains Karl Wilhelm Fricke, *Die DDR-Staatssicherheit* (Cologne: Verlag Wissenschaft und Politik, 1989), which appeared before the fall of the Wall and thus does not contain new archival material. Jens Gieseke's recent *Mielke-Konzern: Die Geschichte der Stasi 1945-1990* (Stuttgart: Deutsche Verlags-Anstalt, 2001) is a useful introduction. For an introduction to East Germany's state security in English, see David Childs and Richard Popplewell, *The Stasi: the East German Intelligence and Security Service* (Houndmills: MacMillan, 1996).
2. Monika Tantzscher, "'In der Ostzone wird ein neuer Apparat aufgebaut'" *Deutschland Archiv* (Hereafter *DA*) 31 (1998): 49-52. See also her "Die Vorläufer des Staatssicherheitsdienstes in der Polizei der Sowjetischen Besatzungszone: Ursprung und Entwicklung der K-5," *Jahrbuch für Historische Kommunismusforschung* 7 (1998): 125-156. The two other directorates were the Main Directorate for Training and the Main Directorate for the German *Volkspolizei*.
3. Fricke, *Die DDR Staatssicherheit*, 24-25. Clemens Vollnhalls, "Das Ministerium für Staatssicherheit," in *Der SED-Staat: Neues über eine vergangene Diktatur*, ed. Jürgen Weber (Munich: Olzog Verlag, 1994), 54; Monika Tantzscher, "In der Ostzone," 54.
4. In November 1951, Mielke ordered the MfS to gather information and pictures on the members of the provincial executives of the LDPD, the CDU, the NDPD, the FDJ, and the VdgB; BStU, ZA, # 100828. November 15, 1951 Directive 1/51 from Mielke to the Minister of State Security in Brandenburg. The department charged with monitoring the broader population, Department VIa, was initially small. The BStU's internal researcher on this topic, Herr Wiedmann, defines Department VIa as an "extremely small apparatus"; Interview with Herr Wiedmann, April 28, 1997, Berlin. Following the revolution of 1953, the MfS greatly expanded its internal monitoring duties by creating "information groups" within the MfS. See the following chapter.
5. *Neues Deutschland* January 28, 1950.

6. Soviet authorites, on the other hand, were heavily involved in monitoring the eastern German population. As the former head of the KGB's German department writes: "MGB units . . . came under intense pressure from Moscow to control the population." David Murphy, Sergei Kondrashev, and George Bailey, *Battleground Berlin* (New Haven: Yale University Press, 1997), 36. Unfortunately, the scarcity of sources on the Soviet security apparatus in Germany prevent a systematic description of its activities.

For an outstanding overview of the institutionalized suspicion in Stalin's Soviet Union—including the associated obsession with western subversion—see Vojtech Mastny, *The Cold War and Soviet Insecurity* (New York: Oxford University Press, 1996).

7. Jens Gieseke, *Die hauptamtlichen Mitarbeiter der Staatssicherheit* (Berlin: Ch. Links, 2000), 86-87. Gieseke's work provides more reliable data than earlier treatments such as Clemens Vollnhalls, "Das Ministerium für Staatssicherheit," in *Sozialgeschichte der DDR*, ed. Hartmut Kaelble, Jürgen Kocka and Hartmut Zwahr (Stuttgart: Klett-Cotta, 1994), 502 and Jens Gieseke, "Die Hauptamtlichen 1962," *DA* 27 (1994): 940.

8. BStU, ZA, SdM 1921, 74. "Referat des Genossen Staatssekretär auf der Dienstbesprechung am 5.8.1955."

9. BStU, ZA, SdM 1921, 75. "Referat des Genossen Staatssekretär auf der Dienstbesprechung am 5.8.1955."

10. Helmut Müller-Enbergs, *Inoffizielle Mitarbeiter des MfS in der DDR* (Berlin: Ch. Links, 2001), 30.

11. BStU, ZA, SdM 1921, 74-75. "Referat des Genossen Staatssekretär auf der Dienstbesprechung am 5.8.1955."

12. Fricke, *Die DDR-Staatssicherheit*, 39-42. Leo Bauer and Günter Stempel are two of many who mention the presence of Soviets in their arrest proceedings.

13. Erich Mielke acknowledged the help that the Soviets had accorded in the creation of the MfS; Erich Mielke, "Mit hoher Verantwortung für den zuverlässigen Schutz des Sozialismus," *Einheit* 1 (1975): 45. The internal MfS history also states that the Russian "Chekists" helped in the founding years; BStU, ZA, VVS JH3 001-133/80. *Studienmaterial zur Geschichte des Ministeriums für Staatssicherheit* (hereafter Studienmaterial), 16-17.

14. There is presently no overview of the structure of the MfS during its early years. Although the research branch of the former MfS archive in Berlin has been working on one, the overview is slated to be released only to the internal research branch of the archive. (Telephone interview with Herr Wiedmann of the BStU, February 26, 1997) There are at present only unreliable overviews of the organization in Bernhard Sagolla, *Die Rote Gestapo* (Berlin: Hansa Druck, 1952) produced by the Fighting Group Against Inhumanity, and *Der Staatssicherheitsdienst* (Bonn: Bundesministerium für Gesamtdeutsche Fragen, 1962). Sagolla's overview of the MfS cites Department II as responsible for the financial affairs of the MfS (Sagolla, 5), although Department II was actually responsible for spying in West Germany (BStU, ZA, GVS 447/51, #100016. 11 December 1951 Order Nr. 67/51 from Zaisser).

For an overview of the MfS in its final years, see BStU, *Die Organisationsstruktur des MfS* (Berlin: BStU, 1995).

For an introduction to the Stasi documents themselves and their value for the study of GDR history, see Joachim Gauck, *Die Stasi-Akten: Das unheimliche Erbe der DDR* (Reinbek bei Hamburg: Rowohlt Taschenbuch Verlag, 1991) and Roger Engelmann, "Zum Quellenwert der Unterlagen des Ministeriums für Staatssicherheit," in *Aktenlage:*

Die Bedeutung der Unterlagen des Staatssicherheitsdienstes für die Zeitgeschichtsforschung, ed. Klaus-Dietmar Henke and Roger Engelmann (Berlin: Ch. Links Verlag, 1995).

15. As of November 3, 1951, Department W dealing with the Wismut mining operation became an independent administration with the rights of a provincial MfS administration; BStU, ZA, #100012. November 3, 1951 Order Nr. 56/51 from Zaisser.

16. There were originally sixteen *Abteilungen*; BStU, ZA, GVS 1233/52, # 100041. October 1, 1952 directive on *Aktion Sonne* from Mielke to the *Bezirke* leadership. Sagolla states that there were eighteen, whereas *Der Staatssicherheitsdienst* (Bonn: Bundesministerium für Gesamtdeutsche Fragen, 1962) claims there were seventeen. See Sagolla, *Die Rote*, 5-6 and *Der Staatssicherheitsdienst*, 18-19.

17. Interview with Dr. R. Turber, former MfS Officer in Department V and later Department XX, Berlin, May 31, 1995.

18. BStU, ZA, GVS 1233/52, #100041. October 1, 1952 directive on *Aktion Sonne* from Mielke to the *Bezirke* leadership. Department III had four sections 1) planning, development, and finance 2) industry 3) light industry and trade and supply, 4) agriculture; BStU, ZA, GVS 3530/53. November 16, 1953 Directive 37/53 Generalmajor Last to leader of Department XIII. Until the further release of documents, the operations of Department II must remain somewhat of a mystery.

19. The prototype organization for the GDR's foreign espionage was the Institute for Economic Research. Its work was brought to a standstill by West Germany's Federal Ministry for the Protection of the Constitution in the "Vulkan affair" of 1953. See David Dallin, *Soviet Espionage* (New Haven: Yale University Press, 1955), 343; Peter Siebenmorgen, *"Staatssicherheit" der DDR*, 91.

20. BStU, ZA, GVS 525/52, Tgb.Nr. 952/52, #101166. April 21, 1952 letter from Mielke to Gutsche, Minister for State Security in Saxony. Memoir literature also points to Department VIII as responsible for internal arrests; Günter Fritzsch, *Gesicht zur Wand* (Leipzig:Benno Verlag, 1993), 44. For details on the actual arresting procedure, see Fricke, *Politik und Justiz*, 218-235.

21. BStU, ZA, GVS 542/52, #100030. April 24, 1952 Order Nr. 60/52.

22. Siegfried Mampel, *Der Untergrundkampf des Ministeriums für Staatssicherheit gegen den Untersuchungsausschuss Freiheitlicher Juristen in Berlin (West)* (Berlin: Der Berliner Landesbeauftragte für die Unterlagen des Staatssicherheitsdienstes der ehemaligen DDR, 1994), 24; *Der Staatssicherheitsdienst* (Bonn: Bundesministerium für Gesamtdeutsche Fragen, 1962), 46 also indicates that kidnappings in the West were carried out by Departments V and VIII; *Der Staatssicherheitsdienst* (Berlin: UfJ, 1956), 91, contains a reprint of a report from the Berlin Police *Präsidium* from November 13, 1952 on the kidnapping of Dr. Linse from West Berlin which states that Department VIII of the MfS, headed by Morgenthal, carried out the kidnapping. In the above cited interview of May 31, 1995, Dr. Turber confirmed that section 5 of Department V was responsible for "Western operations."

23. BStU, ZA, GVS 462/51, #100843. December 18, 1951 Instructions. GVS 525/52, #101166. April 21, 1952 Instructions for May 1 and 8, 1952; BA-P, DO 1 11/752, 27. September 28, 1950 report from Danisch, deputy leader of *Volkspolizei* in Saxony, to the Ministry of the Interior, Berlin; BA-P, DO 1 11/1150, 3-5. *Volkspolizei* reports from September 15 to October 9, 1950 from Saxony-Anhalt; BA-P, DO 1 11/24, 40-41. January 31, 1953 report from the head of the *Volkspolizei* Maron to the Soviet Control Commission, Chrenow.

24. BA-P, DO 1 11/1150, 3-5. *Volkspolizei* reports from September 15 to October 9, 1950 from Saxony-Anhalt; BA-P, DO 1 11/24, 40-41. January 31, 1953 report from the head of the *Volkspolizei* Maron to the Soviet Control Commission, Chrenow.

25. BStU, ZA, GVS 8/50, #101091. September 20, 1950 "Richtlinien über die Erfassung von Personen, die eine feindliche Tätigkeit durchführen und die von den Organen des Ministeriums für Staatssicherheit festgestellt wurden," issued by the head of the Department of Registration and Statistics, confirmed by Mielke.

26. BStU, ZA, GVS 8/50, #101091. September 20, 1950 "Richtlinien über die Erfassung von Personen, die eine feindliche Tätigkeit durchführen und die von den Organen des Ministeriums für Staatssicherheit festgestellt wurden," issued by the head of the Department of Registration and Statistics, confirmed by Mielke.

27. BStU, ZA, GVS 10/50, #101091. September 20, 1950 "Richtlinien zur Erfassung der durch die Organe des Ministeriums für Staatssicherheit der DDR verhafteten Personen," issued by the head of the Department of Registration and Statistics, confirmed by Mielke.

28. BStU, ZA, GVS 10/50, #101091. September 20, 1950 "Richtlinien zur Erfassung der durch die Organe des Ministeriums für Staatssicherheit der DDR verhafteten Personen," issued by the head of the Department of Registration and Statistics, confirmed by Mielke.

29. BStU, ZA, GVS 9/50, #101091. September 20, 1950 "Richtlinien über die Erfassung der geheimen Mitarbeiter, der Informatoren und der Personen, die konspirative Wohnungen unterhalten," issued by the Head of the Department of Statistics and Registration, confirmed by Mielke.

The terms *Geheime Mitarbeiter* and *Informanten* were replaced by the mid-1960s with the terms unofficial coworker (*Inoffizieller Mitarbeiter*) and societal coworker for state security (*Gesellschaftlicher Mitarbeiter Sicherheit*); Fricke, *Die DDR-Staatssicherheit*, 98.

30. BStU, ZA, GVS 9/50, #101091. September 20, 1950 "Richtlinien über die Erfassung der geheimen Mitarbeiter, der Informatoren und der Personen, die konspirative Wohnungen unterhalten," issued by the Head of the Department of Statistics and Registration, confirmed by Mielke.

31. BStU, ZA, GVS 9/50, #101091. September 20, 1950 "Richtlinien über die Erfassung der geheimen Mitarbeiter, der Informatoren und der Personen, die konspirative Wohnungen unterhalten," issued by the Head of the Department of Statistics and Registration, confirmed by Mielke.

32. BStU, ZA, GVS 9/50, #101091. September 20, 1950 "Richtlinien über die Erfassung der geheimen Mitarbeiter, der Informatoren und der Personen, die konspirative Wohnungen unterhalten," issued by the Head of the Department of Statistics and Registration, confirmed by Mielke. These files have yet to be located in the BStU.

33. BStU, ZA, GVS 27/50, # 101092, November 2, 1950 Directive I/IVa/50, signed by Mielke.

34. BStU, ZA, May 25, 1951 Order from Walter to the MfS in all provinces.

35. BStU, ZA. *Studienmaterial*, 21.

36. BStU, ZA, Tgb. Nr. 423/51. May 4, 1951 Directive 7/51, Mielke to Gartmann, *Chefinspekteur* of the MfS in Brandenburg.

37. BStU, ZA, GVS 462/51, #100843. December 18, 1951 regulation for the December 20 and 21, 1951 from Mielke to Fruck, Administration of Greater-Berlin; BStU,

ZA, GVS 525/52, #101166. April 21, 1952 regulation for May 1 and 8, 1952 from Mielke to Gutsche, *Chefinspekteur* of the MfS in Saxony.

38. BStU, ZA, #100030. April 24, 1952 Order Nr. 60/52 from Zaisser.

39. The stenographic transcript of the trials are in SAPMO-BA, ZPA, IV 2/13/625, 1-371, and SAPMO IV 2/13/627, 1-257 respectively.

40. BStU, ZA, GVS 2523/53, #100896. February 23, 1953 Directive 8/53, Operation Karo.

41. Wolfgang Eisert, "Zu den Anfängen der Sicherheits-und Militärpolitik der SED-Führung 1948 bis 1952," in *Volksarmee schaffen—ohne Geschrei*, ed. Bruno Thoss (Munich: R. Oldenbourg Verlag, 1994), 184-185.

42. Heinrich Hoffmann, a vice president of the DVdI, took over from Zaisser as head of the HVA in April 1950; Eisert, "Zu den Anfängen," 189.

43. Rüdiger Wenzke, "Auf dem Wege zur Kaderarmee," in *Volksarmee schaffen—ohne Geschrei*, ed. Bruno Thoss, 242.

44. The air force in 1950 numbered only twenty-six pilots; Eisert, 189.

45. Wenzke, "Auf dem Wege," 248.

46. Eisert, "Zu den Anfängen," 186; Wenzke, "Auf dem Wege," 243.

47. BA-P, DO 1 11/1121, 70. 17 September 1950 report entitled: "Stimmungen in Wahlversammlugen."

48. Wenzke, "Auf dem Wege," 243.

49. Eisert, "Zu den Anfängen," 186.

50. Author Collective, *Geschichte der Deutschen Volkspolizei* vol.1 (1945-1961) (Berlin [East]: VEB Deutscher Verlag der Wissenschaften, 1987), 166-167.

51. Author Collective, *Geschichte*, 169.

52. Author Collective, *Geschichte*, 169.

53. Falco Werkentin, *Politische Strafjustiz in der Ära Ulbricht* (Berlin: Ch. Links Verlag, 1995), 26.

54. Hermann Weber, *DDR. Grundriss der Geschichte* (Hannover: Fackelträger, 1991), 44.

55. Werkentin, *Politische*, 26.

56. Werkentin, *Politische*, 35. The Politbüro, a body elected by the Central Committee, was the highest executive organ of the SED. On the evolution of the structure of the SED in this period, see Monika Kaiser, "Die Zentrale der Diktatur—organisatorische Weichenstellungen, Strukturen und Kompetenzen der SED-Führung in der SBZ/DDR 1946 bis 1952," in *Historische DDR-Forschung: Aufsätze und Studien*, ed. Jürgen Kocka (Berlin: Akadamie Verlag, 1993), 83-86, and Peter Ludz, *The Changing Party Elite in East Germany* (Boston: MIT Press, 1972), 122.

57. Ludz, *The Changing*, 28.

58. Ludz, *The Changing*, 41.

59. SAPMO-BA, ZPA, IV 2 13/419, pp. 8, 18, 23. Undated report from the Ministry of Justice (circa 1952).

60. Werkentin, *Politische*, 28.

61. Werkentin, *Politische*, 176.

62. SAPMO-BA, ZPA, NL 182/1134, 176. Undated *Instrukteur* report on a trip to Osterburg and Salzwedel (circa 1950).

63. Werkentin, *Politische*, 177. On the integration of the released prisoners into GDR society, see Michael Buddrus, "'...im Allgemeinen ohne besondere

Vorkommnisse': Dokumente zur Situation des Strafvollzugs der DDR nach der Auflösung der sowjetischen Internierungslager 1949-1951," *DA* 29 (1996): 10-34.

64. Karl Wilhelm Fricke, *Politik und Justiz in der DDR* (Cologne: Verlag Wissenschaft und Politik, 1979), 207.

65. Fricke, *Politik*, 208.

66. Werkentin, *Politische*, 185.

67. Fricke, *Politik*, 212.

68. Fricke, *Politik*, 206.

69. The work of the Soviet Military Tribunals effectively came to an end when the GDR was founded, although they still ruled in exceptional cases such as those involving western spies. The Soviet Union continued to play an influential role in GDR justice, however. Throughout the 1950s, the GDR Ministry of Justice reported to the Soviet Control Commission with analyses of the justice situation in the GDR; Weber, *DDR. Grundriss der Geschichte*, 44.

70. The full text of the GDR constitution is reprinted in Horst Hildebrandt, *Die deutschen Verfassungen des 19. Und 20. Jahrhunderts* (Paderborn: Ferdinand Schöningh, 1971), 195-232.

71. ACDP, III-013-793. March 6, 1952 CDU *Ostbüro* report by Wilhelm Rost.

72. Manfred Agethen, "Die CDU in der SBZ/DDR 1945-52," in *Bürgerliche Parteien in der SBZ/DDR*, ed. Manfred Agethen and Jürgen Fröhlich (Cologne: Verlag Wissenschaft und Politik, 1994), 35.

73. Agethen, "Die CDU," 35.

74. ADL, LDPD #13822. Protocol of the executive sitting of the LDPD *Kreis* association for Borna on May 22, 1950.

75. ADL, LDPD #142499. March 28, 1950 position paper of the LDPD *Ortsgruppe* Gera on the question of the elections.

76. SAPMO-BA, ZPA, IV 2/15/15, "Befreundete Parteien." Undated Report entitled: "Bemerkenswerte blockpolitische Erscheinungen in den Kreisen Sachsens" (c. 1950).

77. Weber, *DDR. Grundriss der Geschichte*, 45.

78. ADL, LDPD #2782. Protocol of the sitting of the acting executive of the LDPD provincial association of Thuringia on March 17, 1950.

79. Siegfried Suckut, "Die Entscheidung zur Gründung der DDR," *VfZ* 39 (1991): 134.

80. Peter Lapp, *Wahlen in der DDR* (Berlin: Verlag Gebr. Holzapfel, 1982), 16.

81. Richter, *Die Ost-CDU*, 246.

82. Michael Richter, "Vom Widerstand der christlichen Demokraten in der DDR," in *"Gefährliche politische Gegner,"* ed. Brigitte Kaff (Düsseldorf: Droste, 1995), 118.

83. See Karl Wilhelm Fricke, *Opposition und Widerstand in der DDR* (Cologne: Verlag Wissenschaft und Politik, 1984), 68. Stempel was released in 1956.

84. Richter, *Die Ost-CDU*, 293.

85. Fricke, *Politik*, 240. For an introduction to the SED's use of justice for political ends, see Werkentin.

86. *Konrad-Adenauer-Stiftung*. Statistics prepared by Frau Nestler. Investigation number 94RK01. These statistics are preliminary and thus do not represent all those arrested. Nevertheless, the trend in arrests is important. In 1950, there were 406 recorded arrests. After 1950, the largest number of CDU arrests took place in 1953 (296) followed

by 1951 (272) and 1952 (252). The number of arrests in 1950 was significantly larger than other years.

87. Richter, *Die Ost-CDU*, pp. 228, 239.

88. Michael Richter, "Vom Widerstand," in Kaff, *"Gefährliche,"* 115.

89. See Erich Ebert's report in Kaff, *"Gefährliche,"* 226.

90. The arrests included the provincial CDU chair in Saxony-Anhlat, Erich Fascher, and the Mecklenburg Minister of Finance, Dr. Siegfried Witte. Richter, *Die Ost-CDU*, 230-240. At the January 25 sitting of the Potsdam city assembly, the CDU protested against the political persecution of its members. "In der Sitzung war die Frage aufgeworfen worden, wie sich die CDU einem ungesetzlichen Terror weiter beugen soll"; Fritz Reinert, *Protokolle der Landesblockausschusses der antifaschistisch-demokratischen Parteien Brandenburgs 1945-50* (Weimar: Verlag Hermann Böhlaus Nachfolger, 1994), 308, 328. See also Fricke, *Opposition und Widerstand*, 65.

91. BLHA, Ld.Br. Rep. 202G, Amt für Information Nr.66, 564. June 1, 1950 letter to *Amt für Information*, signature illegible.

92. BLHA, Ld.Br.Rep 202G, Amt für Information Nr. 59, 395. May 30, 1951 memorandum for *Amt für Information* from Wagner.

93. Richter, "Vom Widerstand der christlichen Demokraten in der DDR," in *Verfolgt—verhaftet—verurteilt*, ed. Günther Scholz (Berlin: Westkreuz Verlag, 1990), 46-47.

94. Richter, *Die Ost-CDU*, 304. Many of these students had complained of the SED university reforms announced at the Second Party Congress, which aimed to make Marxism-Leninism the basis of higher education. The CDU student groups at the University of Leipzig rejected the compulsory lectures on Marxism-Leninism, and suggested working vigorously to counter these measures; ACDP, VII-013-1421. Position of the extended executive of the CDU University group at the University of Leipzig on the situation of universities in the GDR.

95. Richter, "Vom Widerstand," 46-47.

96. BLHA, Ld.Br. Rep 202G, Amt für Information, Nr. 59, 395. May 30, 1951 memorandum for the *Amt für Information* from Wagner.

97. Gerhard Papke, "Die Liberal-Demokratische Partei Deutschlands in der Sowjetischen Besatzungszone und DDR 1945-52," in *"Bürgerliche Parteien,"* ed. Manfred Agethen and Jürgen Fröhlich, 41.

98. Sagolla, *Die Rote*, 46.

99. SAPMO-BA, ZPA, IV 2/4/106, ZPKK, 3. Undated party declaration on the Field affair.

100. The report from the trial against Herwegen, Brundert, and the others, Friedrich Methfessel, Hermann Müller, Leopold Kaatz, Ernst Simon, Paul Heil, Ernst Pauli, and Heinrich Scharf, is found in SAPMO-BA, ZPA, JIV 2/202/60.

101. As early as 1948, Max Fechner had suggested that trials of economic criminals should be conducted in factories; Franz-Josef Kos, "Politische Justiz in der DDR. Der Dessauer Schauprozess vom April 1950," *VfZ* 44 (1996): 397.

102. Kos, "Politische," 414.

103. Willi Brundert, *Es begann im Theater . . . "Volksjustiz" hinter dem eisernen Vorhang* (Berlin: Verlag J.H.W. Dietz GmbH, 1958), 10.

104. Brundert, *Es begann*, 49.

105. Brundert, *Es begann*, 49.

106. Peter Bloch, *Zwischen Hoffnung und Resignation* (Cologne: Verlag Wissenschaft und Politik, 1986), 165.

107. Agethen, "Die CDU," 59.

108. Bloch, *Zwischen*, 182.

109. ACDP, VII-011-3026. September 1, 1950 letter from Alfred Gruner to all CDU provincial executive members in Saxony Anhalt.

110. THSA, IV 4.08/214. February 23, 1950 letter from KPKK, Weber, to LPKK in Erfurt.

111. THSA, IV 4.08/214. February 23, 1950 letter from KPKK, Weber, to LPKK in Erfurt.

112. Richter, *Die Ost-CDU*, 222.

113. SAPMO-BA, ZPA, IV 2/15/15, "Befreundete Parteien." Report entitled: "Bemerkenswerte blockpolitische Erscheinungen in den Kreisen Sachsens." There is no date on the document, but it is clear from the context that it is 1950.

114. BA-P, DO 1 11/1150, 15. September 16, 1950 report Nr. 4 by HVDVP task force.

115. BA-P, DO 1 11/1121, 70. September 17, 1950 report entitled: "Stimmungen in Wahlversammlungen."

116. BA-P, DO 1 11/1121, 70. September 17, 1950 report entitled: "Stimmungen in Wahlversammlungen."

117. Richter, "Vom Widerstand der christlichen Demokraten," 112. Richter, "Vom Widerstand," in Kaff, *"Gefährliche,"* 120. See as well the drop in CDU membership in 1950 documented below.

118. Richter, *Die Ost-CDU*, 278-279.

119. Richter, *Die Ost-CDU*, 279.

120. See Norbert Sommer's report in Kaff, *"Gefährliche,"* 240. He began to engage in underground resistance due to the "totale Unsicherheit."

121. Norbert Sommer's report in Kaff, *"Gefährliche,"* 240.

122. ADL, #2929. March 30, 1951 report from Werner Westermann, CDU mayor of Waldersleben, regarding the resistance group "Michael" in Halberstadt, Saxony-Anhalt.

123. ADL, #2929. June 7, 1951 letter from Otto to Naase. The group was arrested in 1951.

124. ADL, #2509. August 16, 1956 letter from Brandt (Uelzen branch) to the *Ostbüro* of the FDP.

125. ACDP, III-013-792. Unsigned report of August 7, 1951.

126. ADL, #2527. June 1954 monthly report of *Büro* Anton.

127. Richter, *Die Ost-CDU*, 289.

128. ACDP, VII-012-1704. Undated report on CDU work in preparation for the 1951 referendum.

129. Richter, *Die Ost-CDU*, 363.

130. Richter, *Die Ost-CDU*, 392.

131. Richter, *Die Ost-CDU*, 392.

132. ADL, LDPD #2779. Protocol of working conference of *Kreis* association chairs and secretaries with Dr. Loch on February 26, 1951.

133. Gerhard Papke, "Die Liberal-Demokratische Partei Deutschlands in der Sowjetischen Besatzungszone und DDR 1945-52," in *"Bürgerliche" Parteien in der SBZ/DDR*, ed. Manfred Agethen and Jürgen Fröhlich (Cologne: Verlag Wissenschaft und Politik, 1994), 42.

134. Papke, "Die Liberal-Demokratische," 42.

135. Hermann Weber, *Parteiensystem zwischen Demokratie und Volksdemokratie* (Cologne: Verlag Wissenschaft und Politik, 1982) , 513.

136. AdsD, SPD-PV-Ostbüro 0370/I. Undated report on Gerlach's comments in the party executive.

137. This information was provided verbally to the author by his caseworker in the BStU, Frau Karin Göpel, Berlin, July 10, 1996.

138. Stephan Zeidler, "Zur Rolle der CDU (Ost) in der inneren Entwicklung der DDR 1952-53," M.A. thesis, University of Bonn, 1994, 18.

139. One of the first studies to employ this material was Wolfgang Eckelmann, *FDGB Intern: Innenansichten einer Massenorganisation der SED* (Berlin: Treptower Verlag, 1990).

140. Richter, *Die Ost-CDU*, 389.

141. Mary Fulbrook has taken issue with Armin Mitter and Stefan Wolle, who, in *Untergang auf Raten* (Munich: Bertelsmann Verlag, 1993) argue that the GDR never enjoyed internal legitimacy, and was therefore akin to a latent civil war. See Fulbrook, *Anatomy of a Dictatorship* (Oxford: Oxford University Press, 1995), 172.

142. Eisert, "Zu den Anfängen," 187.

143. MLHA, IV L 2/4/1217, 22. LDPD Information bulletin of February 1, 1950.

144. MLHA, IV L 2/4/1217, 22. LDPD Information bulletin of February 1, 1950.

145. MLHA, IV L 2/4/1179, "Landesleitung der SED Mecklenburg." May 4, 1950 report by LPKK Mecklenburg.

146. BLHA, Ld. Br. Rep. 202G, Amt für Information Nr. 56, 250. Report entitled: "Analyse der Tätigkeit der bürgerlichen Parteien LDP und CDU im Kreise Angermünde in den Monaten Januar und Februar 1950."

147. BLHA, Ld. Br. Rep. 202G, Amt für Information Nr. 56, 254. Report entitled: "Analyse der Tätigkeit der bürgerlichen Parteien LDP und CDU im Kreise Angermünde in den Monaten Januar und Februar 1950."

148. BLHA, Ld. Br. Rep. 202G, Amt für Information Nr. 56, 260. Report entitled: "Analyse der Tätigkeit der bürgerlichen Parteien LDP und CDU im Kreise Angermünde in den Monaten Januar und Februar 1950."

149. BA-P, DO 1 11/1121, 140. October 18, 1950 report entitled: "Bericht über die Vorkommnisse während der Vorbereitungen und Durchführung der Volkswahl in der Deutschen Demokratischen Republik v. 15.9 - 15.10.50."

150. BA-P, DO 1 11/1121, 140. October 18, 1950 report entitled: "Bericht über die Vorkommnisse während der Vorbereitungen und Durchführung der Volkswahl in der Deutschen Demokratischen Republik v. 15.9 - 15.10.50."

151. BA-P, DO 1 11/1121, 76. September 28, 1950 report entitled: "Stimmungen in Wahlversammlungen und Kundgebungen."

152. BA-P, DO 1 11/1121, 76. September 28, 1950 report entitled: "Stimmungen in Wahlversammlungen und Kundgebungen."

153. BA-P, DO 1 11/1150, 45. September 18, 1950 report Nr. 13 by HVDVP task-force.

154. The *Volkspolizei* noted complaints regarding repression in three reports. In comparison, hostility to the Oder-Neisse border was mentioned in two reports, and there was no recorded complaints regarding the economic situation. These reports are found in BA-P, DO 1 11/1121.

155. AdsD, SPD-PV-Ostbüro 0421. September 25, 1951 report from *Kreis* Teltow.

156. AdsD, SPD-PV-Ostbüro 0361/2. November 23, 1951 report from *Stadt* and *Kreis* Waren/Müritz; AdsD, SPD-PV-Ostbüro 0361/2, May 22, 1951 report; AdsD, SPD-PV-Ostbüro 0361/2, 0361/1. August 1, 1950 letter.

157. FNA, VII "SBZ/DDR." Undated report of time in Bautzen.

158. BA-P, DO 1 11/1150, 46. September 18, 1950 report Nr. 13 by HVDVP taskforce.

159. ACDP, VII-013-1421. Extract from May 2, 1950 memorandum of the bishop of Evangelical Lutheran provincial church of Saxony.

160. MLHA, IV L 2/12/525, Landesleitung der SED Mecklenburg, Sicherheit, 10. Transcript of Ulbricht's speech from August 1950.

161. MLHA, IV L 2/12/525, Landesleitung der SED Mecklenburg, Sicherheit, 16. Transcript of Ulbricht's speech from August 1950.

162. Richard Bessel, "Die Grenzen des Polizeistaates," in *Die Grenzen der Diktatur*, ed. Richard Bessel and Ralph Jessen (Göttingen: Vandenhoeck & Rupprecht, 1996), 241.

163. Bessel, "Die Grenzen," 241.

164. Bessel, "Die Grenzen," 241.

165. BStU, ZA, GVS 213/53, #100860. October 30, 1952 Directive 2/53.

166. BStU, ZA, GVS 2920/53, #100874. September 19, 1953 Directive 30/53.

167. After the June 17, 1953 revolution, the MfS was downgraded to a Secretariat for State Security. See the following chapter.

168. See the following chapter on the extensive SfS efforts to increase its support in the population.

169. Fricke, *Politik*, 215; Werkentin, *Politische*, 181.

170. BA-P, DO 1 11/1625. November 29, 1951 letter from Hahn, Weidlich, Pfeuffer, and Plaschke of Hauptverwaltung DVP.

171. Fricke, *Politik*, 246-250.

172. Fricke, *Politik*, 251.

173. Fricke, *Politik*, 254.

174. SAPMO-BA, ZPA, IV 2/13/433. October 18, 1951 report by Staatliche Verwaltung der Justiz, signature illegible.

175. Kos, "Politische," 429.

176. BA-P, DO 1 11/1121, 24. September 22, 1950 report entitled: "Stimmungen in Wahlversammlungen und Kundgebungen."

177. BA-P, DO 1/11/1121. September 26, 1950 report entitled: "Stimmungen in Wahlversammlungen und Kundgebungen."

178. BA-P, DO 1 11/1150, 13. September 16, 1950 report by HVDVP taskforce.

179. AdsD, SPD-PV-Ostbüro 0370/I. Summer 1951 report on LDP.

180. BA-P, DO 1 11/1121, 76. September 28, 1950 report entitled: "Stimmungen in Wahlversammlungen und Kundgebungen."

181. See the reports in BA-P, DO 1 11/1121.

182. BA-P, DO 1 11/1121, 139. October 18, 1950 report: "Vorkommnisse während der Vorbereitungen und Durchführung der Volkswahl in der Deutschen Demokratischen Republik v. 15.9.-15.10.50."

183. BA-P, DO 1 11/1121, 63. September 26, 1950 report entitled: "Stimmungen in Wahlversammlungen und Kundgebungen."

184. BA-P, DO 1 11/24, February 27, 1952 report from Seifert, Generalinspekteur of the *Volkspolizei* to *Staatssekretär* Warnke.

185. BLHA, Ld.Br.Rep.202G, Amt für Information Nr.56, 253. "Analyse der Tätigkeit der bürgerlichen Parteien LDP und CDU im Kreise Angermünde in den Monaten Januar und Februar 1950."

186. BLHA, Ld.Br.Rep.202G, Amt für Information Nr.56, 253. "Analyse der Tätigkeit der bürgerlichen Parteien LDP und CDU im Kreise Angermünde in den Monaten Januar und Februar 1950."

187. AdsD, SPD-PV-Ostbüro 0361/2. Excerpts from March 26, 1952 LDPD report to the Soviet Control Commission in Erfurt.

188. ACDP, III-013-630/3. March 5, 1952 report by Hermann Hieke, 3.

189. AdsD, SPD-PV-Ostbüro 0357 I. November 3, 1950 report on the conduct of the election in the SBZ.

190. ACDP, III-013-630/3. March 5, 1952 report by Hermann Hieke, 3; AdsD, SPD-PV-Ostbüro 0357I. November 3, 1950 report on the conduct of the election in the SBZ.

191. THSA, Bestand 5, 218, MdI, Landesbehörde der *Volkspolizei* 130. Various police reports.

192. BA-P, DO 1 11/369, 3. January 29, 1951 report Hauptabteilung Schutzpolizei.

193. Weber, *DDR. Grundriss*, 45.

194. ADL, #2924. November 11, 1950 extracts from the trial of Müller and others.

195. AdsD, SPD-PV-Ostbüro 0368 a-c. October 17, 1950 report from "Source 13 688/8" entitled: "Schlussbericht der Widerstandsbewegung Sachsens."

196. AdsD, SPD-PV-Ostbüro 0368 a-c. October 17, 1950 report from "Source 13 688/8" entitled: "Schlussbericht der Widerstandsbewegung Sachsens."

197. BA-P, DO 1 11/752, 14. September 20, 1950 task force order from deputy head of the *Volkspolizei* for Saxony-Anhalt, Dombrowsky, to the Criminal Police department of the *Volkspolizei* in Saxony-Anhalt; AdsD, SPD-PV-Ostbüro 0368 a-c. October 17, 1950 report from "Source 13 688/8" entitled: "Final report of the Saxony resistance movement against the so called elections of October 15, 1950."

198. BA-P, DO 1 11/752, 14. September 20, 1950 task force order from deputy head of the *Volkspolizei* for Saxony-Anhalt, Dombrowsky, to the Criminal Police department of the *Volkspolizei* in Saxony-Anhalt; AdsD, SPD-PV-Ostbüro 0368 a-c. October 17, 1950 report from "Source 13 688/8" entitled: "Final report of the Saxony resistance movement against the so called elections of October 15, 1950."

199. BA-P, DO 1 11/752, 30. October 4, 1950 report from Department K in the *Volkspolizei* to the chief of police for the GDR Maron regarding operation "Gustav."

200. BA-P, DO 1 11/752, 30. October 4, 1950 report from Department K in the *Volkspolizei* to the chief of police for the GDR Maron regarding operation "Gustav."

201. BA-P, DO 1 11/1121, 23. October 18, 1950: "Bericht über die Vorkommnisse während der Vorbereitungen und Durchführung der Volkswahl in der Deutschen Demokratischen Republik v. 15.9.-15.10.50."

202. The demonstrations in Saalfeld have received treatment in Andrew Port's "When workers rumbled: the Wismut upheaval of August 1951 in East Germany" *Social History* 22 (1997): 145-173. In his account, which relies primarily on MfS and local Party documentation, Port adopts very much a *Resistenz* approach to the uprising. The account presented here relies on police records—which are often more detailed than the party documentation provided by Port—and demonstrates the underlying fundamental hostility to the SED's instruments of control.

203. For more on the Wismut mining operation, see Naimark, *The Russians*, 238-250 and Rainer Karlsch, *Allein bezahlt? Die Reparationsleistungen der SBZ/DDR 1945-1953* (Berlin: CH. Links Verlag, 1993).

204. August 17, 1951 report "Überfall auf das VPKA Saalfeld," (Attack on the *Volkspolizei* district office Saalfeld) by General Inspector Mayer, deputy head of the *Volkspolizei* (hereafter "Attack on the *Volkspolizei* district office") BA-P, DO 1 11/08, 27.

205. August 17, 1951 report "Überfall auf das VPKA Saalfeld," (Attack on the *Volkspolizei* district office Saalfeld) by General Inspector Mayer, deputy head of the *Volkspolizei* (hereafter "Attack on the *Volkspolizei* district office") BA-P, DO 1 11/08, 27. See also the undated report: "Bericht über die im Auftrag des Chefs durchgeführte Untersuchung über die Ursachen der Vorkommnisse im VPKA Saalfeld in der Nacht vom 16. zum 17.8.1951" (Report commissioned by the head of the *Volkspolizei* on the investigation into the reasons for the events in the *Volkspolizei* district office Saalfeld during the night of August 16 to 17, 1951), by the deputy head of the *Volkspolizei* in Thuringia , *Volkspolizei* Inspector Flechtner (hereafter "Report commissioned by the head of the *Volkspolizei*"), BA-P, DO 1 11/08, 37-38.

206. "Report commissioned by the head of the *Volkspolizei*," 37.

207. "Attack on the *Volkspolizei* district station," 28.

208. "Attack on the *Volkspolizei* district station," 28.

209. "Attack on the *Volkspolizei* district station," 28.

210. "Report commissioned by the head of the *Volkspolizei*," 39.

211. "Attack on the *Volkspolizei* district station," 28.

212. "Report commissioned by the head of the *Volkspolizei*," 40.

213. "Report commissioned by the head of the *Volkspolizei*," 64.

214. "Attack on the *Volkspolizei* district station," 28. The market square in Saalfeld where the police station was located was the gathering point for workers awaiting transport to the Wismut mining operation.

215. "Attack on the *Volkspolizei* district station," 28.

216. August 19, 1951 report entitled: "Vorläufiger Schlussbericht über die Ereignisse in Saalfeld bis zum 19.8.1951 -12:00 Uhr," (Preliminary report on the events in Saalfeld up to August 19, 1951, 12:00),by the head of the *Volkspolizei* in Thuringia, König (Hereafter "Preliminary report").

217. "Report commissioned by the head of the *Volkspolizei*," 40.

218. "Report commissioned by the head of the *Volkspolizei*," 42.

219. BA-P, DO 1 11/1124, 29-32. August 18, 1951 Hauptabteilung K report entitled: "Besondere Vorkommnisse in Saalfeld."

220. "Preliminary report" 68.

221. Considering the proximity of dates, it is possible that the riot in Saalfeld caused the MfS leadership to establish Department W (ismut) as an independent administration, with all the rights of a provincial MfS administration. "Befehl Nr. 56/51" from Zaisser, November 3, 1951. #100012. BStU, ZA.

222. "Preliminary report." 65.

223. "Preliminary report." 65.

224. "Preliminary report." 68.

225. "Report commissioned by the head of the *Volkspolizei*," 42-43.

226. "Report commissioned by the head of the *Volkspolizei*," 42-43.

227. "Report commissioned by the head of the *Volkspolizei*," 43.

228. "Report commissioned by the head of the *Volkspolizei*," 43.
229. "Report commissioned by the head of the *Volkspolizei*," 70.
230. "Report commissioned by the head of the *Volkspolizei*," 69.
231. SAPMO-BA, ZPA, DY 30 IV 2/9.02/76, 35 July 15, 1952 special report from the Amt für Information.

Chapter 5

The "Building of Socialism" and Its Consequences, 1952–1953

The SED's declaration of the "building of socialism" (*Aufbau des Sozialismus*) in the summer of 1952 began the process which led to revolutionary upheavals throughout East Germany the following year. At the July 1952 Second Party Conference the SED declared: "The political and economic conditions, as well as the consciousness of the working class and the majority of workers, have sufficiently developed, so that the building of socialism has become the main task of the German Democratic Republic."[1] The SED vowed to take a hard line against any opponent of socialism: "We [i.e., the SED] must be aware that the heightening of the class war is unavoidable. The working classes must break the resistance of enemy forces."[2] The SED further outlined that the main instrument for the "building of socialism" would be the "power of the state" (*Staatsmacht*).[3] The instruments of the *Staatsmacht* which were to carry out the "building of socialism" were the MfS, the *Volkspolizei*, and the judicial system, all of which the SED dominated.[4]

The "building of socialism" caused major changes to East German society. Some elements of the "building of socialism," such as securing the border with West Germany, establishing armed forces, and changing university curricula, had been implemented prior to the SED's Second Party Conference, but the SED now called for their progress to be rapidly increased.[5] Other elements were first introduced with the Second Party Conference. Farmers were to be forced onto agricultural production collectives, a campaign against the Christian churches and their supporters was to be carried out, and increased restrictions were to be applied to independent businesses.[6] Furthermore, the SED Central Committee now emphasized heavy industry in its economic plans at the expense of the consumer industries.[7] The "building of socialism" affected all sections of GDR society.

The declaration of the "building of socialism" had consequences for the SED itself, as in future the party would concentrate on developing cadres. The SED introduced a system of schooling cadres so that the party would have ideologically reliable members throughout the entire party apparatus.[8] The schooling was divided into three sections: (1) the schooling of functionaries at special boarding schools, (2) participation of party members at annual party seminars, and (3) ongoing personal study under the guidance of the party.[9] The SED membership did not react uniformly to the "building of socialism." Ilko-Sascha Kowalczuk has identified five groups within the party: (1) a group of members that acted reserved, preferring not to take a position on the party's new course. This was the largest of the five groups, (2) a group which fully supported the acceleration towards Communism, (3) a group of skeptics who doubted whether the timing for this policy was right, given the economic situation and the "consciousness" of the population, (4) a group which rejected the "building of socialism," and (5) a group of members who supported the new course, and expected the removal of all "bourgeois" elements in the population.[10] Because of the purges that had taken place in 1951-1952, the Central Committee and Politburo were staffed with reliable party members, all of whom supported the "building of socialism." Misgivings about the party's course in these higher levels first materialized in June 1953.[11]

The SED Central Committee undertook several measures to ensure the proper execution of the "building of socialism." First, it removed any potential opposition to its program from the provincial governments by eliminating the five provinces in the GDR and replacing them with fourteen regional districts called *Bezirke*.[12] Second, the SED Central Committee outfitted the police, MfS, and judicial apparatus with the necessary tools to conduct the transformation and eliminate resistance to the changes. In the judicial system, the SED Central Committee took advantage of the creation of *Bezirke* to remove "excess" jurists created by the administrative changes. One hundred and four "less reliable" judges were removed from their positions. By the fall of 1952, all *Bezirk* court directors were SED members. Furthermore, all of these directors (except the director of the Dresden *Bezirk* court who had studied law in the empire of William II) were products of the SED-dominated educational program for becoming a "people's judge."[13] The police, already firmly under the control of the SED, also underwent changes to prepare it for the increased tasks ahead. On July 29, 1952, the SED issued "measures for the improvement of the work of the German *Volkspolizei*" which called for the recruitment of volunteers to help with police duties, developing a system of volunteer surveillance of residences (*Hausvertrauensleute*), and improved arming of the police.[14]

The MfS was also improved in preparation for increased duties. In the fall of 1952, Mielke issued the first comprehensive MfS guidelines dealing with the recruitment and running of unofficial informants from the general population. The first guidelines dealing with informants, dated September 9, 1950, as outlined above, was vague. Guideline 21/52 of November 20, 1952 provided significantly more detail, such as reminders to MfS officers to provide cigarettes and snacks during meetings with unofficial informants to make them feel more relaxed.[15] These guidelines, however, did not call for blanket surveillance of the population, but rather called for a concentrated expansion of the informant net to deal with elements in the population likely to resist the "building of socialism." The main targets in this regard were the churches and the non-Marxist parties. The MfS cloaked its interest in these organizations stating that they provided important "reserve troops of the Anglo-American secret services" in the GDR.[16] To streamline the fight against the non-Marxist parties and the churches, the MfS amalgamated Department VI, which had been responsible for these targets, with Department V which was responsible for underground opposition in general.[17] The MfS leadership warned that "reaction-ary" elements in the non-Marxist parties had often been underestimated in the past, and that secret coworkers should be found to penetrate these parties.[18]

In conjunction with the "building of socialism," the MfS conducted a campaign against the churches in the GDR, and particularly the Protestant church youth group *Junge Gemeinde*. After the Second Party Conference, a more extensive section for church work was established within Department V of the MfS, which contributed to the arrests of 175 members of various religious groups between August and December 1952.[19] On November 11, 1952 Mielke issued the first orders to observe members of the *Junge Gemeinde* and to employ informants to penetrate its leader-ship.[20] In early 1953, the MfS arrested fifty pastors, deacons, and lay preachers and expelled 300 school children who belonged to the *Junge Gemeinde*.[21] The vigorous campaign against church organizations continued until the announcement of the "New Course" by the SED on June 11, 1953.[22]

Due to the tense Cold War, the MfS continued to target anti-Communist or-ganizations based in West Berlin.[23] Guideline 21/52 stated: "The main goal [for informants] is always to penetrate the centers of the enemy [anti-Communist groups in West Germany—GB] or the groups set up by him, in order to determine enemy plans early, make enemy activity impossible, and expose agents."[24] Indeed, *all* examples of informant recruitment in the guideline dealt with western anti-Communist organizations.[25]

The creation of a five km deep demarcation zone along the border with West Germany in the early months of 1952 had demonstrated that the SED would not hesitate to use its disciplinary apparatus to carry out its program. According to CDU reports, police troops used excessive force to evacuate from the demarcation zone elements deemed "unreliable." The Eisenach CDU group stated that the evacuation measures often went against "democratic conformity to law," and complained that many of those affected were not given even forty-eight hours to evacuate their properties. These members also complained that in general the methods of the SED and the "state police" were "regrettable."[26] In 1956, those affected by the evacua-tion measures were still demanding an official explanation as to their removal.[27]

Having outfitted the instruments of control with the necessary tools, the SED Central Committee then proceeded to eliminate both actual and potential opponents to the "building of socialism." The legal basis for the elimination of these opponents was the "law for the protection of the people's property and other societal property" which came into force on October 2, 1952.[28] According to this law, even the smallest economic infraction could be punished with at least one year in penitentiary. The first paragraph of the law read: "Theft, embezzlement or any other removal of state property or collective property, or of property belonging to societal organizia- tions, will be punished with one to five years penitentiary."[29]

The SED applied the law broadly and abundantly. In October 1952, 283 people were tried under the law; in November, 745 were tried; in December, 1,391 were tried; in January 1953, 1,900 were tried; in February, 2,303 were tried; and in March 1953, a staggering 3,572 were tried.[30] Overall, the number of prisoners in the GDR increased from 30,000 in 150 prisons in July 1952 to 61,377 in 200 prisons by May 1953.[31] Moreover, the application of this law affected not only "undesirable" societal sections such as owners of private businesses. In the Leipzig *Bezirk* court, 228 of the 377 tried under this law from October 1952 to April 1953 were workers, and only eight were independent business owners.[32] Not only were large numbers affected, but the punishments were also severe. A worker who stole a few coal bri- quettes, for example, was sentenced to one year in prison. Another worker who stole 3/4 kg of sauerkraut from his work place paid for his crime with one year in the Zwickau prison.[33] Some LDPD members left the party out of disgust that a drunkard who had thrown a barrel of oil down a set of stairs was being tried for committing an economic crime.[34] The SED bestowed strict penalties on justice functionaries who did not hand down verdicts of the maximum penalty under the law.[35]

Farmers also experienced the brutal implementation of the "building of social- ism," with the SED making little distinction between farmers with large land hold- ings—in theory the class enemy—and those with small land holdings—the pre- sumed ally. Between August 1952 and January 1953, SED judges presided over 583 trials against farmers with large land holdings, 311 against farmers with medium- sized land holdings, and 353 against farmers with small land holdings.[36] The sen- tences in these instances were also severe. It was not uncommon for an accused farmer to receive ten years in prison for failing to fill the SED-set quota for pro- duce.[37]

Realizing the negative effect on the population, Dr. Melsheimer, chief public prosecutor of the GDR, approached the Central Committee of the SED in April 1953 suggesting a more cautious use of the law. Referring to the increasing number of those arrested under this law, Melsheimer stated: "This means that in the first three months of the year 1953 alone, 7,775 people have acted against the people's property. This means further that if the number of sentencings do not increase in the coming months, 40,000 people will be sitting in penitentiary by the end of the year for breaking the [law for the protection of the people's economy.] That is indeed unbearable."[38] Melsheimer's suggestions were not acted upon, however, in face of Ulbricht's desire for the rigorous implementation of the "building of socialism." In January 1953, the Central Committee department dealing with justice stated: "*Kreis* judicial instruments in the *Bezirke* often do not treat anti-democratic activity ac- cording to Article 6 of the constitution of the GDR and Control Council Directive 38, but rather as normal transgressions committed because of personal reasons. . . .

criminals set free."[39] In May 1953, Ulbricht warned all judicial and prison employees about leniency in the judicial system: "The party organization must investigate the ideological reasons behind decisions which are politically wrong . . . and in membership meetings it must deal with every sign of forgiveness towards the class enemy."[40] Ulbricht's phrase was almost identical to the wording of the resolution of the SED's Second Party Congress: "The party and each individual member of it must exercise great revolutionary attentiveness and conduct a decisive battle against tendencies of forgiveness towards enemies of the party and the people."[41] The Second Party Congress ushered in a hard line against real and potential enemies of Communism in the GDR.

Reaction to the "Building of Socialism" Prior to the Revolution

The Non-Marxist Parties and the "Building of Socialism"

The general membership of the non-Marxist parties had misgivings about their parties' support for the "building of socialism," revealing that the *Gleichschaltung* process had yet to be fully completed by 1952. Because there are no reports of the local level of the CDU prior to June 17, 1953, it is difficult to ascertain the reaction of the CDU membership to the "building of socialism," but there is other evidence which suggests a negative reaction.[42] The CDU had difficulty finding "progressive" candidates to participate in the 6th Party Conference in October which officially recognized the "building of socialism."[43] Following the conference, the general secretary of the CDU, Gerald Götting, announced that investigation committees would be established in the party to ensure that all members were "reliable." The MfS was to assist the CDU in this process.[44] As a result of these investigations, many CDU members were arrested and/or expelled from the party. It appears, therefore, that sections of the CDU membership disapproved of the party's support for the "building of socialism."

Removing CDU opposition, real and potential, to the "building of socialism" was also at the center of the show trials the SED conducted against the CDU in Erfurt and Gera during the winter of 1952-1953. In December 1952 at the *Bezirk* court of Erfurt, the SED sentenced seven CDU members who had contact with the western CDU to between eight and fifteen years in prison.[45] Other show trials against CDU members in Gera and again in Erfurt took place following the first show trials of 1952. The campaign to remove opponents and intimidate potential opponents continued in 1953. The MfS conducted searches of CDU offices, including its headquarters, and arrested the CDU Foreign Minister of the GDR, Georg Dertinger, on January 13, 1953 for allegedly conspiring with West Germany to absorb the GDR. Dertinger was sentenced the following year to fifteen years in prison. He was amnestied in 1956.[46]

The muted response of CDU members to these arrests and trials is testimony to the *Gleichschaltung* process within the CDU. It should be remembered that resistance activity increased in the CDU after the removal of Kaiser and during the wave of arrests in 1950. This quiet reaction, and as will be seen the lack of CDU participation on June 17, indicates that SED repression had succeeded in removing democratic anti-Communist resistance in the CDU by 1953.

Reports from lower-level LDPD groups to the leadership of the party indicate that there was also limited opposition in the LDPD to the party's support of the "building of socialism." In *Kreis* Eberswalde, *Bezirk* Frankfurt/Oder, the LDPD reported that the mood in the membership was very negative. Members simply could not understand the leadership's support for the "building of socialism."[47] The members of the LDPD in *Kreis* Borna also criticized the party's position, believing that there would be no room for a non-socialist party in the "building of socialism." In *Kreis* Erfurt-Stadt, the LDPD representative complained: "Some of our members do not agree with the 'building of socialism,' and added that they were considering dissolving the party."[48] The LDPD in *Kreise* Bergen-Putbus and Greifswald also stated that the membership opposed the "building of socialism."[49] In a sampling of five LDPD *Bezirk* groups conducted for this study, three groups mentioned resistance by the LDPD membership to the "building of socialism," and two did not contain documents on the subject.[50]

The remaining elements of the non-Marxist parties which had not yet been co-opted into the Communist system also vigorously opposed the rearmament outlined in the "building of socialism." The CDU in Schwerin estimated that 20 percent of CDU members opposed an East German People's Army (*Volksarmee*) for a variety of reasons, including the threat of civil war, the fear that the army would serve Russian interests, its negative effect on the economy, and the lack of a need for an army as West Germany did not constitute a threat.[51] The SED attributed the 9,211 (6.6 percent) drop in LDPD membership between July 31 and November 20, 1952 primarily to the creation of armed forces.[52] The issue of rearmament played an important role in the LDPD Leipzig *Kreis* conference of May 26, 1952. During the conference, the members voted on the following resolution: "The LDP recognizes the necessity of defending our Republic, including by means of national armed forces." Thirty-eight members supported the resolution, thirty-seven voted against it, and nineteen withheld their vote.[53] The members who voted against the resolution expressed concern that the creation of armed forces would bring closer the possibility of war.[54] The SED recognized that there was opposition within the non-Marxist parties to armed forces. In a report on these parties issued after the Second Party Conference, the SED stated: "There is still large resistance in the CDU and LDP membership with regard to armed forces."[55]

The churches especially took issue with the founding of an army. On June 22, 1952, a letter from the Magdeburger Synode was read in all Protestant churches in Magdeburg pleading for God's help so that Germans would not fire upon one another. Many ministers encouraged youths not to take up weapons, and offered them protection in the church. In the overwhelming majority of *Gemeinden* in *Bezirk* Magdeburg, ministers spoke out against armed forces.[56]

There is evidence to suggest that the general population also rejected rearmament, perhaps because this was the clearest symbol of the division of Germany and the prelude to a possible civil war. The LDPD *Land* association for Thuringia reported that the entire LDPD membership rejected remilitarization, as did wide sections of the population.[57] The following incidents support the LDPD analysis. At a factory meeting in Erfurt on June 26, 1952, which 100-120 people attended, three people spoke out strongly against the GDR and the creation of armed forces, and were greeted with loud applause. Those in attendance adopted a proposal against national armed forces and the *Volkspolizei*, and demanded the removal of a banner in the factory which read: "Women, encourage your husbands to defend the homeland. You will be helping to maintain peace."[58] On the day following the meeting, the cultural director of the plant spoke with one of those who criticized the armed forces to "show her the error of her ways." When, after half an hour, she had not returned to her post, the other workers began to form a demonstration column, believing she had already been arrested. Upon her return, she was greeted with cries of joy and celebrated as a martyr.[59] In Auerbach, the SED issued a questionnaire in the Falkensteiner Gardinenfabrik which was to be filled out by young males, and not women or the disabled. The factory workers protested, believing that the survey would provide the basis for a conscription list. Approximately fifty youths gathered in front of the factory shouting: "We do not want a conscription law, but an election law. We will not fill out the questionnaire because we do not want to be conscripted."[60] Graffiti against remilitarization appeared throughout the GDR. In Bad Berka, *Kreis* Weimar, someone painted slogans against rearmament such as: "Count us out. Hold on to your husbands tightly. Hold on to your sons tightly" on seven different sites in the town, including the office of the local SED secretary.[61]

Popular Reaction to the "Building of Socialism": Origins and Roots of the June 17, 1953 Revolution

Before the Second Party Conference, the SED Central Committee created a new department within the Central Committee called *Abteilung Leitende Organe der Parteien und der Massenorganisationen* (Leading Organs of the Parties and the Mass Organizations—LOPM). This department was responsible for controlling and guiding all lower levels of the party, the other parties in the GDR, and the mass organizations. The LOPM department received situation reports from local party organizations on the party and the population, and prepared reports for the Politburo and the Central Committee on a variety of themes, ranging from agriculture to internal security. In addition, the LOPM department organized *Instrukteur* (Instructor) brigades to travel to the lower levels of the party in order to verify the accuracy of lower-level reports.[62] This department became the most important department in the Central Committee of the SED.[63] For an understanding of the overall situation in the GDR, these reports are more revealing than the records of the Politburo and the Central Committee. There exist no transcripts of the Politburo meetings of this period, but only indexes of the topics discussed. The transcripts of the Central Committee sittings are useful, but do not provide the insight into popular developments available in LOPM reports. Nevertheless, the reaction of certain Central Committee members to developments in the GDR can be revealing. On the basis of the documents generated by the LOPM, Armin Mitter, Stefan Wolle, and Ilko-Sascha Kowalczuk have provided new evidence on unrest in the population, and the motivation behind this unrest, in the period preceding the revolution in June 1953.[64] The following account relies on the evidence presented in their work and on police documents and situation reports from the non-Marxist parties.

By the end of 1952, there were already signs that dissatisfaction in the broad population was boiling over as a result of the "building of socialism." It is important to stress that although these protests were linked to the economic situation, they quickly turned into fundamental political resistance. The economic situation was admittedly abysmal, however. Workers had to contend with material shortages in factories, lacking supplies of energy, ineffective machines, a shortage of tools, and few spare parts.[65] Workers were also affected by the fact that falling production meant that their wages remained low.[66] This trying situation did not hinder the Central Committee from declaring at the Second Party Conference that workers should expect to work longer hours. The SED leadership voiced its intention to increase work norms, in an attempt to decrease production costs at a sitting of the Council of Ministers in August 1952: "The first task is the reduction of production costs. . . . If we don't achieve this, we will not be able to make any progress towards Socialism."[67] The emphasis on heavy industry at the expense of consumer industry prescribed in the "building of socialism" contributed to a drop in living standards. During the first half of 1953, basic goods such as butter, fruit, and vegetables were difficult to obtain.[68]

With Christmas rapidly approaching, the SED rewarded its loyal factory bosses with generous bonuses of a full month's salary, while workers received a tiny bonus, if anything.[69] Enraged factory workers walked off the job in Weissenfels, Glauchau, Schkopau, Plauen, Cottbus, Berlin, and Magdeburg.[70] At the massive Karl-Liebknecht-Werk in Magdeburg, roughly 2,000 workers left work on December 13, 1952 due to the uneven distribution of the Christmas bonuses.[71] The protests reached beyond mere monetary considerations, however, as reflected in the reports of three Instructor brigades that the Central Committee sent out to Magdeburg to investigate the disturbances there.[72] The fact that the Central Committee sent out these three brigades attests to its concern for the situation in Magdeburg. During a strike at the Magdeburger Werft in December 1952, the brigades noted that workers criticized the press and the SED's view of democracy, and compared GDR conditions to those of the Nazi dictatorship.[73] Demonstrators voiced similar political slogans at the Ernst Thälmann and Karl Marx plants in Magdeburg.[74] Worker protests and criticisms of the regime continued in April 1953. In Rathenow factory workers complained: "We do not have democracy. If somebody says something, he ends up in Siberia. These government measures would not be possible in any capitalist country. There would be strikes and rebellion." And: "In the press, everything is presented to the people so wonderfully, but in reality everything is a disgrace."[75] It is notable that as early as the fall of 1952 strikers and protestors consistently coupled economic demands with political demands for the removal of the government, a task that East Germans knew could be accomplished through free elections.

Basic resistance to the SED program in East Germany was also visible in rural regions affected by the creation of agricultural collectives (*Landwirtschaftliche Produktionsgenossenschaften*—LPG). It was not only farmers with large land holdings, called *Grossbauern* in SED vocabulary, who were reluctant to join LPGs, but also farmers with small land holdings, known as "working farmers" (*werktätige Bauern*) in SED vocabulary, who presumably were to benefit from pooling resources.[76] During a farmers' meeting in Friedrichsaue, *Kreis* Seelow/Mark, the vast majority of the fifty new farmers (*Neubauern*, landless workers who had received land in the land reform of 1945) in attendance protested the founding of an LPG. After the meeting, those who supported the LPG and those against began to brawl in a bar in town.[77] In Neukirche, the new farmer Alwin Weiss was skeptical about LPGs, stating after a meeting that he had been in the Soviet Union and had seen what could be expected from a similar agricultural strategy.[78] In *Landkreis* Leipzig, one farmer with small land holdings said: "As a long-time Comrade, I am happy with the building of socialism, and especially that the village has not been left behind. But I am very worried. Of the 17 new farmers, I am the only one who supports the collectives. Even our comrades are opponents and would rather throw down their party books. . . . They have already called me 'Russian slave' and other such things."[79] A police report from September 1952 provides important evidence that not only farmers with large land holdings opposed the LPGs. The initial draft of this report attributed the recent 40 percent rise in crime in agricultural regions to the "class enemy," a clear reference to farmers with large land holdings. The draft was revised to state that the crimes were a result of "among others, the class enemy."[80] By January 1953, only 3.2 percent of farmers with small land holdings had joined an LPG.[81] Moreover, between September 1952 and January 1953, more "working farmers" than *Grossbauern* fled the GDR.[82]

The SED faced great difficulty in implementing its agricultural strategy. Founding meetings for the creation of collectives were regularly disrupted. In Burkhardswalde, *Bezirk* Dresden, and Reinsberg, *Kreis* Neuruppin, farmers opposed to the founding of the LPG disrupted its founding meeting and prevented the establishment of the collective. A minister in *Kreis* Meiningen disrupted the founding of an LPG there.[83] It should also not be assumed that all farmers who joined the LPGs did so out of support for the agricultural collectives. At the founding of an LPG in *Bezirk* Erfurt, one agricultural worker made clear his reasons for joining the LPG: "There are only two [other] paths, either into prison or over the border."[84] In a CDU survey of eighty *Kreise* throughout the GDR, *all* of the *Kreise* reported either rejection or skepticism toward the LPGs.[85] Even in the agricultural north, in *Kreise* such as Greifswald, Prenzlau, Usedom, and Rostock, LPGs were unpopular, demonstrating that the SED had failed to establish solid political roots in the region despite its land reform.[86] However, the *Bezirke* which reported the most difficulties regarding the agricultural programme since January 1953 were Leipzig, Potsdam, Frankfurt/Oder, Dresden, and Magdeburg.[87]

Due to the resistance in the countryside, the SED was forced to use its judicial system to implement its agricultural programme. Between August 1, 1952 and January 31, 1953, over 1200 trials were conducted against farmers.[88] The SED also sent out party Instructors to work closely with the press to convince the population of the benefits of the SED's agricultural policy.[89]

The *Volkspolizei* was gravely concerned about the situation in the countryside. The police, alarmed at the 40 percent rise in crimes in agricultural regions over the previous year, attributed the rise to sabotage of the agricultural program of the "building of socialism."[90] The police furthermore listed the security of LPG foundings as its primary duty: "The help of the *Volkspolizei* is particularly important at the establishment of new LPG's."[91] This task was likely to be difficult, given the strained relationship between farmers and the *Volkspolizei*. In September 1952, the police complained that the amount of contact between "working farmers" and the *Volkspolizei* was very low.[92] The SED recommended that the *Volkspolizei* work more closely with farmers in order to overcome the existing shortcomings, hoping that the SED *Volkspolizei* would be able to create a situation whereby "every member of the agricultural collectives feels that the *Volkspolizei* is his assistant and his friend."[93]

Farmers' protests against entry into the LPGs revealed both economic and political motivation. At a gathering of farmers to establish an LPG in *Gemeinde* Kyritz, one speaker talked of his positive experience in the Soviet Union, only to be met by people shouting him down. During the discussion afterwards, even farmers with small land holdings expressed their reluctance to join the LPG fearing they would lose land.[94] Similarly in Markkleeberg/Ost a new farmer stated: "I am outraged at how our government acts. . . . I do not want to be a slave in the collective. I haven't worked day and night for other people. I'd rather throw everything in and hang myself than join the collective."[95] But opposition to the LPGs often revealed a more fundamental resistance to the SED. On August 18, at another public farmers' meeting in Friedrichsaue, those in attendance diverted attention away from the LPG issue on the agenda, and instead brought up issues such as the arming of the *Volkspolizei*, the recently introduced requirement of a passport to enter the other zones of Germany, and the SED's desire for armed forces. These issues led to general criticism of the SED. One member in attendance accused the SED first secretary of the region of being an enemy of the people because the first secretary demanded that he shoot at his western German brother in the event of war. Others criticized the judicial system. One person said that a friend told him that an investigation had been started against him and that his arrest was imminent, to which another person replied: "Fritz, forget it. Just remember who did it. The day is coming when we will take our revenge."[96] One woman even suggested that all SED functionaries should receive a good beating with a crowbar.[97] The events at this meeting led to several arrests, and the matter was taken up by the MfS for further investigation. In Hagenwander, the SED revealed political resistance in the population by attributing the unwillingness of local farmers to found an LPG to the influence of RIAS.[98] At a general meeting in Kleinow-Westprignitz, farmers shouted down the SED speaker with cries of: "We do not need schooling. We want to conduct our meeting. Away with him!" Others, *Grossbauern*, stated: "With the expression 'working farmers,' they just want to see hate spread among us, and they build their power on this hate. Through the expression 'working farmer,' war is brought into the village. We are all German farmers."[99] In Piskowitz near Zahren, similar thoughts were echoed. One *Grossbauer* said: "There is no such thing as a "working farmer" or a *Grossbauer*, only German farmers."[100] Sometimes the anger of farmers was uncontrollable. In *Gemeinde* Gösslow, *Kreis* Hagenow, one *Grossbauer* was so angry with the SED that he threatened the local SED party secretary: "I'll hang you all one day. For you, I've already got the rope ready."[101] In Loburg, *Bezirk* Magdeburg, at a meeting to expand the local LPG, one farmer yelled at the local SED functionary during his talk on the reasons to expand: "You lie. Why don't you tell us the truth?"[102]

The political nature of resistance in agricultural regions was a general phenomenon in the GDR. During a seminar on possible dangers for the upcoming harvest, the *Volkspolizei* reported: "The biggest danger for the harvest is enemy activity. . . . An important method of enemy activity is to influence our 'working farmers,' especially through RIAS' smear, so that they lose faith in the whole project [i.e., building socialism]."[103] A section within the SED membership itself expressed their doubts about the viability of the reforms, not solely because of the economic situation, but because of the "present state of consciousness in the population."[104] This "consciousness" was a euphemism for popular rejection of the SED. In fact, the extent of instability in the countryside caused Ulbricht to order the head of the *Volkspolizei*, Karl Maron, to increase protection of the collectives.[105]

By May 1953, the Central Committee of the SED was forced to admit the failure of the collectivization strategy. The Central Committee halted the establishment of new LPGs, and instructed existing ones not to accept new members.[106] In defence of these measures, Ulbricht stated during a conference with the MfS: "If, by the harvest, we have . . . properly worked through all these problems in individual agricultural collectives; if the mistakes have been corrected; . . . if we are successful in overcoming this backwardness and correcting certain mistakes, then our harvest will be a success. At the harvest, we will see that a much larger number of working farmers will want to join the agricultural collectives."[107] Ulbricht was aware of both the failure and unpopularity of the agricultural policies implemented since the Second Party Conference.

SED members in *Bezirk* Schwerin noted that arrests in the agricultural sector contributed to this resistance to the SED. During a sitting of the SED control commission for *Bezirk* Schwerin in March 1953, one member asked: "Why do we have so many [farmers] that flee to the West?" Another member answered: "Agents try to penetrate our ranks. They sow the seeds for these people to flee the Republic by telling them that they will be locked up and other things."[108] The arrests did cause concern in the population. In Basedow, Mecklenburg, the arrest of one farmer led to a protest which saw the village gather 300 signatures for his release. The protest was successful, and the farmer released.[109] SPD reports from their sources in the GDR between the summer and fall of 1952 emphasize that oppression caused the large majority of the population to oppose the regime.[110]

Due to the deep hostility in the population, the MfS took extra measures in February 1953 for the protection of leading SED functionaries. In the same month the Politburo issued a resolution which stated: "Uninterrupted day and night protection is to be guaranteed to all members of the Politburo of the Socialist Unity Party of Germany through escorts from the Ministry for State Security."[111] Furthermore, the first and second party secretaries in the *Bezirke* received permits to carry weapons, and all "undesirable" elements were removed from the Berlin neighbourhood of Pankow where the most important SED functionaries lived, in order to better secure the area.[112] Even prior to the revolutionary uprising of 1953, the population had shown signs that their rejection of the SED program rose above economic considerations.

The Descent Toward June 17, 1953

Despite signs of unrest, the SED believed that the situation in the GDR was stable enough to continue its "building of socialism." At the thirteenth sitting of the Central Committee, held on May 14, 1953, the Central Committee of the SED called for "increased work norms of 10 percent by June 1."[113] Increased work norms translated into increased number of hours worked, without a corresponding increase in wages. Although these norms did not become law until June 2, the call for the increase on May 14 meant that factory party chairmen would feel obliged to have their workers "voluntarily" raise the production level before the law came into effect.[114] The increased norms caused strikes as early as May 1953. In Leipzig, 900 workers at the iron and steel pouring works marched out of the factory on May 16.[115] There were also short work stoppages due to the norms at the end of May and beginning of June in Eisleben, Fürstenwalde, Chemnitz, and Borna.[116] In an analysis issued following the revolution, the SED Central Committee recognized these disturbances as a precursor to the revolution in June:"The first signals were that in a large number of factories, even before the publication of the communique [of June 9 announcing the New Course—GB], there were short strikes, mainly against the administrative increase in norms which had been ordered."[117] The SED took little notice of these disturbances, however. In an analysis of the background to the revolution Marshall Sokolovskii, the Soviet Deputy Defense Minister, Vladimir Semyenov, head of the Soviet High Commission in the GDR, and Pavel Yudin, Chairman of the Soviet Control Commission in the GDR wrote: "In December and January-February 1952 [sic] there were isolated incidents of small and short-lived workers' strikes within a few enterprises; these, however, did not catch the attention of the . . . SED and [Soviet Control Commission] organs."[118]

The Soviet Union, which closely monitored the situation in the GDR, realized that the stability of the GDR was at risk in the early summer of 1953. From the end of 1952 through the first four months of 1953, the Soviet Control Commission in East Germany did research into the attitude of the East German population and found that the population was not only discontent, but that it was "facing the regime with increasing hostility."[119] The Soviet Union therefore called three leading members of the SED to Moscow. On June 2, Fred Oelssner, Walter Ulbricht, and Otto Grotewohl travelled to Moscow to meet with the interim leadership of the Communist Party of the Soviet Union which had replaced Stalin after his death in March 1953: Nikita Khruschchev, Lavrenty Beria, W.M. Molotov, G.M. Malenkov, and W.S. Semyonov.[120] The Soviet leadership minced no words with their German counterparts: "There is serious dissatisfaction in the majority of the population, including the workers, farmers, and intellectuals, regarding the economic and political measures which have been introduced in the GDR."[121] It was clear to the Moscow leadership that political developments had contributed to the unrest. Based on its analysis, the Soviet Union forced the SED to slow down the "building of socialism." One of the main changes suggested by the Soviets was the adoption of a more lenient approach to the religious community. In a disguised order to the SED, the Soviets explained: "It should be kept in mind that repression of the church . . . can only contribute to strengthening religious fanaticism in residual sections of the population, and to increasing their dissatisfaction."[122]

Apparently surprised by this information on its own population, the Central Committee took measures upon the return of its leadership from Moscow to improve its knowledge on the mood of the population. Central Committee displeasure with the information gathering system became evident on June 12, when Karl Schirdewan, head of the *Leitende Organe der Parteien und der Massenorganisationen* branch, ordered a special group of three members of the LOPM branch to produce daily reports on the mood of the population based on reports from the SED *Bezirk* leadership, from the central leadership of the mass organizations, from the party instructors, and from the various departments within the Central Committee apparatus.[123] It is important to emphasize that Schirdewan's order did not involve instructions to use MfS reports, further demonstrating that MfS information gathering on the GDR population was deficient in the early years of the organization.

The SED Politburo heeded the advice of the Soviet Union by recommending in a communiqué of June 9 that the government adopt a "New Course."[124] Two days later, the government announced in its newspaper *Neues Deutschland* that a "New Course" would be embarked upon. The news of the impending "New Course" spread quickly throughout East Germany in the two days following the issuing of the communique and on June 11, *Neues Deutschland* sold out within a few hours of appearing on newsstands, with some people in Berlin paying up to thirty times the regular price to obtain a copy.[125] The "New Course" entailed a relaxation of the collectivization of agriculture, the end of the persecution of church members and the *Junge Gemeinde*, and the elimination of restrictions on private business owners. There was no mention of a reduction of work norms, however.[126]

In recognition of the abuse of basic rights, the government also announced that a release of prisoners would take place and that there would be a general increase in

Rechtssicherheit (legal security).[127] The Soviet authorities in Germany had recognized the role that arrests had played in popular discontent. In an analysis of the roots of the revolution, high-ranking Soviet officers in Germany attributed the uprising to the lack of basic consumer goods combined with legal insecurity: "This [i.e., material shortages] was joined by the measures taken by the [Central Committee of the SED], as part of their mistaken policy of liquidating the petit and middle bourgeoisie of both city and country, which in some places took the rather ugly forms of insular administrative planning and mass repressions, directed also at workers."[128] The Soviets indicated that the excesses might have been the result of over zealous local authorities: "In a number of instances, SED district and regional committees completely supplanted government organs, bringing under their authority police operations, arrests, the day-to-day administration of enterprises, etc."[129]

The population interpreted the "New Course" as an admission of weakness by the government and therefore began to act, believing that an opportunity existed to affect political change. Even before the widespread disturbances of June 17, isolated work stoppages and other disturbances, often with clear political overtones, took place in the GDR. About 200 people gathered in front of the prison in Stralsund to demand the release of prisoners there on June 12.[130] On the same day in the Mathias-Thesen-Werft in Wismar, workers began demanding free elections and the resignation of the government.[131] Some elementary school teachers took advantage of the announcement to tear down from the school walls all pictures of Wilhelm Pieck, the president of the GDR.[132] On June 15 near Leipzig, forty workers of the VEB Sowahr in Rosslau went on strike for one hour. On the morning of the sixteenth at the Warnow-Werft in Warnemünde, one protestor scrambled up the side of a building and hung a large sign demanding the removal of the increased norms and free and secret elections.[133] In Berlin, about 900 demonstrators gathered in front of the prison on Barnimstr at 9 am demanding the release of prisoners.[134]

A dramatic protest against the government occurred in Brandenburg on June 12 when six workers appeared at the *Kreis* public prosecutor's office and demanded the release of their boss who had been jailed for not having paid taxes. After the request was rejected, the workers proceeded to the prison in the middle of town and began protesting. Within an hour, the crowd had swelled to over 5,000 demonstrators. The demonstrators demanded free elections and the resignation of the government.[135]

The Politburo and Central Committee gradually came to recognize discontent in the population, but the members refused to abandon the course. At the Politburo sitting of June 13, Grotewohl emphasized that the SED would not "give up," and stressed that the Politburo had to demonstrate that the raised norms and "frugalness" were not mistakes.[136] By June 15, the Central Committee was visibly nervous. Schirdewan ordered more information on the population to be collected, especially in industrial centers: "At present, the Central Committee does not possess *Bezirk* overviews on certain important sites, such as Leuna-Werke, Buna, Bitterfeld, Mansfeld, Karl-Marx-Stadt, the border regions, and large factories in Berlin."[137]

Thus, there were isolated protests in the industrial centers of the north and south of the GDR at the beginning of June with the most dramatic protests taking place in Brandenburg. The desire for political change was, however, common in the protests prior to the revolution. In an LOPM report summarizing the reports of the *Bezirk* level party reports on June 12, the authors stated that typical opinions of protesting workers were: "Now the GDR is bankrupt." And: "Now those at the top realize that they're at their end."[138] Despite these protests, the SED leadership refused to reduce the norms.[139]

Rural regions also experienced unrest on the eve of the revolution. In an increasing number of LPGs, farmers indicated their desire to be rid of the agricultural collectives and met with only isolated protests by other farmers for their views.[140] Moreover, the rural population also interpreted the "New Course" as a chance to affect political change. In some districts, entire villages gathered in local pubs and drank to the health of the West German chancellor Konrad Adenauer.[141] On June 13 at a village gathering in Eckolstädt, after joyously receiving four farmers released from prison, those in attendance demanded free elections and the resignation of the government.[142] In Muchow, *Kreis* Ludwigslust, during the night of June 16 to 17, farmers demanded the removal of the SED mayor.[143] In Schmergow, Rathenow, and Jessen, demonstrators demanded the release of imprisoned farmers. The SED in *Bezirke* Gera and Schwerin noted an increase in "enemy arguments" and increasing calls for an end to the SED.[144]

These open demonstrations of political resistance were not isolated phenomena. All *Bezirke* reported oppositional activity in the villages, ranging from "drunken fests" to demonstrations, all of which revealed a hostility toward the government. It is therefore not surprising that all *Bezirke* also reported an increased number of attacks against SED functionaries in rural regions.[145] On June 15, Central Committee member Karl Schirdewan, dismayed by the situation in the countryside, sent instructions to all SED *Bezirk* heads criticizing the reports of negative occurrences in the rural population: "Certain *Bezirke*, such as Gera, Halle, Wismut have provided good analysis of the situation taking into account present opportunities. The other *Bezirke* limit themselves to repeating the well-known daily reports, without providing true analysis."[146] Armin Mitter and Stefan Wolle have concluded that rural disturbances particularly shocked the Central Committee because it was in those regions that the Central Committee had expected the most loyalty.[147]

The historians Arnulf Baring and Torsten Diedrich argue that the protests in the summer of 1953 did not become political until the afternoon of June 17, and that, therefore, the uprising should not be interpreted as revolutionary from the outset.[148] For the purposes of this study, it is important to establish the fact that political demands accompanied economic demands in demonstrations leading up to the June 17 uprising.

The Revolution

The State of the Literature

The first major work on the June 17 uprising was Stefan Brant's *Der Aufstand: Vorgeschichte, Geschichte und Deutung des 17. Juni 1953* (Stuttgart: Steingrüben Verlag, 1954), a work based on eyewitness accounts and personal experience, as Brant himself took part in the uprising. The work claims to be based on SED documents, but the lack of footnotes means it is impossible to verify this claim. It is in any case extremely unlikely that the author would have been able to obtain access to substantial amounts of SED material in 1954. Brant's work is therefore an unreliable, memoir-type account. Nevertheless, he was the first to suggest that the events of June 17 represented more than an uprising, but were rather a revolution.[149] Brant also noted that the uprising involved a variety of social groups because, although workers started the uprising, the GDR had been "ripe" for unrest.[150]

The first academic work on the topic, Arnulf Baring's *Der 17. Juni 1953* (Cologne: Kipenheuer & Witsch, 1965), which appeared in English as *Uprising in East Germany: June 17, 1953* (Ithaca: Cornell University Press, 1972), concluded that the uprising was primarily a workers' uprising, and that economic demands prevailed:

> There is danger in paying too much attention to the large scale demonstrations which took place in certain towns, for they tend to create the impression that June 17 was a popular uprising. In fact, the eyewitness reports prove conclusively that this was not the case. It was the industrial workers—actively supported by the youth of the GDR—who were responsible for the events of June 17. They started the rising and were the dominant factor in every major demonstration. By contrast, the farmers were involved only in isolated incidents, and the middle classes and the intelligentsia played little or no part in the day's events.[151]

There were two factors that hindered Baring's analysis: the lack of a sufficient source base and the interpretation of the uprising in isolation. These two are related, for the opening of the archives has revealed that the uprising took place within a longer period of turmoil. Examining unrest before, during, and after the uprising suggests that disturbances in the summer of 1953 involved various societal groups. Karl Wilhelm Fricke and Ilse Spittmann's, *17. Juni 1953: Arbeiteraufstand in der DDR* (Cologne: Edition Deutschland Archiv, 1982) contributed more information to the debate, but took essentially the same position as Baring, arguing that the uprising was exclusively a workers' revolt which centered on economic demands.

The first major work to appear after 1989 on the June 17 uprising was Torsten Diedrich's *Der 17. Juni 1953: Bewaffnete Gewalt gegen das Volk* (Berlin: Dietz Verlag, 1991) which dealt with the military response to the uprising, and especially the role of the GDR's People's Police in Barracks (*Kasernierte Volkspolizei*). Like Baring, Diedrich believed that "one clearly cannot come to the conclusion that the

June 17 uprising was a popular revolt."[152] Treating the uprising in isolation was the primary reason for this conclusion, but it was also likely a result of an unscientific use of sources, and an insufficient source base. Diedrich limited his research to police reports and the odd SED report to describe the uprising, but his account does not satisfy the requirements of historical scholarship. His citation of sources is sparse, and the few citations provided are vague. Diedrich provides only the archival call number for the record group without the precise location or description of the document. As some of these record groups contain hundreds of documents, it is impossible to know which documents Diedrich has used, and therefore to judge their value. Diedrich's account of the uprising is vague and in some instances incorrect. Through a scientific use of similar sources to the ones used by Diedrich, combined with records from the MfS, CDU, and LDPD, especially in the period following the uprising, this study challenges Diedrich's contentions that the uprising was exclusively a workers' uprising and that it did not represent political resistance.[153] Gerhard Beier's *Wir wollen freie Menschen sein* (Cologne: Bund Verlag, 1993) added documents from the East German Free German Trade Union and western archives to the debate in support of Diedrich's analysis of the nature of the uprising, as well as the earlier interpretations of Baring, Fricke, and Spittmann.

The first work to offer new evidence that the uprising was more than a workers' protest was Manfred Hagen's *DDR- Juni 1953* (Stuttgart: Franz Steiner Verlag, 1992). Based primarily on eyewitness reports in letters to himself from those who had been involved in the uprising, Hagen offered an in-depth look at all aspects of the uprising and its progress throughout the days of June 16 and 17. Hagen's thoroughness allowed him to contend that other social groups were involved in the uprising. He found, for example, that workers often encountered other protesting groups on the streets already, not groups which joined the workers only after they saw them protesting.[154] Through these examples, Hagen demonstrated that the middle class, technical intelligentsia, farmers, youth, and women all played an important role in the uprising. Hagen therefore employs the term *Volkserhebung* (popular uprising) to describe the events of June 17 in the GDR. The eyewitness reports should not substitute for archival evidence, however.[155]

With the publication of Armin Mitter and Stefan Wolle's *Untergang auf Raten: Unbekannte Kapitel der DDR-Geschichte* (Munich: Bertelsmann Verlag, 1993) historians were presented with a radical interpretation of June 17, based on the most thorough use of sources to date. The work attempted to trace the decline of the GDR through key episodes in East German history: the June 17, 1953 uprising, the destalinization of 1956 and the events in Hungary, the building of the Wall in 1961, and the Prague Spring of 1968.[156] For the first episode, Mitter and Wolle sought to answer the following question: "Was June 17 a workers' revolt or a people's revolt? Did the population protest in the streets and squares of the German Democratic Republic against the decaying standard of living or for the abolition of the Communist regime?"[157] By expanding the discussion to include the prelude to, and the aftermath of, the uprising and introducing much new archival material, Mitter and Wolle offered a convincing argument that June 17 was more than a workers' revolt, preferring the term *revolutionäre Erhebung* (revolutionary uprising). They argued that the population concluded from the events that the SED rested on Soviet power, that "the GDR was an artificial product of the Cold War without internal legitimacy."[158] The present work comes to similar conclusions regarding the nature of the uprising, based on an entirely different set of documents—documents which have an advantage over the MfS files presented by Mitter and Wolle in that they are accessible. During January 1990, when the "Citizens' Committee" occupied the MfS headquarters in Berlin, Mitter and Wolle were able to access and photocopy archival material relating to the uprising. The archival holdings were allegedly lost during the transfer of files in 1990 from the MfS archives to the German Federal Agency for the Files of the State Security Service of the former GDR.[159] These files are now only available from Mitter and Wolle. Unlike the MfS files in Mitter and Wolle's work, the police records on which the present study is based are publicly verifiable.

Mary Fulbrook argues that the uprising cannot be categorized so neatly. She feels that economic issues in favor of better living conditions and anti-communist motives were too closely related for historians to be able to separate. In analyzing the character of the uprising, Fulbrook concludes: "A debate which counterposes economic dissatisfaction (economist strikes in favor of better living conditions) to political demands (anti-communism, unification with the West) . . . fails to capture the ways in which these were so closely interrelated as to be almost inseparable."[160] Fulbrook's claims notwithstanding, historians must work in terms of priority. The danger in Fulbrook's approach is to raise economic concerns to an artificially elevated motive for resistance. Were better living conditions the reason for simultaneous demonstrations and strikes in over 350 sites in the GDR on June 17, 1953? Could one make the counterfactual argument that if the GDR had satisfied the material situation of the population, the uprising would not have taken place? A report by an SED member after his trip to Halle in July 1953 helps to prioritize the issues: "The main slogans that the enemy brings into the factories and spreads in the countryside, which are cleverly disguised as smaller, more immediate economic demands but which are increasingly brought to the fore, are: free elections, release of all political prisoners since 1945, apolitical unions."[161] It is important not to confuse the sparks which set off the uprising with the powder keg of fundamental political resistance. Historians of June 17, 1953 would do well to keep in mind what George Rudé has championed: "The immediate—or even long term—causes of popular participation in revolution is one thing; popular ideology that infuses that participation, and without which there can be no popular revolutionary activity at all, is something else."[162]

There were much deeper issues at work during the summer of 1953 than economic demands. Furthermore, to emphasize economic aspects of the uprising is to downplay the development of the repression apparatus in eastern Germany from the end of the war. The uprising demonstrated a fundamental lack of trust in the system of government which was, no doubt, partially related to economic difficulties attributed to the regime. However, the history of repression in the GDR and Soviet zone was crucial in transforming opposition to government economic policies into fundamental resistance to the political system. Police, MfS, CDU, and LDPD documentation from the days and months of the revolution and following the revolution—documentation not cited by Fulbrook—attest to the political nature of the demonstrations and the importance of SED repression in popular motivation to resist.

Another ground-breaking work on the revolution was Ilko-Sascha Kowalczuk, Armin Mitter, and Stefan Wolle's richly documented *Der Tag X, 17. Juni 1953: Die "Innere Staatsgründung" der DDR als Ergebnis der Krise 1952/54* (Berlin: Ch.Links Verlag, 1995).[163] This work augmented the conclusions in *Untergang auf Raten* that the June 17 uprising was a popular revolutionary upheaval and proposed that the SED and the Soviets drew the conclusion from the events of 1952-1953, particularly the June uprising, that the GDR had to be "internally founded" to ensure that a repetition of the disturbances would not be possible. The SED thus expanded its security and repression apparatus. This analysis has expanded the context of the uprising, based primarily on LOPM documents, to include events up to 1954.

The Outbreak

The spark for the revolution came from construction workers in East Berlin, although, as has been proven throughout this study, the underlying willingness to resist was already well established. On the morning of June 15, angered not only that the 10 percent norm increase had not been retracted in the "New Course," but that the FDGB newspaper *Tribüne* justified the raise in norms and indicated that a retraction of the norms would not occur, construction workers on the site of a future hospital in the Berlin district of Friedrichshain forced the party chair for the work site to draft a resolution to be handed to Grotewohl. The resolution read: "We colleagues of the construction site of the Friedrichshain hospital of VEB *Industriebau* turn to you, Mr. Minister President, asking that you take note of our concerns. We believe that the 10 percent norm increase is a great hardship for us. We demand that our construction site be exempted from the raised norms. . . . Considering the agitated mood of all employees, we demand a completely satisfactory response on these difficult matters, and await your position until tomorrow noon."[164] As arranged over beer during the previous Saturday's construction workers' boat excursion on the beautiful lakes of southern Berlin, members from other construction sites attended this meeting of the Friedrichshain hospital construction workers. Through these attendees, word spread quickly to other construction sites and by the end of the 15th, construction workers throughout Berlin anxiously awaited Grotewohl's response.[165]

On the following day, June 16, Grotewohl's personal secretary announced that Grotewohl would not be taking a position on the resolution right away because the question of work norms required lengthy consultation with various levels of the party.[166] To deliver the message to the construction workers at the hospital in Friedrichshain, the party sent out fifteen instructors who explained that a retraction of the norms would not take place. Between 400 and 500 construction workers from the Friedrichshain site attended the meeting, joined by 200 workers from the construction site of Fernheizwerk.[167] During the meeting with the Instructors, the director of the construction site had the entrance to the site locked. The construction workers immediately became suspicious that they would be arrested, causing two workers from the nearby massive Stalinallee construction site to return to their comrades and enlist assistance. They arrived breathless, reporting that "construction workers of the Friedrichshain hospital were locked up and being held against their will."[168] Roughly one hour later, between 8 and 9 am, a column of construction workers from Block 40 on the Stalinallee appeared at the hospital construction site and forcefully opened the gate. Workers from both sites then joined together in a demonstration of about 700 people which snaked its way through the city, leaving the Friedrichshain hospital along Stalinallee until they reached Alexanderplatz, just a stone's throw from the Communist party archives where future historians would read about their actions. They turned west crossing the Spree river at Mühlendammbrücke, and marching along Breitestrasse to Marx-Engles Platz, turning onto the storied avenue Unter den Linden within sight of the enormous Berlin Cathedral. Normally boisterous and belting out songs, the crowd passed the gaudy Soviet embassy in complete silence. At the Brandenburg Gate, they turned and marched along Wilhelmstrasse with its bombed-out embassies from the Third Reich, finally reaching the House of Ministries located on Leipzigerstrasse.[169]

As demonstrators marched to the House of Ministries, a building last occupied by Hermann Goering's Air Ministry, their numbers increased more than sevenfold, reaching at least 5,000 by the time they reached the House of Ministries.[170] Women and children are clearly visible in pictures of this marching column.[171] By the time the crowd had gathered in front of the House of Ministries, they had already begun to call for free elections and the resignation of the government.[172] The police recognized the political nature of the demonstration, reporting that the demonstrators' began voicing "anti-democratic" demands such as a general strike on June 17 and the overthrow of the government.[173] Fritz Selbmann, the minister for steel industry and mining, tried to quell the crowd by stating that the norms were to be rescinded, but the crowd shouted Selbmann down.[174] Although there was a general desire to remove the government, the demonstration of June 16 in front of the House of Ministries suffered from a lack of leadership. Between 2 and 3 pm, due to the lack of leadership and the intense summer heat, the demonstrators began to disperse, but not before several demonstrators appealed to the crowd to hold a general strike the following day.[175]

The present historiography has not adequately dealt with the evening of June 16 in East Berlin, as various episodes from that evening demonstrate the revolutionary nature of the uprising.[176] Upon leaving the House of Ministries, the demonstrators headed back along the path they had come and continued further towards Warschauer Bridge and finally to Oberbaum Bridge, where at 7:30 the demonstration began to disperse.[177] Along the way towards Oberbaum Bridge, demonstrators ripped down SED symbols, such as FDJ flags and SED posters.[178] On

Chausseestrasse, the demonstrators threw the driver of an FDJ truck out and used its loud speaker to broadcast demands like "Down with the SED" and "Overthrow of the government."[179] Although the demonstrators began to disperse at 7:30 pm, this did not signal the end of the disturbances. At 8:12 pm, a new marching column of about 1,000 people formed on the Stalinallee and began marching towards the center of the city. They ripped down flags and propaganda boards of the SED on construction sites along the Stalinallee, yelled slogans such as "Down with the SED," and attacked a monument to Stalin.[180] By 9:50 pm with the rain driving down and lightning brightening the sky, the demonstrators, now totalling 3,000, tore down SED flags and posters on Marx-Engels-Platz. [181] Shortly thereafter, demonstrators turned over a government truck,[182] and at Bersarin square, some demonstrators even tried to break into the houses of SED functionaries.[183] Torsten Diedrich argues that West Berliners who crossed the border to join the demonstrations "implanted" the political slogans of June 17 and, as evidence, he states that there were no demands for the fall of the government on June 16.[184] Diedrich's conclusion is not supported by the events of June 16.

The *Volkspolizei* were extremely nervous about the developing situation. At 9:50 pm, the Berlin police called for reinforcements from Potsdam, Magdeburg, and even from as far away as Leipzig,[185] ordered an extra 200 officers to guard the *Volkspolizei* presidium in Berlin, and extra troops to guard the offices of the public prosecutors.[186] The allotment of these reinforcements provides evidence of what the *Volkspolizei* felt would be targets of the demonstrators—the instruments of the repression apparatus where prisoners were being held. The *Volkspolizei* was eventually able to disperse the crowds on the evening of the 16th, reporting that by 11 pm, the situation in East Berlin was stable.[187] The police were careful not to use their weapons and to avoid arrests where possible, as they were fearful that the situation would escalate.[188]

At 4:30 pm on June 16, the American Radio in the American Sector (RIAS) reported for the first time on the disturbances in Berlin. The ninety-second clip called the disturbances a "mass demonstration," and claimed that the *Volkspolizei* had not dared to disperse the crowd. For the rest of the day, and throughout the morning of the 17th, RIAS continually played this message. By the 17th, wide sections of the GDR had been well informed of the disturbances in Berlin.[189]

Other cities apart from Berlin experienced disturbances on 16 June. Three hundred people in VEB Hammerschuh in Döbeln went on strike.[190] At RAW "Einheit" in Engelsdorf near Leipzig, workers demanded the release of all political prisoners, the conducting of secret elections, and the resignation of the government.[191] In fact, all *Bezirke* reported work stoppages or factory disturbances and noted that these disturbances involved political demands.[192] Thus, although construction workers incited further disturbances in Berlin, the rest of the GDR was clearly restless and showed a willingness for action. Indeed, on the following day, demonstrations across the GDR began simultaneously with those in Berlin.

On the night of June 16, the Politburo hastily organized a meeting (*Parteiaktivtagung*) in the Friedrichstadt-Palast of the most reliable party members for Greater

Berlin in order to deal with the unrest. The Politburo announced that the "obligatory" raising of the norms would be rescinded, and that the Politburo would appeal for a voluntary increase of the norms instead. On that night, Ulbricht stated: "In today's sitting, the Politburo of the SED resolved to recommend to the government that the directives of the individual ministries for the obligatory increasing of work norms be lifted. We believe that an increase in work norms can only take place on a voluntary basis."[193] The norms were therefore to be rescinded. For this reason, demonstrators' demands on the following day centerd around the removal of the government and free elections.[194] Diedrich's argument that protests on June 17 were largely the result of workers' confusion as to whether or not the norms would actually be rescinded[195] is not as convincing as that of Mitter and Kowalczuk, who claim that Ulbricht's speech was a provocation for another reason: It did not announce changes to the system of rule.[196]

June 17, 1953 in Berlin

East Berlin erupted on June 17, 1953, a rainy Wednesday. The earliest strike in Berlin took place at 6:35 am, when between 250 and 300 workers at the Fortschritt Werk III began marching towards the Stalinallee.[197] At 6:40, workers at the railway outfitting works Friedrichshain and Bremsenwerk threw down their tools.[198] Striking workers from various other factories such as RFT Treptow, RFT Edison-Strasse, ABUS Lichtenberg, and Kabelwerk Köpenick also poured out of the factories and began the long walk to the city center.[199] The most dramatic marching column came from Hennigsdorf, where workers from two large factories walked 27 km to join the demonstrations in Berlin, bypassing the Walter Ulbricht soccer stadium where they tore down the gigantic letters spelling his name. Many of the workers arrived in Berlin still wearing their protective glasses that they had put on that morning in front of the sweltering factory ovens.[200] As early as 7 am, striking workers shouted political demands. At approximately 7:15 am, striking workers of the Kabelwerk Oberspree shouted: "Down with the police, the *Volksarmee*, and the government!"[201] At 7:25 am, a crowd of between 400 and 500 workers heading towards Strausberger Platz—the gathering destination announced by demonstrators in front of the House of Ministries on the previous day[202]—from Lichtenberg shouted: "We are at the end of our torture. We demand free elections."[203] At 8:45 am, two columns of demonstrators marching towards Marx-Engels-Platz shouted: "We do not need a *Volkspolizei*, we will free ourselves."[204] The demands of demonstrators in other areas of Berlin also went beyond economic considerations. Although there were calls for the reduction of the work norms, demonstrators also called for free elections, the overthrow of the government, the end of the SED, and the release of all political prisoners.[205] The police revealed that the political nature of the revolution was a general phenomenon in Berlin: "The demands and placards of the *early morning hours* demonstrated the strong presence of provocateurs in the demonstration,"[206] whereby in this context SED vocabulary "provocateurs" referred to an opponent other than "regular" striking workers. Around 7:50 am, between 300 and 500 people smashed through a chain of blue-shirted police officers and Free German Youth members on Strausberger Platz, shouting: "We want to be free workers. We are at the end of our torture. Free elections."[207] By 8:18 am, the police reported that all demonstrators had left Strausberger Platz.[208] The demonstrators began marching towards the previous day's target, the House of Ministries. Political demands occupied a prominent place in the demonstrations of the early morning hours of June 17. Of the police posts around Berlin that reported on the slogans of the demonstrators, none mentioned economic slogans prior to the demonstrators' arrival at the House of Ministries.[209]

The issue of whether or not June 17 was a workers' uprising continues to be debated. It is unlikely that a definitive breakdown of the social backgrounds of the demonstrators can be compiled because of the lack of sources on this topic, but archival sources do reveal that the workers met with widespread moral and physical support in their demonstrations. Historians should therefore look beyond the fact that workers made up the largest societal group in the demonstrations to the deeper issue of why broad sections of society took part in the demonstrations. It is prudent, therefore, to revise the arguments of Baring, Fricke, and Diedrich to take into account the participation of a variety of social groups in the demonstrations. In Berlin, other people constantly joined marching workers in the streets. The police reported that one group of about 1,000 construction workers near Strausberger Platz was "joined by passers-by on the streets who marched along with them."[210] At 8:17 am, near the Café Warschau in Berlin, a group of between 300 and 400 women joined the demonstrations shouting against the creation of a *Volksarmee*.[211] Eye witnesses also report the strong support that demonstrators received from people along the streets.[212] In a recollection of the events on June 17, *Volkspolizei* commander Koch stated: "More and more . . . people, who had nothing to do with the construction workers, appeared on the scene."[213]

Along the way to the House of Ministries, demonstrators attacked members of the FDJ, damaged *Volkspolizei* cars, ripped down the Communist slogans and pictures that blanketed Berlin's buildings, and often wrote their own slogans on the reverse side.[214] One group of demonstrators even tried to throw some FDJ members into the river, but were prevented from doing so by other demonstrators.[215] Other demonstrators, not as violent, simply ripped the party symbol from those wearing it,[216] and constantly subjected the police to verbal abuse, often calling them "traitors of the working class."[217] By 10 am, there were thousands of demonstrators in the streets of East Berlin heading towards the House of Ministries, cramming into subway trains (many, the station administrators noted, without a valid ticket), or already demonstrating in front of the building.[218] Political slogans adopted early that morning, such as "free elections," adorned demonstrators' placards here as well.[219]

Upon arrival at the House of Ministries, a regiment of the MfS lifted demonstrators off their feet with water cannons.[220] Few of the members of the government dared to speak to the crowd, Walter Ulbricht and Otto Grotewohl preferring to watch the unfolding of events from the comfort of the Soviet headquarters in Karlshorst.[221] Only Fritz Selbmann, the minister for iron and steel works and mining, Robert Havemann, a professor at the University of Berlin, and state secretary Heinz Brandt emerged from the House of Ministries to talk to the crowd, but the hostile audience quickly drowned them out.[222] The popular resistance to the regime would not be quelled by speeches. At roughly 11:00 am, the *Volkspolizei*, with the assistance of Soviet tanks which had been posted at the Brandenburg Gate early in the morning of the 17th, began dispersing the outer edges of the crowd.[223] At 1 pm, the Soviets declared a state of emergency and vigorously dispersed the crowd, although avoiding excessive force.[224] The protestors scattered in all directions, running for cover behind anything that looked like it might provide some protection— newspaper and snack kiosks set up nearby, barrels littered around the square, and massive piles of rubble still left from the war.

Demonstrators in Berlin also targetted the *Volkspolizei* presidium at Alexanderplatz, where an angry crowd of between 4,000 and 5,000 armed with rocks tried to storm the building. While police officers on Alexanderplatz tried unsuccessfully to disperse the crowd using billy clubs, one police officer was stabbed. Throughout the skirmishing, workers at a finance office on Alexanderplatz cheered when demonstrators threw stones at the police, and called the police "dogs" when they dispersed the crowd. The crowd on Alexanderplatz was finally dispersed after 1 pm with the announcement of a state of emergency and the arrival of the Soviets.[225]

The police had not been able to disperse the crowd on their own in part because they had received an order not to use their weapons against the demonstrators. A police report by General Koch after the revolution explained why no order to use firearms had been given: "A bullet can, and this has been demonstrated throughout history, lead a world into catastrophe." He stated that the goal of those operating "behind-the-scenes" was to provoke and demonstrate confrontation between state and people; thus use of weapons would have played into their hands. It seems that the training of the police was also an issue, for Koch commented: "The officers' level of training for active duty is insufficient."[226] Torsten Diedrich has further suggested that the SED's uncertainty about the reliability of its security apparatus caused the SED to be cautious in employing its own troops during the revolution.[227]

Targets and Demands of Demonstrators Outside Berlin

An analysis of the targets and demands of demonstrators reveals that the revolution reached far beyond economic considerations. Legal insecurity, which was characteristic of life in eastern Germany from 1945 and which had been exacerbated in the months prior to the disturbances, demonstrated itself in the widespread attacks to free prisoners from the buildings of the SED's repression apparatus: the *Volkspolizei* buildings, prisons, judicial buildings, party buildings and, to a lesser extent, MfS buildings. Furthermore, the demonstrators' demands revealed a desire for change in the political system. In the vast majority of disturbances, the demonstrators demanded free elections, fully aware that such elections would rid themselves of the SED regime.

Bezirk Magdeburg

At 9:30 am in Magdeburg, workers at the VEB Schwermaschinebau Ernst Thälmann, Karl-Liebknecht-Werk, and Dimitroff Werk went on strike. In the Karl-Liebknecht-Werk, where workers had gone on strike in December 1952 because of the Christmas bonuses, workers yelled at police officers of the small police station in the factory and attacked the head of the station.[228] Roughly 8,000 workers from the three sites gathered together to form a marching column, and began marching towards the city, shouting through megaphones: "Workers, lay down your work. Down with the government."[229] As was common during the revolution, they were joined by supporters in town.[230] At approximately 10:15, demonstrators stormed the city council building and the FDGB building, and beat up several FDGB functionaries. At 10:55, while some demonstrators stormed the FDJ building, others headed to the SED *Bezirk* headquarters and the building of the newspaper *Volksstimme*. The demonstrators then turned their attention to the *Volkspolizei* prison, first beating a *Volkspolizei* officer before storming the building.[231] The demonstrators, by this time somehow having managed to obtain fourteen rifles, set the front gate of the prison on fire, but were unable to free the prisoners due to the arrival of Soviet troops at 12:30 pm.[232] However, demonstrators freed prisoners awaiting transport in a train at the railway station.[233]

Demonstrators also targeted other sites in the area around Magdeburg where prisoners were being held. Demonstrators stormed the police station and justice building in Magdeburg-Sudenburg, releasing a total of twenty prisoners at a cost of the lives of two police officers.[234] According to one participant, most of the police officers fled to the roof of the police station, but, after hearing that the Soviets were making their way to the police station, began shooting into the crowd, killing four people and injuring eight. Soviet tanks then arrived at about 11:30 am and tried, with the help of a few warning shots, to disperse the demonstrators. As the crowd refused to disperse, the Soviets fired into the crowd, causing most of those gathered to flee.[235] Another center of unrest was the prison on Moritzplatz in Magdeburg-Neustadt, where demonstrators released between fifty and sixty prisoners. It was necessary for the Soviets to use force here as well to disperse the demonstrators.[236] The fighting on the streets of Magdeburg led to the deaths of two police officers, one MfS Officer, four demonstrators, and the injuries of forty-two others.[237]

Rural regions of *Bezirk* Magdeburg experienced limited unrest. The most significant demonstration occurred in Gommern, where at 4 pm, several hundred people stormed the prison and released some of the prisoners. In Salzelnen, several houses hung banners reading: "Germans awake! The hour has come."[238] In total, 32,000 people took part in demonstrations in *Bezirk* Magdeburg.[239]

Bezirk Dresden

In *Bezirk* Dresden, the main plants to strike were LOWA Waggonwerk Görlitz, EKM Maschinenbau, and the Nagemawerk Sachsenwerk Niedersedlitz where 1,000 workers turned their backs on the factory. Workers in *Bezirk* Dresden targeted sites similar to those in Magdeburg. In Niesky, demonstrators stormed the local SED building, dragged out the first SED secretary for the region, and beat him to the point where he required hospitalization. Demonstrators also attacked the MfS building, yelling at the *Volkspolizei* who guarded the building: "You pigs want to shoot at workers!" After the *Volkspolizei* fired warning shots, someone yelled: "They only have blanks!" The crowd then attacked the *Volkspolizei* with rocks and beer bottles. The *Volkspolizei* did not fire on the demonstrators, however, as their taskforce leader had instructed them not to,[240] and retreated to the local police station. Fifteen border guards who had been sent from Bautzen assisted the police in preventing the crowd from storming the police station. After an hour and a half, the crowd retreated and mounted a renewed attack on the MfS building. They stormed the MfS building, disarmed the few officers who remained in the building, and locked up four of the officers, including the leader of the branch, in dog cages located on site.[241]

Similarly, demonstrators in the nearby town of Görlitz focused their anger on freeing prisoners. The number of demonstrators swelled as workers were joined by "thousands of people" from the town,[242] as they made their way to the detention center for those awaiting trial. The leader of the detention center, Dörich, who had been up since 5:15 am preparing to defend his installation, opened the window of his office and heard the muffled noise of the crowd grow louder and louder as the crowd approached. On his instructions, one of his assistants clambered out to the main gate where he locked the two huge wooden doors while another locked the keys to all the cells in a safe. The demonstrators swarmed the prison, hurling rocks at the windows while chanting: "Free the political prisoners" and scaling the fence. After the crowd had broken through the first outer barriers, the leader of the prison tried to negotiate with the crowd. The discussions lasted for twenty minutes, after which time the crowd became more unruly and pushed into the building, where the demonstrators broke open the cells on the lower levels of the complex and freed all prisoners in the installation.[243] The building of the Soviet commander and the MfS building in town were also stormed. During the storming of the MfS building, demonstrators attacked SED functionaries and ripped down posters and slogans.[244] After the storming of city hall and the local courthouse, demonstrators armed with axes forced the SED mayor to sign a form ordering the release of all prisoners.[245]

In Dresden, thirty members of the Sachsenwerk Niedersedlitz factory who the previous day had been in Berlin on an educational outing on the Stalinallee and witnessed the calls of the construction workers for a general strike on June 17 brought word of the unrest in Berlin, sparking a walkout of roughly 1,000 workers. The strikers headed towards the Abus-Werk factory to garner support and were joined en route by workers from Hutfabrik Niedersedlitz, Gardinenfabrik Dobritz, Kamerawerke Zeiss-Ikon, and Berufsschule Mügelner Strasse. The SED, clearly out of touch with the workers, attempted to placate the remaining workers in the Niedersedlitz factory by sending one of their leading functionaries, Otto Buchwitz, to discuss international diplomacy. The speech convinced those workers who had returned to their posts to join the strike. At approximately 4 pm, the *Volkspolizei* notified the Soviet officer for Dresden that the crowd was heading towards the theater square to hold a rally. Upon hearing the news, the Soviet officer announced a state of emergency, and, with the help of the *Volkspolizei* , dispersed the crowd with the use of warning shots. No shots were fired on the demonstrators and by 9 pm, order had been restored in Dresden.[246]

Demonstrators' demands in *Bezirk* Dresden centered on political and economic issues. Workers at Sachsenwerk Niedersedlitz demanded the reduction of norms, the removal of the government, and the release of all political prisoners.[247] A delegation from Betrieb Koh-i-Noor demanded German unity and free elections.[248] In Niesky, one of the slogans on the 17th was the demand for the dissolution of the *Volkspolizei* in Barracks and the *Staatspolizei*.[249] At LOWA Görlitz Werk, where one third of the plant left to take part in demonstrations, workers demanded a reduction in store prices, higher wages, and removal of the increased norms. Of those who stayed behind, one worker who was acting as speaker for the group told the local party leader that the government should resign because it had lost the trust of the workers. He also recommended that new and secret elections be held and that the union and party representatives in the factory should resign. All workers eventually left the plant.[250]

Political resistance was made evident in *Bezirk* Dresden on June 17 by demands for the permitting of the SPD. Görlitz witnessed the greatest degree of SPD activity on June 17, as demonstrators publicly refounded the SPD on Lenin square in the center of town[251] and then quickly disappeared for fear of arrest. At other sites in Görlitz, such as the fine optics plant and the hospital, "initiative committees" of the SPD were formed.[252] In VEB Lowa, speakers at a rally demanded the unity of Germany, free elections, and the revival of the SPD.[253] The countryside surrounding Görlitz also experienced SPD activity. At least one SPD group was formed, and several SED members demanded to have their SPD membership books back.[254] SPD influence overall in the revolution was of considerable concern to the SED. Horst Sindermann, leader of the Central Committee Agitation and Propaganda department said in October 1953: "We should examine how it is that agents of the SPD *Ostbüro* have a relatively large influence with the working masses compared to other agents."[255]

Bezirk Leipzig

In Leipzig, demonstrators attacked the police station and the prison, but the police successfully defended the buildings against the crowd.[256] Demonstrators in the streets of Leipzig attacked the FDGB building, the FDJ building, the radio building, and the *Volksstimme* building.[257] In Delitzsch near Leipzig, approximately 300 people stormed the local police station. In Düben, 300 people failed in their attempt to storm the city hall.[258] Demonstrating Leipzigers demanded the abolition of the government, the introduction of democratic rights and freedoms, and free and democratic elections.[259] *Bezirk* Leipzig also experienced SPD activity. Heinz Neumann, an SPD member who had been expelled from the SED in 1951, led striking workers in the precision tool factory in Schmölln in singing the SPD song: "Brüder, zur Sonne, zur Freiheit."[260]

Heidi Roth's local history of the uprising in *Bezirk* Leipzig emphasizes that although workers comprised the main social group during the revolution, other social groups participated. Roth therefore concludes that June 17 in *Bezirk* Leipzig was a popular uprising.[261] Roth concluded that the increasing legal insecurity and forced implementation of the socialist program caused both affected and unaffected to oppose the regime,[262] conclusions that support the evidence presented in this study.

Bezirk Potsdam

The most dramatic disturbances in *Bezirk* Potsdam occurred in Brandenburg. The starting point for the demonstrations here was the Bau Union in the Stahl-und Walzwerk Brandenburg, where between 500 and 700 people left their work at about 7:30 am on June 17. It is worth remembering that by this time, demonstrators in Berlin had only started to gather at Strausberger Platz, but had not yet begun marching towards the House of Ministries. The outbreak of disturbances occurred, therefore, virtually simultaneously in Berlin and Brandenburg. The Stahl-und Walzwerk workers burst into nearby factories and urged workers to join the demonstration. By 9:30 am, the number of demonstrators had risen to between 12,000 and 15,000.[263] Demonstrators first attacked the *Kreis* SED building, where they attacked SED members and threw propaganda material and telephones out of the windows. The second party secretary for the district narrowly avoided being thrown out of a third story window.[264] The demonstrators then proceeded to the prison on Steinstrasse, storming the prison and the local court house located in front of the prison, and freeing roughly forty prisoners. During this attack, demonstrators stripped several *Volkspolizei* officers and severely beat them.[265] The revolution in Brandenburg was so extensive that the police candidly admitted that they thought that the government had fallen.[266]

After releasing the prisoners, the demonstrators stormed the FDGB building and threw documents out of the windows. The crowd then demonstrated in front of the House of German-Soviet Friendship before reaching the police station, where the police greeted the crowd with warning shots. The shots provoked the crowd into a frenzy, resulting in between fifty and eighty demonstrators successfully breaking into the station. The demonstrators were likely spurred on by overhearing one police officer shout to his subordinates who were protecting the building: "Don't shoot. Don't shoot. The *Kreis* office said not to." Once inside, demonstrators beat several police officers and SED functionaries, with one demonstrator going so far as to smash open the head of a member of the SED with a wooden stick. Soviet troops, which appeared at roughly 12:30, were needed to free the police station of demonstrators.[267] Afterwards, the police complained about the orders not to use their weapons.[268]

The demonstrations in Brandenburg reveal broad hostility to the judicial system. After demonstrators had freed all prisoners in the prison on Steinstrasse, the crowd began chanting for Judge Benkendorf to be handed over to them. One member of the crowd felt that it was unnecessary for Benkendorf to be handed to the crowd, but rather that he should be locked up because he would "be hanged tomorrow in any case." The demonstrators did, in fact, catch Benkendorf, and, after thoroughly beating him, dragged him through town. Benkendorf narrowly escaped death due to the presence of a doctor nearby who treated him for his injuries. During the demonstrations, the demonstrators also jailed the public prosecutor.[269]

A large demonstration also took place in Hennigsdorf, near Berlin. Many of the nearly 4,000 demonstrators from LEW Henningsdorf attacked FDGB buildings and the local courthouse and freed the prisoners held in the court prison before continuing their journey to Berlin.[270] In Potsdam, workers at the Karl-Marx-Werk first went on strike at 2:30 pm, a late start that local SED functionaries speculated resulted from viewing Soviet tanks heading towards Berlin provoked the strike. The striking workers demanded the resignation of the government, the removal of the newly introduced work norms, lower store prices, and free elections.[271]

Political demands accompanied economic ones in demonstrations in *Bezirk* Potsdam. The police reported that the most common slogans were: "Free elections, removal of norms reduction in prices [in state stores], removal of the zonal boundaries, fall of the government, and tanks out of Berlin."[272] The call for free elections, the fall of the government, and the removal of zonal boundaries reflected popular desire to be rid of the Communist system in East Germany.

Bezirk Halle

Demonstrators throughout *Bezirk* Halle attacked buildings and personnel associated with the SED and attempted to free prisoners. In both Rosslau and Quedlinburg, the police office and the prison were stormed.[273] The course of the revolution in Rosslau in particular made evident the popular nature of the revolution. Striking workers at the Rosslauer Schiffswerft gathered early in the morning and demanded the resignation of the government and the freeing of political prisoners. At 9:30 am, three-fourths of the employees (about 1,600) streamed out of the plant heading towards the town center, and along the way the crowd "grew quickly" to number between 3,000 and 4,000 people, as "many petit bourgeois" elements joined the workers.[274] In Eisleben, the police station and detention center for those awaiting trial were stormed and the prisoners released, following which the demonstrators proceeded towards a prison camp in Volksstaedt. They did not reach their destination because Soviet soldiers dispersed the approximately 1,000 strong crowd.[275] In Merseburg, the police station, prison, and MfS buildings were stormed, their interiors destroyed, and prisoners in all sites released.[276] Demonstrators attacked police officers on the streets in Weissenfels.[277]

In *Kreis* Bitterfeld, the entire complement of the VEB Farbenfabrik in Wolfen—between 5,000 and 6,000 workers—laid down their work on the morning of June 17 and, at 8 am, marched to the nearby Filmfabrik. En route, a "large number of inhabitants from Wolfen" joined the workers, who forcefully entered the Filmfabrik. The demonstration then swelled to nearly 10,000 people. The crowd proceeded to the Elektrochemischen Kombinat to join with workers there. At 10:30

am, this group marched towards the police station in Bitterfeld, attacking various SED functionaries along the way, including the local SED secretary for propaganda, who was knocked down and dragged along with the demonstration as a trophy.[278] Upon arrival at the police station, a delegation, identifying itself as an "SPD delegation," demanded to see the books of the prison to determine if there were any political prisoners there. The demonstrators freed an undetermined number of prisoners before attacking the MfS *Kreis* building and the FDJ *Kreis* building.[279] Clearly unnerved, the police described the situation in Bitterfeld that morning as such "that there were no organs left that could be considered to embody the state's authority."[280]

In Halle itself, workers at the Waggonfabrik gathered to discuss a strike at 6 am. This meeting, it should be emphasized, took place before any action had been undertaken in Berlin. At 6:30 am, several workers demanded in front of the crowd of 2,000 workers removal of the increased work norms, reduction of store prices, and the resignation of the government. At 10:20 am, the crowd began heading towards the center of town. During their march, workers from Ifa-Karrosserieweri, Maschinenfabrik Halle, and MTS-Reparaturenwerkstatt joined the demonstrators. The crowd grew from 2,000 to 6,000 due to the additional workers and, according to the police, "many members of the petit bourgeoisie."[281] At Reileck square, protestors pried the eight metre picture of Stalin off a nearby wall and watched it slam into the middle of the square below, where thousands of eager demonstrators trampled it beneath their feet.[282] In Halle, protests took place in front of three sights where prisoners were being held: Halle prison I, Halle prison II, and the building of the justice administration. Other SED buildings were attacked, however, including the MfS building, the FDJ building, the police office, and the SED building.[283] During these protests, several police officers and a judge were beaten up. Halle is one of the few instances where there is clear evidence of the use of weapons to quell unrest, as demonstrators attempting to enter Halle prison I and the police station were kept out through the use of weapons.[284] In the words of one SED report: "In Halle, calm and order were first reestablished after armed units from the Soviet army and the *Volkspolizei* were employed and shots fired."[285] During the fighting in Halle, Erna Dorn, a former Nazi concentration camp commander, was freed from one of the prisons and took an active part in the demonstrations.[286] The SED made great use of the propaganda value of this incident, holding up Dorn's release and participation in the demonstrations as evidence that the revolution had been a cloaked "fascist putsch." Following a trial, Dorn was beheaded on October 1, 1953 in Dresden.[287]

Attacks on jurists, as had occurred in Halle and Brandenburg, offer evidence that repression was a leading cause behind resistance. In Rosslau, a similar occurrence took place to the one in Halle. Demonstrators successfully penetrated the police station and the prison and freed all prisoners. In the process, they identified and badly beat the *Kreis* district attorney.[288]

Demands of demonstrators were fairly uniform throughout *Bezirk* Halle. Workers at the Otto-Brosowski-Schacht in *Kreis* Eisleben did not demonstrate in the streets, but elected a strike leadership who demanded the removal of the government, lowering of prices, and the release of prisoners. The *Volkspolizei* acknowledged the importance of political demands for these demonstrators stating that the "fascist leadership" issued "extreme demands, including the resignation of the government."[289] In *Kreis* Rosslau, workers at the Rosslauer Schiffswerft went on strike demanding the removal of the government and the freeing of political prisoners.[290] At the RAW in Halle, workers went on strike demanding that the government resign because it no longer held the trust of the population, and that food prices be lowered.[291] After witnessing the extent of the revolution, the police in Merseburg indicated a fundamental hostility to the regime by stating that they were unaware of "the true attitude of a large part of the workers."[292]

Bezirk Halle also experienced SPD activity on June 17. During the strike of about 4000 workers at the sprawling Leuna factory "Walter Ulbricht," demonstrators called for the reestablishment of the SPD, prior to taking to the streets and ripping down all Communist slogans and pictures of all party functionaries.[293] At the Soda factory in Bernburg, signs bearing the slogan "We demand the permitting of the SPD in the eastern zone" were hung up.[294]

Bezirk Gera

In the town of Gera, about 200 workers of the VEB Roto-Record held a meeting at 8 am on June 17, at which a resolution was issued demanding a reduction of prices in stores, reduction of norms, dissolution of the MfS, release of political prisoners, and the end of the government. The workers then left the factory to gather support from workers at other factories such as the compress works, Firma weber, EKM boiler construction, Thuringian carpet works, WMW Union Gera, TEWA and RFT. The demonstrators then headed to various SED sites. By 1 pm, with the addition of workers from other factories, the number of demonstrators had grown to about 6,000.[295] In Greiz, one car drove through town with the banner "Freedom—down with the government."

In nearby Weida, approximately 1,500 people took part in demonstrations, shouting: "This is not the will of the people. The *Spitzbart* must go." *Spitzbart* was the common derogatory name for Ulbricht. Demonstrators also attacked the police station here yelling: "Count your days."[296] The police report on the occurrences in Weida is notable for the manner in which it formulated the development of events. The police reported that one protestor went from factory to factory "and took advantage of the mood of the population" to get others to join the strike.[297] The phrasing suggests that there was an underlying hostility to the government which could be taken advantage of.

The revolution in Jena reveals the extent to which the population had come to despise the SED and its instruments of control. Over 20,000 agitated demonstrators stormed buildings of the National Front, the local branch of the German Soviet Friendship Society, the SED, and the MfS,[298] throwing files onto the streets.[299] Throngs cheered when across town the manager of a theater smashed with a hammer the lit letters S-E-D which adorned the theater.[300] Demonstrators also attacked the prison and released between fifty and sixty prisoners there. The regional police chief regretted that his subordinates had "misinterpreted" orders from headquarters to understand that employing "all means" to prevent the storming of the prison did not include use of force. During the storming of the prison, four police officers were injured and taken to hospital, but doctors at the local hospital refused to treat the police officers. When one police officer was brought in, the doctor yelled "another one of those criminals," and slammed the door of the examining room on his way out. The police officers had to be hurried to a nearby Soviet military hospital.[301]

Bezirk Frankfurt/Oder

At 5 am precisely on June 17, Chief Inspector Grünstein of central headquarters in Berlin telephoned the leader of the regional police office in Frankfurt/Oder, Inspector Kotulan, and told him to prepare his men for whatever may come that day. Kotulan called his subordinates and ordered them into the station by 6 am. Because their guns were broken, the group spent most of the morning prying spare parts off their practice guns to slot into their service revolvers. By mid-morning, the phone was ringing off the hook with reports of disturbances in the district. In virtually every corner under his jurisdiction, Kotulan witnessed some form of disturbance: strikes paralyzed factories, telephone lines were being cut, pictures of the president Wilhelm Pieck ripped off walls and thrown out windows, trucks parked across railway lines to block transportation. Kotulan first rushed reinforcements from his station in Frankfurt to the SED party office in Fürstenwalde where they beat back with billy clubs the roughly seventy demonstrators who had broken in and were threatening the functionaries. Turning their attention to blocking traffic, the demonstrators toppled a statue of Karl Marx on the main square and dragged it to Wilhelm Pieck street. By early afternoon, Kotulan was sending his men out to assist in putting down disturbances all over the region. A few days following the outbreak, Kotulan, breathing a sigh of relief that the disturbances were put down, demanded from his superiors better weapons for his men and schooling in tactical procedures to deal with riots.[302]

Attacks on detention centers also marked demonstrations in Bezirk Frankfurt/Oder. In Fürstenwalde, about 100 people tried to enter the police station, causing the police to call for reinforcements from Seelow.[303] In Angermünde, a group of between 80 and 100 youths demonstrated in front of the SED Kreis building.[304]

Demonstrators from Strausberg near Berlin also focused their anger on a symbol of state repression by marching towards the prison camp in Rüdersdorf. Cement and phosphate workers joined the demonstrators along the way. The commander of the camp was determined that the demonstrators would not succeed in freeing the prisoners there, however. The police report on the occurrence does not clearly state the result of the encounter, but the innuendos suggest that the camp was defended with the use of force: "When the provocateurs showed up in front of the installation and demanded the release of prisoners, [the person in charge] prepared for the rigorous defence of the installation. The security of the installation was guaranteed by clear orders, including the order to shoot."[305]

Demonstrators' demands in *Bezirk* Frankfurt/Oder revolved around political and economic issues. In a tire factory in Fürstenwalde, banners were put up with the slogans: "We demand free and secret elections," "Remove the government," "Abolish the KVP," and "Reduce the prices in the [state] stores by 40 percent." Apart from these general demands, the demonstrators specifically called for revision of the verdicts against two workers.[306] On the night of June 16, 1953, three different sites in Herzfelde, *Kreis* Strausberg, were painted with graffiti reading: "SED must go," "*Volksarmee* must go," and "[State stores] must go."[307] On the following day, these slogans were physically put into practice. In Strausberg, demonstrators attacked and beat one SED member and in the nearby train station at Herzfelde, another SED member was shot at.[308] Railway installations were also centers of unrest. In RAW Basdorf, workers went on strike demanding 40 percent lower prices in the state-run stores and free elections.[309] In Eberswalde, demonstrators spread hand made pieces of paper through the Abus-Kranbau demanding free elections and the fall of the government.[310] The police in *Kreis* Bernau reported that the "free elections" demanded by the demonstrators corresponded to the West German elections.[311] In Bogensee, construction workers of the "FDJ-Hochschule Wilhelm Pieck" revealed that they wanted elections to be held like those in West Germany, stating: "We would then see how popular they are. (They are referring to the government of the GDR)."[312] There can be little doubt that the widespread call for free elections was due to the popular desire to be rid of the Communist system in the GDR.

Bezirk Erfurt

Demonstrations for the release of prisoners occurred in various cities of *Bezirk* Erfurt. In Worbis, demonstrators in front of the *Kreis* court demanded that prisoners be freed.[313] In Apolda, between 500 and 600 people protested on the market square in front of the *Kreis* court demanding the release of prisoners.[314] The judicial system also came under attack in Apolda. On June 17, a government lawyer, Vogel, drove to Jena on a motorcycle, and seeing the unrest there, returned to Apolda and contacted the local court judge. Vogel proposed a meeting to remove all SED members from the *Kreis* court.[315]

In the countryside, demonstrators demanded the release of prisoners and the end of the government. In Mühlhausen, a farmers' assembly took place which attracted 2,500 people to the market square. One of the primary demands of the demonstrators was the release of imprisoned farmers.[316] In the towns of Oberdorla and Altengottern, farmers also demonstrated for the release of prisoners.[317] Demonstrations in the countryside were likely more widespread than reported. One police report stated that: "Even in small localities of the *Bezirk*, agents and provocateurs were active. In Tunzenhausen, for example, a gathering took place at which 100 people took part." At this demonstration, protestors called for the release of all economic criminals and the peaceful unification of Germany.[318] At a farmers' demonstration in Sömmerda, demonstrators demanded free all-German elections and economic changes.[319]

Striking workers also demanded the release of prisoners and the end of the Communist system in the GDR. Workers from the VEB Rheinmetall Sömmerda demonstrated on the market square demanding a reduction in norms and release of political prisoners. In RFT Funkwerk, Erfurt, the tool construction section of the plant went on strike demanding the release of one of their members who had been arrested.[320] In Heiligenstadt, the leader of the VEB Mewa, gave a speech in which he strongly condemned the conduct of the government and demanded its removal.[321]

Bezirk Erfurt also witnessed SPD activity on June 17. In Niedersedlitz people wrote slogans on the side of a school in support of the demonstrators, reading: "Long live the SPD" and "The SPD still lives."[322] In *Kreis* Arnstadt, the SED party secretary in Behringen stated that several comrades suggested to him that it might be better to form an SPD group because the SED had made mistakes. He added that he felt "isolated" by those members who wanted to establish an SPD group.[323]

Bezirk Cottbus

Release of prisoners was at the center of demonstrations in the city of Cottbus. Early in the morning of June 17, emerging from the steam and the massive black engines, workers from the railway outfitting works Cottbus laid down their work and began marching through town.[324] The crowd moved towards the detention center for those awaiting trial but Soviet soldiers prevented them from entering the building.[325] Blaming elements that were roughly equivalent in their eyes, "youths and prostitutes," the police reported on a small demonstration later in the day that quickly grew as people from town joined and marched through town shouting: "Down with the government," "Freedom for all prisoners," "Reduction of the norms and [state run store] prices." The crowd forced its way through the narrow streets to the detention center where security forces barred all entrances just before the arrival of the demonstrators, and hurried to the telephones barking orders for reinforcements. The extra police arrived from nearby stations and met with fierce resistance to their attempts to break up the demonstration. Fearful of a successful storming of the detention center, the Soviets called in the tanks, causing some demonstrators to flee in fear and others to viciously attack the Soviet soldiers. Even with warning shots, it took over two hours to disperse the crowd. The presence of the Soviets meant that the police did not have to call in the "air police," the nascent East German air force stationed in Cottbus that had been at the ready since early morning.[326] In nearby Lübben, demonstrators attacked the local police station.[327] There is also evidence that prisoners themselves were restless. In *Bezirk* Cottbus, the police, nervous because prisoners in the prison work camps were becoming unruly, called for additional reinforcements.[328]

In the countryside, demonstrators also targeted buildings associated with SED repression. Indeed, the first disturbance in the *Bezirk* came from a group of about 250 *Grossbauern* in Jessen who demonstrated in front of the *Kreis* administration building and demanded the release of all imprisoned *Grossbauern*, something that the public prosecutor agreed to do. During the demonstration, the demonstrators happened upon a member of the *Volkspolizei* and ripped the gun out of his hand. They also planned to go to the prisons in Herzberg and Liebenwerda to free farmers there, but, for reasons not mentioned in police reports, did not carry out this plan.[329] In Lübbenau, demonstrators demanded freedom of press and speech.[330]

The police report on a demonstration in the agricultural region of *Gemeinde* Sielow in *Kreis* Cottbus, reveals in chilling fashion the underlying widespread resistance to the SED regime in the countryside: "In the late evening hours of 17 June, a demonstration column was formed in *Gemeinde* Sielow, *Kreis* Cottbus. SED members were attacked and struck down. The ring leaders opened the doors of the volunteer fire department and began ringing the fire siren. Due to this, a large part of the village population gathered on the village square. The ring leaders called for the murder of active comrades of the SED and also tried to organize the plundering of certain police officers' homes. We only became aware of these occurrences the following day, and therefore conducted an operation against the ring leaders on the evening of 18 June."[331]

Bezirk Rostock

There were geographically limited disturbances in *Bezirk* Rostock on June 17, mainly in the shipbuilding district along the coast where over 2,000 workers went on strike. These also revealed political resistance and issues related to repression. In Rostock itself, there was an attempt at an easier method of releasing prisoners. One person phoned the prison and, posing as a local authority, ordered the release of all economic criminals.[332] During a demonstration in Sievershagen, one farmer yelled: "Up to now, we have been muzzled, now we can breathe freely."[333] In Volkswerft Stralsund, there were also political slogans, where workers demanded: "We need parties, and not just an SED" and one worker blacked out the name Walter Ulbricht on the slogan hanging on a ship that vowed to finish the ship before Walter Ulbricht's next birthday. Following the disturbances, the police called for both weapons and a telephone lines repair truck, because the cut lines had severely hindered their ability to coordinate activities in the region.[334]

Bezirk Schwerin

In Güstrow, *Kreis* Schwerin, approximately fifty workers gathered in front of the *Kreis* court and demanded the release of the former owner of a chair factory in town.[335] Otherwise, there were no major disturbances. Although there were fewer disturbances here, the SED recognized that there was anger similar to that expressed in other regions of the GDR. The SED in *Bezirk* Schwerin reported that the LPGs were unreliable during the revolt and that many of those who worked on the agricultural collectives sympathized with the striking workers.[336]

Bezirk Neubrandenburg

The only site of significant unrest in *Bezirk* Neubrandenburg was Teterow, where about 400 people demonstrated in front of the prison demanding the release of prisoners. The police reported that many pamphlets appeared on the streets of the

Bezirk with slogans like: "Down with Ulbricht," "We demand free elections," and "Russians out."[337]

Bezirke Karl-Marx-Stadt and Suhl

Although there was unrest in these *Bezirke*,[338] there were no serious disturbances.[339]

The CDU and LDPD During the Revolution

A telegram from the leadership of the CDU to the SED Central Committee claiming its support of the government on June 17 reflected the views of a majority of its membership.[340] There were, however, isolated incidents of CDU participation in the revolution. In *Bezirk* Erfurt, *Kreis* Heiligenstadt, the CDU deputy chair of the *Kreis* council, stated that the SED should resign and that the CDU should take over the leading role.[341] A CDU factory chair in Heiligenstadt agreed, saying: "If the government makes mistakes, then it must be dissolved."[342] In Ershausen, Steinbach, and Arenshausen, the CDU had already prepared a list for new elections to the *Gemeinde* assemblies.[343] In a sugar factory in Wismar, *Bezirk* Rostock, CDU members were aggressive toward SED members and supported the strike.[344] Soviet sources also reveal that there were elements in the CDU that felt the CDU should form the government in light of the failures of the SED.[345] There were, on the other hand, CDU members who supported the SED and attempted to disperse crowds and bring the demonstrations to an end.[346] These members certainly chose the safer option. The former chair of a CDU group in *Kreis* Rudolstadt was executed out-of-hand for his participation in the revolution.[347]

There was also a certain amount of LDPD activity during the revolution. Dr. Hans Loch, chair of the LDPD in the GDR, acknowledged LDPD involvement in the revolution: "There were also certain members of our party [the LDPD] who had an idea of taking over leadership on [June 17]."[348] In Magdeburg, one of the leaders of the uprising was an LDPD member and in Ebersbach, the CDU and LDP replaced the SED mayor.[349] An LDPD member of city council in Kranichfeld, *Kreis* Weimar-Land, *Bezirk* Erfurt demanded that all citizens of Kranichfeld who where in prison should be immediately released.[350]

Overall, however, CDU/LDPD participation in the demonstrations was negligible. In *Bezirk* Leipzig, out of fifty-nine "ring leaders," three were SED, one LDPD, one former CDU, and sixteen FDJ.[351] After extensive study of the documents of the non-Marxist parties, Leo Haupts has concluded that the non-Marxist parties did not firmly support the SED on June 17, but they did not actively resist the regime either.[352] Haupts' conclusion is supported by police records. Of 2,916 people arrested between June 17 and June 30 for their part in the revolution, only 4.6 percent were members of the CDU or LDPD.[353] The lack of resistance can be attributed to the fact that the non-Marxist parties had been coopted into the Communist system by 1953, as outlined in the previous chapter.

The Nature of the Revolution

Although workers initiated the disturbances on June 17, the latent hostility to the regime was visible in the manner in which these demonstrators gained support from other sections of society. The participation of other societal elements in the demonstrations has already been established in the above discussions of *Bezirke* Magdeburg, Leipzig, Halle, and Berlin. The other *Bezirke* reported similar occurrences. According to a police report on demonstrations in Cottbus: "The demonstrators quickly gained adherents during the march through town."[354] A theme common to the police reports on Halle was the willingness of other people in the city to join the demonstrations. In Stadtroda, people eagerly joined the 200 protesting workers on the streets. Police also complained of the trucks transporting demonstrators between Gera and Greiz: "Over 50 percent of the people in the trucks were in my opinion not Wismut workers, but provocateurs from the population and youths."[355] In *Bezirk* Frankfurt/Oder, other people in town joined construction workers demonstrating at the border crossing of Dahlwitz/Hoppegarten. According to one police report: "When the construction workers, and other sections of the population who had gathered there, tried to break through, the comrades of the border police put an energetic stop to their efforts."[356] In Wittenberge, a demonstration of 400 people "from various societal groups" took place.[357]

A police report from June 18 offers excellent evidence that June 17 was a popular uprising, not exclusively a workers' revolt. This report separated the numbers involved in strikes and those involved in demonstrations as follows:

Table 5.1. Work Stoppages and Demonstrations on June 17, 1953

Bezirk	Work Stoppages or Strikes	Number of strikers	Demon- strations	Number of demonstrators
Potsdam	45	40,250	32	53,350
Frankfurt/O	18	8,000	7	9,000
Cottbus	13	5,000	6	5,000
Dresden	35	24,200	5	49,000
Leipzig	3	1,400	5	30,000
K-Marx-Stadt	7	1,200	—	—
Erfurt	6	15,000	7	15,000

Table 5.1. Continued

Bezirk	Work Stoppages or Strikes	Number of Strikers	Demon-strations	Number of Demonstrators
Gera	30	15,000	10	51,900
Suhl	1	70	—	—
Halle	56	60,000	14	94,000
Magdeburg	59	—	42	32,000
Rostock	—	—	—	—
Neubran-den-burg	—	—	—	—
Total	**313**	**170,120+**	**129++**	**339,450++**

+ excluding Magdeburg and Berlin
++ excluding Berlin
Source: BA-P, DO 1 11/45, 11. June 18, 1953 report #166 on the events of June 17,
1953.

Although these were preliminary figures, a trend is nevertheless discernible.
The chart indicates that in seven out of nine *Bezirke* where disturbances took place
(excluding Suhl because the disturbances were negligible and Magdeburg because
of the missing data), there were more demonstrators than strikers. Only in one
Bezirk (Karl-Marx-Stadt) did a strike occur without an accompanying demonstration. Thus, in seven *Bezirke*, even if all strikers had joined a demonstration—and
this was not the norm, as some strikers simply went home[358]—other members of the
community would have had to join to make up the total number of demonstrators.
This finding corroborates the police records on the events presented in the above
discussion, which noted the participation of other townspeople in the worker-incited
demonstrations.[359]

Police statistics on arrests after the revolution also suggest the participation of
other sections of society in the demonstrations of June 17 but, because these numbers represent but a small percentage of the number that took part in the revolution,
the results should be treated cautiously. Between June 17 and June 22, the police
arrested 3,791 people for their part in the disturbances on 17 June.[360] By 25 June,
2,269 remained in the custody of the *Volkspolizei*; the others were either released
or handed over to the MfS.[361] Of the 2,269 prisoners, the social background of
2,065 was recorded as in Table 5.2.

Table 5.2.   Social background of those arrested by *Volkspolizei* for involvement in June 17 disturbances (initial findings)

Social Group	Percent of Those Arrested
Workers	68.6
Government/Intelligentsia	13.4
Tradesmen	3.8
LPG farmers	0.7
Small and middle farmers	3.6
Large farmers	0.7
Businessmen	1.9
Unemployed	2.4
Other	4.9

Source: BA-P, DO 1 11/758, p. 18. June 25, 1953 report by Weidlich, head of the investigation branch of the *Volkspolizei*, on arrests of those involved with the "fascist provocation."

In a final summary of those arrested for participating in the demonstrations, similar numbers were reported; see table 5.3.

Table 5.3.   Social background of those arrested by *Volkspolizei* for involvement in June 17 disturbances (final summary)

Social Group	Percent of Those Arrested
Workers	65.3
Government/Intelligentsia	13
Tradesmen	4.3
LPG Farmers	0.3
Small and Middle Farmers	1.9
Large Farmers	0.5
Businessmen	0.4
Unemployed	1.7
Other	12.6

Source: BA-P, DO 1 11/758, p. 34. June 25, 1953 report by Weidlich, head of the investigation branch of the *Volkspolizei*, on arrests of those involved with the "fascist provocation."

Although workers made up the largest societal section which took part in the revolution, there is overwhelming evidence to suggest involvement from other sections of society. It is therefore inappropriate to continue to characterize June 17 exclusively as a "workers' revolt," and more appropriate to acknowledge the participation of a cross-section of East German society.[362] These statistics reveal further that the demonstrators cannot be dismissed as rowdy youths.[363] Of 2,645 people arrested between June 17 and June 30 for their part in the revolution, 10.4 percent were under the age of eighteen; 27.6 percent were between eighteen and twenty-four; and 62 percent were above the age of twenty-four.[364]

It is also important to address the interpretation of certain historians that the uprising was not revolutionary, because it had ended before the Soviets arrived. The sources suggest that both Baring's and Diedrich's arguments that the uprising had basically ended prior to the arrival of Soviet troops contain weaknesses.[365] Baring was forceful in his argument: "But let no one imagine that the rising was actually put down by the Soviet troops. By the time they were deployed, the revolutionary wave had already begun to ebb. The Soviet intervention was not a turning point, it merely served to mark the end of the day's events: the demonstrators had run out of steam; their rising had come to a standstill before it had really gotten off the ground."[366]

Although Baring's conclusion can be explained by the appearance of his work prior to 1989, and therefore a lack of sources, it is odd that Diedrich would come to this conclusion as well, considering his own evidence suggests that the revolution was far from over by the time the Soviets arrived. His assertion that the uprising had begun to wind down because the demonstrators lacked concrete objectives, cannot be applied universally to the GDR.[367] The danger in Diedrich's approach is, of course, to minimize the revolutionary character of the uprising.

Although the Soviets declared a state of emergency at 1 pm in Berlin, there are a variety of examples of disturbances late in the day on June 17. In Eisenberg, workers at the VEB Schamotte Werk first went on strike at 2 pm. Only at 3 pm did workers of the steel work in Silbitz go on strike and proceed to occupy various posts around town, including the SED building and the central telephone switchboard.[368] Centerd around the coal burning plant "Matyas Rakosi," named after the Stalinist dictator of Hungary, in the industrial area of *Bezirk* Cottbus, Lauchhammer, the *Volkspolizei*, overwhelmed by the number of demonstrators and their brandishing of axes and spades, had to call on the support of the Soviets.[369] It was not until late in the evening that Soviet tanks first appeared on the streets of Lauchhammer.[370] In fact, it was not until 5 pm on June 17 that the Soviet commander in *Kreis* Eberswalde declared a state of emergency, because the situation had become so serious by then.[371] Similarly, the Soviet commander did not declare a state of emergency in *Bezirk* Frankfurt/Oder until 8 pm.[372] In Halle, demonstrators began gathering again at 6 pm on the main square.[373] Moreover, the account of the revolution outside Berlin reveals, on several occasions, that the Soviets were *required* to bring an end to disturbances. There is evidence, therefore, to bring into question the contention that the uprising had exhausted itself before the arrival of Soviet troops. Future local histories will likely assist in clarifying this issue.

It should be noted that in some instances, the appearance of the Soviets caused further disturbances. In Eberswalde, at EKM Finow, at about noon on June 17, 300 workers and clerks stopped working. They refused to work as long as Soviet troops occupied the plant, insisting that it was unreasonable to expect them to work under

Soviet aegis eight years after the end of the war. When the workers returned to their jobs, they demanded that nobody from the factory be arrested for their views. Should this occur, the workers threatened, they would stop working once again.[374] In Potsdam, construction workers became incensed later in the day of the 17th when they saw tanks driving through Potsdam on their way to Berlin.[375]

The revolution did not affect the GDR uniformly. The northern *Bezirke* of the former province of Mecklenburg experienced significantly fewer disturbances on June 17 than the other *Bezirke* (see table above). This trend in regional resistance was evident previous to the revolution, as demonstrated by the *Volkskongress* vote of 1949 and the 1946 elections. The sites where disturbances occurred correspond to the *Kreise* which reported higher than average "no" votes in the *Volkskongress* election.[376] Police reports on the October 1950 election reported less interest in the election in Saxony and Thuringia than in Mecklenburg.[377] Nevertheless, sites of rural unrest during the revolution, and especially after it as will be seen, corresponded largely to where LPGs had been established.[378] The revolution affected those sites most, where the forced implementation of the SED's programme had taken place.

The June 17 revolution was an act of popular political anti-Communist resistance which had been caused in large part by Soviet and SED repression. A cross-section of East German society took part in the storming of prisons and demanded free elections, which would have rid them of the Communist system. Certainly, demonstrators voiced economic demands, but in eleven of fourteen *Bezirke* they also called for free elections and the end of the SED, and through their *actions* showed that the fate of prisoners in the GDR lay at the center of the demonstrations. Had economic demands been the overriding concern, one would expect the demonstrators to have been content to protest in factories and perhaps on city squares, rather than at prisons, police stations, and court houses. The deputy head of the *Volkspolizei* listed the following as the most common demands of demonstrators throughout the GDR: (1) reduction of the work norms, (2) reduction in prices of state store wares, (3) removal of agricultural quotas, (4) release of prisoners, (5) free elections, (6) against the SED, (7) resignation of the government, (8) removal of zonal boundaries.[379] The similarity of the demands, especially their political content, provided the SED Central Committee with "evidence" that West Germany had organized the demonstrations. As a Central Committee analysis stated: "The agent-provocateurs from West Berlin succeeded in misusing the workers for their political smear slogans."[380] Soviet officers in East Germany also claimed that the commonality of the demands and their "anti-state" character were a result of western behind-the-scenes maneuvering.[381] The widespread attacks on the repression apparatus were intimately entwined with the political slogans. In essence, the political nature of the revolution was a result of the demonstrators' desire for protection of basic rights. Events in East Germany in the months and years following the revolution, along with secret police reports on the population, support this conclusion, and it is to this evidence that we should now turn.

Notes

1. Resolution of the Second Party Conference, printed in *Dokumente der Sozialistischen Einheitspartei Deutschlands* (Vol. IV) (Berlin [East]: Dietz Verlag, 1954), 73.

2. Resolution of the Second Party Conference, printed in *Dokumente der Sozialistischen Einheitspartei Deutschlands* (Vol. IV) (Berlin [East]: Dietz Verlag, 1954), 73.

3. Resolution of the Second Party Conference, printed in *Dokumente der Sozialistischen Einheitspartei Deutschlands* (Vol. IV) (Berlin [East]: Dietz Verlag, 1954), 73.

4. On the SED takeover of these instruments, see Chapters 3 and 4.

5. Ilko-Sascha Kowalczuk and Armin Mitter, "'Die Arbeiter sind zwar geschlagen worden, aber sie sind nicht besiegt,'" in *Der Tag X: Die 'Innere Staatsgründung' der DDR als Ergebnis der Krise 1952/1954*, Ilko-Sascha Kowalczuk et al. (Berlin: Ch. Links Verlag: 1995), 35.

6. Kowalczuk and Mitter, "Die Arbeiter," 35.

7. Kowalczuk and Mitter, "Die Arbeiter," 36. It is likely that the Soviet Union ordered the increased emphasis on heavy industry and the armed forces to meet its own Cold War needs; Manfred Hagen, *DDR—Juni '53* (Stuttgart: Franz Steiner Verlag, 1992), 24. In any case, the "building of socialism" could not have been carried out without Stalin's consent. See Dietrich Staritz, "Die SED, Stalin und der 'Aufbau des Sozialismus' in der DDR," *DA* 24 (1991): 686-700.

8. Hermann Weber, *DDR.Grundriss der Geschichte* (Hannover: Fackelträger, 1991), 53.

9. Weber, *DDR. Grundriss*, 53.

10. Kowalczuk, "Wir werden siegen, weil uns der grosse Stalin führt," in Kowalczuk et al., *Der Tag X*, 195-196.

11. Kowalczuk, "Wir werden siegen," 195-196.

12. The transformation was accomplished through a law issued on July 23, 1952 entitled "law on the further democratization of the state's instruments in the provinces of the GDR." Armin Mitter and Stefan Wolle, *Untergang auf Raten* (Munich: Bertelsmann Verlag, 1993), 32.

13. Falco Werkentin, *Politische Strafjustiz in der Ära Ulbricht* (Berlin: Ch. Links Verlag, 1995), 31.

14. Werkentin, *Politische*, 80.

15. BStU, ZA, GVS 1855/52, #101097. Guideline 21/52 of November 20, 1952, 39.

16. BStU, ZA, GVS 1855/52, #101097. Guideline 21/52 of November 20, 1952, 1.

17. BStU, ZA,GVS 1221/52, #100848. Directive 17/52/V/C of September 26, 1952 and Directive 6/52/V/E of September 17, 1952. Section C of the amalgamated department was responsible for the LDPD, Department E for the CDU and churches.

18. BStU, ZA,GVS 1221/52, #100848. Directive 17/52/V/C of September 26, 1952 and Directive 6/52/V/E of September 17, 1952. Section C of the amalgamated department was responsible for the LDPD, Department E for the CDU and churches.

19. Stefan Wolf, "Die 'Bearbeitung' der Kirchen in der Sowjetischen Besatzungszone und der DDR durch die politische Polizei und das Ministerium für Staatssicherheit bis 1953," in *Die Ohnmacht der Allmächtigen. Geheimdienste und politische Polizei in der modernen Gesellschaft*, ed. Bernd Florath et al. (Berlin: Ch. Links Verlag, 1992).

20. Hermann Wentker, "'Kirchenkampf' in der DDR 1950-1953," *VfZ* 42 (1994), 110. The *Volkspolizei* also assisted in the campaign against the *Junge Gemeinde*.

21. Christoph Klessmann, *Die doppelte Staatsgründung* (Göttingen: Vandenhoeck & Rupprecht, 1982), 267.

22. Wolf, "Die Bearbeitung," 200-201.

23. The integration of West Germany into the western Alliance through the Bonn and European Defence Community treaties of 1952 and the failure of the "Stalin notes" contributed to the Cold War tension. On March 10, 1952, Stalin sent notes to the three western Allies proposing a united, neutral Germany. Whether Stalin's notes were a ruse, or a genuine attempt to solve the German question continues to be debated. See Gerhard Wettig, "Die Stalin-Note vom 10. März 1952 als geschichtswissenschaftliches Problem," *DA* 25 (1992): 157-167, and "Stalin and the SED leadership, 7 April 1952," in the *Cold War International History Project Bulletin* Issue 4 (Fall 1994), 35.

24. BStU, ZA, GVS 1855/52, #101097. Guideline 21/52 of November 20, 1952, 27.

25. BStU, ZA, GVS 1855/52, #101097. Guideline 21/52 of November 20, 1952, 27.

26. ACDP, VII-013-1361. June 10, 1952 protocol of Eisenach *Kreis* council sitting. This record group contains a variety of reports on the general discontent with the evacuations.

27. ACDP, VII-041-001/4. September 5, 1956 letter from CDU *Kreis* association Bad Salzungen to the CDU *Bezirk* association for Suhl.

28. Mitter and Wolle, *Untergang*, 35.

29. Werkentin, *Politische*, 68.

30. Werkentin, *Politische*, 69.

31. Hagen, *DDR*, 26.

32. Heidi Roth, "Der 17. Juni im damaligen Bezirk Leipzig," *DA* 24 (1991): 576.

33. Werkentin, *Politische*, 71.

34. ADL, LDPD #15848. November 1952 working report of LDPD *Kreis* association for Bergen.

35. Werkentin, *Politische*, 70.

36. Werkentin, *Politische*, 81.

37. Werkentin, *Politische*, 82-84.

38. Quoted in Mitter and Wolle, *Untergang*, 47.

39. SAPMO-BA, ZPA, IV 2/13/409, Abteilung Staat und Recht. January 19, 1953 judicial report signed by Matter and Trotz, employees of the central commission for state control.

40. BA-P, DO 1 11/1560, 218-220. May 5, 1953 letter from Ulbricht to all party organizations of the justice instruments and the prisons.

41. *Dokumente der SED*, 70.

42. Stephan Zeidler, "Zur Rolle der CDU (Ost) in der inneren Entwicklung der DDR 1952-53," M.A. thesis, University of Bonn, 1994, 18.

43. Zeidler, "Zur Rolle," 24.

44. Zeidler, "Zur Rolle," 28-29.

45. Franz-Josef Kos, "Der Erfurter Schauprozess und die beiden Nachfolgeprozesse 1952/53," in *"Gefährliche politische Gegner,"* ed. Brigitte Kaff (Düsseldorf: Droste, 1995), 126-130.

46. Michael Richter, "Vom Widerstand der christlichen Demokraten in der DDR," in *Verfolgt-verhaftet-verurteilt*, ed. Günter Scholz (Berlin: Westkreuz Verlag, 1990), 48-52. See also Joachim Franke, "Der Fall Dertinger und seine parteiinternen Auswirkungen: Eine Dokumentation," *DA* 25 (1992): 286-298.

47. ADL, LDPD #12887. November 1, 1952 report from LDPD *Kreis* association for

Eberswalde to the *Bezirk* association, Frankfurt/Oder.

48. ADL, LDPD #14734. August 27, 1952 protocol of the sitting of the *Kreis* executive for Erfurt-Stadt.

49. ADL, LDPD #15848. October 1952 report from the LDPD in *Kreis* Bergen-Potbus. ADL, LDPD #31926. November 10, 1952 report from *Bezirk* Schwerin LDPD to the LDPD leadership; ibid., LDPD # 15848. September 17, report from *Kreis* Greifswald LDPD to *Bezirk* Rostock.

50. The *Bezirke* analyzed were Halle, Potsdam, Rostock, Frankfurt/Oder, and Schwerin. The documents on Halle and Potsdam did not contain information on reaction of the membership to the "building of socialism."

51. ACDP, VII-013-1361. Undated report by the CDU *Bezirk* association for Schwerin.

52. SAPMO-BA, ZPA, DY 30 IV 2/15/3. October 4, 1952 report on the situation in the other parties.

53. SAPMO-BA, ZPA, DY 30 IV/2/9.02/75, Amt für Information, 63. *Informmitteilung* Nr.II 95/52 of May 30, 1952.

54. SAPMO-BA, ZPA, DY 30 IV/2/9.02/75, Amt für Information, 63. *Informmitteilung* Nr.II 95/52 of May 30, 1952.

55. SAPMO-BA, ZPA, DY 30 IV 2/15/3. August 16, 1952 report on the situation in the other parties.

56. SAPMO-BA, ZPA, DY 30 IV 2/9.02/76, Amt für Information. *Informmitteilung* II/117/52 of July 2, 1952 on activities of the church.

57. AdsD, SPD-PV-Ostbüro 0370/I Copy of LDPD *Land* association for Thuringia report to the Soviet Control Commission on February 8, 1952.

58. SAPMO-BA, ZPA, DY 30 IV 2/9.02/76, 26. Amt für Information *Informmitteilung* Nr. II/126/52 of July 8, 1952. SPD reports also indicated resistance to East German armed forces. See ADSD, SPD-PV-Ostbüro 0361/1. August 12, 1952 report.

59. SAPMO-BA, ZPA, DY 30 IV/2/9.02/76, Amt für Information, 26. *Informmitteilung* Nr. II 126/52 of July 8, 1952.

60. SAPMO-BA, ZPA, DY 30 IV 2/9.02/75, Amt für Information. April 1, 1952 special report entitled: "Proteste wegen angeblicher Stammrollenerfassung."

61. SAPMO-BA, ZPA, DY 30 IV 2/9.02/75, Amt für Information. Special Report, *Informmitteilung* II/100/52 of June 5, 1952.

62. Armin Mitter, "Der 'Tag X' und die 'Innere Staatsgründung,'" in Kowalczuk et al, *Der Tag X*, 29-30.

63. Ilko-Sascha Kowalczuk, "'Wir werden siegen, weil uns der grosse Stalin führt!' Die SED zwischen Zwangsvereinigung und IV. Parteitag," in Kowalczuk et al. *Der Tag X*, 195.

64. Kowalczuk, Mitter, and Wolle, *Der Tag X*, passim.

65. Ilko-Sascha Kowalczuk and Armin Mitter, "Die Arbeiter sind zwar geschlagen worden, aber sie sind nicht besiegt! Die Arbeiterschaft während der Krise 1952/53," in Kowalczuk et al., *Der Tag X*, 39-40.

66. Kowalczuk and Mitter, "Die Arbeiter," 40.

67. Kowalczuk and Mitter, "Die Arbeiter," 42.

68. Torsten Diedrich. *Der 17. Juni 1953* (Berlin: Dietz Verlag, 1991), 40-41. For an introduction to the condition of workers in the GDR at this time, see Peter Hübner, *Konsens, Konflikt und Kompromiss. Soziale Arbeiterinteressen und Sozialpolitik in der SBZ/DDR 1945-1970* (Berlin: Akademie Verlag, 1995), and Jeffrey Kopstein, *The Politics of Economic Decline in East Germany* (Chapel Hill: University of North Carolina Press, 1997).

69. Diedrich, *Der 17. Juni*, 40-41.

70. Kowalczuk and Mitter, "Die Arbeiter," 44

71. Kowalczuk and Mitter, 'Die Arbeiter,' 44.

72. The reports are cited in Kowalczuk and Mitter, "Die Arbeiter," 44, footnote 75, and 46, footnotes 78 and 80.

73. Kowalczuk and Mitter, "Die Arbeiter," 45.

74. Kowalczuk and Mitter, "Die Arbeiter," 45.

75. Quoted in Kowalczuk and Mitter, "Die Arbeiter," 46.

76. ACDP, VII-013-1361. Two unsigned reports, one dated August 8, 1952 and the other September 2, 1952 on the agricultural situation.

77. BA-P, DO 1 11/24, 29-31. October 23, 1952 report of *Volkspolizei* investigative committee on events in Friedrichsaue.

78. BA-P, DO 1 11/24, 45. March 26, 1953 report summarizing the reports of all *Bezirk* levels of the *Volkspolizei* by Seifert, general inspector of the *Volkspolizei*, to Maron, Zaisser, Chrenow, and Ministry of the Interior.

79. SAPMO-BA, ZPA, DY 30 IV 2/9.02/76, Amt für Information. Informmitteilung II/153/52 of August 15, 1952 entitled "Tätigkeit des Gegners."

80. BA-P, DO 1 11/24, 8. September 11, 1952 draft proposal to all *Bezirk* heads of the *Volkspolizei* from the Ministry of the Interior (author not specified) entitled: "Die Situation auf dem Lande."

81. Armin Mitter, " 'Am 17.6.1953 haben die Arbeiter gestreikt, jetzt aber streiken wir Bauern.' Die Bauern und der Sozialismus," in Kowalczuk et al., *Der Tag X*, 87.

82. Mitter, "Am 17.6.1953," 88.

83. MLHA, IV 2/4/611, Amt für Information. June 9, 1952 special report on conditions in the *Gemeinde* Gösslow, *Kreis* Hagenow.

84. BA-P, DO 1 11/409, 65. July 13, 1953 report from Kober, head of the *Bezirk* Erfurt police to the Berlin *Volkspolizei*.

85. ACDP, VII-013-1361. August 8, 1952 report for Götting on the agricultural situation.

86. Bauerkämper argues that the continuing economic problems in the countryside prevented the SED from creating solid political allegiance there; Arnd Bauerkämper, "Die Neubauern in der SBZ/DDR 1945-1952," in *Die Grenzen der Diktatur*, ed. Richard Bessel and Ralph Jessen, (Göttingen: Vandenhoeck & Ruprecht, 1996), 128.

87. BA-P, DO 1 11/24, 45. March 26, 1953 report summarizing the reports of all *Bezirk* levels of the *Volkspolizei* by Seifert, general inspector of the *Volkspolizei*, to Maron, Zaisser, Chrenow, and the Ministry of the Interior.

88. Mitter, "Am 17.6.1953,' 86. For a breakdown of these sentences, see above.

89. Quoted in Mitter, "Am 17.6.1953," 89.

90. BA-P, DO 1 11/24, 8. September 11, 1952 draft proposal to all *Bezirk* heads of the *Volkspolizei* from the Ministry of the Interior (author not specified) entitled: "Die Situation auf dem Lande."

91. BA-P, DO 1 11/24, 8. September 11, 1952 draft proposal to all *Bezirk* heads of the *Volkspolizei* from the Ministry of the Interior (author not specified) entitled: "Die Situation auf dem Lande."

92. BA-P, DO 1 11/24, 9. September 11, 1952 draft proposal to all *Bezirk* heads of the *Volkspolizei* from the Ministry of the Interior (author not specified) entitled: "Die Situation auf dem Lande."

93. BA-P, DO 1 11/24, 13. September 11, 1952 draft proposal to all *Bezirk* heads of the *Volkspolizei* from the Ministry of the Interior (author not specified) entitled: "Die Situation

auf dem Lande."

94. BA-P, DO 1 11/24, 9. September 11, 1952 proposal to all *Bezirk* heads of the *Volkspolizei* entitled: "Die Situation auf dem Lande."

95. SAPMO-BA, ZPA, DY 30 IV 2/9.02/76, Amt für Information. *Informmitteilung* II/153/52 of August 15, 1952 entitled: "Tätigkeit des Gegners."

96. BA-P, DO 1 11/24, 29-31. October 23, 1952 report of the *Volkspolizei* investigative committee on events in Friedrichsau.

97. BA-P, DO 1 11/24, 29-31. October 23, 1952 report of the *Volkspolizei* investigative committee on events in Friedrichsau.

98. BA-P, DO 1 2/4, 45. March 26, 1953 report by Seifert, general inspector of the *Volkspolizei* to Maron, Zaisser, Chrenow, and the Ministry of the Interior.

99. SAPMO-BA, ZPA, NL 182/888. Undated report entitled: "Bericht über einige Erscheinungen des Verhaltens antidemokratischer grossbäuerlicher Kräfte bei den Generalversammlungen der Bäuerlichen Handelsgenossenschaften."

100. SAPMO-BA, ZPA, NL 182/888. Undated report entitled: "Bericht über einige Erscheinungen des Verhaltens antidemokratischer grossbäuerlicher Kräfte bei den Generalversammlungen der Bäuerlichen Handelsgenossenschaften."

101. MLHA, IV 2/4/611, Amt für Information. June 9, 1952 special report on conditions in the *Gemeinde* Gösslow, *Kreis* Hagenow.

102. BA-P, DO 1 11/409, 21. Undated report by *Bezirk* levels of *Volkspolizei* on "reactionary activities" at founding meetings for LPG's.

103. BA-P, DO 1 11/409. May 11, 1953 report on seminar topics for the police. One of the topics was entitled: "Gefahren für die Ernte."

104. Kowalczuk, "Wir werden siegen," 195.

105. BA-P, DO 1 2/4, pp. 50-51. March 26, 1953 letter from Ulbricht to Maron.

106. Mitter, "Am 17.6.1953," 95.

107. Quoted in Mitter, "Am 17.6.1953," 95.

108. MLHA, IV 2/4/502. Protocol of the BPKK sitting of March 4, 1953.

109. AdsD, SPD-PV-Ostbüro 0361. December 30, 1952 report from Mecklenburg.

110. See the reports contained in AdsD, SPD-PV-Ostbüro, 0361.

111. Mitter and Wolle, *Untergang*, 27.

112. Mitter and Wolle, *Untergang*, 27.

113. Kowalczuk and Mitter, "Die Arbeiter," 46.

114. Kowalczuk and Mitter, "Die Arbeiter," 46.

115. Kowalczuk and Mitter, "Die Arbeiter," 47.

116. Hagen, *DDR*, 28-29.

117. SAPMO, ZA, IV 2/202/15, 29. July 20, 1953 report entitled: "Analyse über die Vorbereitung, den Ausbruch und die Niederschlagung des faschistischen Abenteuers vom 16.- 22.6.53." This document is now available, translated in English, in the *Cold War International History Project Bulletin* Issue 5 (Spring 1995), 11. Document obtained by Christian Ostermann, translated by Helen Christakos.

118. This document appears in translation in the *Bulletin* of the Cold War International History Project, Spring 1995, 10. The document was obtained by Vladislav Zubok and translated by Danny Rozas.

119. Gerhard Wettig, "Sowjetische Wiedervereinigungsbemühungen im ausgehenden Frühjahr 1953?" *DA* 25 (1992): 945.

120. For a detailed analysis of the Soviet Union's German policy during this transition period, see Mark Kramer's three-part article, "The Early Post-Stalin Succession Struggle and

Upheavals in East-Central Europe: Internal-External Linkages in Soviet Policy Making," *Journal of Cold War Studies* 1 (1999): Vols. 1-3.

121. Mitter and Wolle, *Untergang*, 55. On the role of the interim leadership in the Soviet Union after Stalin's death, and in particular Beria's role in implementing the "New Course" in East Germany, see Kramer, "The Post-Stalin"; Vojtech Mastny, *The Cold War and Soviet Insecurity* (New York: Oxford University Press, 1996), 178-190; and Amy Knight, *Beria, Stalin's First Lieutenant* (Princeton: Princeton University Press, 1993).

122. Mitter and Wolle, *Untergang*, 57. The Soviet resolution prepared for the SED members in Moscow is reprinted in Rolf Stöckigt, "Ein Dokument von grosser historischer Bedeutung vom Mai 1953," *Beiträge zur Geschichte der Arbeiterbewegung* 32 (1990): 649-663.

123. Mitter and Wolle, *Untergang*, 78.

124. Hagen, *DDR*, 33.

125. Mitter and Wolle, *Untergang*, 63.

126. *Neues Deutschland* June 11, 1953

127. *Neues Deutschland* June 11, 1953.

128. See note 118 above *Cold War International History Project Bulletin*, Spring 1995, 17. Unfortunately, the translation of this document is poor.

129. See note 118.

130. SAPMO-BA, ZPA, DY 30 IV 2/5/524. June 14, 1953 daily report VI signed by Schirdewan.

131. Kowalczuk and Mitter, "Die Arbeiter," 50.

132. SAPMO, ZA, IV 2/202/15, 62. July 20, 1953 report entitled: "Analyse über die Vorbereitung, den Ausbruch und die Niederschlagung des faschistischen Abenteuers vom 16.- 22.6.53."

133. Hagen, *DDR*, 36.

134. BA-P, DO 1 11/306, 128. July 5, 1953 report from the prison to the political department of the *Volkspolizei*.

135. Mitter and Wolle, *Untergang*, 77. See also SAPMO-BA, ZPA, DY 30 IV 2/5/524. June 14, 1953 daily report VI signed by Schirdewan.

136. Mitter and Wolle, *Untergang*, 80.

137. Quoted in Mitter and Wolle, *Untergang*, 80.

138. Kowalczuk and Mitter, "Die Arbeiter," 49-50.

139. Christoph Buchheim speculates that the Central Committee could not reduce the norms, because of its economic obligations to the Soviet Union; Christoph Buchheim, "Wirtschaftliche Hintergründe des Arbeiteraufstandes vom 17. Juni 1953 in der DDR," *VfZ* 38 (1990): 415-433.

140. Mitter, "Am 17.6.1953," 102.

141. Mitter, "Am 17.6.1953," 102.

142. Mitter, "Am 17.6.1953," 104.

143. MLHA, IV 2/4/587, 41. SED *Bezirk* leadership BPKK report on enemy activity 1952-1956. Analysis of June 17 and its aftermath.

144. Mitter, "Am 17.6.53," 107-109.

145. Mitter, "Am 17.6.53," 106.

146. Mitter and Wolle, *Untergang*, 79.

147. Mitter and Wolle, *Untergang*, 79.

148. Diedrich. *Der 17. Juni*, 83; Arnulf Baring, *Uprising in East Germany* (Ithaca: Cornell University Press, 1972), 74.

149. Stefan Brant, *Der Aufstand: Vorgeschichte, Geschichte und Deutung des 17. Juni 1953* (Stuttgart: Steingrüben Verlag, 1954), 303.

150. Brant, *Der Aufstand*, 304-306.

151. Baring, *Uprising*, 52-53. Baring also stated that only a small number of workers took part, between 5.5 percent and 6.8 percent of the work force.

152. Diedrich, *Der 17. Juni*, 149.

153. For other weaknesses in Diedrich's work, see Armin Mitter, "Der "Tag X" und die 'Innere Staatsgründung,'" 12.

154. Hagen, *DDR*, 199.

155. Hagen lists twenty-six instances of storming of locations where prisoners were being held. Some of the locations named are not verified in documentary material, and there are at least ten other locations where prisons were stormed which Hagen does not mention. Hagen, *DDR*, 172. The locations which Hagen does not mention are Hennigsdorf, Quedlinburg, Fürstenwalde, Rüderstadt, Apolda, Jessen, Gommern, Lübben, Preschen, and Worbis. Additionally, Hagen (and Diedrich) mention only 2 MfS stations being attacked, but there were at least six. Hagen, *DDR*, 172; Diedrich, *Der 17. Juni*, 278

156. Mary Fulbrook in particular has taken issue with this approach, believing that 1989 could not be read off of 1953; that there was not a constant, if latent, state of civil war in the intervening thirty-five years. Mary Fulbrook, *Anatomy of a Dictatorship* (Oxford: Oxford University Press, 1995), 172.

157. Mitter and Wolle, *Untergang*, 160.

158. Mitter and Wolle, *Untergang*, 162.

159. Interview with Armin Mitter, November 11, 1996, Berlin. For a discussion of the Stasi archive and its holdings, see my "Update on the Stasi files" in the *Cold War International History Project Bulletin* Issue 12/13 (Fall/Winter 2001): 348-350.

160. Fulbrook, *Anatomy*, 178.

161. Quoted in Kowalczuk and Mitter, "Die Arbeiter," 67.

162. Harvey Kaye, ed., *The Face of the Crowd: Studies in Revolutionary, Ideology and Popular Protest. Selected Essays of George Rudé* (Toronto: Harvester Wheatsheaf, 1988), 77.

163. This work appeared as part of the series *Forschungen zur DDR-Geschichte* which is presently the venue for the most valuable research on East Germany.

164. Quoted in Mitter and Wolle, *Untergang*, 89.

165. Mitter and Wolle, *Untergang*, 87-88.

166. Mitter and Wolle, *Untergang*, 90.

167. BA-P, DO 1 11/304, 258. July 13, 1953 report by the political department of the *Volkspolizei Präsidium* in Berlin entitled: "Der Beginn der Streikbewegung in der Stalinallee." See also Mitter and Wolle, *Untergang*, 91. Mitter and Wolle's account is based on an MfS report on the origin of the uprising, also from July.

168. BA-P, DO 1 11/304, 258. July 13, 1953 report by the political department of the *Volkspolizei Präsidium* in Berlin entitled: "Der Beginn der Streikbewegung in der Stalinallee."

169. BA-P, DO 1 11/304, 107. June 17, 1953 report of the operations staff of the *Volkspolizei Präsidium* entitled: "Auszug aus dem Lagebericht Nr. 167 des Operativstabes PdVP vom 16.6.1953, von 07:00 bis 24:00." In *Untergang auf Raten*, Mitter and Wolle describe a slightly different route, but their information is based on an MfS report a month after the uprising. This police report of the following day is more reliable; Mitter and Wolle, *Untergang*, 91. Diedrich does not mention the construction workers being locked up; Die-

drich, *Der 17. Juni*, 59-60.

170. BA-P, DO 1 11/304, 107. June 17, 1953 report of the operations staff of the *Volkspolizei Präsidium* entitled: "Auszug aus dem Lagebericht Nr. 167 des Operativstabes PdVP vom 16.6.1953, von 07:00 bis 24:00." Mitter and Wolle claim that 10,000 participated in the demonstration on June 16, but do not provide a citation for this claim; Mitter and Wolle, *Untergang*, 93. Diedrich claims 2,000 participated, but does not provide a citation; Diedrich, *Der 17. Juni*, 60.

171. Hagen, *DDR*, 38.

172. Kowalczuk and Mitter, "Die Arbeiter," 56.

173. BA-P, DO 1 11/304, 259. July 13, 1953 report by the political department of the *Volkspolizei Präsidium* in Berlin entitled: "Der Beginn der Streikbewegung in der Stalinallee."

174. Hagen, *DDR*, 44.

175. Hagen, *DDR*, 45.

176. Baring, *Uprising*, and Fricke in "Der Arbeiteraufstand," in *17. Juni 1953: Arbeiteraufstand in der DDR*, ed. Karl Wilhelm Fricke and Ilse Spittmann (Cologne: Verlag Wissenschaft und Politik, 1982), 12-13 simply did not have the sources to be comprehensive. Diedrich provides more detail, but his account suffers from a lack of proper citation, and he has missed some important police reports; Diedrich, *Der 17. Juni*, 63.

177. BA-P, DO 1 11/304, 108. June 17, 1953 report of the operations staff of the *Volkspolizei Präsidium* entitled: "Auszug aus dem Lagebericht Nr. 167 des Operativstabes PdVP vom 16.6.1953, von 07:00 bis 24:00."

178. BA-P, DO 1 11/304, 108. June 17, 1953 report of the operations staff of the *Volkspolizei Präsidium* entitled: "Auszug aus dem Lagebericht Nr. 167 des Operativstabes PdVP vom 16.6.1953, von 07:00 bis 24:00."

179. BA-P, DO 1 11/304, 259. July 13, 1953 report by the political department of the *Volkspolizei Präsidium* in Berlin entitled: "Der Beginn der Streikbewegung in der Stalinallee."

180. BA-P, DO 1 11/304, 110. June 17, 1953 report of the operations staff of the *Volkspolizei Präsidium* entitled: "Auszug aus dem Lagebericht Nr. 167 des Operativstabes PdVP vom 16.6.1953, von 07:00 bis 24:00."

181. BA-P, DO 1 11/304, 110. June 17, 1953 report of the operations staff of the *Volkspolizei Präsidium* entitled: "Auszug aus dem Lagebericht Nr. 167 des Operativstabes PdVP vom 16.6.1953, von 07:00 bis 24:00."

182. BA-P, DO 1 11/304, 111. June 17, 1953 report of the operations staff of the *Volkspolizei Präsidium* entitled: "Auszug aus dem Lagebericht Nr. 167 des Operativstabes PdVP vom 16.6.1953, von 07:00 bis 24:00."

183. BA-P, DO 1 11/304, 111. June 17, 1953 report of the operations staff of the *Volkspolizei Präsidium* entitled: "Auszug aus dem Lagebericht Nr. 167 des Operativstabes PdVP vom 16.6.1953, von 07:00 bis 24:00."

184. Torsten Diedrich, "Zwischen Arbeitererhebung und gescheiterter Revolution in Berlin und der DDR" in *Jahrbuch für Historische Kommunismusforschung* (Berlin: Akademie Verlag, 1994), 299.

185. BA-P, DO 1 11/34, 55. June 16, 1953 unsigned report entitled: "Getroffene Massnahmen."

186. BA-P, DO 1 11/34, 55. June 16, 1953 unsigned report entitled: "Getroffene Massnahmen."

187. BA-P, DO 1 11/34, 111. June 16, 1953 unsigned report entitled: "Getroffene Mass-

nahmen."

188. BA-P, DO 1 11/304, 261. July 13, 1953 report from the political department of the *Volkspolizei Präsidium* in Berlin entitled: "Der Beginn der Streikbewegung in der Stalinallee."

189. RIAS was careful not to call for a general strike though, largely because its American owners were not sure of the results of such an occurrence in the tense Cold War of 1953; Hagen, *DDR*, 37.

190. SAPMO-BA, ZPA, JIV 2/202/14. June 17, 1953 report entitled: "Über die Lage am 17.6.53 in Gross-Berlin und der DDR."

191. Kowalczuk and Mitter, "Die Arbeiter," 54.

192. Mitter and Wolle, *Untergang*, 93.

193. Quoted in Kowalczuk and Mitter, "Die Arbeiter," 56.

194. Kowalczuk and Mitter, "Die Arbeiter," 57.

195. Diedrich, *Der 17. Juni*, 64.

196. Kowalczuk and Mitter, "Die Arbeiter," 57.

197. BA-P, DO 1 11/304, 102. June 17, 1953 summary report of *Volkspolizei* Hauptabteilung K on updates from various *Volkspolizei* posts around Berlin on June 17, 1953 (signature illegible).

198. BA-P, DO 1 11/304, 102. June 17, 1953 summary report of *Volkspolizei* Hauptabteilung K on updates from various *Volkspolizei* posts around Berlin on June 17, 1953 (signature illegible).

199. SAPMO-BA, ZPA, JIV 2/202/14. June 17, 1953 Central Committee report entitled: "Über die Lage am 17.6.53 in Gross-Berlin und der DDR."

200. Hagen, *DDR*, 48-49.

201. SAPMO-BA, ZPA, JIV 2/202/14. June 17, 1953 report entitled "Über die Lage am 17.6.53 in Gross-Berlin und der DDR."

202. Diedrich, *Der 17. Juni*, 64.

203. BA-P, DO 1 11/304, 103. June 17, 1953 summary report from *Volkspolizei* Hauptabteilung K on updates from various *Volkspolizei* posts around Berlin on June 17, 1953 (signature illegible).

204. BA-P, DO 1 11/304, 105. June 17, 1953 summary report from *Volkspolizei* Hauptabteilung K on updates from various *Volkspolizei* posts around Berlin on June 17, 1953 (signature illegible).

205. SAPMO-BA, ZPA, JIV 2/202/14. June 17, 1953 report entitled: "Über die Lage am 17.6.53 in Gross-Berlin und der DDR."

206. BA-P, DO 1 11/304, 262. July 13, 1953 report by the political department of the *Volkspolizei Präsidium* in Berlin entitled: "Der Beginn der Streikbewegung in der Stalinallee." Italics added.

207. BA-P, DO 1 11/304, 104. June 17, 1953 summary report of *Volkspolizei* Hauptabteilung K on updates from various *Volkspolizei* posts around Berlin on June 17, 1953 (signature illegible). See also the document of 17.6.1953 by Karl Nohr, of the executive of the Free German Trade Union, reprinted in Wolfgang Eckelmann et al, *FDGB Intern* (Berlin: Treptower Verlagshaus GmbH, 1990), 19. Manfred Hagen's account of the uprising in Berlin relies almost exclusively on eyewitness reports or letters to the author in 1989. The police reports presented here as evidence are more reliable.

208. BA-P, DO 1 11/304, 105. June 17, 1953 summary report of *Volkspolizei* Hauptabteilung K on updates from various *Volkspolizei* posts around Berlin on June 17, 1953 (signature illegible). These sources offer evidence that Diedrich and Baring are incorrect to point

to an "escalation" in the uprising from demonstrations concerned solely with economic conditions in the morning to political issues in the afternoon; Baring, pp. 74-75.

209. BA-P, DO 1 11/304, 262. July 13, 1953 report by the political department of the *Volkspolizei Präsidium* in Berlin entitled: "Der Beginn der Streikbewegung in der Stalinallee."

210. BA-P, DO 1 11/304, 102. June 17, 1953 summary report of *Volkspolizei* Hauptabteilung K on updates from various *Volkspolizei* posts around Berlin on June 17, 1953 (signature illegible).

211. BA-P, DO 1 11/304, 105. June 17, 1953 summary report of *Volkspolizei* Hauptabteilung K on updates from various *Volkspolizei* posts around Berlin on June 17, 1953 (signature illegible).

212. Hagen, *DDR*, 48.

213. BA-P, DO 1 11/304, 298. Undated personal report of Comrade Commander Koch, political department.

214. BA-P, DO 1 11/304, 104. June 17, 1953 summary report of *Volkspolizei* Hauptabteilung K on updates from various *Volkspolizei* posts around Berlin on June 17,1953 (signature illegible).

215. BA-P, DO 1 11/304, 105. June 17, 1953 summary report of *Volkspolizei* Hauptabteilung K on updates from various *Volkspolizei* posts around Berlin on June 17, 1953 (signature illegible).

216. BA-P, DO 1 11/304, 105. June 17, 1953 summary report of *Volkspolizei* Hauptabteilung K on updates from various *Volkspolizei* posts around Berlin on June 17, 1953 (signature illegible).

217. BA-P, DO 1 11/304, 105. June 17, 1953 summary report of *Volkspolizei* Hauptabteilung K on updates from various *Volkspolizei* posts around Berlin on June 17, 1953 (signature illegible). Baring describes June 17 as an orderly demonstration against economic conditions in the morning which escalated into riotous, revolutionary demonstrations in the afternoon. As evidence, he states that during the morning of the 17th, only SED members who had behaved badly in the past were beaten up, whereas in the afternoon, anyone wearing a party symbol fell victim to the mob; Baring, *Uprising*, 75. Clearly, Baring has erred on this point.

218. SAPMO-BA, ZPA, JIV 2/202/14. June 17, 1953 report entitled: "Über die Lage am 17.6.53 in Gross-Berlin und der DDR." SED estimates on the number of demonstrators in front of government buildings on June 17 in Berlin (25,000) correspond to Soviet estimates (30,000). See Christian Ostermann, "New Documents on the East German Uprising of 1953," *Cold War International History Project Bulletin* Issue 5 (Spring 1995): 13; Hagen, *DDR*, 49.

219. SAPMO-BA, ZPA, JIV 2/202/14. June 17, 1953 letter from Albert Norden to Walter Ulbricht.

220. SAPMO-BA, ZPA, JIV 2/202/14. June 17, 1953 report: "Über die Lage am 17.6.53 in Gross-Berlin und der DDR."

221. Mitter and Wolle, *Untergang*, 104.

222. Mitter and Wolle, *Untergang*, 104. Fricke, "Der Arbeiteraufstand," 12.

223. BA-P, DO 1 11/304, 264. July 13, 1953 report by the political department of the *Volkspolizei Präsidium* in Berlin entitled: "Der Beginn der Streikbewegung in der Stalinallee"; Hagen, *DDR*, 110.

224. Hagen, *DDR*, 110. According to Soviet sources, only 33 demonstrators were killed and 132 wounded throughout the GDR; June 20, 1953 report from Grechko, Tarasov, Opera-

tions Division, Main Operations Administration, General Staff of the Soviet Army to Bulganin, reproduced in Christian Ostermann (ed.), *The Post-Stalin Succession Struggle and the 17 June 1953: The Hidden History* (Washington: National Security Archive, 1996), Document #20. Many of these documents are reprinted in Ostermann's invaluable *Uprising in East Germany* (New York: Central European University Press, 2001).

225. SAPMO-BA, ZPA, JIV 2/202/14. June 17, 1953 report entitled: "Über die Lage am 17.6.53 in Gross-Berlin und der DDR"; BA-P, DA 1 11/304, pp. 301-307. Undated personal report of Comrade Commander Koch, political department.

226. BA-P, DO 1 11/304, 301-7. Undated personal report of Comrade Commander Koch, political department.

227. Diedrich, *Der 17. Juni*, passim.

228. Richard Bessel, "Die Grenzen des Polizeistaates," in *Die Grenzen der Diktatur*, ed. Richard Bessel and Ralph Jessen (Göttingen: Vandenhoeck & Ruprecht, 1996), 243. It is important to correct Bessel's suggestion that the scorn of the population was directed primarily at *Volkspolizei* stations with prisoners. There were several instances like the above mentioned case where attacks on *Volkspolizei* officers occurred where the motive of releasing prisoners was absent. Attacks and insults against the police were evident during the Berlin demonstrations, noted above. Popular attacks on the police did not simply aim to release prisoners, but were an act of resistance against this instrument of the regime's apparatus.

229. BA-P, DO 1 11/45, 1. Extracts from the *Bezirk* police situation reports for the period of 0:00 to 17:00 on June 17, 1953, signed by head of operations staff, Weidhase. Diedrich reports that only 5,000 demonstrators took part, but his citation cannot be verified for he does not provide a description of the document, only the archival record group number; Diedrich, *Der 17. Juni*, 112.

230. SAPMO-BA, ZPA, JIV 2/202/14. June 17, 1953 report entitled: "Über die Lage am 17.6.53 in Gross-Berlin und der DDR."

231. BA-P, DO 1 11/45, 1. Extracts from the *Bezirk* police situation reports for the period of 0:00 to 17:00 on June 17, 1953, signed by the head of the operations staff Weidhase.

232. SAPMO-BA, ZPA, JIV 2/202/14. June 17, 1953 report entitled "Über die Lage am 17.6.53 in Gross-Berlin und der DDR"; BA-P, DO 1 11/45, 1. Extracts from the *Bezirk* police situation reports for the period of 0:00 to 17:00 on June 17, 1953 signed by the head of operations staff Weidhase.

233. BA-P, DO 1 11/45, 1. Extracts from the *Bezirk* police situation reports for the period of 0:00 to 17:00 on June 17, 1953 signed by the head of operations staff Weidhase.

234. BA-P, DO 1 11/45, 1. Extracts from the *Bezirk* police situation reports for the period of 0:00 to 17:00 on June 17, 1953, signed by head of operations staff Weidhase.

235. AdsD, SPD-PV-Ostbüro 0436b #03347. Undated report by a worker of the Karl-Liebknecht Werk Magdeburg who took part in the uprising and later fled to the West.

236. AdsD, SPD-PV-Ostbüro 0436b #03347. Undated report by a worker of the Karl-Liebknecht Werk Magdeburg who took part in the uprising and later fled to the West.

237. SAPMO-BA, ZPA, JIV 2/202/14. June 17, 1953 report entitled "Über die Lage am 17.6.53 in Gross-Berlin und der DDR."

238. BA-P, DO 1 11/45, 2. Extracts from the situation reports of the *Bezirk* police for the period of 0:00 to 17:00 on June 17, 1953 signed by head of operations staff Weidhase.

239. BA-P, DO 1 11/45, 11. June 18, 1953 report #166 on the events of June 17, 1953 by Gönstein, deputy head of the *Volkspolizei*.

240. BA-P, DO 1 11/305, 75. June 29, 1953 update report from *Bezirk* Dresden police.

241. BA-P, DO 1/11/305, pp. 245-247. July 1, 1953 report from the *Bezirk* Halle

Volkspolizei on the June 17, 1953 demonstrations; ACDP, VII-013-1300. June 22, 1953 report from CDU *Kreis* association of Niesky to the CDU; ACDP, VII-011-1300. June 17, 1953 report from *Bezirk* association for Dresden to Götting. This detail is not available in the party sources in the central archive. See SAPMO-BA, ZPA, JIV 2/202/14. June 17, 1953 report entitled: "Über die Lage am 17.6.53 in Gross-Berlin und der DDR."

242. BA-P, DO 1/11/305, 67. June 29, 1953 report from *Bezirk* Dresden police.

243. BA-P, DO 1 11/305, 49-50. June 29, 1953 update report from *Bezirk* Dresden police.

244. BA-P, DO 1 11/45, 7. Extracts from the *Bezirk* police situation reports for the period 0:00 to 17:00 on June 17, 1953, signed by head of operations staff Weidhase.

245. BA-P, DO 1 11/45, 68. Extracts from the *Bezirk* police situation reports for the period 0:00 to 17:00 on June 17, 1953, signed by head of operations staff Weidhase.

246. BA-P, DO 1/11/305, 72-73. June 29, 1953 update report from *Bezirk* Dresden police.

247. BA-P, DO 1/11/305, 70. June 29, 1953 update report from *Bezirk* Dresden police.

248. SAPMO-BA, ZPA, JIV 2/202/14. Report on the situation in *Bezirk* Dresden for June 17 and 18, 1953.

249. ACDP VII-013-1300. Report of 22.6.53 from CDU *Kreisverband* Niesky to the CDU leadership; ACDP VII-011-1300 Report of 17.6.53 from *Bezirksverband* Dresden to Götting.

250. BA-P, DO 1/11/305, 70. June 29, 1953 update report from *Bezirk* Dresden police.

251. SAPMO-BA, ZPA, DY 30 IV 2/5/546, 239 Report on June 17, 1953 based on reports from the *Bezirke*.

252. SAPMO-BA, ZPA, DY 30 IV 2/5/535, 7. June 17, 1953 report from the *Bezirk* leadership in Dresden.

253. AdsD, SPD-PV-Ostbüro 0434b. June 22, 1953 report on Görlitz strikers, reconfirmed in reports by sources 20984, and 20924.

254. SAPMO-BA, ZPA, DY 30 IV 2/5/596, 42. July 20, 1953 report on the events of June 17, 1953.

255. Helmut Bärwald, *Das Ostbüro der SPD* (Krefeld: SINUS, 1991), 78.

256. BA-P, DO 1 11/45, 10. Extracts from the situation reports of the *Bezirk* police for the period 17:00-24:00 on June 17, 1953 signed by the head of the operations staff Weidhase. This report provides an example of the discrepancy between the police reports and the SED reports. The central SED analysis of the situation in Leipzig stated that the demonstrators had occupied the police station; SAPMO-BA, ZPA, JIV 2/202/14. June 17, 1953 report entitled: "Über die Lage am 17.6.53 in Gross-Berlin und der DDR."

257. BA-P, DO 1 11/45, 10. Extracts from the *Bezirk* police situation reports for the period 17:00-24:00 on June 17, 1953, signed by the head of the operation staff Weidhase.

258. BA-P, DO 1 11/45, 10. Extracts from the *Bezirk* police situation reports for the period 17:00-24:00 on June 17, 1953, signed by the head of the operation staff Weidhase.

259. Heidi Roth, "Der 17. Juni im damaligen Bezirk Leipzig," *DA* 24 (1991): 583.

260. Franz Walter et al., eds., *Die SPD in Sachsen zwischen Hoffnung und Diaspora* (Bonn: JHW Dietz, 1993), 455.

261. Heidi Roth, "Der 17. Juni im damaligen Bezirk Leipzig," *DA* 24 (1991): 583.

262. Roth, "Der 17. Juni," 576. Roth does not address the period prior to the "building of socialism," and therefore does not sufficiently take into account the loss of trust in the government prior to 1952.

263. BA-P, DO 1 11/304, 281. June 23, 1953 *Instrukteur* report. Diedrich reports that

5,000 people took part in the demonstrations, but because Diedrich does not provide a description of the document which provided him with this number, it is not possible to compare his source to the one presented here; Diedrich, *Der 17. Juni*, 105.

264. BA-P, DO 1 11/304, 281. June 23, 1953 *Instrukteur* report.

265. BA-P, DO 1 11/304, 283. June 23, 1953 *Instrukteur* report.

266. BA-P, DO 1 11/304, 283. June 23, 1953 *Instrukteur* report.

267. BA-P, DO 1 11/304, 282. June 23, 1953 *Instrukteur* report. Diedrich reports that only "some" demonstrators penetrated the police station. His incomplete citations, again, do not allow for an evaluation of his source, but it is extremely unlikely that it is more reliable than the one presented here; Diedrich, *Der 17. Juni*, 106.

268. BA-P, DO 1 11/304, pp. 281-282. June 23, 1953 *Instrukteurbericht*.

269. BA-P, DO 1 11/304, pp. 281-282. June 23, 1953 *Instrukteurbericht*.

270. SAPMO-BA, ZPA, JIV 2/202/14. June 17, 1953 report entitled "Über die Lage am 17.6 in Gross-Berlin und der DDR."

271. SAPMO-BA, ZPA, JIV 2/202/14. June 29, 1953 report from the SED *Bezirksleitung* for Potsdam entitled: "Bericht über die Vorgänge in der Stadt Potsdam ab 17.6.1953."

272. BA-P, DO 1 11/304, 397. June 28, 1953 report from *Bezirk* Potsdam police on the uprising.

273. BA-P, DO 1 11/304, 3. June 28, 1953 report from *Bezirk* Potsdam police on the uprising.

274. BA-P, DO 1 11/305, 240. July 1, 1953 report from *Bezirk* Halle police on the course of the fascist provocation in B*ezirk* Halle on 17.6.53.

275. BA-P, DO 1 11/305, 244. July 1, 1953 report from *Bezirk* Halle police on the course of the fascist provocation in *Bezirk* Halle on 17.6.53.

276. BA-P, DO 1 11/305, 245-246. July 1, 1953 report from Halle *Bezirk* police on the course of the fascist provocation in *Bezirk* Halle on June 17, 1953.

277. BA-P, DO 1 11/45, 3. Extracts from the *Bezirk* police situation reports for the period 0:00 to 17:00 on June 17, 1953 signed by head of operations staff Weidhase.

278. SAPMO-BA, ZPA, JIV 2/202/15, 6. July 20, 1953 report "Analyse über die Vorbereitung, den Ausbruch und die Niederschlagung des faschistischen Abenteuers vom 16.-22.6.1953."

279. BA-P, DO 1 11/45, 3. Extracts from the situation reports of the *Bezirk* police for the period 0:00 to 17:00 on June 17, 1953, signed by the head of the operations staff Weidhase.

280. BA-P, DO 1 11/305, 247. July 1, 1953 report from *Bezirk* Halle police on the course of the fascist provocation in *Bezirk* Halle on June 17, 1953.

281. BA-P, DO 1 11/305, 239. July 1, 1953 report from *Bezirk* Halle police on the course of the fascist provocation in *Bezirk* Halle on June 17, 1953.

282. Hagen, *DDR*, 67.

283. BA-P, DO 1 11/45, 3. Extracts from the *Bezirk* police situation reports for the period 0:00 to 17:00 on June 17, 1953 signed by head of operations staff Weidhase; SAPMO-BA, ZPA, JIV 2/202/14. June 17, 1953 report entitled: "Über die Lage am 17.6. in Gross-Berlin und der DDR."

284. BA-P, DO 1 11/45, 4. Extracts from the situation reports of the *Bezirk Volkspolizei* from June 17, 1953, for the period 0:00-17:00; BA-P, DO 111/305, 242 July 1, 1953 report of Halle *Bezirk* police on the course of the fascist provocation in *Bezirk* Halle on June 17, 1953. This detail is not available in SED reports in the central archive, which state simply that prisoners were freed from the police station; SAPMO-BA, ZPA, JIV 2/202/14. June 17,

1953 report entitled: "Über die Lage am 17.6.53 in Gross-Berlin und der DDR."

285. SAPMO-BA, ZPA, JIV 2/202/15, 6. July 20, 1953 report "Analyse über die Vorbereitung, den Ausbruch und die Niederschlagung des faschistischen Abenteuers vom 16.-22.6.1953."

286. Diedrich, *Der 17. Juni*, 123.

287. Karl Wilhelm Fricke, "Todesstrafe f:ur Magdeburger 'Provokatuer.' SED Rachejustiz nach dem Aufstand vom 17. Juni 1953," *DA* 26 (1993): 527.

288. BA-P, DO 1 11/305, 245-246. July 1, 1953 report from *Bezirk* Halle police on the course of the fascist provocation in *Bezirk* Halle on June 17, 1953.

289. BA-P, DO 1 11/305, 238. July 1, 1953 report from the Halle *Bezirk* police on the course of the fascist provocation on June 17, 1953 in *Bezirk* Halle.

290. BA-P, DO 1 11/305, 238. July 1, 1953 report from the Halle *Bezirk* police on the course of the fascist provocation on June 17, 1953 in *Bezirk* Halle.

291. BA-P, DO 1 11/1435, 12. Report on overview of the situation with railway installations on June 17, 1953.

292. BA-P, DO 1 11/305, 245-246. July 1, 1953 report from Halle *Bezirk* police on the course of the fascist provocation in *Bezirk* Halle on June 17, 1953.

293. AdsD, SPD-PV-Ostbüro 0434b One report from Quelle 20718, the other an unsigned report II on June 17, 1953.

294. AdsD, SPD-PV-Ostbüro 0434b, (#03347). Report from Quelle 3-622/1

295. BA-P, DO 1 11/45, 8. Extract from the *Bezirk* situation reports for the period 0:00 to 17:00 on June 17, 1953, signed by Weidhase, head of operations staff. The documents do not provide information on how the uprising was brought to an end.

296. BA-P, DO 1 11/45, 8. Extract from the *Bezirk* situation reports for the period 0:00 to 17:00 on June 17, 1953, signed by Weidhase, head of operations staff.

297. BA-P, DO 1 11/45, 8. Extract from the *Bezirk* situation reports for the period 0:00 to 17:00 on June 17, 1953, signed by Weidhase, head of operations staff.

298. BA-P, DO 1/11/306, 243. July 1, 1953 report from *Bezirk* Halle police on the course of the fascist provocation in *Bezirk* Halle on June 17, 1953.

299. BA-P, DO 1 11/45, 159. June 22, 1953 report of HVDV Hauptabteilung K signed by Werthmann and Rodis.

300. Hagen, *DDR*, 67.

301. BA-P, DO 1 11/45, 159. June 22, 1953 report of HVDV Hauptabteilung K signed by Werthmann and Rodis; BA-P, DO 1 11/45, 10. Extracts from the situation reports of the *Bezirk* police for the period from 17:00 to 24:00 on June 17, 1953 signed by head of operations staff Weidhase; BA-P, DO 1 11/758, 37. July 20, 1953 Hauptabteilung K report on poor examples of party work in and around June 17.

302. BA-P, DO 1 11/305, 1-18. June 29, 1953 report: "Analysis of the events since 16 June 1953" from Kotulan, head of the *Bezirk* Frankfurt/Oder police to the head of the *Volkspolizei in Berlin.*

303. BA-P, DO 1 11/45, 4. Extracts from the *Bezirk* police situation reports for the period 17:00 to 24:00 on June 17, 1953, signed by head of operations staff Weidhase.

304. BA-P, DO 1 11/305, 17a. June 29, 1953 report: "Analysis of the events since 16 June 1953" from Kotulan, head of the *Bezirk* Frankfurt/Oder police to the head of the *Volkspolizei in Berlin.*

305. BA-P, DO 1 11/305, 23. June 29, 1953 report from the *Bezirk* Frankfurt/Oder police to the operations staff of the *Volkspolizei.*

306. BA-P, DO 1 11/305, 22. June 29, 1953 report from the *Bezirk* Frankfurt/Oder po-

lice to the operations staff of the *Volkspolizei.*

307. BA-P, DO 1 11/305, 21. June 29, 1953 report from the *Bezirk* Frankfurt/Oder police to the operations staff of the *Volkspolizei.*

308. BA-P, DO 1 11/45, 4. Extracts from the *Bezirk* situation reports for the period 0:00 to 17:00 on June 17, 1953 signed by head of operations staff Weidhase.

309. BA-P, DO 1 11/305, 19. June 29, 1953 report from the *Bezirk* Frankfurt/Oder police to the operations staff of the *Volkspolizei.*

310. BA-P, DO 1 11/306, 18. June 29, 1953 report by *Bezirk* Frankfurt/Oder police chief Kotulan entitled: "Auswertung der Ereignisse seit dem 16.6.1953."

311. BA-P, DO 1 11/305, 19. June 29, 1953 report from the *Bezirk* Frankfurt/Oder police to the operations staff of the *Volkspolizei.*

312. BA-P, DO 1 11/305, 19. June 29, 1953 report from the *Bezirk* Frankfurt/Oder police to the operations staff of the *Volkspolizei.*

313. THSA, IV 4.01/124. June 24, 1953 report from SED Apolda *Kreis* leadership to BPKK Erfurt.

314. BA-P, DO 1 11/306, 280-282. June 29, 1953 report of the *Bezirk* Erfurt police on the events since June 17, 1953.

315. THSA, IV 4.02/124, KPKK. June 24, 1953 letter from Rotter to BPKK Erfurt.

316. BA-P, DO 1 11/306, 281. June 29, 1953 report from *Bezirk* Erfurt police on events since June 17.

317. BA-P, DO 1 11/306, 281. June 29, 1953 report from *Bezirk* Erfurt police on events since June 17.

318. BA-P, DO 1 11/306, 282. June 29, 1953 report from *Bezirk* Erfurt police on events since June 17.

319. BA-P, DO 1 11/306, 281. June 29, 1953 report from *Bezirk* Erfurt police on events since June 17.

320. BA-P, DO 1 11/306, 280-282. June 29, 1953 report of *Bezirk* Erfurt police on the events since June 17, 1953.

321. THSA, B IV 2/4-49, Bezirksparteiarchiv der SED Erfurt. June 16, 1953 report entitled: "Bericht über das Verhalten von Parteiorganisationen, leitende Functionäre, und Mitglieder unserer Partei während des faschistischen Putschversuches in der Zeit des 17.6.53."

322. AdsD, SPD-PV-Ostbüro 0434b (#03350) from Quelle 13.7.53. Buschfort argues that *Ostbüro* was surprised by the uprising and therefore did not play a role during it. See Wolfgang Buschfort, *Das Ostbüro der SPD* (Munich: R. Oldenbourg Verlag, 1991), passim.

323. THSA, B IV 2/4-49, Bezirksparteiarchiv der SED Erfurt. September 3, 1953 report entitled: "Analyse über die Ereignisse während des und nach dem 17.6.53 in Bezirk Erfurt."

324. BA-P, DO 1 11/305, 102. June 27, 1953 report from the Cottbus *Bezirk* police to the head of the *Volkspolizei.*

325. BA-P, DO 1 11/305, 102. June 27, 1953 report from the Cottbus *Bezirk* police to the head of the *Volkspolizei.*

326. BA-P, DO 1 11/305, 102. June 27, 1953 report from the Cottbus *Bezirk* police to the head of the *Volkspolizei.*

327. BA-P, DO 1 11/305, 102. June 27, 1953 report from Cottbus *Bezirk* police to the head of the *Volkspolizei.*

328. BA-P, DO 1 11/305, 102. June 27, 1953 report from Cottbus *Bezirk* police to the head of the *Volkspolizei.*

329. BA-P, DO 1 11/305. June 27, 1953 report from the Cottbus *Bezirk* police to the head of the *Volkspolizei.*

330. ACDP VII-011-1268. Situation report of June 18, 1953 from CDU *Kreisverband* Calau to the CDU leadership.

331. BA-P, DO 1 11/305, 102. June 27, 1953 report by the *Bezirk* Cottbus police entitled: "Auswertung der Ereignisse seit dem 16. Juni 1953."

332. BA-P, DO 1 11/305, 7. June 27, 1953 report by the *Bezirk* Cottbus police entitled: "Auswertung der Ereignisse seit dem 16. Juni 1953."

333. Mitter, "Am 17.6.53," 111.

334. BA-P, DO 1 11/304, 337. June 26, 1953 report from the *Bezirk* Rostock police chief Ludwig.

335. MLHA, IV L/2/4/587, 40. June 20, 1953 analysis of the situation in *Bezirk* Schwerin due to the "fascist adventure," signed by the SED *Bezirk* leadership;MLHA, IV 2/4/587, Bezirksleitung der SED, 41. "Analyse über die Lage im *Bezirk* Schwerin am 17.6.1953" by *Bezirk* leadership of SED.

336. MLHA, IV 2/4/587, 44. June 20, 1953 analysis of the situation in *Bezirk* Schwerin due to the "fascist adventure," signed by the *Bezirk* SED leadership.

337. BA-P, DO 1 11/304, 361. June 27, 1953 report from Neubrandenburg *Bezirk* police, signed by inspector Münchow.

338. See the locations listed in Kowlaczuk, Mitter, and Wolle, *Der Tag X*, 338-340.

339. SAPMO, ZPA, JIV 2/202/14. June 17, 1953 report entitled: "Über die Lage am 17.6.1953 in Gross-Berlin und der DDR."

340. This telegram is in SAPMO-BA, ZPA, DY 30 IV 2/5/545. The telegram was signed by August Bach, Hans-Paul Garter-Gilmans, Charlotte Hallscheidt, Max Reutter, Dr. Heinrich Toeplitz, Dr. Gerhard Descyk, Gerald Götting, Dr. Reinhold Lobedanz, Luitpold Steidle, Erich Wächter, and Josef Wujciak.

341. THSA, B IV 2/4-49, 9. September 3, 1953 report on the events during and after June 17, 1953 in *Bezirk* Erfurt.

342. THSA, B IB 2/4-48. July 1953 letter from KPKK Heiligenstadt to BPKK Erfurt.

343. THSA, B IV 2/4-48, Bezirksparteiarchiv der SED Erfurt.

344. Leo Haupts, "Die Blockparteien in der DDR und der 17. Juni 1953," *VfZ* 40 (1992), pp. 396-397.Udo Wengst, "Der Aufstand am 17. Juni 1953 in der DDR," *VfZ*41 (1993), 300.

345. June 27, 1953 report from Lieutenant General Fedenko, Operations Division, Main Operations Division, General Staff of the Soviet Army, to Lieutenant General Pavlovsky, reproduced in Ostermann, *The Post-Stalin,* Document #25.

346. Haupts, "Die Blockparteien," 398; Wengst, "Der Aufstand," 289. *Kreis* Saalkreis CDU supported the suppression of the uprising; Wengst, "Der Aufstand," 294. The CDU *Kreis* chair for Gera helped disperse crowd; Wengst, "Der Aufstand," 296.

347. SAPMO-BA, ZPA, DY 30 IV 2/5/560, 6. July 1,1953 summary of the important events from the *Bezirk* reports of June 30, 1953. Of approximately 1,600 individuals tried for their participation in the uprising, two were executed. One of those executed was the former National Socialist concentration camp commander Erna Dorn; the other a worker from Magdeburg, Ernst Jennrich. The GDR's supreme court sentenced Jennrich to death on October 6, 1953. He was beheaded on March 20, 1954. For details on his case, see Karl Wilhelm Fricke, "Todesstrafe für Magdeburger 'Provokateur,' *Deutschland Archiv* 26 (1993): 527-531.

348. ADL, #2367. FDP Ostbüro report from August 1953.

349. ADL, #2367. FDP Ostbüro report from August 1953.

350. THSA, B IV 2/4-48/1. June 23, 1953 report by SED sekretariat for Weimar-land

on strikes and demonstrations between June 16 and June 21, 1953.

351. Roth, "Der 17. Juni," 573-583

352. Haupts, "Die Blockparteien," 42.

353. BA-P, DO 1 11/758, 4. July 2, 1953 report by Weidlich, head of the investigation department of the *Volkspolizei*, on those arrested in connection with the "fascist putsch."

354. BA-P, DO 1 11/305, 102. June 27, 1953 report from the Cottbus *Bezirk* police to the head of the *Volkspolizei*.

355. BA-P, DO 1 11/45, 243. Extracts from the *Bezirk* police situation reports for the period 0:00 to 17:00 on June 17, 1953 signed by Weidhase, head of operations staff.

356. BA-P, DO 1 11/45, 9. Extracts from the *Bezirk* police situation reports for the period 17:00 to 24:00 on June 17, 1953, signed by head of operations staff Weidhase.

357. MLHA, IV 2/4/587. "Analyse über die Lage in *Bezirk* Schwerin am 17. Juni 1953" by the *Bezirk* leadership of the SED.

358. See the reports in BA-P, DO 1 11/304,305,and 306, and DO1 11/45.

359. Soviet sources offer different numbers, but suggest a similar trend. Soviet military official reported 132,169 strikers in the GDR on June 17, but 269,460 demonstrators. June 27, 1953 report from Lieutenant General Fedenko, Operations Division, Main Operations Administration, General Staff of the Soviet Army, to Lieutenant General Pavlovsky, reproduced in Ostermann, *The Post-Stalin,* Document #25.

360. BA-P, DO 1 11/758, 18. June 25, 1953 report by Weidlich, head of the investigation branch of the *Volkspolizei* on arrests of those involved with the "fascist provocation."

361. BA-P, DO 1 11/758, 18. June 25, 1953 report by Weidlich, head of the investigation branch of the *Volkspolizei* on arrests of those involved with the "fascist provocation.".

362. The intellegentsia and students tended to be critical of the regime during the disturbances, but generally did not actively participate. See Anke Huschner, "Der 17. Juni 1953 an Universitäten und Hochschulen der DDR," *Beiträge zur Geschichte der Arbeiterbewegung* 33 (1991): 690-691. In his recent history of opposition in East Germany, Ehrhart Neubert also stresses the broad participation in the uprising. Unfortunately, he does not provide sources for his contention. See Ehrhart Neubert, *Geschichte Geschichte Opposition in der DDR 1949-1989* (Bonn: Bundeszentrale für politische Bildung, 2000), 86.

363. Baring stresses the youth component in demonstrations; Baring, *Uprising*, 52-52

364. BA-P, DO 1 11/758, 5. July 2, 1953 report by Weidlich, head of the investigation department of the *Volkspolizei*, on those arrested in connection with the "fascist putsch."

365. Diedrich, *Der 17. Juni*, 157.

366. Baring, *Uprising,*76.

367. Diedrich, *Der 17. Juni*, 157.

368. BA-P, DO 1 11/45, 240. Extract from the *Bezirk* police situation reports for the period 0:00 to 17:00 on June 17, 1953, signed by head of operations staff Weidhase.

369. BA-P, DO 1 11/45, 5. Extracts from the *Bezirk* police situation reports for the period 0:00 to 17:00 on June 17, 1953 signed by head of operations staff Weidhase.

370. BA-P, DO 1 11/305, 102. June 27, 1953 report from the *Bezirk* police in Cottbus entitled "Auswertung der Ereignisse seit dem 16. Juni 1953."

371. BA-P, DO 1 11/306, 18. June 29, 1953 report from the *Bezirk* Frankfurt/Oder police chief Kotulan entitled "Auswertung der Ereignisse seit dem 16.6.1953."

372. BA-P, DO 1 11/45, 9. Extracts from the *Bezirk* police situation reports for the period 0:00 to 17:00 on June 17, 1953 signed by head of operations staff Weidhase.

373. BA-P, DO 1 11/45, 4. Extracts from the *Bezirk* police situation reports for the period 0:00 to 17:00 on June 17, 1953 signed by Weidhase, head of operations staff.

374. BA-P, DO 1 11/305, 18. June 29, 1953 report from *Bezirk* Frankfurt/Oder police to the operations staff of the *Volkspolizei*.

375. SAPMO-BA, ZPA, JIV 2/202/14. June 29, 1953 report on the events in the city of Potsdam on June 17, 1953.

376. See chapter three.

377. See chapter four.

378. See Mitter, "Am 17.6.53," passim.

379. BA-P, DO 1 11/45, 12. June 18, 1953 report Nr. 166 on the events on June 17, 1953, signed by Grünstein, deputy to the head of the *Volkspolizei*. A Free German Trade Union analysis came to a similar summary of the demands. Wolfgang Eckelmann, Hans Hermann Hertle, and Rainer Weinert, *FDGB Intern* (Berlin: Treptower Verlagshaus, 1990), 26. ACDP, VII-011-1268. The vast majority of situation reports from CDU *Bezirk* organizations in this signature mention that the demand for free elections permeated the uprising.

380. SAPMO-BA, ZPA, JIV 2/202/14. June 17, 1953 report entitled: "Über die Lage am 17.6.53 in Gross-Berlin und der DDR."

381. June 17, 1953 report from Grechko, Tarasov and Malinin (Operations Division, Main Operations Administration, General Staff of the Soviet Army) to N.A. Bulganin, in Ostermann, *The Post-Stalin Succession Struggle*, Document #15.

Chapter 6

The Aftermath of the Revolution: Repression and Popular Resistance

Disturbances in the GDR after the Revolution

Strikes and disturbances continued to rip through the GDR throughout the week following the revolution. Indeed, in *Bezirk* Cottbus more workers went on strike on June 18 (14,983) than did on June 17 (11,017),[1] and Soviet sources estimate that overall in the GDR, more workers went on strike on June 18 (218,700) than on June 17 (132,169).[2] Moreover, prominent in the disturbances in the week following the uprising, like the disturbances of June 17, were issues of repression and the end of the Communist system in East Germany. Let us turn our attention to each *Bezirk*.

Bezirk Cottbus
    The city of Cottbus was a center of unrest following the uprising. On June 18, striking workers from VEB Kraftverkehr Cottbus proclaimed: "We demand free discussions without personal disadvantages. We demand truly free and secret elections in the GDR and all Germany."[3] Demonstrations took place in front of the Cottbus prison where the crowd demanded the release of political prisoners.[4] In total, forty-seven factories went on strike in *Bezirk* Cottbus on June 18, and by the 19th, only twenty-nine of those had returned to normal operation. At two of the factories that returned to normal operation, VEM Cottbus and VEM Anlagebau, workers gathered to observe five minutes of silence for those who had been shot the previous day.[5]
    Aware of the demonstrators' interest in the fate of prisoners in East Germany,

the *Volkspolizei* evacuated the prison work camp in Preschen on the night of June 17-18. The police successfully transported the prisoners to a prison in Cottbus by the morning. Police reports indicate that the prisoners were well behaved, but "were astounded by the significant movements of Soviet troops."[6] However, the police were unable to complete the evacuation of the prison camp in Drewitz and were forced to leave about 200 prisoners in the camp. On June 18, about 400 people gathered around the camp and demanded the release of prisoners. Because most of the police force had already left for the new site, the police guarding the camp immediately called for a KVP company and tank unit to protect the site. The additional forces arrived just as demonstrators began to attack the fences of the camp.[7]

Bezirk Potsdam

Work stoppages and disturbances also occurred in *Bezirk* Potsdam in the aftermath of the revolution. In Potsdam itself, workers walked off the job in major factories such as Karl-Marx-Werk, the railway outfitting works, DEFA, and APAG on June 18 but all factories were back to normal by the following day.[8] Abus Wildau and Thälmann Werk in Brandenburg also continued to strike on June 18. On the same day, demonstrators stormed the LPG office in *Gemeinde* Gülpe, *Kreis* Rathenow, and beat up the SED mayor.[9] In Kunstfaserwerk Friedrich Engels, workers attempted to form a strike committee as late as June 20.[10]

Bezirk Frankfurt/Oder

At the Bau Union Spree in *Kreis* Fürstenwalde, a majority of the factory's complement went on strike on June 18 demanding that political prisoners be freed.[11] On the construction site of Stalinstadt, very few workers showed up to their jobs on June 18 because they were planning a demonstration for 4 pm to free prisoners. Arrests of the leaders, however, prevented the demonstration from taking place.[12] Political slogans were also evident in *Bezirk* Frankfurt/Oder. In addition, 430 construction workers from the Güldendorf construction site went on strike after meeting and adopting a resolution which demanded the end of the government.[13]

Bezirk Dresden

In *Bezirk* Dresden, workers at Sachsenwerk Niedersedlitz still had not returned to their jobs by June 18.[14] No other major disturbances or work stoppages were reported.

Bezirk Rostock

Unlike June 17, *Bezirk* Rostock experienced considerable unrest in the week after the revolution. On June 19 in Warnow-Werft Warnemünde, workers issued the following demands: removal of the Grotewohl government, release of the factory head, reduction of norms, "not one cent" for the KVP, and the lifting of the state of emergency.[15] The police sent one company of the para-military troops in the *Volkspolizei* (Department HV A) to Warnemünde to quell the unrest but badly underestimated the number of troops required to put down the large demonstration.

The police were therefore forced to call for the backup of the KVP.[16]

In support of these striking workers, about 230 workers from Bootswerft Gehlsdorf—Rostock, went on strike demanding: (1) same wages as in Warnow-Werft, (2) reduction of norms, (3) release of imprisoned colleagues, and (4) removal of Soviet tanks from the streets of Berlin and Rostock. Receiving no indication that the demands would be met, 200 workers went on strike the following day, adding to their list of demands free elections, a lifting of the state of emergency, and flying the flag at half mast in memory of a demonstrator who had been shot.[17]

The port of Stralsund on the Baltic coast also experienced unrest following the uprising. At 9:45 am on the 18th, about 200 workers of the Schiffsbau and Reparaturwerft Stralsund went on strike and stayed away from work until 2 pm when Soviet troops arrived and ended the walkout.[18] In Bau Union Küste, Schwedenschanze, workers went on strike almost simultaneously with Schiffsbau Stralsund. Here, the strike leadership demanded punishment of those who were involved with the laws that led to the lowering of the living standards, substantial improvement in living standards, the release of their arrested colleagues, free and secret democratic elections with the licensing of all parties, and removal of the KVP from factories and public places.[19] About 2,200 workers went on strike in *Kreis* Stralsund on June 18.[20]

Calls for the end of the government were also central to other strikes after June 17. During a strike at Mathias Thesen Werft in Wismar on June 18, one demonstrator shouted: "Our elections are not free elections. We can't really talk of democracy."[21] Another protestor demanded that the "government should and must disappear."[22] The anger at the government meant that SED functionaries also had to be cautious in the aftermath of the uprising. On June 20, twenty people attacked the SED party secretary from *Kreis* Rostock shouting: "You've ruled up to now. Now we rule."[23]

Bezirk Erfurt

At the VEB Ifa-Schlepperwerk in Nordhausen, approximately 1,200 of the 2,204 workers went on strike on June 18 demanding the removal of the government and the end of state of emergency.[24] In SAG-Betrieb Pelz in Erfurt, workers went on strike issuing only one demand: "Free all-German elections."[25] VEB Optima in Erfurt and EKM-Werk Feuerungsbau in Erfurt went on strike on June 18 in solidarity with workers who had been shot in Berlin during the demonstrations.

Unrest in *Bezirk* Erfurt continued into the week following the uprising. On June 19, all 3,000 workers at RFT-Funkwerk Erfurt, and 2,500 of the 4,000 workers of VEB Optima in Erfurt went on strike.[26] In Weimar, demonstrators occupied the central telephone exchange and built barricades.[27] In isolated cases throughout the *Bezirk*, SED party members were "terrorized."[28] It was not until June 20 that the police in Erfurt reported that a day had passed without strikes or work stoppages.[29]

Bezirk Halle

In contrast to the boisterous demonstrations and storming of prisons on June

17, *Bezirk* Halle was fairly quiet in the week following the revolution. No demonstrations took place, and most factories were at full strength by June 18. Only Lowa-Ammendorf, Ifa-Karrosseriewerk, Diamalt, EKM Hohenthurm, and "several" small factories continued to strike on June 18.[30] The railway outfitting plant also went on strike temporarily.[31] In the evening of June 18, a crowd gathered on the Halle market square, but 200 armed *Volkspolizei* and KVP units dispersed the demonstrators before any major disturbances could took place, although not without a cost. One bystander was shot during the dispersal.[32]

Vigorous police measures prevented major disturbances in *Bezirk* Halle following the revolution. To prevent a demonstration in the unsettled Waggonfabrik, units of the KVP occupied the plant on the morning of June 19 and handed out pamphlets stating that the KVP would not tolerate any demonstrations, and that they would continue to occupy the plant until "workers who want to get back to work can do so safely."[33] These measures were adopted in Ifa-Karrosseriewerken and EKM-Hohenthurm as well.[34]

In the Mansfeld-Kombinat, a majority of workers went on strike on June 18, although workers had not gone on strike on June 17.[35] Apparently, the second SED party chair of the *Bezirk* was able to convince the workers to return to the plant by the 19th. On the same day, however, new strikes broke out in Sangerhausen, where the Thomas-Münzer-Schacht, the machine factory Sangerhausen, Mifa, and other small factories went on strike. Police measures helped force workers back to the factories by June 20.[36]

Bezirk Magdeburg

On June 18, the workers at Magdeburg plants RAW, Elmo, Kupferwerk, and all Kaliwerke left their jobs. In the outlying *Kreise* Oschersleben and Gardelegen, workers returning to Magdeburg tore down flags and banners, called for a general strike, and tried to storm the control point at Weissenborn.[37] In *Gemeinde* Egeln, *Kreis* Strassfurt, opponents of the regime demonstrated their support for the revolution, and their view of its nature, by laying at a war memorial a wreath with a ribbon reading: "June 17 1953—To the victims for freedom and human rights."[38] In Wernigerode, the SED's attempt to convince striking workers not to hold a demonstration fell on deaf ears, but the "warning shots from the Friends," convinced the striking workers not to organize a demonstration.[39] By June 20, 90 percent of factories in Magdeburg were back at full strength.[40]

Bezirk Neubrandenburg

Unrest in *Bezirk* Neubrandenburg was most prevalent at construction sites. At the construction site Gross-Dölln, 1,700 workers went on strike on June 18 and simply went home rather than march through town.[41] At the construction site Bau-Union-Nordost, workers threatened to strike but did not carry through on the threat.[42] In the countryside of this *Bezirk*, no demonstrations took place, but there was a massive exodus from the LPGs in the days following the uprising.[43]

Bezirk Suhl

Although farmers dissolved a large number of LPGs, there were no disturbances in Suhl following the revolution.[44]

Bezirk Gera

Most factories had returned to normal operation by the morning of June 18. In the town of Gera, only the construction site Maxhütte and the section of the Zeiss plant that had started the strike on June 17 remained on strike.[45] In *Kreise* Rudolstadt and Eisenberg, only one factory in each *Kreis* experienced work stoppages in the week following the uprising.[46] On June 19, there was a short work stoppage by truck drivers delivering food supplies.[47]

Bezirk Schwerin

No major disturbances occurred in *Bezirk* Schwerin following the revolution. In Grabow, a demonstration took place in front of city hall during which the SED *Kreis* secretary was attacked.[48] Otherwise, there were only "agitated discussions" and threats to demonstrate.[49]

Bezirk Leipzig

Six *Kreise* in *Bezirk* Leipzig experienced work stoppages: Döbeln, Delitzsch, Geithain, Wurzen, Eilenburg, and Leipzig-Land, making the strikes in this *Bezirk* more widespread on June 18 than on June 17. The SED also noted that on 18 June, "enemy activity" spilled over into the countryside.[50] On June 22, there were isolated attempts to strike, and a number of LPGs dissolved.[51]

Bezirk Karl-Marx-Stadt

Construction worker strikes in Freiberg and Werdau were the only instances of unrest on June 18 in *Bezirk* Karl-Marx-Stadt. The SED leadership was able to convince the workers in Werdau not to hold a demonstration.[52]

Although the demonstrations and disturbances in the GDR were not as widespread in the week following the June 17 revolution, they nonetheless reveal that the situation in the GDR was extremely unstable. Indeed, in some instances only through arrests, the occupation of factories, and Soviet assistance was the SED able to prevent demonstrations in the week following the revolution. Even during these limited disturbances, however, political demands invariably accompanied economic demands, and demonstrators continued to exhibit concern for prisoners in the GDR. Not until one week after the uprising could the MfS report, with some relief: "The situation in Berlin and the German Democratic Republic was completely quiet on June 24. No occurrences, strikes, demonstrations etc. took place."[53]

As might be expected from the extent of unrest, the SED faced an enormous task in attempting to garner support in the aftermath of the revolution. The Politburo believed that the revolution was largely related to economics, and therefore believed that improving the material situation in the GDR would placate the population. The Politburo announced on June 25 that there would be significant improvements in living standards, and arranged for several measures to ease day to day burdens, including, importing extra foodstuffs from the Soviet Union, reducing public transit prices, and setting aside funds to rebuild living accommodations and to improve hygenic conditions in factories.[54] The Politburo, however, had erred in its analysis of the situation, for, in the words of an MfS employee: "Above all things, the dissatisfaction in the population is so large, it is unlikely we can ever make it up."[55] The MfS officer's observations were confirmed by strikes that ripped through the GDR's industrial heartland three weeks after the announcement of improved living conditions. The site most affected by strikes was Bunawerk in Schkopau, *Bezirk* Halle, where political considerations were clearly at the forefront of workers' demands. From July 15 to 17, over 5,000 of the 16,000 workers at Bunawerk went on strike and demanded (1) free, all-German elections as quickly as possible, (2) the release of all political prisoners, (3) new elections for the union leadership, (4) until such elections, no union dues to be paid, and (5) removal of the party from the union.[56]

An important example of the dominance of political issues over economic ones comes from the reaction of the population towards the food packets that the United States was supplying to the eastern German population in the aftermath of the uprising.[57] When the SED confronted people who intended to accept these packets with arguments that the SED was improving the standard of living in the GDR, East Germans replied that they were going to pick up the packets not because they needed food, but to show support for the American policy. In *Bezirk* Cottbus, the *Volkspolizei* were put on alert because of the thousands of workers threatening to leave for Berlin to pick up the packets.[58]

The strike in Jena at the Zeiss works optic plant on July 7, 1953 also demonstrated political considerations. The first point of the thirty-three-point program that the strikers adopted demanded free, secret elections in Germany.[59] One MfS report summarized the situation at the Jena plant as the following: "Over and over we see that in meetings where reactionary elements speak against the government and its measures, a large number of workers are won over to their goals."[60] An SED Instructor in *Bezirk* Halle recognized the true situation in the GDR in his report from the beginning of July: "The main slogans that the enemy cleverly disguises as smaller economic demands, and that he brings more and more frequently into factories and spreads more and more frequently in the countryside, are: Free elections, Release of all political prisoners since 1945, apolitical union"[61]

As indicated in the above report, the countryside was turbulent in the wake of the uprising. In *Bezirk* Halle, one farmer shouted at the mayor: "On 17 June, the workers went on strike. Now we farmers are going to strike." The head of the *Volkspolizei* operations staff lamented that these sentiments were widespread in the countryside.[62] At the end of July in *Bezirk* Gera, farmers still demanded the end of the government, free elections, and the release of prisoners.[63] At a farmers' meeting in Kribitz, *Kreis* Plauen, one farmer shouted his demand for political change: "Gentlemen, it is five minutes past twelve. The day of reckoning is almost here. RIAS, that is the station. All the people in the eastern zone who fight for human rights are locked up. My wife was sentenced to five years in prison for this."[64] These were not uncommon occurrences. At another gathering, one farmer said: "Why isn't Ulbricht locked up? We do not need these puppet figures. We want to choose our own government," and received tumultuous applause for his words.[65] Popular opposition to the SED's agricultural strategy was also visible in the massive dissolution of the agricultural collectives. In *Bezirk* Neubrandenburg, the police reported: "Since the events of 17 June . . . there has been a movement towards dissolving the LPGs in nearly all *Kreise*."[66] In *Kreis* Weimar-Land, there was a major exodus from the LPGs Trommlitz and Kottendorf, during which farmers departed under the slogan: "We want to be free farmers again."[67] At the fourteenth Sitting of the Central Committee on June 21, Otto Grotewohl acknowledged the catastrophic situation in the countryside: "The careful analyses that lay before us demonstrate that . . . hundreds of thousands of farmers have left their farms and fled to the West."[68] The rejection of the LPGs was a common phenomenon in the GDR. On July 15 alone, 217 out of 5,000 LPGs were dissolved and by the end of July, 10 percent of the LPGs had been dissolved, and a further 10 percent reported a massive exodus of membership.[69] Considering that a state of emergency was in effect until July 11, this was a significant demonstration against the LPGs.[70]

The police were gravely worried by the number of attacks on SED functionaries in agricultural collectives in the aftermath of June 17. In October and November 1953, SED members in *Gemeinde* Wüstenmark, Harlow, Jahna, Kospoda, Gladow, Seelow, Oranienburg, Werneuchen, Frauenhain, and Klingenberg were attacked, often with billy clubs, and left to find their own way to the hospital. In several instances, chairmen of the collective farm were shot dead.[71] In *Gemeinde* Melchow, celebrations marking the thirty-sixth anniversary of the October revolution were continually interrupted by boos and whistles. After the event, the main speaker was beaten up. These episodes prompted Karl Maron, head of the police force, to write to Walter Ulbricht pleading for the vacant positions in rural police stations to be filled.[72]

Due to the presence of this fundamental hostility to the SED, it is not surprising to find that the SED's propaganda events designed to "prove" that the population was loyal to the regime were ineffective. The population overwhelmingly rejected these events.[73] SED functionaries who went into factories in the aftermath of the uprising to talk on the situation were often drowned out.[74] When Ulbricht came to the Leuna works to talk to workers there, workers who had been invited to a discussion with Ulbricht were not interested in hearing what he had to say, but rather demanded that he release all political prisoners and separate the party from the union.[75] An LOPM report summarizing the general situation among the working class in the GDR from June 23, 1953 acknowledged that the speeches of functionaries met with such hostile reaction because of the lack of trust in the government.[76] In June 1953, Grotewohl admitted that the government had to win back the trust of the population, but that this could not be accomplished by mere demonstrations.[77]

The Non-Marxist Parties in the Aftermath of the Revolution

Although the CDU and the LDPD had become instruments of the SED by 1953, there was hostility in the general membership to the leadership's support for the "building of socialism." It is difficult to characterize this hostility as resistance, however, because the protests tended to be directed against certain aspects of the "building of socialism," rather than the Communist system itself. Religious CDU members, for example, tended to be the most critical because of the SED's campaign against the *Junge Gemeinde*.[78] Resistance in the CDU and LDPD had been broken by 1953, but oppositional elements continued in the parties until the end of the GDR.[79]

Following the uprising, the CDU general secretary Götting met with all CDU *Bezirk* associations. The protocols from these meetings provide insights into the tensions between the general membership and the leadership of the party. The CDU membership in *Bezirke* Karl-Marx-Stadt, Potsdam and Leipzig expressed dismay that the party had supported the SED's "leading role" claim and that the party had participated in the campaign against the *Junge Gemeinde*.[80] Indeed, a report on the situation in the CDU after the revolution stated that there were "substantial" criticisms due to the campaign against the *Junge Gemeinde*.[81] In *Bezirke* Suhl and Rostock, members also criticized the party for not practising more independent politics.[82] Two local CDU groups in Halle even complained that Nuschke should not have agreed to unity lists in 1950.[83] In a report written by Götting after his meetings with the *Bezirk* groups, Götting acknowledged that he had undertaken the visits because of "serious accusations" by lower levels of the party against the leadership, including demands for resignations and new elections to the CDU leadership.[84] The impression he formed from these meetings, however, was that CDU members desired improvement in Block work.[85] Because of the negligible participation of the CDU during the uprising, and the lack of CDU interest in a new political system—only the improvement of the Communist system—one cannot consider grumblings in the CDU after the uprising to be resistance. From 1953 on, the CDU had oppositional elements, but was not a home for anti-Communist resistance as it had been previously.

The LDPD also experienced isolated protests by its members in the aftermath of the uprising. LDPD members who spoke out against the leadership tended to emphasize that the LDPD was not independent. In one locality, one LDPD member left the party because he felt it shared equally in the responsibility for the situation in the GDR, and would pay the price in another revolt, stating: "No, I'm not taking part anymore. I don't want to be hanged, like they're going to hang you all one day."[86] The LDPD in *Kreis* Dessau also reported that party members had lost faith in the leadership of the party.[87] The LDPD in *Kreise* Saalkreis, Rosslau, Halle, and Greifswald also expressed their displeasure with the LDPD leadership.[88] In a sampling of five *Bezirke* conducted for this study, four LDPD *Bezirk* associations indicated opposition in the membership to the leadership of the party.[89]

Opposition still lingered in the LDPD into 1954. Johannes Dieckmann, deputy chairman of the LDPD, reported in April 1954 that reports from LDPD members repeatedly stated that they were opposed to unity list elections like the fall of 1950. Dieckmann further reported that there was a considerable portion of the LDPD membership who wanted an election system as practiced in Bonn.[90]

Popular Concern with Legal Insecurity

This study has demonstrated that one of the primary causes behind the June 17 revolution was legal insecurity. The evidence suggests that this issue continued to preoccupy the population in the aftermath of the uprising. On July 29, Max Fechner, the Minister of Justice, called for a strengthening of "our democratic adherence to the law," stating: "In the recent past, verdicts have been handed down which have no relation to the crime committed,"[91] and, indeed, the verdicts were extraordinarily harsh. In *Gemeinde* Poplitz, one woman was sentenced to six years in prison for selling eggs in West Berlin. In *Kreis* Schwerin, the population complained because cigarette factory workers had been sentenced to three years in prison for smoking on a break, the irony apparently lost on the judge.[92]

Situation reports of the non-Marxist parties in the aftermath of the uprising point to the destabilizing effect of legal insecurity. These reports reveal that districts most affected by disturbances on June 17 and in the days following the revolution also expressed the most concern for legal security in its aftermath. In *Bezirk* Halle, which experienced the second most demonstrations or strikes between June 16 and 21 (after *Bezirk* Magdeburg), legal insecurity was at the center of popular discontent. CDU members in Bitterfeld reported that legal insecurity was the primary topic of discussion in the population,[93] and suggested placing the MfS under the Ministry of the Interior as had been done in the Soviet Union, in order both to help with administrative costs and to increase the population's trust in the state. Reports of torture chambers in the MfS building in Bitterfeld caused much unrest in the population.[94]

The CDU and LDPD in other centers in *Bezirk* Halle reported popular concern with legal insecurity. In the city of Halle, the CDU reported that the population simply did not trust the MfS or the *Volkspolizei*.[95] At an LDPD meeting in Sellin in July 1953, LDPD members argued that the *Volkspolizei* was a state within a state, and that as a result, trust in the government had been lost.[96] In *Kreis* Bernburg, the trust in the government had been irreparably shaken due to judicial practice. People here stated that "the years behind bars for innocent people, and the tears of farmers, craftsmen and private business owners could never be made up." The population criticized in particular arresting procedures, saying it took "one night to lock someone up, but weeks to release them."[97]

Because of Fechner's support for the workers' right to strike on June 17, which he voiced in a *Neues Deutschland* article, he was replaced as Minister of Justice on July 16, 1953 by Hilde Benjamin.[98] Popular response to the appointment of Hilde

Benjamin as the new Minister of Justice demonstrates the extent to which the population in *Bezirk* Halle was concerned with judicial practice. Eleven CDU *Kreis* associations in *Bezirk* Halle went so far as to call the appointment of Hilde Benjamin a "provocation of the population,"[99] because of her involvement in the harsh sentencing practices during the "building of socialism." The LDPD in Köthen reported that the population lost confidence in the government through measures such as appointing Benjamin Justice Minister.[100] In *Kreis* Artern, the population overwhelmingly rejected Benjamin as Justice Minister because they saw her as responsible for the harsh sentences prior to the revolution and believed that the SED was returning to the Old Course.[101] People in *Kreis* Eisleben also rejected the appointment of Benjamin.[102] Furthermore, the population in *Bezirk* Halle reacted strongly to the establishment of communal living units called "House and Court Societies" (*Haus- und Hofgemeinschaften*) because they considered them a method of "political supervision."[103] One LDPD member, commenting on the advertisement in a movie theater which portrayed the living units as centers in the fight against agents, spies, and provocateurs, stated: "Due to these ads, wide sections of the population believe that these are installations for surveillance, and they are therefore rejected by the population."[104]

In *Bezirk* Potsdam, the *Bezirk* which experienced the third most disturbances during the revolution, the non-Marxist parties reported deep popular concern regarding legal insecurity. The LDPD in Potsdam reported that the population desired trials of government officials, especially those involved in the judicial apparatus: "People have repeatedly expressed the hope that those in . . . middle and lower administrations (especially the justice administration) will be held accountable for their conduct."[105] The CDU echoed these sentiments: "The number one demand, expressed over and over, is the introduction of legal security in the Republic."[106] There was a similar reaction in *Bezirk* Potsdam to the founding of *Haus- und Hofgemeinschaften*. In *Kreis* Gransee, at the founding of the communal living units, people stated: "When we no longer have to fear that we will be picked up, and when we are allowed to speak, then we'll go along with everything."[107]

The CDU in *Bezirk* Magdeburg, which had experienced the most disturbances in the GDR during the revolution, did not report legal insecurity as the most pressing issue, but rather the lack of coal.[108] Legal insecurity still played a role in the *Bezirk*, however. In *Gemeinde* Vogelberg, there was "great unrest" on the LPG because of a rumor that the SED had compiled a list of fifteen farmers who were to be sent to prison. That the farmers immediately believed the rumor demonstrates the pervasiveness of lawlessness.[109] The communal living units in Magdeburg were also rejected as "centres to spy on us."[110]

In *Bezirk* Dresden, the centers of greatest unrest, Niesky and Görlitz, continued to show their concern for legal security in the aftermath of the revolution. In Görlitz, during a talk by MfS members to the workers of the Lowa plant, one of the workers stood up and asked why the MfS felt it had to keep files on GDR citizens. The MfS officers denied the practice, after which the workers produced some of these MfS files which had been taken during the storming of the MfS building on

June 17. The workers then threw them on the floor and burned them. The workers also produced what they believed to be a torture device which had been taken from the building and destroyed it with a welding torch.[111] The CDU in Niesky reported that the population was very critical of the MfS.[112]

In *Bezirk* Frankfurt/Oder, the CDU reported that MfS measures were worse than those of the Gestapo and demanded changes to its practices. These members wanted guarantees of legal security in the constitution.[113] The CDU in Frankfurt/Oder concluded that MfS practices contributed to popular opposition and estimated that the SED was backed by only 8-10 percent of the population.[114]

The population in *Bezirke* which witnessed limited or no activity on June 17 also expressed concern regarding *Rechtsunsicherheit* in the aftermath of the uprising. On July 16, 1953, the CDU *Bezirk* association for Suhl recommended a relaxation of the application of the "law for the protection of the people's economy," saying that the harsh sentences agitated the population. This CDU group even brought into question whether judges properly applied the infamous Article 6 of the constitution. To improve the judicial system, the CDU in Suhl recommended that Communist ideology in the judiciary be tempered: "It is especially important to implement a unified administration of justice in the Republic. The administration of justice should closely follow laws, and avoid expanding the application of laws according to a certain ideology"[115]

LDPD situation reports from Schwerin taken between May and October 1953 reveal that the population was still alarmed by the abuse of German women by Russian forces after the war. These reports also concluded that although there were no demonstrations in the region on June 17, "there was still plenty of dissatisfaction."[116] The LDPD noted that past suppression continued to have a negative effect on the population, reporting that people did not "speak openly and freely."[117] Another LDPD member warned of "great unrest" in the population because the police did not always provide a reason for arrest within twenty-four hours, as required by the constitution.[118]

The CDU in *Bezirk* Gera also brought up issues of legal security in their conversation with Götting. The CDU here was concerned for CDU members that were sentenced during the Erfurt trials. In *Kreis* Zeulenroda, the population complained of public prosecutor Schletta's remark that it was a pleasure for him to sentence a capitalist to twenty years in prison.[119] The LDPD *Kreis* association for Gera-Stadt went so far as to adopt a resolution stating: "The arresting practices of public prosecutors and the courts are untenable. The respect for personal freedom is often frighteningly low."[120]

In the city of Jena, *Bezirk* Gera, which had experienced widespread disturbances on June 17, legal insecurity was an issue following the uprising. At a meeting between Johannes Becher and members of the Jena intelligentsia on July 9, 1953, which approximately eighty people attended, the audience sharply criticized the conduct of the MfS. Professor Knöll, a winner of the GDR's national prize, and Professor Hämel, rector of the Friedrich Schiller University, supported the public's stance by emphasizing that the judicial system and the *Volkspolizei* were to protect the people, and were not to be used as an instrument of the power apparatus. They received extensive applause for their comments. Hämel provided insight into the situation in the GDR when he explained: "It is unacceptable that every time a black car stops in front of the house in the evening, you have to grab your day bag."[121]

In *Kreis* Freital, *Bezirk* Leipzig, the population demanded a "true" press and the dissolution of the MfS and *Volkspolizei* in barracks.[122] This fear was echoed at a meeting of the *Kreis* executive Borna on July 1, 1953 where one LDPD member commenting on June 17 stated: "Every citizen was frightened and didn't dare express his true opinion. He did not want to run the risk of holding the wrong political opinion."[123]

Perhaps the most striking feature of the reports of the non-Marxist parties in the aftermath of the uprising is the absence of mention about the material situation of the population. Only the CDU in Magdeburg specifically commented on the lack of coal as a source of unrest.[124] In contrast, the *Bezirke* Potsdam, Karl-Marx-Stadt, Schwerin, Gera, Rostock, Halle, Cottbus, Leipzig, Frankfurt/Oder, Suhl and Dresden all reported concern regarding legal insecurity. In Halle and Potsdam, where the second and third most disturbances had taken place, legal security was clearly at the forefront of people's concerns. CDU *Kreis* leaders emphasized the importance of legal security at a conference of CDU *Kreis* leaders in the GDR in the summer of 1953. The *Kreis* leaders reported that the population rejected the lies in the SED press, disapproved of the conduct of those in administration positions, was displeased with the demarcation zone, desired an improved agricultural situation, and desired freer access to West Berlin. However, the main concern in the population was the "strengthening of legal security in the Republic." The CDU *Kreis* leaders summarized: "People demand over and over that every person arrested must be informed as to the reason for the arrest. His next of kin must also be informed as to the reason for the arrest."[125] The CDU *Kreis* leaders insisted that this issue be addressed as quickly as possible.

Popular concern with legal security can only partially be dismissed as a result of the arrests which took place throughout the GDR in the aftermath of the revolution. In *Bezirk* Karl-Marx-Stadt, five of seven *Kreise* emphasized restoring legal security, although only five people had been arrested by June 30.[126] In Suhl, where legal insecurity preoccupied the population, only one person had been arrested by June 30.[127] In Halle, the arrests of 712 people in connection with the revolution (137 were immediately released) likely contributed to the emphasis on legal security, but in Potsdam, where there was clear emphasis on the need for legal security, there had been only 230 arrested, of which twenty-seven were immediately released.[128] Furthermore, sentencings in the GDR in the months following the uprising were mild.[129] Popular emphasis on legal security which was reflected in the reports of the non-Marxist parties was a reaction to systematic repression over an extended period of time, not a reaction to a recent phenomenon.

The Eisenberg Circle

The motives behind the establishment of the only known organized resistance group between 1953 and 1955, the Eisenberg Circle, reflected those concerns of the population made evident in the reports of the non-Marxist parties. The Eisenberg Circle began in September/October 1953 as a loose collection of five or six high school students from Eisenberg who were reacting to the expulsion of other students for being members of the *Junge Gemeinde* and the general "Stalinization" of the school curriculum.[130] One of the founders recalled that SED repression in general, not solely against the *Junge Gemeinde*, contributed to deep fear in the population.[131]

The founding members of the Eisenberg Circle were Thomas Ammer, Johann Frömel, Günter Schwarz, Reinhard Spalke, and Ludwig and Wilhelm Ziehr.[132] Initially, the group, unsure of a course of action, spent the first few months discussing a name for the group and what actions it should undertake. The group had considered naming itself the Stauffenberg Circle in recognition of the officer who had attempted to assassinate Hitler in the Wolf's Lair on July 20, 1944, but rejected the name for fear that, if arrested, GDR authorities would charge members of the group with planning assassinations. The group had no firm political agenda, although all members desired free elections and the return of a state based on the rule of law.[133]

Within a few months of its founding, the Eisenberg Circle had begun its first modest actions against the regime, including tearing down SED propaganda and symbols and distributing anti-Communist material. The Eisenberg Circle contacted West Berlin anti-Communist organizations like the KgU and the *Ostbüro* of the SPD to procure material. At the end of 1955, the group undertook more daring resistance by breaking into the local museum to procure arms but the raid failed because the museum had only old guns, for which ammunition was not available.[134] Shortly after that action, the group took up contact with Peter Herrmann, Rudolf Rabold, Ludwig Götz, and Roland Peter, oppositional students from Eisenberg studying at the University of Jena. To reduce risk of arrest, the two groups maintained their independence, whereby members of one group were not necessarily known by the other group. The groups had loose organizational structures; they did not hold elections or membership meetings. On January 21, 1956 the Eisenberg Circle undertook its first major action by burning down a shooting range of the East German army near Eisenberg.[135] The Eisenberg Circle continued its resistance work until February 1958 when the MfS began arrests of the group's members. One of the founders attributed the group's longevity to the basic support in the population for its endeavors.[136]

State Reaction to the Revolution

The Judicial Apparatus

When Hilde Benjamin took office as Minister of Justice on July 16, she signalled that she would run a strict judicial system. Benjamin criticized the previous Minister of Justice, Max Fechner, for his "dangerous" ideas that the uprising was simply a strike, not a fascist putsch: "In judicial practice since 17 June, there have been tendencies towards a new criminal law."[137] She warned that the "provocateurs of 17 June" would not be seen through these "rose coloured glasses."

Benjamin's stance ran counter to the general trend in the Central Committee towards a milder system of justice. Rudolf Herrnstadt's draft Central Committee resolution after the uprising entitled "The New Course and the Renewal of the Party" demonstrates high-level concern for an improved relationship between the judicial system and the population: "It is important to create a GDR whose prosperity, social justice, legal security, national traits, and atmosphere of freedom will meet with the approval of all honest Germans."[138] Furthermore, between June and October 1953, the SED released 23,853 prisoners in the GDR.[139] The SED also wanted to be careful not to add to the hostility of the population through severe judicial measures against the demonstrators of June 17. Of the 13,000 people arrested for their part in the demonstrations, only approximately 1,600 were sentenced.[140] In September 1953, the Politburo, still concerned about the hostility in the population, ordered the High Court to issue milder sentences against economic criminals.[141] Even Hilde Benjamin acknowledged that some sentences were too harsh and that these sentences did little to strengthen trust in legal security in the GDR.[142]

Relaxation in the judicial field did not meet with universal approval of the MfS nor the *Volkspolizei*. During a conference with Benjamin in September 1953, an MfS representative complained that the *Bezirk* Madgdeburg court had reviewed 4,027 cases and reversed decisions in 2,295 cases.[143] The representative complained: "In so doing, not only those who committed small economic crimes are amnestied, but reactionaries and enemies of the GDR are also let out of prison. . . . Public prosecutors and the courts . . . consider the GDR government's 'New Course' an excuse to be soft on criminals. Many cases illustrate that since the events of 17 June, the judicial apparatus has gone to the opposite extreme."[144]

The head of the investigative unit of the *Volkspolizei* also disapproved of the trend in judicial practice in the aftermath of the uprising. He complained of three tendencies in recent sentences: (1) unjustifiably mild sentences against provocateurs and ring leaders of June 17, (2) unjustified release of other sentenced criminals, and (3) inappropriate judicial practice in the application of the "law for the protection of the people's economy." To support his contention, he cited the example of a demonstrator in Magdeburg who had stormed the police station and threatened the police officers there with a knife, but who was not sentenced.[145]

The MfS After the Uprising

The most important result of the disturbances in the GDR in the summer of 1953 was the expansion of the SED's instruments of control. At the 15th Plenum of the SED, held between July 24 and 26, the SED called for a more complete system of monitoring and controlling the population. The importance of the 15th Plenum in the history of the GDR has received attention in Armin Mitter, Ilko-Sascha Kowalczuk, and Stefan Wolle's *Der Tag X: Der 17. Juni 1953,* in which the authors argue that the crisis of 1953 led to the "internal founding of the state" (*Innere Staatsgründung*) in order to prevent future disturbances which would require Soviet assistance and further undermine the legitimacy of the SED. Some measures that the SED adopted included the creation of interior troops such as factory militias (*Kampfgruppen*) and a "rapid reaction" motorized police unit with over 4,000 men.[146]

The MfS also underwent significant changes as a result of the "internal founding of the state." At the 15th Plenum, the Central Committee expelled the Minister for State Security, Wilhelm Zaisser, and Rudolf Herrnstadt, editor of *Neues Deutschland,* from the SED for having challenged the leadership of the party.[147] The SED then dissolved the MfS as an independent ministry and transferred it to the Ministry of the Interior as a Secretariat for State Security (*Staatssekretariat für Staatssicherheit* [SfS]).

As part of the expanded control apparatus, the SfS vastly increased its information-gathering apparatus on the GDR population. In August 1953, Wollweber established information groups within the SfS.[148] An MfS report outlined the information groups as follows: "The information group in the *Bezirk* administration [of the SfS—GB] examines and evaluates the incoming reports on a daily basis. On the basis of these reports, a situation report is to be produced. The situation report is to be forwarded to the head of the *Bezirk* administration, to the information group in the [SfS headquarters—GB] and to the first secretary of the SED *Bezirk* leadership. From the reports of the information groups in the *Bezirk* administrations, the information group in the [SfS headquarters—GB] produces a situation report on the GDR for the head of the SfS, for the Politburo, and for the government."[149] These information groups collected and evaluated reports of informants from the general population. The SfS was careful not to repeat mistakes of the past, when reports from party members tended to present an inaccurate picture of the mood of the population. In instructions outlining the procedure for collecting information, Heinz Tilch, the head of the new information service (*Informationsdienst*) noted that unofficial informants from the general population should be used to collect information on the mood of the population, rather than "official sources" such as factory party chairmen, because "real enemies do not usually show their true colours to functionaries."[150] In outlining the advantages of informal sources, Tilch wrote: "An informant who is a mechanic in a factory, for example, will be able to bring us useful information on the mood of workers. . . . Because nobody will know that he has contact to the SfS, workers will talk to him exactly how they talk to other colleagues."[151] In warning against the use of reports from factory party chairmen, Tilch revealed the popular distrust of the party by stating that workers did not talk, or only rarely talked, to party functionaries.[152] The SfS still used official sources in assessing the mood of the population, but these were second in importance to unofficial informants' reports.

The most important factor in improved monitoring of the GDR's population was a reliable informant network. In the Politburo resolution of September 9, 1953, the Politburo had emphasized that the SfS information net was exceptionally weak, and called for an increased and more reliable informant net.[153] The Secretary for State Security was aware of the deficiencies in the informant net. Four days before the Politburo resolution, Wollweber had called for a substantially increased informant net and better-qualified informants,[154] complaining: "Apart from the poor quality of the information network, the network does not have sufficient numbers, and is therefore incapable of uncovering enemies in all sections of GDR society."[155] Unlike Directive 21/52 of 1952 which emphasized obtaining informants who could penetrate western organizations, this directive focused on widening the informant net in important economic and administrative sites in the GDR.

To increase the informant base, however, the SfS realized that it would have to overcome popular rejection of this instrument of control. It should be remembered that during the revolution of June 17, demonstrators attacked MfS installations in Bitterfeld, Görlitz, Niesky, Jena, Merseburg, and Halle,[156] and it is likely that the number of MfS installations attacked would have been greater had the MfS had a larger system of internal surveillance. To overcome the basic distrust, the SfS embarked on a venture most peculiar for a Communist secret service; it undertook a public relations campaign. The campaign began in November 1953 when Wollweber stressed to his subordinates the need for greater popular involvement in information gathering, suggesting that SfS officers speak in factories and other sites.[157] The speech launched a series of unprecedented appearances by Wollweber himself. In November, he talked to Wismut workers. In December, he spoke at an SED public meeting in the mechanized weaving mill in Zittau. In January 1954, he spoke in a Berlin brake factory, in February at a steel sheet plant in Berlin-Adlershof and in the Weimar administration school, in April at a factory rally in Ludwigsfelde, in August in H.F. Werk Köpenick and Leuna Werk Walter Ulbricht, in September in the House of German-Soviet Friendship, Köpenick, in December in Mansfeld Combine, and in March 1955 at a rally in Kröllwitz.[158] During these appearances, which continued into 1956, Wollweber played up the important role of the SfS in fighting western anti-Communist organizations like the SPD *Ostbüro*, the KgU, and the UfJ, and he appealed to GDR residents to support this work by reporting on any "enemy" activity in the GDR. During his speech to the administration school in Weimar, Wollweber stated that the best manner to defend against the enemy was the "personal vigilance" of each citizen of the GDR.[159]

As part of the campaign to gain public confidence, the SfS increased its propaganda activities. In July 1954, the SfS created a new section in its apparatus, the "Agitation" branch, headed by General Bormann. The SfS outlined the duties of the

"Agitation" branch as the systematic informing of the GDR population on the activity of the SfS so that the "vigilance of all workers and . . . the willingness to work for the instruments of state security will be increased."[160] The "Agitation" branch organized speeches in factories, administrations, and on radio; published brochures; mounted exhibits; and produced documentary films which heaped praise on the SfS.[161] As Wollweber stated during an SfS conference in August 1954: "The political importance of our work must be continually emphasized."[162] The "Agitation" branch used all means at its disposal to justify the existence of the SfS to the public. In its efforts to stress the need for the SfS in the face of an enemy like the Gehlen Organization, the "Agitation" branch prepared arrests of mock Gehlen agents, who were really SfS agents who had been exposed and were therefore no longer of use to the SfS. The "Agitation" branch used these exposed agents to conduct staged arrests and trials of "imperialist agents."[163] Operation *Pfeil* (Arrow) against the Gehlen Organization was accompanied by a carefully coordinated propaganda plan.[164] The SfS also took special measures for the fifth anniversary of the agency, planning for SfS representatives to be in large factories during the week of February 1 to 6, 1955 in order to discuss the "political importance" of the SfS, and showing a documentary film on the SfS in movie theaters the following week.[165]

To increase popular loyalty to the SfS, the SfS addressed a leading issue behind resistance. The SfS took careful measures to reduce wrongful arrests and to improve treatment of its prisoners, aware that these occurrences had tarnished the SfS's image. In August 1953, a member of the Department of Registration and Statistics in the SfS commented: "In the past, thousands of people were interrogated in the investigation departments. But at the same time, the former MfS did not know how to find the right people. Arrests were handled thoughtlessly."[166] Wollweber himself issued a stern warning to his subordinates: "If anyone treats a prisoner unlawfully to reach his goal more easily, he will be punished. If anyone puts a person in prison only to show he's getting results, he will be punished."[167] Mielke supported Wollweber's position by stating that a "trusting relationship" had to be established between the SfS and the working class.[168]

During the SfS campaign in the fall of 1953 to expose enemy agents in the GDR, Wollweber warned that *only* agents should be fearful of arrest in the GDR: "There should be no shock effect for the population. People should not feel that a wave of arrests is moving through the GDR, or that we are at the beginning of such a wave. . . . The population must believe that the instruments of state security aim for, and hit, the right targets. The population must believe this, *then they will support us.*"[169] Wollweber even went so far as to use the radio to allay people's fears. During one broadcast, Wollweber stated: "A wave of arrests is not taking place. There are carefully targeted strikes against important sites of enemy activity."[170] The following year, the SfS still considered the "fight against wrongful arrests" one of its main duties because "wrongful arrests create enemies."[171] It appears that the SfS did act more cautiously following the revolution. In April 1954, the SfS reported that it had arrested fewer people than during the same period the previous year.[172]

These attempts to soften the image of the SfS were not always successful. During the May Day parade of 1955 in Potsdam, one spectator swore at the SfS troops as they paraded by, and had to be restrained from breaking through the barriers to attack them. A housewife from Suhl expressed similar sentiments during the May Day parade there, saying "here come the dangerous ones" when the SfS officers paraded past.[173]

Overall, however, it is difficult to determine if the SfS campaign to increase public support was successful. The numbers of secret informants working for the SfS had increased by 1955,[174] but there appear to have been many who were simply on the rolls but not active. In November 1954, 50 percent of the informants working for *Bezirk* Potsdam had no contact to the SfS.[175] The following year, Wollweber complained that too many informants were SED members and that there were many informants who were inactive. Wollweber referred to these informants as "ballast."[176]

Robert Gellately's pathbreaking arguments regarding the Gestapo form an interesting point of comparison for the postwar East German secret police. Gellately exploded the myth that the Gestapo had an army of informants that held German society in the Third Reich in check by demonstrating that the Gestapo operated with a relatively small apparatus and relied on spontaneous denunciations from the public.[177] SfS need for a large number of secret coworkers suggests that GDR citizens did not spontaneously denounce others to the SfS.

The SfS and the Ostbüro

The SfS campaign against the SPD *Ostbüro* in the aftermath of the revolution provides evidence of the importance of political motive behind the uprising.[178] After the revolution, Wollweber commented that there had been "strong social democratic organizations in factories of the GDR."[179] Due largely to the prevalence of demands for the SPD during the uprising, Wollweber launched a campaign against the *Ostbüro*. The campaign against the *Ostbüro* was not simply a witchhunt for convenient scapegoats,[180] but an attempt to eliminate what the SED believed was a substantial negative influence on the population of the GDR. In August 1953, during a meeting between Wollweber and the heads of all SfS *Bezirk* administrations, certain SfS officers expressed confusion as to the manner in which they should operate. They asked Wollweber whether the SfS should work according to site—a penetration of specific installations in order to monitor for "enemy" activity—or whether it should work according to departmental lines (*Linien*), which would involve a more general investigation to determine which sites were targeted by western organizations for disruption, either through sabotage or propaganda activity. Wollweber felt that the MfS should work offensively: "The question regarding our work in factories, which has been raised here, must be cleared up: Do we work according to specific *Linien* or do we work according to sites? My opinion is that Departments IV and V should concentrate on centres outside the GDR and expose matters there. In the future, the main struggle in factories will be played out between us and representatives of the *Ostbüro*."[181] Wollweber clearly believed that there was considerable interest among East German workers in the SPD, and by extension the alternative political system it represented.

The Lingering Hope for a New Political System

In the years following the uprising, the SfS continued to note the population's desire for an alternative political system. Reports on the population collected by the SfS provide evidence that the population still hoped for the removal of the political system in East Germany into the fall of 1955. There were three events during this period at which this desire was visible: the February 1954 foreign ministers' conference in Berlin, the October 1954 elections in the GDR, and the July 1955 Geneva Conference.

The Berlin Foreign Ministers' Conference, 1954

In February 1954, the foreign ministers of the wartime Allies met in Berlin to discuss the possibility of German reunification. There was keen interest throughout the GDR in the outcome of the Berlin foreign ministers' conference, because the end of the division of Germany and the riddance of the SED political system were at stake. Thus, the refusal of the SED to print the speeches of the western foreign ministers was a source of hostility to the SED. At a sitting of the political committee of the LDPD central executive, one member commented that people continually questioned her as to why only the Soviet foreign minister Molotov's comments were published in the press, and not those of the other foreign ministers. Another LDPD member at the meeting added that people in his *Bezirk* fully supported British foreign minister Anthony Eden's plan for Germany because it would allow free elections. The LDPD member countered these arguments by stating that the elections proposed by Eden were not free, but "Hitler style elections."[182] CDU reports also reveal that East Germans repeatedly rejected the method of elections like those held in the GDR in 1950 for eventual all-German elections.[183]

The result of free elections was clear to workers at the "Torpedo" factory in Bernau. In February 1954, in anticipation of a successful conclusion of the Berlin foreign ministers' conference, workers at the factory began discussing the possibility of a reinstatement of the SPD.[184] Workers at the VEB-Stahlblechbau Berlin Adlershof also hoped that the foreign ministers' conference would bring the end of the Communist system in East Germany. They repeatedly asked why Molotov's speeches were printed in the GDR's newspapers, but not the speeches of Dulles and Eden.[185] According to the SfS, only 20 percent of the workers in the plant supported the GDR's "democratic order."[186] The situation in this plant was so tense that many members of the SED refused to let it be known that they were Party members.[187]

Although these episodes may well be representative, they do not allow for a comprehensive conclusion on popular views of the conference. Because the SfS information gathering apparatus had been established only five months earlier, there are few reports on the population and no comprehensive SfS analyses. Nevertheless, the similarities between SfS, CDU, and LDPD findings is striking. SfS information gathering had improved considerably by the October elections.

The October 1954 Elections in the GDR

The information department within the SfS noted that the population continued to reject the SED manner of conducting elections because it removed from the population the possibility of deciding its political future. In the fall of 1954, both prior to and after the elections, the SfS information department reported popular contempt for the conduct of the elections. A mechanic in Leipzig complained: "Our elections of 17 October have nothing to do with democracy."[188] Another worker summed up the elections as the following: "The results are already determined, whether we vote against or for, or even go to vote at all. The results of the election were already determined at the 4th Party Congress of the SED."[189] One worker from Zschopau lamented for the electoral practice of the Weimar era: "We should conduct elections like we did during the Weimar era. The SED wouldn't know what hit it."[190] In the months prior to the election in Dessau, the LDPD reported that a large part of the population repeatedly asked if the voting would be open or secret.[191]

Employees of the SfS information department noted that rejection of the election was a general phenomenon in the GDR. Significant numbers of election posters were torn down in the period leading up to the election,[192] and SfS workers were also gravely worried about the increased attacks on party functionaries in the period leading up to the elections.[193] In *Bezirk* Schwerin, for example, a member of the SED and a *Kreis* FDJ secretary were beaten up. In Quedlinburg, three members of the National Front who had come to talk on the upcoming elections were beaten up.[194] East Germans also demonstrated their rejection of the upcoming elections by fleeing the GDR or applying to travel to the West during the election. The SfS information department was alarmed that on certain days, the number of people leaving the GDR "illegally" was 50 percent higher than in previous months.[195] The number of applications to travel to West Germany also increased dramatically during the period around October 17, 1954. The SfS information department acknowledged that this increase was likely a result of people wanting to avoid the election.[196]

After the election, there continued to be strong criticism against the SED's electoral practice. In the words of one factory worker: "That wasn't even an election, but just a handing over of a piece of paper."[197] One SfS report summarized: "Relatively strong criticism of the conducting of the election, of the voting ballot, and the lack of pencils comes from all sections of the population."[198] Another SfS summary report echoed these sentiments: "There are sections of the population in each societal group who do not understand why there was nowhere on the ballot to cross off yes or no, and why there were no pencils in the election booths. Enemy elements use this, in association with RIAS arguments, to portray to the population the elections as undemocratic."[199] The phrasing of these reports suggests that the lack of pencils in election booths was a calculated SED maneuver, and not mere coincidence.

Material Shortages

In the first half of 1955, acute material shortages plagued the East German population. Basic foodstuffs such as sugar and products with fat content were scarce, causing extensive lines whenever the products were available. People also complained that the beer had been watered down.[200] In May in *Gemeinde* Altruppin, *Kreis* Neuruppin, 300 people awaited the delivery of butter, forcing police to accompany the shipment to ensure order. In Ecknitz, *Kreis* Pasewalk, the police had to be employed because 100 people were shouting about the lack of goods. In Görlitz, fights broke out in the local state-run store during the selling of butter.[201] There were similar scenes in Brandenburg, Puttlitz, and Luckenwalde, where fights and other disturbances occurred because of the lack of butter.[202] There were also repeated popular complaints about the poor quality of the dark bread. During a visit by a West German delegation to the VEB RFT-Fernmeldewerk in Arnstadt, one female worker approached the delegation with her sandwich in hand and said: "Do you see this dark bread that we have to eat here?"[203] The worker's comments led to her removal from her job. Upon hearing this news, roughly 100 other workers demanded that she be reinstated, threatening to strike if she did not receive her job back. On the following day, the workers went on strike from 7 until 10 am in protest of their colleague's removal, stopping once the arrested worker had been reinstated.[204]

Popular reaction to the shortages illustrate the extent to which the East German population had come to distrust the SED. Rumors abounded that the government was hoarding goods in preparation for an upcoming war.[205] In some instances, people pleaded for the truth on the situation: "Why aren't we told the truth? We don't believe that the present situation is the result of a bad harvest."[206] At a factory in Arnstadt, another worker stated: "It is a disgrace that there is no butter or sugar for sale, and then bad bread on top of that. Nobody should be too surprised that workers are so dissatisfied. We are always lied to. Nobody can tell us that these problems are the result of the previous harvest."[207]

As June 1955 approached, there was an increase in the number of threats in the population of a repetition of June 17. Statements such as: "The second 17 June will be a lot worse than the first." And: "If it keeps on like this, a day like 17 June cannot be far off" were common in factories and workplaces of the GDR.[208] If an uprising were to take place, the SED was to be targeted. In VEB Glaswerk near Suhl, workers stated: "If another 17 June comes, all Comrades will hang."[209] On June 17,

1955 in *Gemeinde* Oberndorf, *Kreis* Apolda, a member of the SED stated: "I am waiting for another 17 June, and then I'm going to get going with a knife. I will cut up like pigs anything that belongs to the SED or anyone wearing a uniform."[210] Several strikes had, in fact, already taken place. In February 1955, eleven sites in the GDR went on strike, followed by four in March. The strikes were a result of the difficult material situation and problems specific to the plants.[211]

The SfS took seriously the threats of another uprising. To secure the GDR on June 17, 1955, the SfS adopted Operation *Bumerang*. Mielke instructed Main Departments I and XIII and Department VII to ensure that their units would be prepared if needed suddenly and that all arms and munition were in perfect working order.[212] In Halle, Leuna, Leipzig, Rostock, Greifswald, Magdeburg, Gera, Jena, Potsdam, Henningsdorf, and Brandenburg, the SfS contacted nearby police stations and ordered them to have their officers at the ready in case the SfS needed to call them in. Wollweber reminded his subordinates that gathering these forces together would have to be done discreetly.[213] Due to the agitated state of the population, Mielke wanted to avoid what had been a primary cause of unrest in the summer of 1953—added repression. He wrote that all departments in the SfS were to carefully follow the guidelines from the leadership, in order to ensure that "wrong or unwarranted measures" did not provoke "dissatisfaction or anger in the population."[214] Wollweber further instructed the Department PS, which was responsible for the protection of party functionaries, to increase protection of SED party members, SED buildings, and the homes of party functionaries. More troops were added to protect these buildings, and increased security was to be furnished on the routes driven by party functionaries.[215] Wollweber also added troops to protect SfS buildings, KVP, and *Volkspolizei* buildings.[216] SfS preparations reveal a fear of popular reprisal against the instruments of SED repression.

The Geneva Conference

In July 1955, the leaders of the Soviet Union, Britain, France, and the United States met in Geneva to discuss the German question. According to SfS reports, the GDR population watched developments in Geneva with great interest, as it had the foreign ministers' conference of 1954 in Berlin. In Jüterbog and Neukirchen, church bells peeled through town on July 18 to mark the beginning of the conference. In a factory near Leipzig, workers observed two minutes of silence in recognition of the beginning of the conference.[217] SfS reports on the population noted the keen interest in the Geneva conference: "On the overall opinion on the Geneva conference, it can be said that besides the four power conference in Berlin, rarely has a political event found such popular interest."[218] The SfS remarked on the numerous discussions in factories prior to and during the conference, noting that because of the overwhelming interest in the Geneva conference, all other concerns of the population had faded into the background.[219] Another report summarized the situation as the following: "The strong interest in the Geneva conference is largely due to the hope for a rapid solution to the German problem. This is true for all sections of society. The difference is that progressive elements are interested in a democratic Germany, while reactionary and enemy elements desire unity along the western model."[220] Situation reports from the CDU echo the views of the SfS reports on the strong interest in the Geneva conference because of its potential impact on the GDR. All available CDU *Bezirk* analyses noted popular desire for a successful conclusion of the Geneva Conference in order that free elections could take place.[221]

East Germans saw in the conference the possibility of an end to the Communist system in the GDR. For this reason, the population consistently demanded that German unity take place on the basis of *free* all German elections. SfS situation reports are replete with quotations from people expressing their desire for free elections. One farmer in Dienstadt near Jena stated: "If free elections come, Adenauer doesn't have to worry because I—and many others—would vote for him."[222] A mechanic at a Machine Loan station in Eilenburg near Leipzig echoed these comments: "If free elections are carried out, the SED would get the least number of votes."[223] One worker in Magdeburg stated that free elections must be carried out, but that all parties should be allowed in the GDR. He was certain that the KPD and the SED would not receive the majority of votes.[224] One worker at a factory near Gera said: "They should just hold a referendum. Then they would see the true will of the people."[225] This desire, SfS employees in the information department acknowledged, was only partly a result of the dissatisfaction with the economic situation and factory shortages.[226] The unpopularity of the SED was not lost on members of the party. One party member who worked in the VEB Landmaschinenbau in Torgau stated: "The population no longer agrees with the government. One sees this most clearly by the fact that no one comes to meetings anymore. If free elections were to take place, the government would fall because everyone would vote for Adenauer."[227]

The desire for free elections in order to remove the Communist system in East Germany was a general phenomenon in the GDR. The SfS information department reported that a great "lack of clarity" existed in wide sections of the population on the manner in which Germany would be united and that they did not understand why free elections on the western model were not possible.[228] The SfS reported that instead of noting the deficiencies in the western manner of conducting elections, people argued that the SED was afraid of free elections because of certain defeat.[229] Although SfS reports attributed the desire for "free elections to change the political structures in the GDR,"[230] solely to farmers with large land holdings, intellectuals, and those from a "bourgeois" background, the SfS's own reports reveal that these sentiments prevailed in all sections of society. The SfS information department report summarizing the popular attitude towards the Geneva conference stated: "There is a great lack of clarity in all sections of the population about the manner of achieving German unity, and the form of a united Germany. Propaganda must be increased to deal specifically with these questions, but also why the carrying out of free elections is presently impossible."[231]

Ernst Wollweber, the head of East German state security from 1953 to 1957, was alarmed by the significant popular interest in free elections. During a conference of the leading members of the SfS in August 1955, he explained:

> We [state security workers] should have no illusions regarding the content of our fight for reunification. There have been these illusions. There have been these illusions in general. We see this in our daily information reports. . . . We should have no illusions—we can't say this on the outside—that the situation is this simple: We hold free elections and then see what happens based on the result of the vote. We are Democrats, but not idiots. We support free elections, if at these elections the working class and its leading Party play the decisive role. We support free elections, where those who do not deserve freedom, do not have freedom.[232]

The significant popular support for free elections had been registered at the highest level of the secret police.

Popular concern for legal security characterized the immediate aftermath of the revolution. Moreover, disturbances in the days and months following the uprising and reports of the non-Marxist parties reveal that legal insecurity actually eclipsed material concerns in the population. The changes to the MfS and judicial apparatus following the revolution further demonstrate that the Politburo realized the negative impact of its repression apparatus, although this did not stop it from expanding the apparatus. In the years following the uprising, the East German population continued to make visible its resistance to the Communist system by calling for free elections, which would have resulted in the end of the SED regime. SED and Soviet repression were intertwined with popular political resistance to Communism in the GDR of the 1950s.

Notes

1. BA-P, DO 1 11/305. June 27, 1953 report from Bezirk Cottbus police.
2. June 27, 1953 report from Lieutenant-General Fedenko, Operations Division, Main Operations Administration, General Staff of the Soviet Army, to Lieutenant-General Pavlovsky, reproduced in Christian Ostermann, *The Post-Stalin Succession Struggle and the 17 June 1953 Uprising in East Germany* (Washington: National Security Archive, 1996), Document #25.
3. Andreas Peter, "Der Juni-Aufstand im Bezirk Cottbus," *Deutschland Archiv* (Hereafter *DA*) 27 (1994): 587.
4. Peter, "Der Juni-Aufstand," 589.
5. SAPMO, ZPA, JIV 2/202/15. SED Central Committee report entitled: "Analyse über die Vorbereitung, den Ausbruch und die Niederschlagung des faschistischen Abenteuers vom 16.-22.6.53," 16.
6. BA-P, DO 1 /11/305, 106. June 27, 1953 report from the Bezirk Cottbus police to the head of the Volkspolizei.
7. BA-P, DO 1 /11/305, 106. June 27, 1953 report from the Bezirk Cottbus police to the head of the Volkspolizei.
8. SAPMO-BA, ZPA, JIV 2/202/14. June 29, 1953 report on the events in the city of

Potsdam beginning on June 17, 1953.

9. BA-P, DO 1 11/758, 39. July 20, 1953 Volkspolizei Hauptabteilung K report on examples of poor party work during the fascist disturbances of June 17, 1953 and in its aftermath.

10. SAPMO, ZPA, JIV 2/202/15. SED Central Committee Report entitled: "Analyse über die Vorbereitung, den Ausbruch und die Niederschlagung des faschistischen Abenteuers vom 16.-22.6.53," 12.

11. BA-P, DO 1 11/305, 22. June 29, 1953 report of the Bezirk Frankfurt/Oder police to the operations staff of the Volkspolizei.

12. BA-P, DO 1 11/305, 17a. June 29, 1953 report of the Bezirk Frankfurt/Oder police to the operations staff of the Volkspolizei.

13. BA-P, DO 1 11/306, 19. June 29, 1953 report from the Bezirk Frankfurt/Oder police chief Kotulan entitled: "Auswertung der Ereignisse seit dem 16.6.1953."

14. SAPMO-BA, ZPA, JIV 2/202/14. Report on the situation in Bezirk Dresden for June 17 and 18, 1953.

15. BA-P, DO 1 11/304, 334. June 26, 1953 report by Bezirk Rostock police chief Ludwig.

16. BA-P, DO 1 11/304, 334. June 26, 1953 report by Bezirk Rostock police chief Ludwig.

17. BA-P, DO 1 11/304, 336. June 26, 1953 report by Bezirk Rostock police chief Ludwig.

18. BA-P, DO 1 11/304, 338. June 26, 1953 report by the Bezirk Rostock police chief Ludwig.

19. BA-P, DO 1 11/304, 338. June 26, 1953 report by the Bezirk Rostock police chief Ludwig.

20. BA-P, DO 1 11/304, 338. June 26, 1953 report by the Bezirk Rostock police chief Ludwig.

21. BA-P, DO 1 11/304, 342. June 26, 1953 report by the Bezirk Rostock police chief Ludwig.

22. BA-P, DO 1 11/304, 342. June 26, 1953 report by the Bezirk Rostock police chief Ludwig.

23. BA-P, DO 1 11/304, 341. June 26, 1953 report by the Bezirk Rostock police chief Ludwig.

24. BA-P, DO 1 11/305, 284. June 29, 1953 report from the Bezirk Erfurt police entitled: "Auswertung der Ereignisse seit dem 17.6.1953."

25. BA-P, DO 1 11/305, 284. June 29, 1953 report from the Bezirk Erfurt police entitled: "Auswertung der Ereignisse seit dem 17.6.1953."

26. BA-P, DO 1 11/305, 284-285. June 29, 1953 report from the Bezirk Erfurt police entitled: "Auswertung der Ereignisse seit dem 17.6.1953."

27. SAPMO, ZPA, J IV 2/202/15. Report of the SED Central Committee entitled: "Analyse über die Vorbereitung, den Ausbruch und die Niederschlagung des faschistischen Abenteuers vom 16.-22.6.53," 12.

28. SAPMO, ZPA, J IV 2/202/15. Report of the SED Central Committee entitled: "Analyse über die Vorbereitung, den Ausbruch und die Niederschlagung des faschistischen Abenteuers vom 16.-22.6.53," 12.

29. BA-P, DO 1 11/305, pp. 284-285. June 29, 1953 report from the Bezirk Erfurt police entitled: "Auswertung der Ereignisse seit dem 17.6.1953."

30. BA-P, DO 1 11/305, 243. July 1, 1953 report on the course of the fascist provoca-

tion on 17.6.1953 in Bezirk Halle.

31. BA-P, DO 1 11/305, 243. July 1, 1953 report on the course of the fascist provocation on 17.6.1953 in Bezirk Halle.

32. BA-P, DO 1 11/305, 243. July 1, 1953 report on the course of the fascist provocation on 17.6.1953 in Bezirk Halle.

33. BA-P, DO 1 11/305, 243. July 1, 1953 report on the course of the fascist provocation on 17.6.1953 in Bezirk Halle.

34. BA-P, DO 1 11/305, 243. July 1, 1953 report on the course of the fascist provocation on 17.6.1953 in Bezirk Halle.

35. BA-P, DO 1 11/305, 244. July 1, 1953 report on the course of the fascist provocation on 17.6.1953 in Bezirk Halle.

36. BA-P, DO 1 11/305, 244. July 1, 1953 report on the course of the fascist provocation on 17.6.1953 in Bezirk Halle.

37. SAPMO, ZPA, JIV 2/202/15. Report of the SED Central Committee entitled: "Analyse über die Vorbereitung, den Ausbruch und die Niederschlagung des faschistischen Abenteuers vom 16.-22.6.53," 7.

38. BA-P, DO 1 11/45, 10. June 22, 1953 report Nr. 170 for the period from 6:00 on June 21, 1953 to 6:00 on 22.6.53.

39. BA-P, DO 1 11/45, 10. June 22, 1953 report Nr. 170 for the period from 6:00 on June 21, 1953 to 6:00 on 22.6.53.

40. BA-P, DO 1 11/45, 10. June 22, 1953 report Nr. 170 for the period from 6:00 on June 21, 1953 to 6:00 on 22.6.53.

41. SAPMO, ZPA, JIV 2/202/15. Report of the SED Central Committee entitled: "Analyse über die Vorbereitung, den Ausbruch und die Niederschlagung des faschistischen Abenteuers vom 16.-22.6.53," 9.

42. SAPMO, ZPA, JIV 2/202/15. Report of the SED Central Committee entitled: "Analyse über die Vorbereitung, den Ausbruch und die Niederschlagung des faschistischen Abenteuers vom 16.-22.6.53," 9.

43. SAPMO, ZPA, JIV 2/202/15. Report of the SED Central Committee entitled: "Analyse über die Vorbereitung, den Ausbruch und die Niederschlagung des faschistischen Abenteuers vom 16.-22.6.53," 9.

44. SAPMO, ZPA, JIV 2/202/15. Report of the SED Central Committee entitled: "Analyse über die Vorbereitung, den Ausbruch und die Niederschlagung des faschistischen Abenteuers vom 16.-22.6.53," 10.

45. SAPMO, ZPA, JIV 2/202/15. Report of the SED Central Committee entitled: "Analyse über die Vorbereitung, den Ausbruch und die Niederschlagung des faschistischen Abenteuers vom 16.-22.6.53," 11.

46. SAPMO, ZPA, JIV 2/202/15. Report of the SED Central Committee entitled: "Analyse über die Vorbereitung, den Ausbruch und die Niederschlagung des faschistischen Abenteuers vom 16.-22.6.53," 11

47. SAPMO, ZPA, JIV 2/202/15. Report of the SED Central Committee entitled: "Analyse über die Vorbereitung, den Ausbruch und die Niederschlagung des faschistischen Abenteuers vom 16.-22.6.53," 11.

48. SAPMO, ZPA, JIV 2/202/15. Report of the SED Central Committee entitled: "Analyse über die Vorbereitung, den Ausbruch und die Niederschlagung des faschistischen Abenteuers vom 16.-22.6.53," 13.

49. SAPMO, ZPA, JIV 2/202/15. Report of the SED Central Committee entitled: "Analyse über die Vorbereitung, den Ausbruch und die Niederschlagung des faschistischen

Abenteuers vom 16.-22.6.53," 13

50. SAPMO, ZPA, JIV 2/202/15. Report of the SED Central Committee entitled: "Analyse über die Vorbereitung, den Ausbruch und die Niederschlagung des faschistischen Abenteuers vom 16.-22.6.53," 13.

51. SAPMO, ZPA, JIV 2/202/15. Report of the SED Central Committee entitled: "Analyse über die Vorbereitung, den Ausbruch und die Niederschlagung des faschistischen Abenteuers vom 16.-22.6.53," 15.

52. SAPMO, ZPA, JIV 2/202/15. Report of the SED Central Committee entitled: "Analyse über die Vorbereitung, den Ausbruch und die Niederschlagung des faschistischen Abenteuers vom 16.-22.6.53," 17.

53. Armin Mitter and Stefan Wolle, *Untergang auf Raten* (Munich: Bertelsmann Verlag, 1993), 108.

54. Armin Mitter and Ilko-Sascha Kowalczuk, "Die Arbeiter sind zwar geschalgen worden," in *Der Tag X*, ed. Ilko-Sascha Kowalczuk, Armin Mitter, and Stefan Wolle (Berlin: Ch. Links Verlag, 1995), 65.

55. AdsD, SPD-PV-Ostbüro 0046 f/a. October 28, 1953 report.

56. Mitter and Wolle, *Untergang*, 134-135.

57. For an analysis of the American strategy behind these packets, see Christian Ostermann, "'Keeping the pot simmering:' The United States and the East German Uprising of 1953," *German Studies Review* 19 (1996): 61-90.

58. ACDP, VII-013-1743. Summary of situation reports of Bezirk association taken between June 17 and July 17, 1953.

59. Armin Mitter, "Die Ereignisse im Juni und Juli 1953 in der DDR," *Aus Politik und Zeitgeschichte* B 5/1991, 36.

60. Quoted in Mitter, "Die Ereignisse," 37.

61. Kowalczuk and Mitter, "Die Arbeiter," 67.

62. BA-P, DO 1 11/1144, 170. December 12, 1953 HVDVP Operations staff report on the situation in the countryside, signed by the head of operations staff Schmidt.

63. Armin Mitter, "Am 17.6.53 haben die Arbeiter gestreikt," in Kowalczuk, Mitter, and Wolle, *Der Tag X*, 116.

64. Mitter, "Die Ereignisse," 35.

65. Mitter, "Die Ereignisse," 35.

66. BA-P, DO 1 11/409, 102. August 3, 1953 from Bezirk Neubrandenburg police to the Volkspolizei in Berlin.

67. BA-P, DO 1 11/758, 36. July 20, 1953 report of Hauptabteilung K on examples of poor party work during June 17 and its aftermath.

68. Quoted in Mitter, "Am 17.6.53," 112.

69. Mitter, "Am 17.6.53," 117.

70. Mitter, "Am 17.6.53," 117.

71. BA-P, DO 1 11/24, 77-78. January 5, 1954 letter from Maron, head of the Volkspolizei, to Ulbricht.

72. BA-P, DO 1 11/24, 81. January 5, 1954 letter from Maron, head of the Volkspolizei, to Ulbricht.

73. Mitter and Wolle, *Untergang*, 113-114.

74. Kowalczuk, "Wir werden siegen," in Kowalczuk, Mitter, and Wolle, *Der Tag X*, 212-213.

75. Mitter and Wolle, *Untergang*, 63.

76. Mitter and Kowalczuk, "Die Arbeiter," 63.

77. Mitter and Wolle, *Untergang*, 114.

78. Stefan Zeidler, "Zur Rolle der CDU (Ost) in der inneren Entwicklung der DDR 1952-53" (M.A. thesis, University of Bonn, 1994), 80.

79. Zeidler, "Zur Rolle," 77.

80. ACDP, VII-013-1743. July 18, 1953 report on the meeting between the CDU association for Bezirk Potsdam and the general secretary of the CDU; ibid., July 9, 1953 report on the meeting between the CDU association for Bezirk Karl-Marx-Stadt and the general secretary of the CDU.

81. Günter Buchstab, "Widerspruch und widerständiges Verhalten der CDU der SBZ/DDR," *Materialien der Enquete-Kommission "Aufarbeitung von Geschichte und Folgen der SED-Diktatur in Deutschland,"* published by the German parliament, Vol. VII/1, 41.

82. ACDP, VII-013-1743. July 3, 1953 report on the meeting between the CDU association for Bezirk Rostock and the general secretary of the CDU; ACDP, VII-013-1743; report on the meeting between the CDU association for Bezirk Suhl and the general secretary of the CDU.

83. ACDP, VII-013-1743. July 24-25, 1953 report on the CDU in Pretzsch and Schmiedeberg.

84. BA-P, DO 1 11/24, 77-78. January 5, 1954 letter from Maron, head of the Volkspolizei, to Ulbricht.

85. BA-P, DO 1 11/24, 77-78. January 5, 1954 letter from Maron, head of the Volkspolizei, to Ulbricht.

86. ADL, LDPD #23534. July 16, 1953 letter from Kreis association Brandenburg-Stadt to Bezirk association for Potsdam.

87. ADL, LDPD #25366. September 29, 1953 working report from the Kreis association Dessau for the month of September.

88. ADL, LDPD #15848. Protocol of Kreis executive meeting on July 6, 1953; ADL, LDP #25366. Working report of Kreis association Saalkreis for October 1953; ibid., September 29, 1953 report from Kreis association Rosslau; ibid., addition to the questionnaire of the Kreis association for Halle for the months of August and September 1953.

89. The Bezirke surveyed were Potsdam, Halle, Leipzig, Rostock, and Frankfurt/Oder. Only Frankfurt/Oder reported no difficulties within the party.

90. ADL, LDPD #L2-28. Protocols of the sitting of the political committee of the central executive of the LDPD on April 6, 1954. These themes were repeated in the February 9, 1954 sitting.

91. AdsD, SPD-PV-Ostbüro 0370/I. December 15, 1953 special information report Nr.3/53 of Ostbüro of the FDP entitled: "Die Liquidierung des Neuen Kurses."

92. ACDP, VII-013-1743. July 18, 1953 report on CDU Bezirk association Potsdam conference with the CDU general secretary.

93. ACDP, VII-013-1743. Report on sitting of extended Kreis association Bitterfeld on July 24 and 25, 1953.

94. ACDP, VII-011-1268. July 7, 1953 situation report from CDU Kreis association Bitterfeld to the CDU leadership.

95. ACDP, VII-011-1268. June 24, 1953 situation report from CDU Bezirk association Halle to the CDU leadership.

96. ADL, LDPD #15848. Protocol of membership meeting of group Sellin on July 13, 1953; Protocol of membership meeting of group Gingst on July 14, 1953 also stated that the trust in the government was lost and that this could not be changed by simply admitting that mistakes had been made.

97. ADL, LDPD #25366. LDPD Kreis association Bernburg supplement a to h for the monthly report of July 1953.

98. Mitter and Wolle, *Untergang*, 141. Fechner was sentenced in 1954 to eight years in prison, and amnestied in 1956.

99. ACDP, VII-011-1268. Situation reports of CDU Kreis association Forst/Lausitz to the CDU leadership.

100. ADL, LDPD #25366. LDPD Kreisverband Köthen supplement to monthly report for July 1953.

101. ADL, LDPD #25366. LDPD Kreis association Artern Monthly report of July 1953. July 25, 1953 to LDPD Bezirk association Halle.

102. ADL, LDPD #25366. LDPD Kreis association Eisleben supplement of July 20, 1953 to monthly report for July.

103. ADL, LDPD #13822. Protocol of LDP Kreis executive meeting for Borna on July 27, 1953. ADL, LDP #25366 says population rejected the communal living units. LDPD Kreis association Köthen supplement to monthly report for July 1953; ibid, #25366. LDPD Kreis association Nebra monthly report of October 1, 1953 to the LDPD Bezirk association Halle.

104. ADL,LDPD #25366. LDPD Kreis association Eisleben supplement to the monthly report for July 1953, July 20, 1953.

105. ADL, LDPD #23534. June 13, 1953 LDPD situation report on New Course from to leadership of the LDPD.

106. ACDP, VII-013-1743. July 18, 1953 report on meeting between functionaries of Bezirk Potsdam and the CDU general secretary.

107. ADL, LDPD #23534. June 19, 1953 situation report from the LDPD Bezirk association Potsdam to the LDPD in Berlin.

108. ACDP, VII-013-1743. Summary from situation reports of the Bezirk associations taken between June 17 and July 17, 1953.

109. BA-P, DO 1 2/4, 80. January 5, 1954 letter from Maron to Ulbricht.

110. ACDP, VII-011-1268. June 17, 1953 report from CDU Kreis association Magdeburg to the CDU leadership.

111. ACDP, VII-013-1743. Report of Bezirk association Dresden conference of June 29, 1953. Kreis association of Görlitz reporting.

112. ACDP, VII-013-1743. Report of Bezirk Dresden conference of June 29, 1953. Kreis association Niesky reporting.

113. ACDP, VII-011-1300. July 1953 report from CDU Bezirk association Frankfurt/Oder to the CDU leadership.

114. ACDP, VII-011-1300. July 1953 report from CDU Bezirk association Frankfurt/Oder to the CDU leadership.

115. ACDP, VII-011-3026. July 16, 1953 memorandum from CDU Bezirk association Suhl to the CDU leadership.

116. ADL, LDPD #31926. Reports from May to October from the LDPD Bezirk association Schwerin on party work.

117. ADL, LDPD #13822. Protocol of sitting of LDPD Kreis association of Borna on September 14, 1953.

118. ADL, LDPD #13822. Protocol of LDPD Kreis executive Borna sitting on July 13, 1953.

119. ACDP, VII-013-1743. July 8, 1953 report on the meeting between the CDU functionaries for Bezirk Gera and the general secretary of the CDU.

120. AdsD, SPD-PV-Ostbüro 0370/I. Special information report Nr.3/53 of Ostbüro of the FDP of December 15, 1953 entitled: "Die Liquidierung des Neuen Kurses."

121. ACDP, VII-013-1743. July 14, 1953 report on talk between Johannes Becher and members of the Jena intelligentsia on July 9, 1953; ACDP, VII-011-1300. July 25, 1953 from CDU Kreis association Jena-Stadt to CDU leadership.

122. ACDP, VII-011-1300. July 1953 report from CDU Bezirk association Dresden, Kreis association Freital, to CDU leadership.

123. ADL, LDP #15848. Minutes of July 1, 1953 Borna Kreis association meeting.

124. ACDP, VII-013-1743. Summary of situation reports of the CDU Bezirk associations taken between June 17 and July 17, 1953.

125. ACDP, VII-013-1743. July 13, 1953 report on meetings of the Kreis secretaries in the previous two weeks.

126. BA-P, DO 1 11/758, 8. July 2, 1953 report on those arrested in connection with the "fascist putsch," by Weidlich, head of the investigation branch in the Volkspolizei.

127. BA-P, DO 1 11/758, 8. July 2, 1953 report on those arrested in connection with the "fascist putsch," by Weidlich, head of the investigation branch in the Volkspolizei.

128. BA-P, DO 1 11/758, 8. July 2, 1953 report on those arrested in connection with the "fascist putsch," by Weidlich, head of the investigation branch in the Volkspolizei.

129. See the section on judicial apparatus below.

130. Patrik von zur Mühlen, "Widerstand in einer thüringischen Kleinstadt 1953 bis 1958. Der "Eisenberger Kreis," in *Zwischen Selbtsbehauptung und Anpassung*, ed. Ulrike Poppe, Rainer Eckert, and Ilko-Sascha Kowalczuk (Berlin: Ch. Links Verlag, 1995), 165.

131. Mühlen, "Widerstand," 164-165.

132. Mühlen, "Widerstand," 166.

133. Mühlen, "Widerstand," 170.

134. Mühlen, "Widerstand," 166.

135. Mühlen, "Widerstand," 166.

136. Mühlen, "Widerstand," 168-169.

137. AdsD, SPD-PV-Ostbüro 0048 f. Report entitled: "Urteile der Bezirksgerichte und der sowjetischen Standgerichte gegen Teilnehmer am Juni Aufstand 1953."

138. SAPMO-BA, ZPA, IV 2/4/391, 221. Resolution of the Central Committee of the SED. The Central Committee rejected this draft in July 1953 due to the alleged Zaisser-Herrnstadt attempt to seize control of the party. See Peter Grieder, *The East German Leadership 1946-1973* (Manchester: Manchester University Press, 1999), 77.

139. Werkentin, *Politische Strafjustiz in der Ära Ulbricht* (Berlin: Ch. Links, 1995), 89.

140. Werkentin, *Politische*, 123.

141. Werkentin, *Politische*, 133.

142. Werkentin, *Politische*, 368.

143. BStU, ZA, SdM 1909, 86. Draft for the conference with Benjamin on September 12, 1953.

144. BStU, ZA, SdM 1909, 86. Draft for the conference with Benjamin on September 12, 1953.

145. BA-P, DO 1 11/758, 9. July 20, 1953 report of the Investigative Unit of the Volkspolizei signed by the head of the unit Weidlich, to the SKK, ZK, and department responsible for penal institutions.

146. Torsten Diedrich, *Der 17. Juni 1953* (Berlin: Dietz Verlag, 1991), 184.

147. An overview of the struggle within the SED in and around the June uprising, complete with reproduction of archival documentation is found in Nadja Stulz-Herrnstadt, *Das*

Herrnstadt Dokument (Reinbek: Rowohlt, 1990). The 15th Plenum also marked an offensive by Ulbricht, whose leadership position had been challenged by both Soviet officials in East Germany and by East German Politburo members, against his detractors within the Politburo. For more on Ulbricht's embattled leadership position, see Kramer, "The Early Post-Stalin," especially nos. 1 and 3, and Peter Grieder, *The East German Leadership 1946-1973* (Machester: Manchester University Press, 1999).

148. BStU, ZA, Allgemeine Sachablage (hereafter AS), 43/58, Vol. 9, 384. Instructions by head of Information branch Tilch.

149. Quoted in Mitter and Wolle, *Untergang*, 146.

150. BStU, ZA, A/S 43/58, Vol. 9, 388. Instructions by Tilch.

151. BStU, ZA, A/S 43/58, Vol. 9, 388. Instructions by Tilch.

152. BStU, ZA, A/S 43/58, Vol. 9, 388. Instructions by Tilch.

153. SAPMO-BA, ZPA, JIV 2/202/62. Resolution of the Politbüro from September 23, 1953, 2-3.

154. BStU, ZA, GVS 2920/53, #100874. Directive 30/53 from Mielke. The Party complained: "The MfS information net is badly organized, both with regards to the people and to their deployment and allocation"; SAPMO-BA, ZPA, DY30 IV 2/12/101. Resolution of the 15th Plenum of the Central Committee, 8.

155. BStU, ZA, GVS 2920/53, #100874. Directive 30/53 from Mielke.

156. SAPMO-BA, ZPA, JIV 2/202/14. "Über die Lage am 17.6.53 in Gross-Berlin und der DDR"; BA-P, DO 1 11/305, pp. 245-247. July 1, 1953 report from Bezirk Halle to Volkspolizei; BA-P, DO 1 11/305, 67. June 29, 1953 report from Bezirk Dresden to Volkspolizei; BA-P, DO 1 11/45, p.3. Extracts from the situation reports of the Bezirk police for the period 0:00 to 17:00 on June 17, 1953 by the head of operations staff Weidhase.

157. BStU, ZA, SdM 2613, 296. Transcript of Wollweber's speech at the Parteiaktiv meeting in the SfS on November 2, 1953.

158. BStU, ZA, SdM 2613, 143, 153, 156, 161, 185, 208, 222, 250, 257, 260.

159. BStU, ZA, SdM 2613, 212.

160. BStU, ZA, SdM 1924, 107. July 10, 1954 proposal for the creation of the department "Agitation of the SfS," signed by General Bormann.

161. BStU, ZA, SdM 1924, 107. July 10, 1954 proposal for the creation of the department "Agitation of the SfS," signed by General Bormann.

162. BStU, ZA, SdM 1921, 172. Remark on the conference which took place at 10:00 am on August 13, 1954.

163. BStU, ZA, SdM 1909 VIII/1, 63. Undated plan for propaganda measures to accompany "Aktion Pfeil."

164. BStU, ZA, SdM 1909 VIII/1, 63. Undated plan for propaganda measures to accompany "Aktion Pfeil."

165. BStU, ZA, SdM 1909 VIII/1, 55. January 4, 1955 proposal resulting from the meeting of the Kollegium committee responsible for events in honour of the 5th anniversary of state security on February 8, 1955.

166. BStU, ZA, SdM 1921, 225. Protocol of the conference between the heads of the Bezirk administrations and the department heads on August 21, 1953.

167. BStU, ZA, SdM 1921, 226. Protocol of the conference between the heads of the Bezirk administrations and the department heads on August 21, 1953.

168. BStU, ZA, SdM 1921, 209. Protocol of the conference between the heads of the Bezirk administrations and the department heads on August 21, 1953.

169. BStU, ZA, SdM 2613, 302. Transcript of Wollweber's speech at the Parteiaktiv

meeting in the SfS on November 2, 1953. Italics added.

170. BStU, ZA, SdM 2612, 105. Undated remark on Wollweber's radio address (1953).

171. BStU, ZA, SdM 1921, 169. Note on the conference held on August 13, 1954 at 10:00 am.

172. BStU, ZA, SdM 1921, 183. Remark on the conference between the heads of the Bezirk administrations and the department heads on April 22, 1954.

173. BStU, ZA, AS 43/58, vol. 3. 21, 29. May 8, 1955 Informationsdienst report.

174. Wollweber stated that the number of secret coworkers had increased to number "several divisions" by 1955. BStU, ZA, SdM 1921, 72. Transcript of Wollweber's speech at the SfS conference on August 5, 1955.

175. BStU, ZA, 1921, 156. Disposition on conference of November 2, 1954.

176. BStU, ZA, SdM 1921, 38. Protocol from the SfS conference on August 5, 1955.

177. See Robert Gellately, *The Gestapo and German Society* (Oxford: Clarendon Press, 1990).

178. The SfS coordinated its offensive against West Berlin-based groups with its internal campaigns to secure the GDR. See Karl Wilhelm Fricke and Roger Engelmann, *"Konzentrierte Schläge:" Staatssicherheitsaktionen und politische Prozess in der DDR 1953-1956* (Berlin: Ch. Links Verlag, 1998).

179. BStU, ZA, SdM 1921, 208. Protocol of the SfS conference between the heads of the Bezirk administrations and the department heads on August 21, 1953.

180. Stefan Wolle has portrayed the campaign against the SPD in this manner. See Stefan Wolle, "'Agenten, Saboteure, Verräter. . .' Die Kampagne der SED-Führung gegen den 'Sozialdemokratismus'," in Kowalczuk, Mitter and Wolle *Der Tag X*, 243-277.

181. BStU, ZA, SdM 1921, 210. Protocol of the SfS conference between the heads of the Bezirk administrations and the departments heads on August 21, 1953.

182. ADL, LDPD #L2-29. Protocol of extraordinary sitting of the political committee of the Central Executive of the LDPD on February 9, 1954.

183. ACDP, III-045-183/7 Undated report from CDU Bezirk Gera to the CDU leadership. Reports before the conference reveal popular optimism that a solution to the German question would be found.The SPD Ostbüro reported deep pessimism after the conference; AdsD, SPD-PV-Ostbüro 0361/2. Summary of reports from February 1954 on Berlin conference; situation report from Dessau of February 20, 1954; situation report from Suhl of February 6, 1954.

184. AdsD, SPD-PV-Ostbüro 0330 Report from Neuer Tag 6.2.54

185. BStU, ZA, SdM 2613, 229. Background report for Wollweber on the situation in VEB Stahlblechbau Berlin Adlershof for his talk on February 4, 1954.

186. BStU, ZA, SdM 2613, 229. Background report for Wollweber on the situation in VEB Stahlblechbau Berlin Adlershof for his talk on February 4, 1954.

187. BStU, ZA, SdM 2613, 230. Background report for Wollweber on the situation in VEB Stahlblechbau Berlin Adlershof for his talk on February 4, 1954.

188. BStU, ZA, AS 43/58, Vol. 11, 218. October 4, 1954 Informationsdienst report.

189. BStU, ZA, AS 43/58, Vol. 11, 218. October 4, 1954 Informationsdienst report.

190. BStU, ZA, AS 43/58, Vol. 11, 324. October 4, 1954 Informationsdienst report. September 21, 1954 Informationsdienst report.

191. ADL, LDPD #25413. Protocol of the Kreis association Dessau meeting on June 11, 1954.

192. BStU, ZA, GVS 1922/54, #100095. October 12, 1954 Information report on the situation in the GDR during the preparations for the elections.

193. BStU, ZA, GVS 1922/54, #100095. October 12, 1954 Information report on the situation in the GDR during the preparations for the elections.

194. BStU, ZA, GVS 1922/54, #100095. October 12, 1954 Information report on the situation in the GDR during the preparations for the elections.

195. BStU, ZA, GVS 1922/54, #100095. October 12, 1954 Information report on the situation in the GDR during the preparations for the elections.

196. BStU, ZA, GVS 1922/54, #100095. October 12, 1954 Information report on the situation in the GDR during the preparations for the elections.

197. BStU, ZA, AS 43/58, Vol. 11, 9. October 26, 1954 Informationsdienst report.

198. BStU, ZA, AS 43/58, Vol. 11, 79. October 26, 1954 Informationsdienst report. October 19, 1954 Informationsdienst report.

199. BStU, ZA, AS 43/58, Vol. 11, 63. October 26, 1954 Informationsdienst report. October 20, 1954 Informationsdienst report.

200. BStU, ZA, AS 43/58 Vol. 2, 187. March 25, 1955 Informationsdienst report.

201. BStU, ZA, AS 43/58 Vol. 3, 203. May 31, 1955 Informationsdienst report.

202. BStU, ZA, AS 43/58 Vol. 3, 220. May 31, 1955 Informationsdienst report.

203. BStU, ZA, AS 43/58 Vol. 3, 38. May 7, 1955 Informationsdienst report.

204. BStU, ZA, AS 43/58 Vol. 3, 38. May 7, 1955 Informationsdienst report.

205. BStU, ZA, AS 43/58 Vol. 2, 187. March 25, 1955 Informationsdienst report.

206. BStU, ZA, AS 43/58 Vol. 2, 187. March 25, 1955 Informationsdienst report. ; BStU, ZA, AS 43/58 Vol. 2, 149. April 1, 1955 Informationsdienst report.

207. BStU, ZA, AS 43/58 Vol. 2, 51. April 19, 1955 Informationsdienst report.

208. BStU, ZA, AS 43/58 Vol. 2, 189. March 25, 1955 Informationsdienst report; ibid., 6. April 29, 1955 Informationsdienst report. There are also numerous references to the possible repetition of June 17 in ibid., AS 43/58, Vol. 4/2, 32-255.

209. BStU, ZA, AS 43/58 Vol. 2, 189. March 25, 1955 Informationsdienst report.

210. BStU, ZA, AS 43/58 Vol. 2, 105. June 17, 1955 Informationsdienst report.

211. BStU, ZA, GVS 1499/55, #100104. June 6, 1955 report from Mielke to the heads of all Bezirk administrations.

212. BStU, ZA, GVS 1500/55, #100104. Directive Nr. 14/55 from June 8, 1955 issued by Mielke.

213. BStU, ZA, GVS 1500/55, #100104. Directive Nr. 14/55 from June 8, 1955 issued by Mielke.

214. BStU, ZA, GVS 1500/55, #100104. Directive Nr. 14/55 from June 8,1955 issued by Mielke.

215. BStU, ZA, GVS 1500/55, #100104. Directive Nr. 14/55 from June 8, 1955 issued by Mielke.

216. BStU, ZA, GVS 1500/55, #100104. Directive Nr. 14/55 from June 8, 1955 issued by Mielke.

217. BStU, ZA, AS 43/58, Vol. 4/1, 54. July 19, 1955 Informationsdienst report.

218. BStU, ZA, AS 43/58 Vol. 4/1, 200. August 4, 1955 Informationsdienst report.

219. BStU, ZA, AS 43/58 Vol. 4/2, 71. July 22, 1955 Informationsdienst report.

220. BStU, ZA, AS 43/58 Vol. 4/1, 205. August 4, 1955 Informationsdienst report.

221. ACDP, VII-013-1262. Undated report of CDU Bezirk association Erfurt to the CDU leadership; July 19, 1955 report from the CDU Bezirk association Magdeburg to the CDU leadership; July 18, 1955 report from CDU Kreis association Burg to the CDU leadership; July 25, 1955 report from CDU Bezirk association Karl-Marx-Stadt to the CDU leadership; political information report 19/55 of November 14, 1955; November 30, 1955 report

from the CDU Bezirk Dresden association to the CDU leadership.

222. BStU, ZA, AS 43/58 Vol. 4/2, 179. July 12, 1955 Informationsdienst report.

223. BStU, ZA, AS 43/58 Vol. 4/2, 255. July 8, 1955 Informationsdienst report.

224. BStU, ZA, AS 43/58 Vol. 4/1, 71. August 19, 1955 Informationsdienst report; ibid., 87. August 16, 1955 Informationsdienst report.

225. BStU, ZA, AS 43/58 Vol. 4/1, 19. August 26, 1955 Informationsdienst report.

226. BStU, ZA, AS 43/58 Vol. 4/1, 20. August 26, 1955 Informationsdienst report.

227. BStU, ZA, AS 43/58 Vol. 5, 319. September 9, 1955 Informationsdienst report.

228. BStU, ZA, AS 43/58 Vol. 7, 4. September 21, 1955 Informationsdienst report.

229. BStU, ZA, AS 43/58 Vol. 7, 6. September 21, 1955 Informationsdienst report. Also BStU, ZA, AS 43/58 Vol. 4/2, 105. July 24, 1955 Informationsdienst report and BStU, ZA, AS 43/58 Vol. 4/1, 202. August 4, 1955 Informationsdienst report.

230. BStU, ZA, AS 43/58 Vol. 7, 7. September 21, Informationsdienst report.

231. BStU, ZA, AS 43/58 Vol. 7, 9. September 21, 1955 Informationsdienst report.

232. BStU, ZA, Sekretariat des Ministers 1921, 73 Transcript: "Rede des Genossen Staatssekretär auf der Dienstbesprechung am 5.8.55."

Chapter 7

Conclusion

A close relationship existed between fundamental anti-Communist resistance and state-sponsored repression in the Soviet Occupied Zone and German Democratic Republic between 1945 and 1955. In the initial years following the war, members of the non-Marxist parties engaged in resistance primarily due to SED and SMAD's encroachment on what they considered to be basic human rights. The land reform of 1945 encountered resistance because of the reform's impact on individual basic rights. Of the non-Marxist parties, the CDU was the most vocal opponent of the manner of the land reform, but sections of the LDPD also resisted the reform. Although the higher levels of the SPD were, in general, more supportive of the land reform, lower levels showed little enthusiasm in carrying it out. The following year, after the fusion of the SPD and the KPD, the most concerted anti-Communist resistance came from members of the SPD. An examination of records on these resisters reveals that repression in the Soviet zone was at the center of resistance motivation. Based on records of the eastern German security apparatus, it is possible for the first time to gauge and periodize this resistance. Between 1946 and 1948, resistance of SPD members in the Soviet zone was the predominant concern of the eastern German security apparatus. Due to a concerted campaign in 1948, the eastern German security apparatus managed to limit SPD resistance, and from 1949 on, organized SPD group activity in the Soviet zone was minimal, but individual SPD members continued to conduct resistance. This finding is confirmed by SPD *Ostbüro* reports on resistance activities in the Soviet zone. Resistance in the LDPD was also a function of repression. The unjust confiscations taking place in the Soviet zone, both in the land reform and the sequestering of industry, met with LDPD resistance, particularly in Thuringia.

The founding of the GDR marked the beginning of the accelerated process of forcing the non-Marxist parties into line. Beginning in 1950, following the acceptance of unity lists and the vigorous MfS campaign to rid the non-Marxist parties of oppositional elements, the non-Marxist parties increasingly became instruments of the SED to carry out the Communist program in East Germany. At the same time, the campaign to remove opposition in these parties led to some members conducting limited, but more vigorous resistance. Oppositional elements lived on within these parties however. The leaderships' support for the "building of socialism" in 1952 did not meet with universal approval of the membership, as demonstrated in the situation reports from the period following the June 17, 1953 uprising.

Popular resistance to Communism in East Germany was a function of the development of the Communist repression apparatus. The lack of sources on popular developments in the initial years after the war (unlike the favorable source situation from 1952 onward) means that historians must look to manifestations of this relationship. Such manifestations include the elections of 1946 and the *Volkskongress* vote of 1949. The first elections do not reveal fundamental hostility to the SED, but do suggest that the party was popular with a minority of the population. The inability of the SED to garner over 50 percent of the vote in any province under extremely favorable conditions suggests this to be the case. More important, the reaction of the SED and SMAD to the election demonstrates that they were displeased with the result and angered at the success of the LDPD and CDU. The situation regarding the *Volkskongress* vote of 1949 was similar. The *Volkskongress* vote visibly unnerved the SED, despite the SED's apparent victory. It is notable, however, that leading politicians in East Germany attributed the "poor" result to legal insecurity. Beginning with the elections of 1950, the source base becomes wider, but still not as advantageous as from 1952 on. Police reports on election-related events prior to the elections of October 1950 reveal that the primary topic raised in these events was legal insecurity. Notably, no concerns regarding the economic situation were raised. The disturbances of August 1951 in Saalfeld provide a case study of the strained relationship between the instruments of control—in this case the *Volkspolizei*—and the population. Although Wismut workers made up the majority of demonstrators, other societal sections participated in this popular expression of hostility towards the *Volkspolizei*.

The revolution of June 17, 1953 laid bare the relationship between popular anti-Communist resistance and repression. The events of June 17 and disturbances afterwards reveal that wide sections of the East German population—not exclusively workers—participated in acts of resistance against the SED regime. Indeed, police records reveal that the main targets of demonstrators were buildings associated with the repression apparatus: *Volkspolizei* offices, court houses, and prisons.[1] The purpose behind these attacks was the freeing of what demonstrators perceived to be wrongfully imprisoned members of their communities. Furthermore, calls for the resignation of the government and free, all-German elections, were present in all *Bezirke* where demonstrations took place. These demands were similar to those voiced by oppositional members of the non-Marxist parties prior to their being forced into line. It was clear to the demonstrators that such elections would bring the end of the Communist system in East Germany. In this light, economic demands of demonstrators were of secondary importance. It is inappropriate, therefore, to characterize June 17 as exclusively a workers' revolt which revolved around economic considerations. Repression by Communist authorities in East Germany (initially Soviet and then SED) over an extended period of time was of greater importance in fuelling political demands during the demonstrations. Documentation collected by the non-Marxist parties in the GDR following the revolution attests to this fact. Lower levels of both the CDU and LDPD, based on independent analyses, noted that legal insecurity was the predominant issue for the population.

Following the revolution, the East German secret police began detailed reporting on the population. SfS reports taken during the Berlin foreign ministers' conference, and to a greater extent during the October 1954 elections and the Geneva Conference of 1955, noted that there was considerable interest in East Germany in free elections. Based on information entering the SfS, even Ernst Wollweber was forced to comment that there was general popular interest in free elections, and by extension the end of the Communist system in East Germany. Analyses compiled by the Secretariat for State Security are confirmed by LDPD and CDU situation reports on the population. One must be careful not to attribute this desire strictly to the difficult economic situation, although material shortages certainly played a role in popular hostility toward the SED. As has been demonstrated in this study, repression played a key role in undermining popular trust in the GDR's political system. Indeed, the SfS leadership showed a concern for the negative impact of unwarranted arrests in the period following the uprising. Nevertheless, the massive expansion of the surveillance apparatus was a direct result of the revolution of June 17, 1953. The MfS informant net would continue to grow at a steady pace until 1972 when closer ties between East and West Germany caused the MfS to accelerate the expansion of its net—a net that expanded until the collapse of the MfS in 1989-1990.[2]

There is at present only one documentary verifiable example of organized anti-Communist resistance in East Germany between 1953 and the end date of this study, 1955. It is worth remembering that this group began to engage in resistance activities because of the repression that they witnesssed in the GDR. While other acts of individual or group resistance may become known as more documentation from the MfS becomes located and catalogued, this is unlikely as the records from post-1953 are already fairly complete. Reasons behind the lack of organized resistance will require further research, but will inevitably return to the June 17, 1953 revolution. The revolution had demonstrated in bloody fashion that it would not be possible to change the political system in East Germany without the acquiescence of the Soviet Union. The failures of international conferences on the German question to change the political system in the German Democratic Republic also contributed to an increased feeling of resignation in the population.[3] Both the SfS and the CDU noted deep popular disappointment in the wake of the failed Geneva Conference. It appeared to East Germans that there was no immediate prospect for a united Germany under the western democratic model. It might indeed be that given these conditions, resistance would have seemed pointless. On the night of August

13, 1961, the SED removed any last vestiges of popular hope that the division of Germany—and thus SED-rule in East Germany—was temporary. On August 13, 1961, East German police troops erected the Berlin Wall. The fact that there was no significant protest in East Germany to the building of the Wall,[4] although this act was equally, if not more, provocative than the increased work norms which had sparked the June 17 revolution, indicates the extent to which the population had resigned itself to the situation in East Germany.

In *My Century*, a brilliant literary journey through the twentieth century, Günter Grass, reflecting on June 17, 1953, writes: "Sometimes, even if decades after the fact, stone throwers do prevail." Grass brings up an intriguing area of investigation—the link between earlier resistance and the revolution of 1989. Resistance in eastern Germany between 1945 and 1955 does indeed provide a useful frame of reference to evaluate resistance in 1989, although, to be sure, studies on the revolution of 1989 continue to emerge, and much more needs to be done to fully understand those events. What is striking about the resistance under investigation in this study is the commonality of desire to remove the Communist system, particularly as expressed in the uprising of 1953 and earlier resisters in the non-Marxist parties. Such was not the case, however, in 1989 when quasi-legal opposition groups pushed for a reformed socialism while demonstrators expressed their desire for the removal of the Communist system.[5] This unique position of members of these groups—in contrast to other dissidents in Eastern Europe who wanted to abandon socialism completely—was a result of their support for the GDR as the better German state because it had outlawed most private ownership, even if it had trampled on basic freedoms.[6]

The underlying roots of resistance also provide intriguing contrasts. In the early period, repression played a dominant role in undermining trust in the regime and in contributing to the fundamentally political nature of the demonstrations of 1953. Economic discontent had its place as well, but the emphasis in the documents on the state's abuse of basic rights as a source of unrest and the general conduct of the demonstrators in June 1953 suggest that repression played a key role in motivation to resist. Several historians have concluded that the roots of the 1989 revolution are to be found in reasons other than economic. As Gale Stokes has written: "The reason so many wanted to flee East Germany was fundamentally not economic, however. They were fleeing a stifling sense of powerlessness, the regime's deadening insistence on capitulation, and the enervating denial of all possibility of idealism and hope."[7] Konrad Jarausch also argues that the lower living standards merely reinforced political frustrations.[8] Other historians speak to the relatively decent living standard in East Germany, and point rather to "utter moral rot" of the regime[9] and to denied rights, including the lack of travel.[10] Thus, the demonstrations of 1989 seem to bear a striking resemblance to those of 1953, in that both were manifestations of political discontent, brought on by a fundamental lack of trust in the regime in which economic dissatisfaction played only a partial role. Indeed, the fundamental political nature of both demonstrations is visible in their slogans. The widespread call for free elections in 1953 seemed to have been updated in 1989 to the fundamentally similar slogan: "We are the people." Other banners and slogans in 1989 related to basic freedoms, including freedom of the press, greater democracy, and dialogue between government and citizens.[11] To be sure, economic demands were much more visible in the demonstrations of 1953, yet the political demands were remarkably similar.

1989 was not 1953, however. Repression in 1989 was far less brutal, the Berlin Wall was a visible reminder of strict travel restrictions, and the Soviet Union had made it clear that it would not intervene in the satellite states. Yet the similarities between the two revolutions suggest that historians would do well to examine the nature of East German society between the two eras through the lens of resistance. Histories that forward the theory that workers in East Germany reigned in the ability of the state to put through its economic program because of threats of strike—a classic *Resistenz* approach—help bring into focus the main issue: If workers held power over the state with their threat to strike; if the state was forced to meet wage and price demands of the population because of these threats; if, in essence, the state bowed to the demands of its workers, why did it remain, in the eyes of the population, fundamentally illegitimate? What would bring millions of people onto the streets of East Germany in 1989 if wage and price demands were, by and large, being met; if it was the population that determined the limits of the state's authority? These answers lie in the investigation of *resistance* in East Germany and the state's lack of popular legitimacy, not in equating accommodation with underlying support of the regime, nor in focusing on *Resistenz* activities that sidestep the issue of why there existed fundamental political resistance to the Communist system.[12]

Whereas 1989 is a useful point of comparison for East German resistance in the postwar decade, so too is resistance in other countries of the Soviet bloc. Resistance in other Soviet bloc countries fell primarily into three categories: (1) armed resistance, (2) semi-legalized resistance in opposition political parties, and (3) open rebellion, including labor unrest. Ukraine, Poland, and the Baltics experienced nothing short of civil war in the years immediately following World War II, as armed resisters fought the Communist takeover of power. The Ukrainian Insurgent Army (Ukrainska povstanska armiia, UPA), which at its peak had over 40,000 members, engaged in high-risk, violent activities against the Soviets in Ukraine, including assassination attempts and the blowing up of railroads and bridges. The UPA also built up a network of contacts to lead an eventual revolution against the Soviet authorities.[13] Overwhelmed by the sheer size of the organization and unable to confront it directly, the Soviets resorted to infiltrating it and bringing it down from within, a task that they had accomplished by 1951.[14] In those parts of Poland with an ethnic Ukrainian population, the UPA conducted a vigorous campaign against Polish authorities (and often regular Poles) and their attempts to "repatriate" Ukrainians from Polish territory. The UPA killed a Polish general in 1947 and systematically burned emptied Ukrainian villages so that Poles would not settle in them.[15] Other areas of Poland experienced fighting between underground resisters—often remnants of the heroic Home Army that had fought so valiantly against the Nazi occupation—and Soviet and Polish authorities, that would claim roughly

30,000 Polish lives and 1,000 Soviet. This fighting dragged on into the 1950s in the southern mountainous region of Poland.[16]

There were no doubt other examples of militant resistance to Soviet occupation in Eastern Europe and to the Communist takeovers. Certainly, western covert operations into Rumania, Albania, and Hungary suggest that there existed local networks, if limited, to be exploited.[17] Apart from rookie efforts by the Fighting Group Against Inhumanity and the rare reference to underground SPD groups with arms, East German resistance in the period under investigation could not be classified as armed resistance to the regime; it did not exist to terrorize the authorities into submission, but rather was characterized by the spreading of pamphlets and word of mouth and, in the case of June 17, taking to the streets. There is no evidence of sustained armed attacks on Communist authorities in East Germany, as occurred in Poland, Ukraine, the Baltics, and perhaps elsewhere.

Similarities in resistance efforts emerge in the milieu of political parties. Most countries of Eastern Europe allowed, at least for a short period, parties other than the Communist party and these non-Communist parties often became rallying centres of resistance. In Poland, membership in the Peasant Party (PSL), under its determined leader, Stanislaw Mikołajczyk, soared to nearly 800,000 members by the summer of 1946—more than the Socialists and Communists combined.[18] At political assemblies, the PSL lashed out at the Communists for establishing a system based on prisons and the collective farm.[19] Indeed, one historian has called the PSL in this period "the lone legal voice for democracy and the rule of law."[20] The line between legal opposition and underground resistance was a fine one, however, and Mikolajczuk's PSL crossed it on several occasions prior to his being forced to flee Poland in October 1947 by contacting the underground, particularly Freedom and Independence (Wolnosc I Niepodleglosc, WIN). Krystyna Kersten summarizes these contacts as follows: "It is difficult to measure the scale of these contacts, or to describe them as cooperation, but there can be no doubt that at certain points the legal and illegal opposition to Communist rule were in touch with each other."[21] This pattern of resistance resonates with the non-Marxist parties in East Germany prior to 1952, members of which were frequently in contact with SPD resisters. The fluidity between the semi-legal opposition in non-Marxist political parties and the underground suggests that historians should reflect upon the distinction between legal opposition in political parties and underground resistance. The experience in Poland and East Germany reveals that the distinction between the two is perhaps unwarranted and that individuals who opposed Communism by speaking out against it in public political assemblies on behalf of a political party may have been simply engaging in but one of their resistance activities. The term "opponent" for members of non-Marxist parties, in many cases, does not capture the extent of resistance in which they were engaged. Although the available evidence suggest such a pattern for Poland and East Germany, the fact that major opposition parties existed in other countries of Eastern Europe, even if briefly—such as the Smallholders Party in Hungary and in Bulgaria, and the Social Democrats in Rumania[22]—suggests that future studies of resistance in these countries would do well to focus on the shift from political opponent to resister.

East German strikes and work stoppages in 1952 and 1953 stand out among labour unrest in other countries of Eastern Europe in the same period due to their political nature. When workers at the Poznański textile mill in Łódź walked off the job in September, sparking a wave of work stoppages encompassing nearly 40 percent of the city's workers, the government could have well feared the worst but the workers' demands centred exclusively on shop floor issues, such as workers' posts in the factory and the number of machines for which each worker was responsible.[23] Earlier strikes in this area, numbering in the hundreds, had centered almost entirely on the immediate concerns of wages and cafeteria food. The political was missing. As Padraic Kenney has summarized: "Labor conflict during this entire period centered not on opposition to or support of a political line but on workplace and community issues."[24] Similarly, work stoppages in Bulgaria and small acts of sabotage in the work place do not reveal political motivation on the part of the perpetrators. Promises by Bulgarian Communist party officials to address the question of work norms sufficed to end the walkout of hundreds of tobacco workers in the Plovdiv and Khaskovo region.[25] In the countryside, Bulgarian peasants hid cereals, rammed iron rods into sheaves, lay down in front of tractors that were to cut "the first co-operative furrow," and even assassinated the chairmen of cooperative farms in three villages in order to halt the government's attempts to collectivize agriculture.[26] Initial research suggests that these opponents did not couple their demands for sweeping political change.

East German work stoppages in 1952 and 1953 bear greater resemblance to the shocking riots of 1951 in Plzeň. Angered by the currency reform of June 1953, Škoda workers marched out of the factory and directly to city hall to the cheers of workers who poured out of nearby factories. The demonstrators occupied city hall and embarked on a rampage against symbols of the regime, including Soviet flags and busts of Vladimir Lenin, Joseph Stalin, and the leader of the Czechoslovak Communists, Klement Gottwald. From the balcony of the city hall, the irate workers demanded the overthrow of the government, free elections, and the end of Communism. As Mark Kramer has written: "The protestors were united mainly by their desire to get rid of Communism."[27] The political nature of the rebellion in Plzeň resonates with the East German disturbances and provides a stark contrast to instances of labor unrest when political aspirations were absent. What remains remarkable about East German labor unrest in 1952 and 1953 compared to other instances in the Soviet bloc—including the bloody Poznań riots of 1956—are the ongoing demand for political change and the sustained period of unrest.

The present study permits a perspective upon the years leading up to the building of the Berlin Wall. In 1956, following Nikita Khrushchev's launch of de-Stalinization in a secret speech at the 20th Party Congress of the Communist Party of the Soviet Union, the East German Politburo renounced the personality cult, and the terrorist methods of Stalinism.[28] The 20th Party Congress relegated the darkest days of Stalinism to the past.

Fundamentally, however, de-Stalinization did not affect political structures in the GDR, as the SED retained its monopoly on power and the non-Marxist parties, which had been fully coopted during the period of this study, continued to be transmission organs of the SED to implement the Communist programme in East Germany. At the LDPD's 7th Party Congress of July 1957, the LDPD supported state takeover (initially only partial) of remaining private enterprises. At the CDU's 9th Party Congress of 1958, it claimed its desire to bring the Christian population closer to the "building of socialism." At its 10th Party Congress in 1960, it officially declared: "The members of the CDU recognize the working class and its party as destined leaders of our nation and place all their force behind the securing and strengthening of the GDR."[29] These parties were clearly not centers of anti-Communist resistance as they had been prior to 1953. It should be expected, however, that future research will find, as has been demonstrated in this study, that the lower level membership of the parties were not always in agreement with the SED's policies, nor those of the leadership.

De-Stalinization in the GDR led to, in general, a milder system of justice, although the SED continued to be strict against political opponents.[30] In 1956, many of those tried for resistance activities in the GDR and Soviet Occupied Zone were amnestied, including the majority of SPD resisters and members of the non-Marxist parties who had been arrested for oppositional activity. Members of the SED who had been expelled during the various purges between 1945 and 1956, including former prominent members of the Central Committee, Franz Dahlem, Anton Ackermann, and Paul Merker, were amnestied. Overall, the number of prisoners in the GDR decreased dramatically. In the first quarter of 1956, there were 48,747 prisoners in the GDR, of whom 13,014 were in prison because of "crimes against the state."[31] This means that 31.2 percent prisoners were political prisoners. By the end of 1958, the total number of prisoners in the GDR had dropped to 22,343, but 8,115 (39.9 percent) of those had been sentenced for "crimes against the state." In other words, although the overall number of prisoners in the GDR fell in the course of 1956, the percentage of political prisoners rose. Between 1958 and 1960, that percentage hovered around 20 percent. By the end of 1960, the percentage of prisoners who had been sentenced for "crimes against the state" rose sharply. Of 23,414 prisoners, 18,198, or 39.5 percent, were "criminals against the state."[32]

The high percentage of "criminals against the state"—the highest percentage since 1953—reflected the Politburo renewed push for the "building of socialism."[33] These efforts were most visible in the countryside, where the Politburo was determined to collectivize agriculture, after the failed attempts of 1952-1953. Erich Mielke, the Minister of State Security, saw the collectivization as a primary duty: "We must focus our informants so that they help us push through all measures on the development of agriculture."[34] As had been the case prior to the uprising of June 17, 1953, state use of repression in 1960-1961 to bring about the realization of the party's program caused increased resentment in the population.[35]

The economic situation deteriorated in 1960-1961, primarily as a result of a lack of production in agriculture during the collectivization phase and industrial difficulties caused by the unrealistic expectations of the Seven Year Plan introduced in 1959.[36] Agricultural difficulties had led to serious supply problems. From March 1961, all *Bezirke* in the GDR had difficulties meeting the food needs of the population. Basic foodstuffs such as bread, milk, and butter were not always available.[37]

East Germans did not have to endure these conditions. In 1960, it was still fairly easy to relocate to West Germany, provided one was willing to leave all possessions, including home and land, to seek a new life in the West. A subway ride from East to West Berlin was all that was required. And indeed, many East Germans chose this option. In 1959, 143,000 East Germans fled to the West; in 1960, that number had risen to 199,000; by August 1961, approximately 160,000 East Germans had fled the GDR.[38] Although further research is needed to determine precisely the nature of popular opinion in the months prior to the building of the Berlin Wall,[39] it appears that the increasing tensions between the Allies of 1958-1961—in particular the failed Khrushchev-Eisenhower summit of 1960—convinced many that there was no immediate prospect of the end of the SED regime through union with West Germany.[40]

Politically and economically unable to tolerate this bleeding of its population, the SED sealed the permeable border between East and West Berlin. The barbed wire that the *Volkspolizei* unrolled on the night of August 13, 1961 was soon replaced by the concrete barrier that knifed through the center of the former German capital.[41] East German resisters now had to contend with the stark reality of a regime that was willing to undertake this step and of an international community unable to prevent it.

Notes

1. The fact that, prior to 1953, the MfS was a small organization that did not concentrate on widespread popular surveillance, but on specific enemy elements in the population such as members of the non-Marxist parties and anti-Communist groups based in West Berlin helps to explain why MfS installations were not a primary target of demonstrators on June 17, 1953.

2. See Bernward Paule, "Die politische Freund-Feind-Differenz als ideologische Grundlage des MfS," *Deutschland Archiv* 26 (1993): 170-184.

3. Hermann Weber, *DDR. Grundriss der Geschichte* (Hannover: Fackelträger, 1991), 74.

4. Mary Fulbrook, *Anatomy of a Dictatorship* (Oxford: Oxford University Press, 1995), 190.

5. See John Torpey, *Intellectuals, Socialism and Dissent: The East German Opposition and Its Legacy* (Minneapolis: University of Minnesota Press, 1995), and Stefan Wolle, "Der Weg in den Zussamenbruch: Die DDR vom Juni bis zum Oktober 1989," in *Die Gestaltung der deutschen Einheit: Geschichte—Politik—Gesellschaft*, ed. Eckhard Jesse and Armin Mitter (Bonn: Bundeszentrale für politische Bildung, 1992), 85.

6. For more on the place of East German intellectuals in the history of East Germany, see John Torpey, *Intellectuals, Socialism, and Dissent* (Minneapolis: University of Minnesota Press, 1995), especially 68.

7. Gale Stokes, *The Walls Came Tumbling Down* (New York: Oxford University Press,

1993), 138.

8. Konrad Jarausch, *The Rush to German Unity* (New York: Oxford University Press, 1994), 24.

9. Daniel Chirot, "What happened in Eastern Europe in 1989?" in *The Revolutions of 1989*, ed. Vladimir Tismaneanu (London: Routledge, 1999), 38.

10. See Charles Maier, *Dissolution* (Princeton: Princeton University Press, 1997), 124, and Dietrich Staritz, "Ursachen und Konsequenzen einer deutschen Revolution," in *Der Fischer Weltalmanach* (Frankfurt: Fischer Taschenbuch-Verlag, 1990), 15.

11. Fulbrook, *Anatomy*, 251.

12. Jeffrey Kopstein in *The Politics of Economic Decline in East Germany* (Chapel Hill: North Carolina Press, 1997) adopting a *Resistenz* approach sees a continues pattern of small acts of worker resistance that reigned in the government's room for maneuver. Whereas Armin Mitter and Stefan Wolle interpret the history of the GDR as a latent civil war in *Untergang auf Raten* (Munich: Bertelsmann Verlag, 1993), Mary Fulbrook in *Anatomy of a Dictatorship* views a society that had, by and large, accommodated itself to the regime.

13. Poltawa, "Our Battle Plan for the Liberation of Ukraine Under the Present Circumstances," in *Political Thought of the Ukrainian Underground 1943-1951*, ed. Peter Potichnyj and Yevhen Shtendera (Edmonton: Canadian Institute of Ukrainian Studies, 1986), 253.

14. Poltawa, "Our Battle," xii. See also Jeffrey Burds, "Agentura: Soviet Informants Network and the Ukrainian Underground in Galicia, 1944-1948," *East European Politics and Societies* 11 (1997): 115.

15. Peter Grose, *Operation Rollback* (Boston: Houghton Mifflin, 2000), 47; Timothy Snyder, "'To Resolve the Ukrainian Problem Once and for All': Ethnic Cleansing of Ukrainians in Poland, 1943-1947," *Journal of Cold War Studies* 1 (1994): 92.

16. Thomas Simons Jr., *Eastern Europe in the Postwar World*, 2nd ed. (New York: St. Martin's Press, 1993), 43.

17. Grose, *Operation Rollback*, 40, 42, 161.

18. Padraic Kenney, *Rebuilding Poland: Workers and Communists 1945-1950* (Ithaca: Cornell University Press, 1997), 51.

19. Bartholomew Goldyn, "Disenchanted Voices: Public Opinion in Cracow, 1945-46," *East European Quarterly* 32 (1998): 142.

20. Kenney, *Rebuilding Poland*, 51.

21. Krystyna Kersten, *The Establishment of Communist Rule in Poland, 1943-48* (Berkeley: University of California Press, 1991), 260.

22. An excellent summary of the political situation in Eastern Europe following WW II is contained in Joseph Rothschild and Nancy Wingfield, *Return to Diversity* (New York: Oxford University Press, 2000), ch. 3.

23. Padraic Kenney, "Working Class Community and Resistance in pre-Stalinist Poland," *Social History* 18 (1993): 38-42. The majority of striking workers were women. See also Padraic Kenney, "The Gender of Resistance in Communist Poland," *American Historical Review* 104 (1999): 399-425.

24. Kenney, *Rebuilding Poland*, 53.

25. Mark Kramer, "The Early Post-Stalin Succession Struggle and Upheavals in East-Central Europe," *Journal of Cold War Studies* 1 (1999): 17.

26. Vladimir Migev, "The Bulgarian Peasants' Resistance to Collectivization 1948-1958," *Bulgarian Historical Review* 25 (1997): 59-68.

27. Kramer, "The Early Post-Stalin," 20. The description of events is based on

Kramer's account in same, 19-20.

28. Weber, *Grundriss,* 75.

29. Weber, *Grundriss,* 80.

30. Following the Hungarian rebellion of October and November 1956, revisionist socialists in the GDR were no longer tolerated. Wolfgang Harich, philosophy professor at Humboldt University and member of the SED, was arrested on November 29, 1956 and sentenced in March 1957 to 10 years in prison. He was amnestied in 1964. High-ranking SED members, including the *Politbüro* member Karl Schirdewan and the Minister for State Security Ernst Wollweber, were also removed due to their opposition to Ulbricht; David Childs, *The GDR: Moscow's German Ally,* 2nd ed. (London: Unwin Hyman, 1988), 53-54.

31. Falco Werkentin, *Politische Strafjustiz in der Ära Ulbricht* (Berlin: Ch. Links Verlag, 1995), 409.

32. Werkentin, *Politische,* 409.

33. Werkentin, *Politische,* 409.

34. Quoted in Mitter and Wolle, *Untergang,* 331.

35. Quoted in Mitter and Wolle, *Untergang,* 327.

36. Weber, *Grundriss,* 91.

37. Mitter and Wolle, *Untergang,* 343.

38. Weber, *Grundriss,* 95.

39. For an introduction, see the chapter "Die DDR zu Beginn der sechziger Jahre: Der Weg ins sozialistische Ghetto," in Mitter and Wolle, *Untergang.*

40. Childs, *The GDR,* 61.

41. On the erection of the Berlin Wall, see Jürgen Rühle and Günter Holzweissig, *13. August 1961. Die Mauer von Berlin* (Cologne: Verlag Wissenschaft und Politik, 1988).

Bibliography

Unpublished Manuscript Sources

Archiv für Christlich-Demokratische Politik in der Konrad-Adenauer-Stiftung, Sankt Augustin, (Archive of Christian Democratic Politics at the Konrad Adenauer Foundation, Saint Augustin)

Record Groups: (1945-1955)

Exil-CDU Sachthemen
Ost-CDU Sekretariat des Hauptvorstandes
Ost-CDU Sachthemen

BV Erfurt	KV Aschersleben	NL W. Seibert
BV Gera	KV Altenburg	NL W. Zeller
BV Halle	KV Eisenach	
BV Magdeburg	KV Greifswald	
BV Rostock	KV Jena	
BV Schwerin	KV Magdeburg	
BV Suhl	KV Worbis	

Archiv der sozialen Demokratie in der Friedrich-Ebert-Stiftung, Bonn Bad Godesberg (Archive of social democracy at the Friedrich Ebert Foundation, Bonn-Bad Godesberg)

Record Group Ostbüro (1945-1956)

Archiv des Deutschen Liberalismus in der Friedrich-Naumann-Stiftung, Gummersbach

(Archive of German liberalism at the Friedrich Naumann Foundation, Gummersbach)

Record Groups: (1945-1955)

Ostbüro

Politischer Ausschuss

LV Brandenburg	BV Frankfurt/Oder	KV Borna
LV Mecklenburg	BV Halle	KV Calau
LV Sachsen-Anhalt	BV Potsdam	KV Dessau
LV Sachsen	BV Rostock	KV Eberswalde
LV Thüringen	BV Schwerin	KV Erfurt

KV Frankfurt/Oder
KV Gera
KV Bad Langensalza
KV Glauchau
KV Gotha
KV Eisleben

Bundesarchiv—Abteilungen Potsdam (Federal Archives—Potsdam branches. Now housed in Berlin-Lichterfelde)

Record Groups: (1945-1953)

Ministerium des Innern - Hauptverwaltung Deutsche Volkspolizei
Ministerium des Innern - Deutsche Verwaltung des Innern

Bundesbeauftragter für die Unterlagen des Staatssicherheitsdienstes der ehemaligen Deutschen Demokratischen Republik, Berlin (Federal commission for the documents of the state security service of the former German Democratic Republic, Berlin)

Record groups: (1945-1955)

Dokumentenstelle
Sekretariat des Ministers
Allgemeine Sachablage

Brandenburgisches Landeshauptarchiv, Potsdam (Brandenburg provincial archives, Potsdam)

Record Groups: (1945-1955)

Amt für Information

Ministerium des Innern
SED Bezirksparteiarchiv
SED Landesvorstand Brandenburg

DeutschlandRadio Archiv, Berlin

Record groups:

Militärwesen, Polizei, Strafvollzug
Justizwesen

Franz Neumann Archiv, Berlin

Binders VII, VIII, and IX

Mecklenburgisches Landeshauptarchiv, Schwerin (Mecklenburg provincial archive, Schwerin)

Record groups: (1945-1955)

Bezirksleitung Schwerin der SED, BPKK
Bezirksleitung Schwerin der SED, Abteilung Sicherheit
Landesleitung der SED Mecklenburg, LPKK
Landesleitung der SED Mecklenburg, Abteilung Sicherheit

Stiftung Archiv der Parteien und Massenorganisationen der DDR im Bundesarchiv, Berlin (Foundation archive of the parties and mass organizations of the GDR in the federal archives, Berlin)

Record groups: (1945-1955)

KPD - Bezirke
KPD - Zentrale Leitende Parteiorgane

SED - Abteilung Parteiorgane
SED - Agitation
SED - Sicherheitsfragen
SED - Staat und Recht
SED - Befreundete Parteien
SED - Zentrale Leitende Parteiorgane - Politbüro
SED - Zentrale Leitende Parteiorgane - Zentralkommittee

NL Walter Ulbricht

Thüringisches Hauptstaatsarchiv Weimar, Weimar (Thuringian provincial archive, Weimar)

Record groups: (1945-1955)

SED Landesleitung Thüringen, LPKK
SED Bezirksleitung Erfurt, BPKK
BPA Erfurt, Landesleitung Thüringen
SED Kreisleitung Apolda KPKK
SED Kreisleitung Mühlhausen KPKK
Ministerium des Innern, Landesbehörde der Volkspolizei Thüringen

Interviews

Hermann Kreutzer, Berlin, April 24, 1995.
Rudolf Turber, Berlin, May 31, 1995.
Karl Schirdewan, Potsdam, March 18, 1995.
Siegfried Mampel, Berlin, April 14, 1995.
Rainer Hildebrandt, Berlin, March 2, 1995

Newspapers

Neues Deutschland (1950, 1953)

Published Primary Sources

Bouvier, Beatrix, and Horst Peter Schulz. "*...die SPD aber aufgehört hat zu   existieren."* Bonn: J.H.W. Dietz, 1991.
Braas, Gerhard. *Die Entstehung der Länderverfassungen in der Sowjetischen Besatzungszone Deutschlands 1946-1947.* Cologne: Verlag Wissenschaft und Politik, 1987.
Das Potsdamer Abkommen: Dokumentensammlung. Berlin: Staatsverlag der DDR, 1980.
Dokumente der Sozialistischen Einheitspartei Deutschlands. Berlin: Dietz Verlag, 1950-58.
Foreign Relations of the United States: The Conferences at Malta and Yalta. Washington, D.C.: U.S. Government Printing Office, 1955.
Foreign Relations of the United States: The Conference of Berlin (Potsdam). Washington, D.C.: U.S. Government Printing Office, 1960.
Hildebrandt, Horst. *Die deutschen Verfassungen des 19. Und 20. Jahrhunderts.* Paderborn: Ferdinand Schöningh, 1971.
Kaff, Brigitte, ed. *"Gefährliche politische Gegner":* Widerstand und Verfolgung in der sowjetischen Zone/DDR. Düsseldorf: Droste, 1995.
Malycha, Andreas. *Auf dem Weg zur SED: die Sozialdemokratie und die Bildung einer Einheitspartei in den Ländern der SBZ: eine Quellenedition.* Bonn: J.H.W. Dietz Nachfolger, 1995.
Mayer, Tilman. *Jakob Kaiser—Gewerkschafter und Patriot. Eine Werkauswahl.* Cologne:

Bund Verlag, 1988.

Ostermann, Christian. "New Documents on the East German Uprising of 1953." *Cold War International History Project Bulletin* 5 (1995): 10-21.

——, ed. *The Post-Stalin Succession Struggle and the 17 June 1953 Uprising in East Germany: The Hidden History.* Washington: National Security Archive, 1996.

——. *Uprising in East Germany.* New York: Central European University Press, 2001.

Reinert, Fritz. *Protokolle der Landesblockausschusses der antifaschistisch-demokratischen Parteien Brandenburgs 1945-1950.* Weimar: Verlag Hermann Böhlaus Nachfolger, 1994.

Scherstjanoi, Elke. "'Wollen wir den Sozialismus?' Dokumente aus der Sitzung des Politbüros des ZK der SED am 6.Juni 1953. " *Beiträge zur Geschichte der Arbeiterbewegung* 33 (1991): 658-680.

Stöckigt, Rolf. "Ein Dokument von grosser historischer Bedeutung vom Mai 1953." *Beiträge zur Geschichte der Arbeiterbewegung* 32 (1990): 648-654.

Suckut, Siegfried. *Blockpolitik in der SBZ/DDR: die Sitzungsprotokolle des zentralen Einheitsfrontausschusses.* Cologne: Verlag Wissenschaft und Politik, 1986.

Weber, Hermann. *DDR. Dokumente zur Geschichte der Deutschen Demokratischen Republik 1945-1985.* Munich: Deutscher Taschenbuch Verlag, 1986.

——. *Parteiensystem zwischen Demokratie und Volksdemokratie: Dokumente und Materialien zum Funktionswandel der Parteien und Massenorganisationen in der SBZ/DDR.* Cologne: Verlag Wissenschaft und Politik, 1982.

Wengst, Udo. "Der Aufstand am 17. Juni 1953 in der DDR. Aus den Stimmungsberichten der Kreis-und Bezirksverbände der Ost-CDU im Juni und Juli 1953." *Vierteljahreshefte für Zeitgeschichte* 41 (1993): 277-321.

Secondary Sources

Agde, Günter. *Sachsenhausen bei Berlin: Speziallager Nr. 7 1945-1950.* Berlin: Aufbau Taschenbuch Verlag, 1994.

Agethen, Manfred. "Der Widerstand der demokratischen Kräfte in der CDU gegen den Gleichschaltungsdruck von sowjetischer Besatzungsmacht und SED 1945-1952." In *Die CDU in der sowjetischen besetzten Zone/DDR 1945-1952*, edited by Alexander Fischer and Manfred Agethen. Sankt Augustin: Konrad-Adenauer-Stiftung.

——."Die CDU in der SBZ/DDR 1945-53." In *"Bürgerliche" Parteien in der SBZ/DDR: Zur Geschichte von CDU, LDPD, DBD, NDPD 1945 bis 1953*, edited by Manfred Agethen and Jürgen Fröhlich. Cologne: Verlag Wissenschaft und Politik, 1994.

Albrecht, Willy. *Kurt Schumacher. Ein Leben für den demokratischen Sozialismus.* Bonn: Verlag Neue Gesellschaft, 1985.

Ammer, Thomas. *Universität zwischen Demokratie und Diktatur.* Cologne: Verlag Wissenschaft und Politik, 1969.

Arlt, Kurt. "Das Wirken der Sowjetischen Militäradministration in Deutschland im Spannungsfeld zwischen den Beschlüssen von Potsdam und der sicherheitspolitischen Interessen Moskaus 1945-1949." In *Volksarmee schaffen - ohne Geschrei: Studien zu den Anfängen einer 'verdeckten Aufrüstung' in der SBZ/DDR 1947-1952*, edited by Bruno Thoss. Munich: R. Oldenbourg Verlag, 1994.

Author Collective. *Geschichte der Deutschen Volkspolizei.* Vol. 1 (1945-1961). Berlin: VEB

Deutscher Verlag der Wissenschaft, 1987.

Baring, Arnulf. *Der 17. Juni 1953.* Cologne: Kipenheuer & Witsch, 1983.

———. *Uprising in East Germany: June 17, 1953.* Ithaca: Cornell University Press, 1972.

Bark, Dennis, and David Gress. *From Shadow to Substance 1945-63.* Oxford: Basil Blackwell, 1989.

Bärwald, Helmut. *Das Ostbüro der SPD.* Krefeld: SINUS, 1991.

———. "Terror als System." in *Verfolgt-verhaftet-verurteilt: Demokratie im Widerstand gegen die Rote Diktatur -Fakten und Beispiele,* edited by Günter Scholz. Berlin: Westkreuz Verlag, 1990.

Bauerkämper, Arnd. "Die Neubauern in der SBZ/DDR 1945-1952: Bodenreform und politisch induzierter Wandel der ländlichen Gesellschaft." In *Die Grenzen der Diktatur: Staat und Gesellschaft in der DDR,* edited by Richard Bessel and Ralph Jessen. Göttingen: Vandenhoeck & Rupprecht, 1996.

Becker, Winfried. *CDU und CSU 1945-1950.* Mainz: V. Hase und Koehler Verlag, 1987.

Behrendt, Armin. *Wilhelm Külz: Aus dem Leben eines Suchenden.* Berlin: Buchverlag Der Morgen, 1968.

Beier, Gerhard. *Wir wollen freie Menschen sein - Der 17. Juni 1953. Bauleute gingen voran.* Cologne: Bund Verlag, 1993.

Benjamin, Hilde, et al. "Der Entwicklungsprozess zum sozialistischen Strafrecht in der DDR." *Staat und Recht* 18 (1969): 1115-1120.

"Berichte über sowjetische Internierungslager in der SBZ." *Deutschland Archiv* 22 (1990): 1804-1810.

Bessel, Richard. "Die Grenzen des Polizeistaates." In *Die Grenzen der Diktatur: Staat und Gesellschaft in der DDR,* edited by Richard Bessel and Ralph Jessen. Göttingen: Vandenhoeck & Rupprecht, 1996.

Bloch, Peter. *Zwischen Hoffnung und Resignation. Als CDU-Politiker in Brandenburg 1945-1950.* Cologne: Verlag Wissenschaft und Politik, 1986.

Bouvier, Beatrix. "Antifaschistische Zusammenarbeit, Selbstständigkeitsanspruch, und Vereinigungstendenz." *Archiv für Sozialgeschichte* 16 (1976): 417-468.

Brant, Stefan. *Der Aufstand. Vorgeschichte, Geschichte und Deutung des 17. Juni 1953.* Stuttgart: Steingrüben Verlag, 1954.

Brill, Hermann. *Gegen den Strom.* Offenbach: Bollwerk Verlag, 1946.

Brundert, Willi. *Es begann im Theater. 'Volksjustiz' hinter dem eisernene Vorhang.* Berlin: Verlag J.H.W. Dietz, 1958.

Broszat, Martin, et al., eds. *Bayern in der NS-Zeit.* Vol. 1-6. Munich: R.Oldenbourg Verlag, 1977-1983.

Broszat, Martin, and Elke Fröhlich, eds. *Alltag und Widerstand—Bayern im Nationalsozialismus.* Munich: R. Piper, 1987.

Broszat, Martin, and Hermann Weber. *SBZ-Handbuch.* Munich: R. Oldenbourg Verlag, 1990.

Buchheim, Christoph. "Wirtschaftliche Hintergründe des Arbeiteraufstandes vom 17. Juni 1953 in der DDR." *Vierteljahrshefte für Zeitgeschichte* 38 (1990): 415-433.

Buchstab, Günter. "Widerspruch und widerständiges Verhalten der CDU der SBZ/DDR." in *Materialen der Enquete-Kommission "Aufarbeitung von Geschichte und Folgen der SED-Diktatur in Deutschland."* Bonn: German Parliament, 1995.

Buddrus, Michael. " '...im Allgemeinen ohne besondere Vorkommnisse': Dokumente zur Situation des Strafvollzugs der DDR nach der Auflösung der sowjetischen Internierungslager 1949-1951." *Deutschland Archiv* 29 (1996): 10-33.

Buhite, Russell. *Decisions at Yalta: An Appraisal of Summit Diplomacy.* Wilmington:

Scholarly Resources Inc., 1986.

Burds, Jeffrey. "Agentura: Soviet Informants Network and the Ukrainian Underground in Galicia, 1944-1948." *East European Politics and Societies* 11 (1997): 89-130.

Buschfort, Wolfgang. *Das Ostbüro der SPD*. Munich: R. Oldenbourg, 1991.

———. *Parteien im Kalten Krieg: Die Ostbüros von SPD, CDU und FDP*. Berlin: Ch. Links, 2000.

Caracciolo, Lucio. "Der Untergang der Sozialdemokraten in der sowjetischen Besatzungszone. Otto Grotewohl und die 'Einheit der Arbeiterklasse' 1945-1946." *Vierteljahrshefte für Zeitgeschichte* 36 (1988): 281-318.

Cassirer, Ernst. *Individuum und Kosmos in der Philosophie der Renaissance*. Leipzig: B.G. Teubner, 1927.

Childs, David. *The GDR: Moscow's German Ally*. 2nd ed. London: Unwin Hyman, 1988.

Childs, David, and Richard Popplewell. *The Stasi: the East German Intelligence and Security Service*. Houndmills: MacMillan, 1996.

Daniel Chirot. "What happened in Eastern Europe in 1989?" in *The Revolutions of 1989*, edited by Vladimir Tismaneanu. London: Routledge, 1999.

Connelly, John. "East German Higher Education Policies and Student Resistance, 1945-48." *Central European History* 28 (1995): 259-298.

Conze, Werner. *Jakob Kaiser: Politiker zwischen Ost und West 1945-1949*. Stuttgart: W. Kohlhammer Verlag, 1969.

Dallin, David. *Soviet Espionage*. New Haven: Yale University Press, 1955.

Der Staatssicherheitsdienst. Bonn: Bundesministerium für Gesamtdeutsche Fragen, 1962.

Diedrich, Torsten. *Der 17. Juni 1953: Bewaffnete Gewalt gegen das Volk*. Berlin: Dietz Verlag, 1991.

Diedrich, Torsten. "Zwischen Arbeitererhebung und gescheiterter Revolution in der DDR." *Jahrbuch für Historische Kommunismusforschung*. Berlin: Akademie Verlag, 1994.

Dietrich, Gerd. *Politik und Kultur in der SBZ 1945-1949*. Berlin: Peter Lang, 1993.

Dijilas, Milovan. *Conversations with Stalin*. New York: Harcourt, Brace and World, 1962.

Dilcher, Gerhard. "Politische Ideologie und Rechtstheorie, Rechtspolitik und Rechtswissenschaft." In *Sozialgeschichte der DDR,* edited by Hartmut Kaelble et al. Stuttgart: J.G. Cotta'sche Buchhandlung Nachfolger, 1994.

Dubré, Louis. "Introduction and major works of Nicholas of Cusa." *The American Catholic Philosophical Quarterly* LXIV (1990).

Eckelmann, Wolfgang, Hans Hertmann Hertle, and Rainer Weinert. *FDGB Intern: Innenansichten einer Massenorganisation der SED*. Berlin: Treptower Verlagshaus, 1990.

Eckert, Rainer. "Die Vergleichbarkeit des Unvergleichbaren. Die Widerstandsforschung über die NS-Zeit als methodisches Beispiel." In *Zwischen Selbstbehauptung und Anpassung: Formen des Widerstandes und der Opposition in der DDR*, edited by Ulrike Poppe, Rainer Eckert, Ilko-Sascha Kowalczuk. Berlin: Ch. Links Verlag, 1995.

———. "Widerstand und Opposition in der DDR: Siebzehn Thesen." *Zeitschrift für Geschichtswissenschaft* 44 (1996): 49-67.

Eisert, Wolfgang. "Zu den Anfängen der Sicherheits-und Militärpolitik der SED-Führung 1948 bis 1952." In *Volksarmee schaffen—ohne Geschrei: Studien zu den Anfängen einer 'verdeckten Aufrüstung' in der SBZ/DDR 1947-1952*, edited by Bruno Thoss. Munich: R. Oldenbourg Verlag, 1994.

Engelmann, Roger. "Zum Quellenwert der Unterlagen des Ministeriums für Staatssicherheit." In *Aktenlage: Die Bedeutung der Unterlagen des*

Staatssicherheitsdienstes für die Zeitgeschichtsforschung, edited by Klaus-Dietmar Henke and Roger Engelmann. Berlin: Ch. Links Verlag, 1995.

Englehart, Stephen, and John Moore Jr., eds. *Three Beginnings: Revolution, Rights, and the Liberal State*. New York: Peter Lang, 1994.

Feige, Hans-Uwe. "Die Leipziger Studentenopposition (1945-48)." *Deutschland Archiv.* 26 (1993): 1057-1067.

Feth, Andrea. "Die Volksrichter," in *Steuerung der Justiz in der DDR*, edited by Hubert Rottleuthner. Cologne: Bundesanzeiger Verlag, 1994.

Finn, Gerhard. *Die politischen Häftlinge der Sowjetzone 1945-1948*. Berlin: Kampfgruppe gegen Unmenschlichkeit, 1958.

Foitzik, Jan. *Inventar der Befehle des Obersten Chefs der Sowjetischen Militäradministration in Deutschland (SMAD) 1945-1949*. Munich: K.G. Saur, 1995.

Franke, Joachim. "Der Fall Dertinger und seine parteiinternen Auswirkungen: Eine Dokumentation." *Deutschland Archiv* 25 (1992): 286-298.

Fricke, Karl Wilhelm, and Ilse Spittmann, eds. *17. Juni 1953: Arbeiteraufstand in der DDR*. Cologne: Edition Deutschland Archiv, 1982.

Fricke, Karl Wilhelm. *Die DDR-Staatssicherheit*. Cologne: Verlag Wissenschaft und Politik, 1989.

Fricke, Karl Wilhelm, and Roger Engelmann. *"Konzentrierte Schläge:" Staatssicherheitsaktionend und politische Prozess in der DDR 1953-1956*. Berlin: Ch. Links Verlag, 1998.

Fricke, Karl Wilhelm. *MfS intern*. Cologne: Verlag Wissenschaft und Politik, 1989.

———. *Opposition und Widerstand in der DDR*. Cologne: Verlag Wissenschaft und Politik, 1984.

———. "Opposition, Widerstand und Verfolgung in der SBZ/DDR." In *Gefährliche politische Gegner": Widerstand und Verfolgung in der sowjetischen Zone/DDR*, edited by Brigitte Kaff. Düsseldorf: Droste, 1995.

———. *Politik und Justiz in der DDR*. Cologne: Verlag Wissenschaft und Politik, 1979.

———. "Todesstrafe für Magdeburger 'Provokatuer.' SED Rachejustiz nach dem Aufstand vom 17. Juni 1953." *Deutschland Archiv* 26 (1993): 527-531.

Friedrich, Thomas. "Aspekte der Verfassungsentwicklung und der individuellen (Grund)-Rechtsposition in der DDR." In *Sozialgeschichte der DDR*, edited by Hartmut Kaelble et al. Stuttgart: J.G. Cotta'sche Buchhandlung Nachfolger, 1994.

Fritzsch, Günter. *Gesicht zur Wand*. Leipzig: Benno Verlag, 1993.

Fulbrook, Mary. *Anatomy of a Dictatorship: Inside the GDR 1949-1989*. Oxford: Oxford University Press, 1995.

Gängel, Andreas. "Die Volksrichterausbildung." In author collective for an "Ausstellung des Bundesministeriums der Justiz." *Im Namen des Volkes? Über die Justiz im Staat der SED*. Leipzig: Forum Verlag, 1994.

Gauck, Joachim. *Die Stasi-Akten. Das unheimliche Erbe der DDR*. Hamburg: Rowohlt, 1991.

Gellately, Robert. *The Gestapo and German Society*. Oxford: Clarendon Press, 1990.

———. "Rethinking the Nazi Terror System: A historiographical analysis." *German Studies Review* 14 (1991): 23-38.

Gieseke, Jens. *Die hauptamtlichen Mitarbeiter der Staatssicherheit*. Berlin: Ch. Links, 2000.

———. *Mielke-Konzern: Die Geschichte der Stasi 1945-1990*. Stuttgart: Deutsche Verlags-Anstalt, 2001.

Gill, David. *Das Ministerium für Staatssicherheit*. Berlin: Rowohlt, 1991.

Gniffke, Eric. *Jahre mit Ulbricht*. Cologne: Verlag Wissenschaft und Politik, 1966.

Goldyn, Bartholomew. "Disenchanted Voices: Public Opinion in Cracow, 1945-46." *East European Quarterly* 32 (1998): 139-166.

Gradl, J.B. *Anfang unter dem Sowjetstern: Die CDU in der SBZ 1945-1948.* Cologne: Verlag Wissenschaft und Politik, 1981.

Graml, Hermann. "Die aussenpolitischen Vorstellungen des deutschen Widerstandes." In *Der deutsche Widerstand gegen Hitler,* edited by W. Schmitthenner and H. Buchheim. Cologne: Kipenheuer & Witsch, 1966.

Gramsch, Robert. "Der Studentenrat im Umbruchsjahr 1948," In *Vergangenheitserklärung an der Friedrich-Schiller-Universität Jena,* edited by Rektor der Friedrich-Schiller-Universität. Leipzig: Evangelische Verlagsanstalt, 1994.

Grebing, Helga, et al. *Zur Situation der Sozialdemokratie in der SBZ/DDR zwischen 1945 und dem Beginn der 50er Jahre.* Schüren: Presseverlag, 1992.

Grieder, Peter. *The East German Leadership 1946-1973.* Manchester: Manchester University Press, 1999.

Grose, Peter. *Operation Rollback: America's Secret War Behind the Iron Curtain.* Boston: Houghton Mifflin, 2000.

Gruner, Gert, and Manfred Wilke. *Sozialdemokraten im Kampf um die Freiheit.* Munich: Piper, 1981.

Hagemann, Frank. *Der Untersuchungsausscuss Freiheitlicher Juristen 1949-1969.* Frankfurt am Main: Peter Lang, 1994.

Hagen, Manfred. *DDR—Juni '53: Die erste Volkserhebung im Stalinismus.* Stuttgart: Franz Steiner Verlag, 1992.

Hahn, Reinhardt. *Ausgedient: Ein Stasi Major erzählt.* Halle: Mitteldeutscher Verlag, 1990.

Hajna, Karl-Heinz. "Zur Bildung der Bezirke in der DDR ab Mitte 1952." *Zeitschrift für Geschichtswissenschaft* 37 (1989): 291-303.

Haritonow, Alexander. "Freiwilliger Zwang." *Deutschland Archiv* 29 (1996): 407-418.

Haupts, Leo. "Die Blockparteien in der DDR und der 17.Juni 1953." *Vierteljahrshefte für Zeitgeschichte* 40 (1992): 383-412.

Henkel, Rüdiger. *Im Dienste der Staatspartei.* Baden-Baden: Nomos, 1994.

Hermes, Peter. *Die CDU und die Bodenreform in der SBZ im Jahre 1945.* Saarbrücken: Verlag der Saarbrücker Zeitung, 1963.

Herwig, Gisela, and Ilse Spittmann, eds. *DDR Lesebuch.* Cologne: Verlag Wissenschaft und Politik, 1980.

Hershberg, James. "Stalin and the SED leadership, 7 April 1952." *Cold War International History Project Bulletin* Fall (1994): 35, 48.

Hoffmann, Peter. *German Resistance to Hitler.* Cambridge: Harvard University Press, 1988.

———. *The History of the German Resistance 1933-1945.* Cambridge: The MIT Press, 1977.

———. *The History of the German Resistance 1933-1945.* 3rd English ed. Montreal: McGill-Queen's University Press, 1996.

———. *Widerstand, Staatsstreich, Attentat.* 4th ed. Munich: R. Piper. 1985.

———. Book review at www.msu.edu/~german/articles/hoffmann1.html (6 Sept.1996).

Hübner, Peter. *Konsens, Konflikt und Kompromiss. Soziale Arbeiterinteressen und Sozialpolitik in der SBZ/DDR 1945-1970.* Berlin: Akademie Verlag, 1995.

Hurwitz, Harold. *Demokratie und Antikommunismus in Berlin nach 1945.* Vol. 1-4. Cologne: Verlag Wissenschaft und Politik, 1983-1990.

Huschner, Anke. "Der 17. Juni 1953 an Universitäten und Hochschulen der DDR." *Beiträge zur Geschichte der Arbeiterbewegung* 33 (1991): 681-692.

Hüttenberger, Peter. "Vorüberlegungen zum 'Widerstandsbegriff.'" In *Theorien in der Praxis des Historikers*, edited by Jürgen Kocka. Göttingen: Vandenhoeck & Ruprecht, 1977.

Itzerott, Brigitte. "Die Liberal-Demokratische Partei Deutschlands." In *Parteiensystem zwischen Demokratie und Volksdemokratie: Dokumente und Materialien zum Funktionswandel der Parteien und Massenorganisationen in der SBZ/DDR*, edited by Hermann Weber. Cologne: Verlag Wissenschaft und Politik, 1982.

Jacobsen, Hans-Adolf. *"Spiegelbild einer Verschwörung": Opposition gegen Hitler und der Staatsstreich vom 20. Juli 1944 in der SD-Berichterstattung*. Stuttgart: Seewald, 1984.

Jarausch, Konrad. *The Rush to German Unity*. New York: Oxford University Press, 1994.

Kaiser, Monika. "Die Zentrale der Diktatur—organisatorische Weichenstellungen, Strukturen und Kompetenzen der SED-Führung in der SBZ/DDR 1946 bis 1952." In *Historische Forschung: Aufsätze und Studien*, edited by Jürgen Kocka. Berlin: Akademie Verlag, 1993.

Kenney, Padraic. *Rebuilding Poland: Workers and Communists 1945-1950*. Ithaca: Cornell University Press, 1997.

———. "Working Class Community and Resistance in pre-Stalinist Poland." *Social History* 18 (1993): 31-51.

———. "The Gender of Resistance in Communist Poland." *American Historical Review* 104 (1999): 399-425.

Kersten, Krystyna. *The Establishment of Communist Rule in Poland, 1943-48*. Berkeley: University of California Press, 1991.

Kershaw, Ian. *The Nazi Dictatorship: problems and perspectives of interpretation*. 3rd ed. New York: E. Arnold, 1993.

Kiliam, Achim. "Die 'Mühlberg-Akten' im Zusammenhang mit dem System der Speziallager des NKWD der UdSSR." *Deutschland Archiv* 26 (1993): 1138-1158.

Kirsch, Henry. *The German Democratic Republic*. Boulder: Westview Press, 1985.

Klessmann, Christoph. *Die doppelte Staatsgründung*. Göttingen: Vandenhoeck & Rupprecht, 1982.

———. "Gegner des Nationalsozialismus. Zum Widerstand im Dritten Reich." *Aus Politik und Zeitgeschichte* B 46/1979.

———. "Zwei Diktaturen in Deutschland—was kann die künftige DDR-Forschung aus der Geschichtsschreibung zum Nationalsozialismus lernen." *Deutschland Archiv* 25 (1992): 601-606.

———. "Opposition und Resistenz in zwei Diktaturen in Deutschland." *Historische Zeitschrift* 262 (1996): 453-479.

Kocka, Jürgen, and Martin Sabrow, eds. *Die DDR als Geschichte*. Berlin: Akademie Verlag, 1994.

Kopstein, Jeffrey. *The Politics of Economic Decline in East Germany*. Chapel Hill: University of North Carolina Press, 1997.

Kos, Franz-Josef. "Der Erfurter Schauprozess und die beiden Nachfolgeprozesse 1952/53." In *"Gefährliche politische Gegner": Widerstand und Verfolgung in der sowjetischen Zone/DDR*, edited by Brigitte Kaff. Düsseldorf: Droste, 1995.

———. "Politische Justiz in der DDR. Der Dessauer Schauprozess vom April 1950." *Vierteljahrshefte für Zeitgeschichte* 44 (1996): 395-429.

Kowalczuk, Ilko-Sascha and Armin Mitter. "'Die Arbeiter sind zwar geschlagen worden, aber sie sind nicht besiegt!' Die Arbeiterschaft während der Krise 1952/1953." In *Der Tag X: Die 'Innere Staatsgründung der DDR als Ergebnis der Krise 1952/1954*, edited by Ilko-Sascha Kowalczuk, Armin Mitter, and Stefan Wolle. Berlin: Ch. Links Verlag,

1995.

Kowalczuk, Ilko-Sascha. "Die studentische Selbstverwaltung an der Berliner Universität nach 1945." *Deutschland Archiv* 26 (1993): 915-926.

———. "Von der Freiheit, Ich zu sagen. Widerständiges Verhalten in der DDR." In *Zwischen Selbstbehauptung und Anpassung: Formen des Widerstandes und der Opposition in der DDR*, edited by Ulrike Poppe, Rainer Eckert, Ilko-Sascha Kowlaczuk. Berlin: Ch. Links Verlag, 1995.

———. " 'Wir werden siegen, weil uns der grosse Stalin führt!' Die SED zwischen Zwangsvereinigung und IV. Parteitag." In *Der Tag X: Die 'Innere Staatsgründung der DDR als Ergebnis der Krise 1952/1954*, edited by Ilko-Sascha Kowalczuk, Armin Mitter, Stefan Wolle. Berlin: Ch. Links Verlag, 1995.

Kramer, Mark. "The Early Post-Stalin Succession Struggle and Upheavals in East-Central Europe: Internal-External Linkages in Soviet Policy Making." *Journal of Cold War Studies* 1-3 (1999): 3-55, 3-38, 3-66.

Krippendorf, Ekkehart. "Die Gründung der LDP in der SBZ 1945." *Vierteljahrshefte für Zeitgeschichte* 8 (1960).

Kuhle, Barbara, and Wolfgang Titz. *Speziallager Nr. 7 Sachsenhausen 1945-1950*. Berlin: Brandenburgisches Verlagshaus, 1990.

Lapp, Peter. *Wahlen in der DDR*. Berlin: Verlag Gebr. Holzapfel, 1982.

Lemmer, Ernst. *Manches war doch anders*. Frankfurt am Main: H. Scheffler, 1968.

Lenk, Kurt. "Probleme der Demokratie." In *Politische Theorien von der Antike bis zur Gegenwart*, edited by Hans-Joachim Leber. Bonn: Bundeszentrale für politische Bildung, 1993.

Leonhard, Wolfgang. *Die Revolution entlässt ihre Kinder*. Cologne: Kiepenheuer & Witsche, 1981.

Lorenz, Thomas. "Die Deutsche Zentralverwaltung der Justiz (DJV) und die SMAD in der Sowjetischen Besatzungszone 1945-1949." In *Steuerung der Justiz in der DDR*, edited by Hubert Rottleuthner. Cologne: Bundesanzeiger Verlag, 1994.

Louis, Jurge. *Die LDPD in Thüringen*. Cologne: Bohlau, 1996.

Löwenthal, Richard. "Widerstand im totalen Staat." In *Widerstand und Verweigerung in Deutschland 1933 bis 1945*, edited by Richard Löwenthal and Patrik von zur Mühlen. Berlin: J.H.W. Dietz, 1982.

Ludz, Peter. *The Changing Party Elite in East Germany*. Boston: The MIT Press, 1972.

Lucas, Scott. *Freedom's War: The American Crusade Against the Soviet Union*. New York: New York University Press, 1999.

Maier, Charles. *Dissolution*. Princeton: Princeton University Press, 1997.

Mallmann, Klaus Michael, and Gerhard Paul. "Resistenz oder loyale Widerwilligkeit? Anmerkungen zu einem umstrittenen Begriff." *Zeitschrift für Geschichtswissenschaft* 41 (1993): 99-116.

Malycha, Andreas. "Der Zentralausschuss der SPD und der gesellschaftpolitische Neubeginn im Nachkriegsdeutschland." *Zeitschrift für Geschichtswissenschaf* 38 (1990): 581-595.

Mammach, Klaus. *Die deutsche antifaschistische Widerstandsbewegung 1933-1939*. Berlin: Dietz, 1974.

Mampel, Siegfried. *Der Untergrundkampf des Ministeriums für Staatssicherheit gegen den Untersuchungsausschuss Freiheitlicher Juristen in Berlin (West)*. Berlin: Der Berliner Landesbeauftragte für die Unterlagen des Staatssicherheitsdienstes der ehemaligen DDR, 1994.

Mason, Timothy. "Arbeiteropposition im nationalsozialistischen Deutschland." In *Die Reihen fast geschlossen*, edited by Detlev Peukert and Jürgen Reulecke. Wuppertal: Hammer, 1981.

Mastny, Vojtech. *The Cold War and Soviet Insecurity*. New York: Oxford University Press, 1997.

Mattedi, Norbert. *Gründung und Entwicklung der Parteien in der Sowjetischen Besatzungszone Deutschlands, 1945-49*. Bonn: Deutscher Bundes-Verlag, 1966.

McCauley, Martin. *The German Democratic Republic since 1945*. London: MacMillan Press, 1988.

Melzer, Ingetraut. *Staats- und Rechtsgeschichte der DDR*. Berlin: Staatsverlag der DDR, 1983.

Merz, Kai-Uwe. *Kalter Krieg als antikommunistischer Widerstand: Die KgU 1948-1959*. Munich: R. Oldenbourg Verlag, 1987.

Meuschel, Sigrid. *Legitimation und Parteiherrschaft in der DDR*. Frankfurt am Main: Suhrkamp Verlag, 1992.

Mielke, Erich. "Mit hoher Verantwortung für den zuverlässigen Schutz des Sozialismus." *Einheit* 1 (1975).

Migev, Vladimir. "The Bulgarian Peasants' Resistance to Collectivization 1948-1958." *Bulgarian Historical Review* 25 (1997): 59-68.

Mitrovich, Gregory. *Undermining the Kremlin: America's Strategy to Subvert the Soviet Bloc, 1947-1956*. Ithaca: Cornell University Press, 2000.

Mitter, Armin. " 'Am 17.6.1953 haben die Arbeiter gestreikt, jetzt aber streiken wir Bauern.' Die Bauern und der Sozialismus." In *Der Tag X: Die 'Innere Staatsgründung der DDR als Ergebnis der Krise 1952/1954*, edited by Ilko-Sascha Kowalczuk, Armin Mitter, Stefan Wolle. Berlin: Ch. Links Verlag, 1995.

———. "Die Ereignisse im Juni und Juli 1953 in der DDR. Aus den Akten des Ministeriums für Staatssicherhiet." *Aus Politik und Zeitgeschichte* 25 (1991): 31-41.

———. "Der 'Tag X' und die 'Innere Staatsgründung der DDR," in in *Der Tag X: Die 'Innere Staatsgründung der DDR als Ergebnis der Krise 1952/1954*, edited by Ilko-Sascha Kowalczuk, Armin Mitter, Stefan Wolle. Berlin: Ch. Links Verlag, 1995.

Mitter, Armin, and Stefan Wolle. *Ich liebe euch doch alle!* Berlin: Elefanten Press, 1990.

Mitter, Armin, and Stefan Wolle. *Untergang auf Raten. Unbekannte Kapitel der DDR-Geschichte*. Munich: Bertelsmann Verlag, 1993.

Möhring, Wolfgang. "Von der Legalität zum Widerstand." In *Vergangenheitserklärung an der Friedrich-Schiller-Universität Jena*, edited by Rektor der Friedrich-Schiller-Universität. Leipzig: Evangelische Verlagsanstalt, 1994.

Mommsen, Hans. "Gesellschaftsbild und Verfassungspläne des deutschen Widerstandes." In *Der deutsche Widerstand gegen Hitler*, edited by W. Schmitthenner and H. Buchheim. Cologne: Kipenheuer & Witsch, 1966.

Moraw, Frank. *Die Parole der "Einheit" und die Sozialdemokratie*. Bonn-Bad Godesberg: Verlag Neue Gesellschaft, 1973.

Morrall, John. *Political Thought in Medieval Times*. London: Hutchinson and Co.Ltd, 1971.

Morsch, Günter. "Streik im Dritten Reich." *Vierteljahrshefte für Zeitgeschichte* 36 (1988): 649-689.

Mühlen, Patrik von zur. "Widerstand in einer thüringischen Kleinstadt 1953 bis 1958. Der 'Eisenberger Kreis'". In *Zwischen Selbstbehauptung und Anpassung: Formen des Widerstandes und der Opposition in der DDR*, edited by Ulrike Poppe, Rainer Eckert, Ilko-Sascha Kowalczuk. Berlin: Ch. Links Verlag, 1995.

Mühlen, Patrik von zur. *Der "Eisenberger Kreis."* Bonn: J.H.W. Dietz Nachfolger, 1995.

Müller, Klaus-Dieter, and Waldemar Krönig, eds. *Anpassung, Widerstand, Verfolgung: Hochschule und Studenten in der SBZ und DDR 1945-1961.* Cologne: Verlag Wissenschaft und Politik, 1994.

Müller, Klaus-Jürgen, ed. *Der deutsche Widerstand 1933-1945.* Paderborn: F. Schoningh, 1986.

Müller, Werner. "SED-Gründung unter Zwang—Ein Streit ohne Ende?" *Deutschland Archiv* 24 (1991): 52-59.

Müller, Werner. "Sozialdemokraten und Einheitspartei." In *Einheitsfront, Einheitspartei: Kommunisten und Sozialdemokraten in Ost- und Westeuropa 1944-1948,* edited by Dietrich Staritz. Cologne: Verlag Wissenschaft und Politik, 1982.

Müller-Enbergs, Helmut. *Inoffizielle Mitarbeiter des MfS in der DDR.* Berlin: Ch. Links, 2001.

Naimark, Norman. "Die Sowjetische Miltäradministration in Deutschland und die Frage des Stalinismus." *Zeitschrift für Geschichtswissenschaft* 43 (1995): 293-307.

———. *The Russians in Germany.* Cambridge: Harvard University Press, 1995.

Neubert, Ehrhart. *Geschichte der Opposition in der DDR 1949-1989.* Bonn: Bundeszentrale für politische Bildung, 2000.

Nietzhammer, Lutz. *Der "Gesäuberte" Antifaschismus: Die SED und die roten Kapos von Buchenwald.* Berlin: Akademie Verlag, 1994.

Orlow, Dietrich. "Delayed Reaction: Democracy, Nationalism and the SPD 1933-1960." *German Studies Review* 16 (1993): 77-102.

Osmond, Jonathan. "Kontinuität und Konflikt in der Landwirtschaft der SBZ/DDR zur Zeit der Bodenreform und Vergenossenschaftlichung 1945-1961." In *Die Grenzen der Diktatur: Staat und Gesellschaft in der DDR,* edited by Richard Bessel and Ralph Jessen. Göttingen: Vandenhoeck & Rupprecht, 1996.

Ostermann, Christian. "Keeping the pot simmering: The United States and the East German Uprising of 1953." *German Studies Review* 19 (1996): 61-89.

Overesch, Manfred. *Hermann Brill: Ein Kämpfer gegen Hitler und Ulbricht.* Bonn: J.H.W. Dietz Nachfolger, 1992.

Papke, Gerhard. "Die Liberal-Demokratische Partei Deutschlands in der Sowjetischen Besatzungszone und DDR 1945-52." In *'Bürgerliche' Parteien in der SBZ/DDR: Zur Geschichte von CDU, LDPD, DBD, NDPD 1945 bis 1953,* edited by Manfred Agethen and Jürgen Fröhlich. Cologne: Verlag Wissenschaft und Politik, 1994.

Paule, Bernward. "Die politische Freund-Feind-Differenz als ideologische Grundlage des MfS." *Deutschland Archiv* 26 (1993): 170-184.

Peter, Andreas. "Der Juni-Aufstand im Bezirk Cottbus." *Deutschland Archiv* 27 (1994): 585-594.

Peukert, Detlev. "Der deutsche Arbeiterwiderstand 1933-1945." *Aus Politik und Zeitgeschichte* B 28-29/1979.

Poltawa, P. "Our Battle Plan for the Liberation of Ukraine Under the Present Circumstances." In *Political Thought of the Ukrainian Underground 1943-1951,* edited by Peter Potichnyj and Yevhen Shtendera. Edmonton: Canadian Institute of Ukrainian Studies, 1986.

Port, Andrew. "When Workers Rumbled." *Social History* 22 (1997): 145-173.

Poutros, Kirsten. "Von den Massenvergewaltigungen zum Mutterschutzgesetz. Abtreibungspolitik und Abtreibungspraxis in Ostdeutschland." In *Die Grenzen der Diktatur: Staat und Gesellschaft in der DDR,* edited by Richard Bessel and Ralph Jessen. Göttingen: Vandenhoeck & Rupprecht, 1996.

Reinert, Fritz. *Blockpolitik im Land Brandenburg 1945 bis 1950.* Potsdam: Brandenburger Verein für Politische Bildung Rosa Luxemburg, 1992.

Remnick, David. *Lenin's Tomb: The Last Days of the Soviet Empire.* New York: Vintage Books, 1994.

Richie, Alexandra. *Faust's Metropolis: A History of Berlin.* New York: Carroll and Graf Publishers, 1998.

Richter, Michael. *Die Ost-CDU 1948-1952. Zwischen Widerstand und Gleichschaltung.* 2nd ed. Düsseldorf: Droste, 1991.

———. "Vom Widerstand der christlichen Demokraten in der DDR." In *"Gefährliche politische Gegner": Widerstand und Verfolgung in der sowjetischen Zone/DDR,* edited by Brigitte Kaff. Düsseldorf: Droste, 1995.

———. "Vom Widerstand der christlichen Demokraten in der DDR." in *Verfolgt-verhaftet-verurteilt: Demokratie im Widerstand gegen die Rote Diktatur -Fakten und Beispiele,* edited by Günter Scholz. Berlin: Westkreuz Verlag, 1990.

Rieke, Dieter. *Sozialdemokraten als Opfer gegen die Rote Diktatur.* Bonn: Friedrich-Ebert-Stiftung, 1994.

Ritscher, Bodo. *Speziallager Nr. 2 Buchenwald.* Weimar-Buchenwald: Gedenkstätte Buchenwald, 1995.

Ritter, Gerhard. *Carl Goerdeler und die deutsche Widerstandsbewegung.* Stuttgart: Deutsche Verlags-Anstalt, 1954.

Roth, Heidi. "Der 17. Juni im damaligen Bezirk Leipzig." *Deutschland Archiv* 24 (1991): 573-583.

Rothfels, Hans. *The German Opposition to Hitler.* Hinsdale: Henry Regency Co., 1948.

Rothschild, Joseph, and Nancy Wingfield. *Return to Diversity.* New York: Oxford University Press, 2000.

Sagolla, Bernhard. *Die Rote Gestapo.* Berlin: Hansa Druck, 1952.

Sandford, Gregory. *From Hitler to Ulbricht:Tthe Communist Reconstruction of East Germany.* Princeton: Princeton University Press, 1983.

Schmädeke, Jürgen, and Peter Steinbach, eds. *Der Widerstand gegen den Nationalsozialismus.* Bonn: Bundeszentrale für politische Bildung, 1994.

Schmädeke, Jürgen, and Peter Steinbach, eds. *Der Widerstand gegen den Nationalsozialismus.* Munich: R. Piper, 1985.

Schneider, Dieter Marc. "Renaissance und Zerstörung der kommunalen Selbstverwaltung in der SBZ." *Vierteljahrshefte für Zeitgeschichte* 37 (1989): 457-497.

Scholz, Gunther. *Kurt Schumacher—Biographie.* Düsseldorf: ELON Verlag, 1988.

Schuller, Wolfgang. *Geschichte und Struktur des politischen Strafrechts der DDR bis 1968.* Ebelsbach: Gremer, 1980.

Schulz, H.J. *Der zwanzigste Juli. Alternative zu Hitler?* Stuttgart: Kreuz Verlag, 1974.

Schwabe, Klaus. *Die Zwangsvereinigung von KPD und SPD in Mecklenburg-Vorpommern.* Schwerin: Friedrich-Ebert-Stiftung, 1994.

Schwarz, Anett, Arianne Riecker, and Dirk Schneider, eds. *Stasi intim: Gespräche mit ehemaligen MfS-Angehörigen.* Leipzig: Forum, 1991.

Schwarz, Josef. *Bis zum bitteren Ende.* Schkeuditz: GNN-Verlag, 1994.

Siebenmorgen, Peter. *"Staatssicherheit" der DDR.* Bonn: Bouvier Verlag, 1993.

Simons, Thomas Jr. *Eastern Europe in the Postwar World.* 2nd ed. New York: St. Martin's Press, 1993.

Snyder, Timothy. " 'To Resolve the Ukrainian Problem Once and for All': Ethnic Cleansing of Ukrainians in Poland, 1943-1947." *Journal of Cold War Studies* 1 (1999): 86-120.

Sommer, Ulf. *Die Liberal-Demokratische Partei Deutschlands.* Munster: Agenda, 1996.

Spielvogel, Jackson. *Hitler and Nazi Germany: A History.* Englewood Cliffs: Prentice-Hall Inc., 1988.

Spittmann, Ilse. *Die SED in Geschichte und Gegenwart.* Cologne: Edition Deutschland Archiv, 1987.

Staritz, Dietrich. "Die SED, Stalin und der 'Aufbau des Sozialismus' in der DDR." *Deutschland Archiv* 24 (1991): 686-700.

———. "Ursachen und Konsequenzen einer deutschen Revolution." In *Der Fischer Weltalmanach.* Frankfurt: Fischer Taschenbuch-Verlag, 1990.

———. *Einheitsfront, Einheitspartei: Kommunisten und Sozialdemokraten in Ost- und Westeuropa 1944-1948.* Cologne: Verlag Wissenschaft und Politik, 1982.

———. *Geschichte der DDR 1949-1985.* Frankfurt am Main: Shurkamp Verlag, 1985.

Steinbach, Peter, ed. *Widerstand: Ein Problem zwischen Theorie und Geschichte.* Cologne: Verlag Wissenschaft und Politik, 1987.

Steinbach, Peter, and Johannes Tuchel, eds. *Widerstand gegen den Nationalsozialismus.* Berlin: Akademie Verlag, 1994.

Steinbach, Peter. "Widerstand—aus sozialphilosophischer und historisch-poliologischer Perspektive." In *Zwischen Selbstbehauptung und Anpassung: Formen des Widerstandes und der Opposition in der DDR,* edited by Ulrike Poppe, Rainer Eckert, Ilko-Sascha Kowalczuk. Berlin: Ch. Links Verlag, 1995.

Steininger, Rolf. *The German Question:The Stalin Notes of 1952 and the Problem of German Unification.* New York: Columbia University Press, 1990.

Stokes, Gale. *The Walls Came Tumbling Down: The Collapse of Communism in Eastern Europe.* New York: Oxford University Press, 1993.

Stössel, Frank Thomas. *Positionen und Strömungen in der KPD/SED 1945-1954.* Cologne: Verlag Wissenschaft und Politik, 1985.

Streit, Josef. "Zur Geschichte der Staatsanwaltschaft der DDR." *Staat und Recht* 8 (1969): 1215-1230.

Suckut, Siegfried. "Der Konflikt um die Bodenreform-Politik in der Ost-CDU 1945." *Deutschland Archiv* 15 (1982).

———. "Die Bedeutung der Akten des Staatssicherheitsdienstes für die Erforschung der DDR-Geschichte." In *Aktenlage: Die Bedeutung der Unterlagen des Staatssicherheitsdienstes für die Zeitgeschichtsforschung,* edited by Klaus-Dietmar Henke and Roger Engelmann. Berlin: Ch. Links Verlag, 1995.

———. "Die Entscheidung zur Gründung der DDR. Die Protokolle der Beratungen des SED Parteivorstandes am 4. und 9. Oktober 1949." *Vierteljahrshefte für Zeitgeschichte* 39 (1991): 125-175.

———. "Innenpolitische Aspekte der DDR-Gründung." *Deutschland Archiv* 25 (1992): 370-383.

———. "Zur Krise und Funktionswandel der Blockpolitik in der sowjetisch Besetzten Zone Deutschlands um die Mitte des Jahres 1948." *Vierteljahrshefte für Zeitgeschichte* 31 (1983): 674-718.

Tantzscher, Monika. "'In der Ostzone wird ein neuer Apparat aufgebaut:' Die Gründung des DDR-Staatssicherheitsdienstes." *Deutschland Archiv* 31 (1998): 48-56.

———. "Die Vorläufer des Staatssicherheitsdienstes in der Polizei der Sowjetischen Besatzungszone." *Jahrbuch für Historische Kommunismusforschung* 7 (1998): 125-156.

Torpey, John. *Intellectuals, Socialism and Dissent: The East German Opposition and Its Legacy.* Minneapolis: University of Minnesota Press, 1995.

Turner, Henry Ashby. *Germany from Partition to Unification*. New Haven: Yale University Press, 1992.

———. *The Two Germanies since 1945*. New Haven: Yale University Press, 1987.

Ueberschär, Gerd, ed. *Der 20. Juli 1944: Bewertung und Rezeption des deutschen Widerstandes gegen das NS-Regime*. Cologne: Bund Verlag, 1994.

Untersuchungsausschuss Freiheitlicher Juristen. *Unrecht als System*. Bonn: Bundesministerium für Gesamtdeutsche Fragen, 1955.

Vollnhals, Clemens. "Das Ministerium für Staatssicherheit." In *Der SED-Staat: Neues über eine vergangene Diktatur*, edited by Jürgen Weber. Munich: Olzog Verlag, 1994.

———. "Das Ministerium für Staatssicherheit." In *Sozialgeschichte der DDR*, edited by Hartmut Kaelble et al. Stuttgart: J.G. Cotta'sche Buchhandlung Nachfolger, 1994.

Walter, Franz et al., eds. *Die SPD in Sachsen zwischen Hoffnung und Diaspora*. Bonn: J.H.W. Dietz, 1993.

Wawrzyn, Liehard. *Der Blaue*. Berlin: K. Wagenbach, 1990.

Weber, Hermann. *DDR. Grundriss der Geschichte 1945-1990*. Hannover: Fackelträger, 1991.

———. *Die Sozialistische Einheitspartei Deutschlands*. Hannover: Verlag für Literatur und Zeitgeschehen, 1971.

———. *Geschichte der DDR 1945-1985*. Frankfurt am Main: Suhrkampf, 1985.

———. *Von der SBZ zur DDR*. Hannover: Verlag für Literatur und Zeitgeschehen, 1968.

Weisenborn, Günter. *Der lautlose Aufstand*. Hamburg: Rowohlt, 1953

Welsh, Helga. "Entnazifizierung und Wiedereröffnung der Universität Leipzig 1945-1946. Ein Bericht des damaligen Rektors Bernhard Schweitzer." *Vierteljahreshefte für Zeitgeschichte* 33 (1985): 339-372.

Wentker, Hermann. " 'Kirchenkampf' in der DDR 1950-53." *Vierteljahrshefte für Zeitgeschichte* 42 (1994): 95-127.

Wenzke, Rüdiger. "Auf dem Wege zur Kaderarmee. Aspekte der Rekrutierung, Sozialstruktur und personellesn Entwicklung des entstehenden Militärs in der SBZ/DDR bis 1952/1953." In *Volksarmee schaffen—ohne Geschrei: Studien zu den Anfängen einer "verdeckten Aufrüstung" in der SBZ/DDR 1947-1952*, edited by Bruno Thoss. Munich: R. Oldenbourg Verlag, 1994.

Werkentin, Falco. *Politische Strafjustiz in der Ära Ulbricht*. Berlin: Ch. Links Verlag, 1995.

Wettig, Gerhard. "Die Stalin-Note vom 10. März 1952 als geschichtswissenschaftliches Problem." *Deutschland Archiv* 25 (1992): 157-166.

———. "Sowjetische Wiedervereinigungsbemühungen im ausgehenden Frühjahr 1953?" *Deutschland Archiv* 25 (1992): 943-958.

Wolf, Stefan. "Die 'Bearbeitung' der Kirchen in der Sowjetischen Besatzungszone und der DDR durch die politische Polizei und das Ministerium für Staatssicherheit bis 1953." In *Die Ohnmacht der Allmächtigen. Geheimdienste und politische Polizei in der modernen Gesellschaft*, edited by Bernd Florath et al. Berlin: Ch. Links Verlag, 1992.

Wolle, Stefan. "'Agenten, Saboteure, Verräter.' Die Kampagne der SED-Führung gegen den 'Sozialdemokratismus'." In *Der Tag X: Die Innere Staatsgründung der DDR als Ergebnis der Krise 1952/1954*, edited by Ilko-Sascha Kowalczuk, Armin Mitter, Stefan Wolle. Berlin: Ch. Links Verlag, 1995.

———. "Der Weg in den Zussamenbruch: Die DDR vom Juni bis zum Oktober 1989." In *Die Gestaltung der deutschen Einheit: Geschichte—Politik—Gesellschaf*, edited by Eckhard Jesse and Armin Mitter. Bonn: Bundeszentrale für politische Bildung, 1992

Zeidler, Stefan. "Zur Rolle der CDU (Ost) in der inneren Entwicklung der DDR 1952-53." M.A. thesis, University of Bonn, 1994.

Zelle, Eberhard. *Geist der Freiheit: Der zwanzigste Juli.* Munich: Hermann Rinn, 1954.

Index

About the Author

Gary Bruce holds a Ph.D. in German history from McGill University. He has attended universities in Canada, Scotland, and Germany. He taught history at McGill University, the University of New Brunswick, and St. Thomas University before his arrival at St. Francis Xavier University, where he is assistant professor of history. He has authored several articles on German history and has traveled extensively in Eastern Germany.

DATE DUE

GAYLORD			PRINTED IN U.S.A.